BELL LIBRARY-TAMU

W9-BZE-603

Philosophy, Biology and Life

ROYAL INSTITUTE OF PHILOSOPHY SUPPLEMENT: 56

EDITED BY

Anthony O'Hear

CAMBRIDGE
UNIVERSITY PRESS

PUBLISHED BY THE PRESS SYNDICATE OF THE UNIVERSITY OF CAMBRIDGE
The Pitt Building, Trumpington Street, Cambridge, CB2 1RP,
United Kingdom

CAMBRIDGE UNIVERSITY PRESS
The Edinburgh Building, Cambridge CB2 2RU, United Kingdom
40 West 20th Street, New York, NY 10011–4211, USA
477 Williamstown Road, Port Melbourne, VIC 3207, Australia

© The Royal Institute of Philosophy and the contributors 2005

Printed in the United Kingdom at the University Press, Cambridge
Typeset by Michael Heath Ltd, Reigate, Surrey

*A catalogue record for this book is available
from the British Library*

Library of Congress Cataloguing-in-Publication Data applied for

ISBN 0 521 67845 5 paperback
ISSN 1358-2461

Contents

Contents

Preface

The papers in this volume are based on the Royal Institute of Philosophy's annual London lecture series for 2004-5. The intention of the series was to focus on a rapidly growing area of interest within philosophy and without. Some have claimed that with the decline of Marxism and Freudianism, Darwinism or, more accurately, neo-Darwinism, has become the dominant intellectual paradigm of the day. And certainly there are many bitter disputes between those who see it as their mission to carry the neo-Darwinist torch before the general public and between those who oppose that vision, often on religious grounds. In fact, as always, things are not nearly as simple as they are often portrayed. For one thing the 'neo-Darwinian paradigm' may not be as seamless and as simple as both its attackers and some of those who seek to defend it would have us believe.

We hope that the papers in this volume, which are written from a number of different perspectives and standpoints, will help to demonstrate that biology and its underlying philosophy are in a state of development which defies the standard stereotypes. Matters are far more complex and far more interesting than one might be forgiven for thinking were one to confine one's attention to public pronouncements on the subject. At the same time, as again we hope the papers demonstrate, the issues discussed, while complex, are not so formidably technical as to exclude all but specialists, and they are also issues which bear directly on our conceptions of human nature and hence of ourselves.

It is a great pleasure to thank those who gave the lectures in the series and who have contributed to this volume. I hope that readers of the volume will be as stimulated and provoked as were those who heard the lectures, and that this volume will itself further one of the most significant debates of our time. My thanks are due to Dr Sophie R. Allen for her help with editing and for compiling the index.

Anthony O'Hear

Notes on Contributors

Rom Harré
Professor of Philosophy at the University of Oxford and Georgetown University, USA.

Gregory Radick
Lecturer in the Division of History and Philosophy of Science, University of Leeds.

Giovanni Boniolo
Professor of Logic and the Philosophy of Science, University of Padova, Italy.

Mary Midgley
Formerly Senior Lecturer in Philosophy, University of Newcastle Upon Tyne.

Michael Ruse
Lucyle T. Werkmeister Professor of Philosophy, Florida State University.

Elliott Sober
Hans Reichenbach Professor and William F. Vilas Research Professor at the University of Wisconsin.

Anthony O'Hear
Weston Professor of Philosophy at the University of Buckingham.

Tim Lewens
Lecturer in the Department of History and Philosophy of Science, University of Cambridge.

John Dupré
Professor of Sociology and Director of Egenis, University of Exeter.

Matthew Ratcliffe
Lecturer in Philosophy , University of Durham.

Friedel Weinert
Senior Lecturer in Philosophy, University of Bradford.

Notes on Contributors

Michael Wheeler
Senior Lecturer in Philosophy, University of Stirling.

David Papineau
Professor of Philosophy, King's College London.

Transcending the Emergence/Reduction Distinction: The Case of Biology

ROM HARRÉ

Introduction

The groups of problems that fall under the titles 'reduction' and 'emergence' appear at the boundaries of seemingly independent and well-established scientific disciplines, such as chemistry and biology, biology and psychology, biology and political theory, and so on. They arise in this way:

1. There is a widespread intellectual 'urge' towards developing a common discourse for adjacent disciplinary practices such as biology and chemistry, biology and psychology, law and psychiatry. To achieve this goal a unified and coherent system of concepts would be required that would be adequate to describe and to explain the phenomena which are the subject matter of both disciplines.
2. There is a discontinuity between the concepts native to each of the adjacent disciplines in that predications from each to a common subject such as a sample of a material substance, or a process or a human being, appear to be incompatible. For example to describe a certain reaction as 'reducing' and to describe it in terms of the quantum states of molecular orbitals is an incompatible predication. For example to say that a brain is thinking and that that brain is taking up glucose is an incompatible predication since the criteria for these assertions are radically different. Or, to say that a human being is ill and to say that a human being is malfunctioning is an incompatible predication, since the former requires the speaker to treat the human being as a person, and the latter as an organism. Just what these various differences amount to will be the main aim of this paper.

I take the program of 'reduction' to be aimed at achieving a common discourse by deleting one or other from the incompatible groups of predicates. Chemical concepts will be replaced *salva veritate* by concepts from physics in the discourse of the transformation of substances, while neurophysiological concepts will replace

1

psychological concepts in the discourse of human behaviour. The program of 'emergence' is aimed at persuading people to abandon the ideal of a common discourse in favour of preserving the conceptual systems already established in the adjacent disciplines

In this paper I will make no attempt to tackle any of the particular forms that the problem of reduction or the problem of emergence take on these and similar boundaries, say physics and engineering. My reason is the advice given to philosophers by Wittgenstein. In the *Philosophical Investigations* and in other writings he suggests that if an intellectual problem is both *intractable*, that is resists the efforts of generations of philosophers to solve, and irresistibly *attractive*, always coming to the fore, then it is probably the manifestation of a grammatical error.

It might arise from falling into a misleading grammatical analogy, in the way that conceptual confusions in cognitive psychology arise by treating beliefs as mental entities. It might come from confusing a grammatical proposition with a scientific hypothesis, in the way that pointless experiments are undertaken in psychology by trying to find empirical grounds for the claim that actions involve intentions.

We bypass the problems by attending to the grammatical errors that brought them into being. This is the technique I propose to use in this discussion, attending to certain fundamental rules of philosophical grammar, rules governing incompatible predications. Because the problems of reduction and of emergence are particularly prominent in philosophy of biology, I propose to center my discussion on biological concepts and their relations to concepts of chemistry, psychology and medicine.

Underlying the very idea of the projects of defending or rejecting both reduction and emergence there lies a neglect of the conditions under which the phenomena to be described and explained are made manifest. An experiment is not a neutral way of providing the scientific community with propositions of the form 'Some A and B'. A psychiatric interview is not a neutral way of bringing out a diagnosis.

I

Some Philosophical Problems of Biology as a Natural Science

The relations between biology and the adjacent disciplines of chemistry and medicine offer a promising field for raising and, one hopes, disposing of the concept pair 'reduction/emergence' which constrain our thinking into 'problems'. A good rule in philosophy, when confronted by a dichotomy such as 'mind or body', 'reduction or emergence' is to drop the dichotomy and start again. The *da capo* move can sometimes reveal a slippery slope down which one slid into believing in the ultimate character of the dichotomy that is causing the trouble.

Intrinsic and Extrinsic Conceptual Problem

Biology presents philosophers with two kinds of problems:

1. *Intrinsic:* There are some problems that seem to invoke the emergence or reduction dichotomy within biology. For example: 'How are the concepts of the anatomy and physiology of animals related to the concepts in use in ethology?' There are also problems based on other dichotomies, such as that between the real and the nominal essences of kinds. For example: 'Are biological species natural kinds?' I will have something to say only about the former.

2. *Extrinsic*: As I remarked above biology is surrounded by at least two other disciplines, chemistry and medicine, each of which has its own vocabulary and preferred modes of explanation. For example: 'How are biological concepts related to concepts from adjacent discourses?' Instead of trying to make sense of debates on these boundaries between advocates of 'reduction' and of 'emergence', I am going to approach these issues from a different direction, by-passing the dichotomy.

My *question* will be: Is there a way of binding the many 'language games' in and around biology into a common discourse, given the apparent incompatibility of joint predications of chemical, biological and psychological attributes to a common subject entity or process within the same discourse?

My *answer* will emerge from an exploration of the internal boundaries between the sub-discourses of biology and the external boundaries between biological discourses and those of adjacent disciplines.

My *procedure* will involve

a. Making a 'grammatical' comparison between the rules for the use of certain groups of biological, non-biological and quasi-biological concepts.

b. Closely examining the rules that constrain predications, in particular those that forbid incompatible predications.

Rom Harré

To implement this strategy I will make use of some leading ideas and distinctions from Ludwig Wittgenstein (1953) and from Niels Bohr (1958).

Boundaries: A Preliminary Sketch

1. By what adjacent disciplinary territories is the domain of biological concepts bounded?

Biology is bounded on one side by chemistry; and on the other side by medicine, the law, religion, economics and so on. The independence of the social sciences is made problematic just in so far as this boundary is seen as permeable, for instance by the concepts of socio-biology, business rivalries as genetically driven male status hierarchy forming rituals, and so on.

However, considerable illumination will come, I hope, from exploring the boundary between biology and medicine, which, in some ways, mediates a larger scale distinction between biology and culture.[1]

2. Medicine and morality

Human beings are discussed by doctors and others as if they were organisms, not subject to the full range of moral concepts, and yet, as people, they are embedded in discourses expressing the principle that they are fully morally protected, and fully morally responsible.

The current trend to biologise human life through the ever widening range of problems that are redefined as medical, raises a nest of moral problems, but presupposes that a boundary issue has been settled, namely that the boundary between biological and other discourse genres apropos of human life has been dissolved or become permeable. How far are the philosophical problems of biology, in particular the debate between emergentists and reductionists, implicated in such issues as the medicalization of morality, and other biologization of traditional systems of social and personal control, through the rise of explanations in terms of genes?

[1] Nor should we forget vetinary science, since this is a discipline where the conceptual boundaries between the vocabularies of animal and human affairs are routinely crossed. To some extent the techniques of vetinary medicine parallel those of human medicine. However, not wholly: there was great fuss in the UK when a vet administered the anaesthetic to a person for an operation in a country hospital!

Transcending the Emergence/Reduction Distinction

Permeability of Discourse Boundaries

There are many pairs of discourses in which the central concepts and rules of grammar are relatively independent of one another. For all practical purposes there are impermeable boundaries. However, in many cases, the boundaries between the domains of application of two systems of concepts are permeable, concepts crossing by one route or another into the adjoining domain.

a. Impermeable boundaries. The discourse of Rugby and the discourse of Astrophysics are impermeable. In World Cup Year, the discourse of Rugby is accessible every day. Concepts like 'supernova', 'black hole', 'big bang' were as conspicuous by their absence, as they are conspicuous in business journalism. A quick glance at the latest journals in Astrophysics reveals not even a Rugby metaphor. There are no 'dropped goals', 'forward passes' or the like.

b. Permeable boundaries. The discourses of Rugby and of Military Campaigns have many cross overs ('The Battle of Waterloo was won on the playing fields of Eton', The Duke of Wellington; 'The Kiwis unveiled their secret weapon', 'The English tactics were soon evident, as they carried their campaign into French territory', and so on).

How permeable are the boundaries between chemical and biological discourses, and between biological and medical conceptual systems? The combination of an impermeable boundary with a strong urge to create a common discourse for two adjoining fields of phenomena, is likely to result in the most intractable versions of the reduction/emergence debate.

Exploring Boundaries

I will approach the boundary issue in the manner of Wittgenstein, exploring the 'grammars' of chemical and biological discourses, and of biological and cultural discourses, and of all three and medical discourse.

The range of conceptual problems is made more complex by the fact that within the boundary of biological discourse, there seem to be sub-boundaries, tempting philosophers to have recourse to reductive strategies within biology, for example proposing to reduce ethology to a branch of genetics. A grammar can be identified by the domain of entities presupposed in admitting the possibility that substantive propositions using this grammar can be assessed for truth-value. For chemistry this presupposition is 'molecule', for biology, 'organism' and for cultural and legal discourses, 'person', for medicine the 'patient'. Our question will be how these discourses are similar and now do they differ, and what is the significance of these similarities and differences.

My plan is to move away from the well-worn problems of reduction and of emergent properties, to aim at casting some light on the differences in discourses that have sparked discussion in terms to reduction and emergence. The argument will involve:

1 Using some familiar distinctions from Wittgenstein to identify the kind of discussion we are engaged in.
2 Reviving, clarifying and applying Niels Bohr's concept of *complementarity*.

Wittgenstein: Hinges and Frames

Niels Bohr remarked that the fact that there is life is not in need of empirical justification. Asserting it identifies the province of biological science in just the way that asserting the existence of the quantum of action identifies the province of fundamental physics.

> 'the very existence of life is to be considered an elementary fact, just as … the existence of the quantum of action has to be taken as basic fact that cannot be derived from ordinary mechanical physics'

(Bohr, 1958:9) I want to connect this observation with a deep insight of Wittgenstein (*On Certainty*), to which I will give my own spin.

There are propositions that share a superficial grammar with empirical statements, but which have the role of setting up the presuppositions or ground rules of a certain discourse. Tiding up Wittgenstein's distinctions for my purposes, it will prove useful to distinguish between 'hinges' and 'frames'.

Hinge propositions, express that which remains fixed while all else changes. As presuppositions that are not subject to empirical test, once taken up they cannot turn out to be right or wrong. Of course, they can be dropped for all sorts of reasons. For example, 'There are extra-Galactic nebulae' is a hinge proposition which expresses what is presupposed in using the principle that the causes of certain hazy marks on photographic plates are distant material objects. It fixes a whole discourse genre That there is life is not the result of an empirical discovery, as if there was a time before which we did not realize there was life, but after a while an able researcher, say Claude Bernard, found out there was. The very idea of there being entities capable of carrying out research makes sense only in a lively world. e.g., 'There is life' expresses what remains unchanged while we replace the creationist assertion 'Animals were created by God' with the Darwinian assertion 'Animal and plants are the product of natural processes'.

Grammatical or *'frame' propositions* fix the rules for using words, though they may look like reports of empirical investigations. Certain propositions express decisions or conventions as to how concepts are internally related to one another into systems, fixing meaning relations. For example, 'Bacteria are neither plants nor animals' and 'Whales are not fish' are grammatical propositions in that they serve to fix the meaning of concepts like 'plant', 'animal', 'fish' and so on. Discovering that some ocean dwelling creatures are viviparous and lactate could have been registered as 'Some fish lactate'. Instead it has been registered as fixing one of the boundaries for the use of the word 'fish'.[2]

Biology seems to involve the following grammar:

a. The *hinge* is the concept of bounded and self-sustaining individuals, separated in some way (for instance by a membrane) from a relatively chaotic environment. That there should be a science of biology presupposes the concept of an organism, a living being. This is one of the hinges on which biology turns. However, biological science makes use of a hierarchy of 'hinges', asserting the existence of cells, organs, organisms, populations and so on.

b. The *grammar* is a complicated multiple hierarchy hard to pin down positively, but it can be characterised negatively. The grammars of biological discourses do not incorporate moral principles. The discourse of 'animal rights' activists, for example, is not part of the science of biology. There are many examples of the use of moral concepts in discourses about animals, from Aesop to animal rights protesters, but they are precisely those in which biological concepts do not figure.

c. It is convenient to take another step beyond Wittgenstein's use of these concepts, to make use of the principle that a grammar is individuated by reference to the type of entity (grammatical subject) that is filling the place of the elementary or atomic individuals of the domain.

The totalized discourse currently considered adequate to human life seems to involve three hinge-specific grammars. There is the

[2] Wittgenstein uses the terms 'hinge' and 'frame' rather carelessly. The way they are used here is an adaptation to assist clear thinking.

molecular grammar, used when we discuss how we are dealing with free radicals by using the anti-oxidants in red wine. There is the organism grammar in which we recommend red wine as a prophylactic for the heart, and there is the person grammar, in which we engage in 'wine talk', disclosing our esoteric knowledge of the rarest vintages.

This paper has two aims:

1. To unify the multiple discourses of biology without making use of reduction, not settling for emergence.
2. To unify the three human oriented grammars without invoking reduction or emergence as philosophical strategies.

To carry out these projects some more philosophical weaponry is needed. It will be found in the writings of Niels Bohr, properly interpreted and supplemented.

Bohr: Complementarity: Incompatible predications

In diagnosing the situation that seems to call for the intractable dichotomy between emergence and reduction I argued that it was characterized by the urge towards a common discourse, with the realization that the domains in question made use of incompatible discourses in the sense that the joint predication of a pair of attributes, one from each discourse, violated some deep rule of philosophical grammar. In many discourses grammar forbids the joint predication to the same 'something' of one from each of two sets of predicates each set having an established use in some discourse that describes or explains that 'something'. So the project of building up the means for a common discourse must fail. There are several kinds of incompatibilities and so several different sets of rules forbidding them. What are the sources of these prohibitions? If one of the grounds is violation of the Principle of Non-Contradiction the project of developing a common discourse is hopeless.

Niels Bohr's Principle of Complementarity is a new rule for constraining joint ascriptions of certain classes of predicates, but one which allows a common discourse to be created. If it can be shown that the problems of creating a common discourse for chemistry and biology and biology and medicine are grounded in the Principle of Complementarity, then a common discourse can be developed not requiring reduction of one set of disjoint predicates to the other. The emergentist can have irreducible groups of predicates without having to give up the advantages of a common discourse.

Transcending the Emergence/Reduction Distinction

What the complementarity of predicates is not:

a. Principle of Non-Contradiction: joint ascription of two predicates that stand in the logical relation of mutual exclusion, that is A entails not-B and B entails not-A, is forbidden. For example, being red and being blue all over cannot be ascribed to the same material thing at the same moment. In this as in many cases the predicates are determinates under the same determinable, hues under the determinable 'colour'.

b. Antinomy: By the use of reason alone it is possible to prove that each of two determinates under the same determinable are properly ascribed to one and the same entity at the same time. For example, Kant thought that there were a priori arguments for ascribing both the predicates, 'being unbounded in time' and 'being bounded in time', to the Universe. However, this would violate the rule of non-contradiction, since they are determinates under the same determinable. The rule to be invoked is a prohibition on the use of reason beyond the bounds of sense. Let us call this the 'Rule of Non-Transcendence'.

What complementarity is:

Two predicates A and B are complementary if:
   a. They are determinates under different determinables
   b. The realization of the conditions or procedures under which predicate A can be manifested or displayed are incompatible with the realization of the conditions or procedures under which B can be manifested or displayed.

For example, precise location and precise momentum cannot be ascribed to a subatomic particle in the same experimental setup. Incompatibility of experimental arrangements means that the set up that is required to bring out attribute of kind A cannot be constructed at the same time and place as the set up required to bring out attribute of kind B. A cloud chamber reveals particle-like phenomena, whereas a diffraction grating reveals wave-like phenomena. No apparatus can be built that would reveal both at once.

Since the prohibition of joint predication concerns determinates from different determinables, say position and momentum, a common discourse using a certain set of problematic predicates in the sense that they are complementary, is made possible by assigning acts of predication for members of each subset of predicates to distinct conditions of display or manifestation of the properties in question.

This procedure permits a complete description of any phenomenon in the domain in question. There is no third conceptual system by means of which a common account of the being in question could be given, compatible with both A and B type concepts.

The common discourse is created by ascribing propensities or affordances to the world. Two incompatible affordances in the sense that each would require a revelatory set up precluding that required to reveal the other, can be jointly predicated of something, since this would be to predicate possibilities, not actualities. We can predicate 'might fall heads' and 'might fall tails' of the same 1 Euro coin at the same time, without contradiction. Which will occur requires a procedure, namely tossing the coin.

Underlying the idea of complementarity is the deeper idea that seemingly segregated predications are compatible if expressed as affordances or possibilities.

In summary,

   i. The rule of non-contradiction allows *either* of a pair of predicates which represent determinates under the same determinable to be predicated at once of the same object, but not both.
   ii. The rule of non-transcendence allows *neither* of a pair of predicates which represent determinates under the same determinable to predicated at one and same time of the same being.
   iii. The principle of complementarity does not allow the joint predication of members of complementary sets of predicates to be predicated of the same 'system', even though they seem to escape the Principle of Non-Contradiction, being determinates under different determinables. However, the fact that they are manifested only under different material conditions or with respect to different procedures for evoking them, means that what we learn from these experiments is what a set up affords or makes possible. The common discourse must, therefore, make use of concepts for *ascribing affordances* rather than for ascribing simple observable properties.

The concept of 'affordance' now needs to be developed. 'How can something be both a wave and a particle?' is a malformed question, if 'wave' and 'particle' are complementary predicates. How to describe the common 'something' from which waves are evoked in a double slit experiment and particles are evoked in cloud chamber experiment will require the introduction of a new concept, the affordance, from the psychology of perception of J. J. Gibson.

An affordance is a disposition of some being to display some definite property when subjected to a certain procedure by a human actor. The world affords particles to one experimental procedure and waves to a different procedure. The world is characterized by its multiple affordances.

a. A substance, system etc., for example, the body of an organism, affords certain possibilities to a human being employing a certain kind of procedure in interacting with it. The procedure might be to hide some food in a maze and measure the length of time an animal took to find it. The procedure might be to weigh the brains of test animals. An animal without a brain is dead and cannot run the maze.

b. An affordance is a disposition, the first clause of which refers to some human activity. A floor affords walking; a recipe affords instructions, a hand affords grasping, an animal or plant in an environment affords behaviour.

The question as to the nature of the 'something' that merits complementary predications dissolves if we realize that only affordances can be jointly predicated of it.

II

Inside the boundary: how are biological concepts to be organised?

We will follow Niels Bohr in holding that there are two major domains of biological concepts, the *anatomical/physiological*, such as 'liver', 'hippocampus', 'body temperature' 'neural transmission' and so on; and *ethological*, such as 'dominance hierarchy', 'ecological niche', 'cooperative hunting', and so on. These seem to cluster into two groups, suggestive of the problem situation that calls for either reduction or emergence. Can we reduce a concept like 'cooperative hunting' to a genetic/neurological concept cluster, or should we say that the propensity to engage in cooperative hunting is emergent on the existence of certain brain structures and hormonal balances?

Bohr argued that biological concepts could be the basis of a unified biological discourse only within the general framework of complementarity. Here is the parallel:

a. The same physical system displays wave-like properties in one experimental set up and particle-like properties in another incompatible experimental arrangement.

b. The same organism displays an integrated and self-maintaining blood circulation under one procedure, vivisection, (Lexicon 1); and is shown to be a member of a dominance hierarchy under a different procedure, observation in the wild, (Lexicon 2) and the two procedures cannot be implemented together.

Bohr's Analysis

Attributes of the Chimpanzee as an Organism:

Context 1 (laboratory: dissection etc.) → (displays oxygen/carbon dioxide exchange)

Context 2 (natural habitat) → (displays capacity for ritual fighting)

We could say that an organism has two complementary sets of affordances: if studied in the laboratory an organism affords proof of vagus nerve stomach secretion control, Pavlov's famous experiment with a surgically prepared dog (the concepts are drawn from Lexicon 1); if observed in the natural environmental an organism affords a status hierarchy display, as observed by Jane van Lawick-Goodall in her study of African wild dog (the concepts are drawn from Lexicon 2).

Organisms can display or afford a biologist attributes in two incompatible environments. There is the laboratory. The animal may be dead or modified so as to be non-viable in its natural habitat, e.g. in physiological experiments the animal is isolated, constrained and surgically manipulated. For example, Pavlov created permanent fistulas through which he extracted the agents and products of digestion. Hales purchased horses on the way to the knackers yard and inserted tubes in the aorta, discovering the diastolic/systolic pattern of blood pressure, killing the animal in the procedure. There is the natural environment. In ethological studies the animal is alive and unconstrained, and able to interact with conspecifics. For example, Lorenz discovered 'imprinting' as he was studying a flock of geese. Tinbergen was watching herring gulls when he made his discovery of 'displacement activities'.

> ... the obvious exclusiveness between such typical aspects of life as the self-preservation and the self-generation of individuals on the one hand and the subdivision necessary for any

physical analysis on the other hand. Owing to this essential feature of complementarity, the concept of purpose, which is foreign to mechanical analysis, finds a certain field of application in biology ... teleological augmentation may be regarded as a legitimate feature of physiological description which takes due regard of the characteristics of life in a way analogous to the recognition of the quantum of action in the correspondence argument of classical physics' (Bohr, 1958: 10).

The pretheoretical concept of purpose must be substituted by a pair of concepts, organic function, the body as a self-sustaining system of organs, and self-organisation, the organism as whole in its natural way of life, each requires a distinct experimental arrangement to bring about the display of the relevant phenomena. (Brock, 2003: 262).

Examples:

1. Horses display fleetness of foot and stamina in races and steeplechasing. They displayed systolic and diastolic blood pressure to Stephen Hales when tied down and opened up, finally dying. No doubt, the blood pressure of a horse is raised in a race but it cannot be displayed in those circumstances.

2. Chimpanzees display the fact that they share 98% of DNA with humans when a portion of a chimp body is subjected to genetic typing. The fact that they engage in fighting and reconciliation was displayed to Franz de Waal during a sustained period of observation of group of chimpanzees in a quasi-natural environment. No doubt, genetic predispositions to 'make up' are inherited by chimpanzees but this fact cannot be displayed in the wild, nor can 'making up' be displayed in a genetic typing experiment.

3. Pavlov's dogs displayed conditioning to a stimulus in the laboratory when they were fed. No doubt, stomach secretions occurred but could not be observed. They displayed the neural mechanisms of stomach secretion when reconfigured by surgery to have a stomach fistula and a dissected out vagus nerve to be cut in the experiment. (Dog died.)

Interim Conclusion:

Anatomy/physiology/genetics can be subsumed into a common discourse with ethology by the use of the concept of complementarity to distinguish and reconcile incompatible conditions of manifestation. There is no need to attempt to reduce the one to other to make a common and complete description possible—just obey the three rules for the constraints of predication.

Outside the Boundary

On one side the subdomains of biology, anatomy and physiology are bounded by chemistry and physics, and on the other side the sub-domains of biology, physiology, anatomy, ethology, genetics and so on are bounded by psychology, sociology and morality, mediated by medicine.

A. The Chemistry-Biology Boundary

Is this boundary permeable by concepts from chemistry through the science of biochemistry? If that science were indeed the chemistry of living beings then this would be a serious issue calling into question the 'grammar' of the relevant hinge concepts 'molecule' and 'organism'. It is easy to show that the question with which this paragraph begins is ill formed. Instead of defining biochemistry as the chemistry of living organisms and their vital processes, we now talk about the 'chemistry of carbon'. Most reactions in this field are performed in laboratories on artifacts. While alcohols, phenols, and so on came to the attention of scientists in living organisms, the chemistry of carbon has simply exploded out of the limited reactions of the mechanism of life.

The domain of biology relative to chemistry is not defined by the kind of chemical reactions that occur in it. The domain is defined by certain 'accidental' groupings of chemical reactions within a confined spatial envelope, the cell and similar entities. We can draw on the writings of Michael Polanyi (1965) for a succinct formulation of the relevant principle.

Polanyi's Principle. Chemical reactions are germane to biology just as far as they occur inside the envelope of a biological individual, be it cell, organ or organism. That such and such chemical processes are life sustaining is not a fact of chemistry, but an accidental historical fact about the composition of the first complex self-replicating molecules in the primeval soup.

It follows from this principle that the identification of a domain of biological chemistry must presuppose the concept of organism. It cannot be based on the intrinsic chemistry of 'organic' compounds, that is the chemistry of carbon. In particular, we cannot draw on the chemistry of carbon to identify organisms.

B. The Biology/Humanity Boundary

Following the Wittgensteinian methodology, our first step will be a surview of the uses of the relevant words, with a view to identifying the hinges and the grammars, distinguishing their propositional expression from empirical, actual or putative fact-stating propositions.

Biology to Culture Unmediated

The strong claim: Human sciences and the liberal arts are reducible via a biological intermediary say, neurophysiology and/or ethology, to branches of biology. This requires that psychological, social, political and moral concepts can be replaced, *salve veritate*, by biological concepts. Rather than revive long running and seeming irresolvable debates if we treat this as an issue about reduction, let us turn to an analysis of the hinge propositions underpinning the debate, to see if there is way of bringing the concept of 'complementarity' to bear to resolve the seeming impossibility of finding a common grammar to forge a common discourse.

The hinge concepts for each domain might be 'organism' as the generic hinge presupposition for the biological domain and 'person' for the hinge on which the discourses of the specifically human domain turn.

The analysis must proceed by looking for telling distinctions in the grammar of '*person*' and '*organism*'

 i. 'Organism' is morally neutral, while 'person' morally loaded. (This is a qualified and contested distinction in 'grammar' by animal rights enthusiasts, vegans etc).
 ii. 'Organism' behaviour requires causal explanations, while 'person' behaviour requires normative explanations. (This is a qualified and contested distinction by orthodox psychologists)

To see how and where we can make use of complementarity to relieve the tension that seems to call for either reduction of moral concepts to biological, for example 'altruism' to 'genetic kinship', or a claim for the emergence of irreducibly moral concepts in the history of homo sapiens, it is illuminating to turn to the other more specific boundary, between medicine as a branch of biology and traditional ways of describing human affairs.

Biology to Culture Mediated by Medicine

The strong claim might be that moral and social problems and predicaments can be transformed into medical problems, subject to

15

diagnosis, treatment and prognosis. The hinge concept for each domain might be 'person' as the generic concept for the specifically human domain, and 'patient' for the medical domain.

How do the grammars of *'person'* and *'patient'* differ?

i. 'Patient' is usually assimilated to 'organism' grammar, that is moral concepts are deleted from medical discourse, and causal concepts used throughout. (This is a qualified and contested distinction, for example by practitioners of 'holistic medicine', alternative therapies, and so on.)

ii. The key to the distinctive grammar of 'person' is the application of the concepts of 'mastery' ('control') and 'autonomy', in every circumstance. 'Moral responsibility' is just one of the concepts subordinate to 'mastery'. For example, moral responsibility for one's actions is tied to the presumption that one can master one's desires and impulses.

In the course of medical treatment and tests (though not in the usual medical consultation) the human being is transformed from a person, with whom and to whom the person grammar is employed, to a patient, about whom some one of the several biological grammars is employed. Such a change of existential status is achieved by handing over personal mastery and autonomy to another person or institution. This can only be done by means of a suitable ritual.

The work of Erving Goffman (1967) drew attention to some of the devices by which the person to patient and back to person transformations are achieved. The discourse of medicine, especially surgery, illustrates this very clearly. Once the person, Mr. Jones, is transformed into a patient, he can be referred to as 'an appendectomy', 'the second heart transplant today' and so on. Rituals of de- and re- personalization are used to achieve the transformation from person to patient to person again. With respect to the grammars of the concepts involved, the transformation amounts to the handing over of both 'mastery' and 'autonomy' to the medical team, for the purposes of the repair of the body as an organic machine.

Medicalization of Morals

This phenomenon has come to be an issue in human affairs, particularly because of the tendency to biologize moral issues by the invocation of genes and by the tendency to medicalize moral and social problems by the invocation of disease concepts. This leads to the consequential use of the concepts of 'diagnosis', 'prognosis', 'treatment' and 'cure', instead of traditional moral concepts like 'responsibility', 'guilt' and 'repentance'.

i. The complex pattern of reasoning to biologize homosexuality, via genetic endowment or some other constituent attribute of human organisms (not persons), has been in the newspapers frequently in recent years. For example, the report in the *London Times* of research at the University of East London which claims support for the use of the blink reflex delays to identify homosexuals. The alleged connection is a common genetic origin of sexual orientation and physiological structures in the eye.

ii. Here is clear example of the invocation of a gene to settle a moral issue. If you do not have the gene can you be blamed for some life demand failure? It is claimed that the 'mothering' gene has been found (in mice). If you do not have the gene can you be blamed for failing to do what we used to think society 'demands', for example looking after your children? And what about 'satyriasis' as another new, gene-based disease? The ex-husband of Halle Berry, the most beautiful woman in the world, a notorious philanderer, was reported to have been diagnosed' as 'suffering sexual obsession syndrome' and sent for treatment! Here we see very clearly how in moving to a discourse in which the hinge propositions turn on the concept of a 'patient', the person concepts such 'mastering one's lusts' and 'freeing oneself from biological impulses', are deleted from the discourse.

iii. Is ADHD a *disease*? Note how the words 'diagnosis' and 'treatment' are prominent in this language game. For example Michael Fitzgerald, of the University of Dublin, claimed to diagnose Lord Byron, the poet and revolutionary hero, through alleged *symptoms* of suffering from ADHD! Imagine if the doctors had had Ritalin then! No *Childe Harold*, and perhaps long delayed Greek independence!

There seems to be something very unsatisfactory in the resolution of the duality of incompatible discourses by adopting a reductive strategy. Nor does emergence seem much better. It is clear that sometimes treatment is the solution to unacceptable behaviour.

Can these antinomies (organism/person; person/patient) be relieved by adopting Bohr's move?

The 'complementarity' move is to point out that the conditions under which a human being displays its organism nature (male or female) and those under which it displays its person nature (him or her) are not realizable in the same procedure, and the relevant procedures cannot be applied together. So, the organic affordances of a human being and the socio-moral affordances are not realizable under the same procedure. In physics, the experimental set-ups cannot be realized at the same place and time. The hierarchical character of human discourse allows some, but not all patient procedures and some but not all person procedures to be carried out at the same time and in the same place.[3] It follows that the complementarity relation is more complex, sometimes mediating between adjoining levels in a hierarchy and sometimes between grammars and their relevant hinges at the same level.

A survey of the examples suggests that person predicates and human organism predicates, including patient predicates are indeed complementary. Being a patient and being a person are complex clusters of affordances. Though they cannot be displayed together they can be predicated together *as affordances*. According to Bohr's prescription, a complete description of a human being requires all three sets of predicates, biological, medical (including malfunctions) and moral (including good and bad behaviour), under the constraints on joint predication of the Principle of Complementarity.

Another General Metaphor for the Relation of the Human Body to Human Culture

The socio-cultural world imposes, directly or indirectly, all sorts of tasks upon its inhabitants. They must brush their teeth, be polite and generous, dig their gardens if they have them, check restaurant bills, and so on. How do they perform these tasks? Well there are rules, first of all. Brush the teeth with an up and down motion; remember that there are 100 cents in the Euro and so on. But more is needed. One needs a toothbrush and a skilled hand. One needs a brain that can process arithmetic, and one needs a strong back, a good eye and a spade to dig the garden properly. Tasks are cultural, tools are material and some of them are organic. What is the 'grammar' of the Task/Tool metaphor? At least it includes thinking of the body as an instrument for the performance of tasks defined in the culture. Just as we need to refer to metallurgy and mechanics in understanding how a piece of steel on a wooden handle can be used to rearrange the soil, so we need to refer to neurophysiology,

---

[3] I am indebted to several people, including Professor Margaret Boden, for drawing my attention to this feature of human affordances.

brain anatomy and connectionist modeling in understanding how a cluster of 10^{11} nerve cells can be used to solve arithmetical problems.

We can go further and distinguish biological from non-biological body projects, in terms of the relevant affordances:

The human body, including all its organs, affords nourishment and reproduction. It affords gymnastics, rugby, music, and even philosophy of biology. In this list we see the increasing dominance of cultural/accidental constraints over what is biological/necessary. Haute cuisine and Michelin stars have come to dominate the conceptions of bread and meat originally developed at the mouth of an Aurignacian cave.

The brain is one among the tools that a person uses to accomplish his or her socio-cultural projects. To adapt a formula of Alan Turing's:

Brain: culture :: racquet : tennis.

In a conceptual system in which persons are ultimate particulars, there is a place for brains and their workings as tools, while in a biological system in which organisms are the basic particulars there is no place for persons. The sciences of culture must include the workings of the brain. But how? My final point is this: The concepts of neuropsychology and associated sciences (tools) are complementary to the concepts of society and culture (tasks). The conditions under which human beings display their neurological nature (affordances) such as taking up radioactive fluorinated glucose in the brain in a PET scan, are incompatible with those under which they display their mathematical skills, their loves and hates, their loyalties and disloyalties, and so on.

Conclusions

1. There is no need to try to use the problematic concept of 'reduction' between incompatible systems of predicates to achieve a complete description of the phenomena in a domain. The ascription of affordances under the constraint of the Principle of Complementarity is sufficient.

2. There is no need to struggle with the problem of giving meaning to the concept of emergence between the properties of two distinct domains. They can be reconciled through the Principle of Complementarity, that is by paying attention to the conditions under which such properties are displayed or manifested.

3. The problems which this principle helps us to bypass, come about by mistakes concerning the grammar of our concepts.

Rom Harré

a. We must expand the rules for the management of incompatible predications to include the Principle of Complementarity.
b. We must beware of treating hinge propositions and grammatical rules as if they were empirical hypotheses.

References

Bohr, N. (1958) *Atomic Physics and Human Knowledge*. New York: John Wyley and Sons.

Brock, S. (2003) *Niels Bohr's Philosophy of Quantum Physics*. Berlin: Logos Verlag, pp. 258–64.

Goffman, E. (1967) *Asylums*. Harmondsworth: Penguin.

Polanyi. M. (1965) *The Knower and the Known*. M. Grene (ed), London: Routledge.

Wittgenstein, L. (1953) *Philosophical Investigations*. Oxford: Blackwell.

Wittgenstein, L. (1974) *On Certainty*. Oxford: Blackwell.

Other Histories, Other Biologies

GREGORY RADICK

1. Taking the counterfactual turn

When philosophers look to the history of biology, they most often ask about what happened, and how best to describe it. They ask, for instance, whether molecular genetics subsumed the Mendelian genetics preceding it, or whether these two sciences have maintained rather messier relations.[1] Here I wish to pose a question as much about what did not happen as what did. My concern is with the strength of the links between our biological science—our biology—and the particular history which brought that science into being. Would quite different histories have produced roughly the same science? Or, on the contrary, would different histories have produced other, quite different biologies?

I shall not endeavour to address the whole of biology or its history. I will concentrate on genetics, the headline-grabbing branch of biology in our time. The claims of this science on our future have given its history an unusually high public profile. Newspaper articles on the completed Human Genome Project came with timelines of genetic achievement, stretching back into the pre-Mendel mists, and forward to a future where, thanks to genetics-based medicine (we were told), the average person will live to more than ninety. Even more recently, the fiftieth anniversary of the introduction of the double-helix model of DNA in 1953 prompted books, symposia, television programmes, even a cover story in *Time* magazine. It also spurred people to wonder out loud about the nature of history. In 2003, we celebrated James Watson and Francis Crick above all. But they inferred the structure of DNA from Rosalind Franklin's remarkable X-ray crystallographic photograph of the B form of DNA. Might Franklin have given the world the double helix?

Earlier versions of this chapter were presented in 2003 to audiences in Leeds and Dublin as well as in London. I am grateful to all who attended on those occasions. I owe particular debts to my Leeds colleagues for their encouragement and suggestions; to the Royal Institute of Philosophy for the initial invitation; and to Jean Gayon, Jonathan Harwood and Richard Lewontin for helpful comments on a draft.
[1] For a survey of the 'Mendel and molecules' debate, see Kim Sterelny and Paul E. Griffiths, *Sex and Death: An Introduction to Philosophy of Biology* (Chicago: University of Chicago Press, 1999), chs. 6 and 7.

21

Gregory Radick

Watson had trained in genetics, Crick in physics. It is tempting to follow Watson himself and ascribe their success to this unique collaboration between different sciences. On this view, the discovery of the double helix awaited the partnering of genetical expertise with X-ray crystallographic expertise. Certainly that is how it happened. But whether it had to happen that way is another matter. A long tradition of counterfactual conjecture to the contrary centres on Franklin. Suppose we could rewind history's tape and keep that photograph out of Watson's hands a little while longer. Unlike Watson, Franklin was no geneticist, and had long thought of DNA as a structural, not a biological, puzzle. But by early 1953, she had given up her long-held prejudices about using structural models and contemplating helices. 'Would it have taken her much longer', asked the distinguished historian of biology Robert Olby, 'to come to the conclusion that the study of the relationship between A and B as helices was the way to go? The answer, though speculative, is surely that it would not.'[2]

Success in science has an air of inevitability about it. Talk of what might have been has an air of speculation about it. This paper aims to show how the critical examination of success in science can make for a less speculative assessment of alternative pasts. The case that will concern me is even more fundamental to our biology than the discovery of the molecular nature of the gene: the discovery of the gene itself. In asking whether we might have had a nongenic biology, I will attempt to illustrate by example just how much evidence from the actual past can be brought to bear on conjectures about possible pasts. Much of what follows will be history filtered through philosophy. At the outset, however, some philosophy leavened with history will help clarify what is, and is not, at stake.

2. The meaning of success

The success of our biology is a thing of wonder. No doubt it holds important lessons about our world and about ourselves. But what lessons? A naïve answer at least has the virtue of clarity. Consider, as an opening bid, that biological success shows (1) that we have got the world about right; and (2) that we could not help but get the world right eventually. More schematically:

[2] Robert Olby, 'Rosy Revised', *London Review of Books* (20 March 2003), 15.

(1) The basic entities, processes and events referred to in our best-confirmed biological theories really exist or occurred; and

(2) The inclusion of those entities, processes and events was inevitable.

Although I shall here be concerned mainly with (2), and then as it applies to just one basic entity, the gene, it is well to begin by noticing that there are several ways of connecting the realism expressed in (1) with the inevitabilism expressed in (2).[3]

The naïve view sketched above holds realism and inevitabilism to be mutually supporting. The items inventoried in our biology are inevitable because they are real, and the existence of these items guarantees their inclusion in a mature biology. So, says the realist-inevitabilist, the inclusion of the gene was inevitable because genes really exist, with something like the properties ascribed to them, and no serious, unhindered attempt to investigate life on Earth could have failed at some point to bump up against them and accord them basic status. But why should we believe that genes are real in the first place? The realist-inevitabilist will appeal in part to historical considerations—in the case of genes, to one of the most famous episodes of simultaneous discovery in the whole of science. As textbooks still proclaim, around 1900, three European botanists, Hugo de Vries, Carl Correns and Erich von Tschermak, independently rediscovered Gregor Mendel's principles of heredity, thus laying the conceptual foundations for genetics.

On the naïve view, the triple rediscovery reveals that, once background knowledge was sufficiently advanced, recognition of the gene was inevitable. The gene forced itself into our theories the moment we were ready to receive it. Mendelism was thus not of our making; and if not for Mendel, and after him De Vries, Correns and Tschermak, then the delivery of the gene would have fallen to others. Contemplating Mendel's long neglect and sudden, multiple rediscovery inspired the anthropologist Alfred Kroeber, writing around 1920, to clumsy eloquence:

> There may be those who see in these pulsing events only a meaningless play of capricious fortuitousness; but there will be others to whom they reveal a glimpse of a great and inspiring inevitability which rises as far above the accidents of personality

[3] This analysis fleshes out the remarks on success, realism and inevitabilism in Ian Hacking, *The Social Construction of What?* (Cambridge, MA: Harvard University Press, 1999), ch. 3, esp. 68-70, 78–80.

as the march of the heavens transcends the wavering contacts of random footprints of clouds on earth. Wipe out the perception of De Vries, Correns, and Tschermak, and it is yet clear that before another year had rolled around, the principles of Mendelian heredity would have been proclaimed to an according world, and by six rather than three discerning minds.[4]

What of those who see in the early history of Mendelism but 'a meaningless play of capricious fortuitousness'? The converse of the naïve, realist-inevitabilist view links scepticism about the existence of genes (antirealism) with scepticism about the inevitability of their inclusion in biological theory (contingentism). Yes, it is conceded, if genes existed, then modern biology would have been bound to include them at some point. But there are reasons, independent of historical considerations, for thinking that genes, as conventionally conceived, do not exist. It follows that if genes are not there in the world to be bumped up against, they cannot be held responsible for the emergence of a scientific consensus in favour of their reality. Where such a consensus holds, it owes its origins and maintenance instead to the contingencies of local history. Within our biological sciences, an unlikely chain of events at the beginning of the century led to belief in genes becoming entrenched while other, rival beliefs, no less well evidenced, went extinct. Since then, admittedly, the idea of the gene has turned out to be a productive one for framing many of our inquiries. But the history of science is strewn with false, useful beliefs (phlogiston, ether). Furthermore, the biological sciences might well have done equally well, or better, within a nongenic framework.

These contrary positions—on the one side, realism-inevitabilism; on the other, antirealism-contingentism—by no means exhaust the possibilities. Swapping the left-hand isms for each other generates two more worth considering. There is, first, antirealism-inevitabilism. By its lights, while belief in genes is unwarranted, the idea of the gene is nevertheless inescapable, once biological inquiry, wherever and whenever begun, has developed to a certain pitch. Gene theory here is seen as a necessary passage point to the future, a gate through which a scientific community must travel if it is to remain successful, not because genes exist—that is something science can never settle—but because human knowledge has a

[4] Alfred Kroeber, 'The Superorganic' (1917), revised 1927 version, reprinted in *Frontiers of Anthropology*, Ashley Montagu (ed.) (New York: Capricorn Books/G. P. Putnam's Sons, 1974), 344–81, quotation on 372–73. The text here reads 'on clouds of earth', which, given the sense of the passage, I take to be a mistake.

certain logic of development. The guiding spirit here is Auguste Comte's, for Comte regarded the postulation of unobservable entities as an unavoidable waystation in the growth of inquiry, marking out a middle, metaphysical stage from an earlier, theological one and a later, culminating, positivist one.

The Comtean has confidence in history. By contrast, the realist-contingentist—occupant of the final position in this quartet—regards history with suspicion. Yes, genes are real, but, says the realist-contingentist, that does not mean their discovery and acceptance was inevitable. If not for past events that could well have turned out differently, we might never have found our way to genes, and our biological sciences would now be nongenic. Maybe this ignorance of genes would have been hobbling, and we would now struggle to understand and control our world much more than we do. But then again, maybe, with genes out of the running, we would have embraced some other, now unknown, but equally real and serviceable entity as basic to our notions of heredity.

I hope the above suffices to suggest that the question of inevitability arises independently of the question of realism. No matter what you think about the ontology of genes, there is room for asking about the inevitability of the idea of the gene within the modern biological sciences. This is not to say that realism and inevitability can be cleanly bracketed off from one another, however. We shall see that they cannot. Moreover, the four positions I have sketched are not equally attractive. The latter two are, for most tastes, decidedly exotic. That leaves the naïve view and its converse, respectively yoking realism to inevitabilism, and antirealism to contingentism. Someone swayed by, say, Evelyn Fox Keller's argument that our biological sciences have outgrown the concept of the gene, and would be better off without it, will probably be inclined to accept a larger role for contingency in the initial canonization of that concept than someone not so swayed.[5] As ever, where logic fears to tread, psychology rushes in.

3. Multiple discovery and gene inevitabilism: the Mendelian convergence

Was a genic biology inevitable? We require well-developed arguments for and against for evaluation. But that is not where we

[5] Evelyn Fox Keller, *The Century of the Gene* (Cambridge, MA: Harvard University Press, 2000). For ontological discussion in a similarly iconoclastic spirit, see John Dupré's chapter in this volume.

stand. The weight of presumption has traditionally come down so much on the side of gene inevitabilism, or on the side of pessimism about counterfactual inquiry (for who can know what might have been?), that gene contingentism has hardly had a look. The main burden of this paper is to shift some of the barriers confronting the gene contingentist at the start.

Let us return, first, to the rediscovery of Mendelism in 1900 as an instance of independent convergence on the genic truth. To the extent that De Vries, Correns and Tschermak arrived at the same conclusions in isolation from each other, and from Mendel, the principles of Mendelian heredity can indeed, as Kroeber suggested, be judged as independent of the precise historical circumstances that carried them into scientific consensus. Note that convergence thus offers, at least in principle, and contrary to global counterfactual pessimism, a straightforward empirical test of inevitability. The greater the number of past trajectories that converged on the same conclusion, and the greater the independence of those trajectories, the more plausible will be the idea that the conclusion was inevitable. Kroeber indeed laid great store by convergence, piling up famous examples of multiple, simultaneous discovery alongside the Mendelian one: Leibniz and Newton converging on the calculus; Darwin and Wallace on evolution by natural selection; and so on. He took it that the best explanation for so much convergence was the inevitability of a discovery or invention, given the accumulation of human knowledge to a certain threshold.[6]

The convergence argument for inevitabilism was not new to Kroeber. It can be found, for instance, nearly a century earlier, in the English historian Macaulay's reflections on science and art.[7] Strikingly, it has become well known in our own time less as an historical argument about the nature of biology than as a biological argument about the nature of history. I refer to the well-known debate between the palaeontologists Simon Conway Morris and the late Stephen Jay Gould. In the contingentist camp is Gould,

[6] Op. cit. note 4, 369–75. On Kroeber's larger purposes in this influential paper, see Abram Kardiner and Edward Preble, *They Studied Man* (New York: Mentor, 1963), 169–72.

[7] For Macaulay, and citations to other instances of the argument from multiple discovery to inevitability, see Robert K. Merton, 'Singletons and Multiples in Science' (1961), reprinted in his *The Sociology of Science: Theoretical and Empirical Investigations*, N. W. Storer (ed.) (Chicago: University of Chicago Press, 1973), ch. 16, 353–4.

arguing that modern animals might well have evolved radically different anatomies, had contingent events at the end of the Cambrian era resulted in a different selection of survivors. In the inevitabilist camp is Conway Morris, arguing that, whatever happened in the Cambrian era, modern animals would look broadly similar to the animals that now inhabit Earth, since natural selection optimizes anatomical design, and the set of optimal designs is narrow. The ace up Conway Morris' sleeve is convergence: over and over again, it seems, independent lineages have evolved the same designs—eyes, wings, fishiness, intelligence, social organization, and so on.[8]

For the inevitabilist, then, much depends on establishing that two or more convergent pathways were in fact independent. Otherwise, the spectre arises of convergence due to the contingent sharing of a local, constraining inheritance. That spectre often proves harder to exorcise than the inevitabilist might hope. Certainly the convergence argument for gene inevitabilism now looks decidedly shaky. Superb historical detective work has revealed the triple rediscovery of Mendelism to be a far more tangled affair than Kroeber supposed. The whole idea that Mendelism amounts to a rediscovery now looks problematic. For one thing, the monk in the garden did not, it seems, regard his work as revolutionizing the science of heredity. Rather, he offered his discovery of a constant, three-to-one ratio of characters in the offspring of hybrid pea plants, and his explanation for this and related ratios, as interesting conclusions salvaged from a failed attempt to produce new species through hybridization. In explaining the ratios, furthermore, Mendel did not postulate the existence of genes. He did introduce a number of ideas later recognizable as 'Mendelian': that alternative characters, such as yellow versus green seed colours, were either 'dominant' or 'recessive' (his terms); and that in hybrid plants, exhibiting just the dominant character but containing factors for the recessive one too, dominant and recessive factors segregated at random into separate gametes. But for Mendel, these factors were

---

[8] The best introduction to the debate is Simon Conway Morris and Stephen Jay Gould, 'Showdown on the Burgess Shale', *Natural History* **107** (December 1998—January 1999), 48–55. See also Gould, *Wonderful Life: The Burgess Shale and the Nature of History* (London: Hutchinson Radius, 1989), esp. ch. 5; Conway Morris, *The Crucible of Creation: The Burgess Shale and the Rise of Animals* (Oxford: Oxford University Press, 1998), esp. ch. 8, and *Life's Solution: Inevitable Humans in a Lonely Universe* (Cambridge: Cambridge University Press, 2003).

not stable atoms of heredity, located in cells and retaining their identities through time. They were not, in short, genes.[9]

'Rediscovery' misleads as a name for what happened around 1900, then, in part because Mendelian principles resembled Mendel's conclusions only in a piecemeal and distorted way. But the fit is even more awkward. There is now little doubt that De Vries, Correns and Tschermak were all aware of Mendel's paper at earlier stages in their research than they later said. The contribution of De Vries, who published first, was arguably the most dependent on a reading of Mendel, for the great Dutch botanist seems to have hit neither on the ratios nor on their explanation independently. Correns does appear to have completed the bulk of his hybridization research before searching the literature and finding the 1866 paper. But he was a former student of Mendel's botanical correspondent Karl von Nägeli, so a prior influence cannot be ruled out. Moreover, the slow gestation of Correns' own paper may well be a sign that the late reading of Mendel brought new clarity. Be that as it may, Correns' trumpeting of Mendel's priority in discovery was probably intended less to bestow honour on Mendel than to take it away from De Vries, an envied rival. (As Correns pointed out, De Vries in his initial paper had quietly abandoned his own vocabulary for Mendel's, though not mentioning Mendel at all.) Tschermak, it seems, did discern the ratios independently of Mendel, but made little of them until he noticed the Mendelian bandwagon starting to roll, then clambered on.[10]

Some mention should be made as well of the small to non-existent roles that De Vries, Correns and Tschermak went on to play in establishing Mendelism as the basis for a new science of heredity. That fell largely to others, notably the Cambridge

[9] The revisionist scholarship on Mendel is summarized in Peter J. Bowler, *The Mendelian Revolution: The Emergence of Hereditarian Concepts in Modern Science and Society* (Baltimore: Johns Hopkins University Press, 1989), ch. 5. An excellent web resource on Mendel and Mendelism, including an annotated translation of the 1866 paper, is MendelWeb; see http://www.mendelweb.org (accessed July 2004).

[10] On 'rediscovery' as an inadequate label for what happened to Mendel's work around 1900, see Robert Olby, 'Rediscovery as an Historical Concept', *New Trends in the History of Science*, R. P. W. Visser *et al.* (eds.) (Amsterdam: Rodopi, 1989), 197–208. See also the more detailed discussion in his *Origins of Mendelism*, 2nd edition (Chicago: University of Chicago Press, 1985), ch. 6. The personal dimension is nicely captured in Robin Marantz Henig, *The Monk in the Garden* (New York: Houghton Mifflin, 2000), chs. 14 and 15.

zoologist William Bateson, of whom more below. For our purposes, the point is that neither independence nor convergence is straightforwardly assessed. We quickly find ourselves asking what criteria have to be met for different historical trajectories to count as independently convergent. How similar do they need to be, in what respects, and why? Other putative cases of independent convergence present similar difficulties. Consider those 'co-discoverers' of evolution by natural selection, Darwin and Wallace. They were different from each other in all sorts of interesting ways. But they shared much as well, including ideas generative of their evolutionary theories, notably the Malthusian population principle and the Lyellian view that history explains biogeography. Even if one overlooks the common inheritances, intellectual and cultural, there remains the fact that Wallace's theory was not strictly identical to Darwin's.[11] On what grounds shall they be declared the 'same' theory? Moving from the history of biology to biology itself, consider the emergence of eyes in animal lineages constituting distant branches of the evolutionary tree. Eyes can be found among the vertebrates, arthropods and molluscs, but not among their common ancestors. Yet, in each phylum, the development of eyes is regulated—so our genic biology teaches—by genes similar enough to work when swapped into organisms belonging to the other phyla. Those eyeless ancestors seem thus to have bequeathed, not eyes, but the biochemical apparatus making eyes possible.[12]

Whatever the general status of convergence arguments for inevitabilism, the convergence argument for gene inevitabilism is wanting. That argument is, however, but one that might be raised against gene contingentism. In the remainder of the paper I shall address three more objections. First, I shall consider whether the failure of Lysenkoism—a nongenic biology that flourished in the mid-twentieth-century Soviet Union—can be counted as an instance of punished divergence from the genic truth. I shall then

[11] On whether Darwin and Wallace converged independently on natural selection, see Gregory Radick, 'Is the Theory of Natural Selection Independent of its History?', *The Cambridge Companion to Darwin*, Jonathan Hodge and Gregory Radick (eds.) (Cambridge: Cambridge University Press, 2003), ch. 6, 149–50.

[12] On convergence and the eye, see Stephen Jay Gould, *Leonardo's Mountain of Clams and the Diet of Worms* (London: Vintage, 1999), ch. 17, 331–2; cf. Simon Conway Morris, *Life's Solution*, op. cit. note 8, 151–73, 193. On the large scope for disagreement about claims for convergence in biology, see Adrian Woolfson's review of the latter, 'How to Make a Mermaid', *London Review of Books* (5 February 2004), 25–6.

Gregory Radick

turn to the question of whether, around 1900, there were serious alternatives to Mendelism that might have served equally well as a basis for a new science of heredity. I shall make a preliminary case for Galtonian biometry, especially as developed by W. F. R. Weldon, as just such an alternative. Finally, I will consider a challenge that puts a new, counterfactualist spin on the familiar topics of theory incommensurability and the theory-ladenness of observations. The worry here is that an intuitively attractive strategy for demonstrating that a losing theory could have been a winner is in fact incoherent.

4. Abandoned alternatives and gene inevitabilism: the Lysenkoist divergence

The twentieth century contains at least one famous and amply documented example of a nongenic biology: Lysenkoism. It ran in parallel with genic biology through the middle decades of the century. It enjoyed enviable institutional clout. Its practitioners took a robustly sceptical stance toward the existence of genes. And it was, by common consent, an utter fiasco. On the face of it, then, the failure of Lysenkoism argues against gene contingentism and for gene inevitabilism. It seems to show that no scientific community deserving of the name can ignore the gene forever. The challenge before the gene contingentist is thus to explain why this is not the right lesson to draw from Lysenkoist failure. But first, a brief review of Lysenkoism is in order.

The movement took its name from the Soviet agrobiologist Trofim D. Lysenko, who in 1936 put his doubts about the gene plainly. What 'we deny', he said, was 'that the geneticists and the cytologists will see genes under the microscope.' Microscopic studies, Lysenko continued, will no doubt reveal structures of interest; but these 'will be particles of the cells, nuclei or chromosomes, and not what the geneticists mean by genes.' In Lysenko's view, the fundamental mistake of 'Mendelism-Morganism' was the notion that heredity could be identified with a mere part of the organism—a bit of chromosome, if T. H. Morgan's school of fruitfly geneticists were to be believed—rather than the whole set of an organism's ever-changing relations with its environment. More perniciously, as Lysenko saw it, the geneticists' false theory of heredity drew support from, and lent support to, a related doctrine: that acquired characters could not be inherited. A major Lysenkoist ambition was to show, on the contrary, that permanent improvements to crop varieties could be engineered through directed transformations of the environment. These views were much debated in the Soviet Union in the 1930s to the mid-1940s. But by the late 1940s, Lysenkoism had won monopoly rights as the Soviet science of heredity. Mendelian genetics was shut down, its leaders marginalized, even imprisoned.[13]

There is a well-known ideological dimension. Although the Bolsheviks had supported genetics from early days, Lysenko gradually tarred it with the brush of elitist, mystifying reaction. Where, according to Lysenko, the revolution needed energetic guidance on rational breeding, the academic geneticists taught that breeders could do nothing but await fortuitous mutations. 'Mendelism-Morganism is built entirely on chance', declared Lysenko, in a notorious 1948 address. 'There is no effectiveness in such science. With such a science it is impossible to plan, to work toward a definite goal; it rules out scientific prediction.' The political credentials of Mendelism-Morganism were little helped by its class affiliation. Unlike Lysenko, the son of peasants, the geneticists came overwhelmingly from bourgeois backgrounds. A further liability was the association with lab-bound fruitflies. As symbols for the otherworldly sterility of academic genetics, flies were second to none. A cartoon from the Soviet periodical press of the era shows a geneticist, pockets full of test tubes of fruit flies, marching arm in arm with a Klansman and a policeman. Another has a fat-cat businessman admiring the flies which, the Lysenkoists alleged, had distracted Soviet scientists from the task of improving agriculture. The geneticists had wanted to learn about flies when the people had needed them to learn about wheat.[14]

[13] For Lysenko in his own words, and in English, the indispensable volume is T. D. Lysenko, *Agrobiology: Essays on Problems of Genetics, Plant Breeding and Seed Growing* (Moscow: Foreign Languages Publishing House, 1954). The quotation is from 'Two Trends in Genetics' (1936–7), 160–94, 186. The whine of axes grinding is never far off in the historiography of Lysenkoism. For a non-Marxist perspective, see David Joravsky, *The Lysenko Affair* (Cambridge, MA: Harvard University Press, 1970). For a Marxist but not uncritical perspective, see Richard Levins and Richard Lewontin, 'The Problem of Lysenkoism' (1976), in their *The Dialectical Biologist* (Cambridge, MA: Harvard University Press, 1985), ch. 7.

[14] The quotation is in T. D. Lysenko, 'The Situation in Biological Science' (1948), in his *Agrobiology*, op. cit. note 13, 515–54, 552. For the cartoons, illustrating a 1949 article entitled 'Fly-Lovers and Man-Haters', see Valery N. Soyfer, *Lysenko and the Tragedy of Soviet Science*, L. and R. Gruliow (trans.) (New Brunswick, NJ: Rutgers University Press, 1994), illustration insert, no. 19.

Gregory Radick

Yet, for all its ideological correctness, Lysenkoism at last fell from favour. Why? According to one of the most senior Western historians of Soviet science, Loren Graham, the Soviets had a belated reality check. He suggests that, as the theoretical and practical failures of the Lysenkoists mounted, and as the excuses for failure became less and less convincing, it became obvious that, to put it bluntly, Lysenkoism was wrong. The abandonment of Lysenkoism thus shows that science is a social construction only within certain bounds. Even totalitarian societies cannot pursue congenial but false sciences forever. Graham compares the Soviets' denial of the realities of the marketplace to their denial of the realities of the gene. 'Despite all the social constructivist support' for Lysenkoist biology and Marxist economics, he argues, 'both have fallen into eclipse. Both the gene and the market have reemerged, and, one is tempted to add, "with a vengeance." Natural and economic realities have obtruded.' Graham lingers especially over the famous image of Khrushchev visiting an Iowa farm in the early 1960s, amazed to learn of its productivity, and of the Mendelian principles that, as Khrushchev was told, guided the development of the American agricultural wonder, hybrid corn.[15]

On Graham's reading, then, the failure of Lysenkoism is a kind of divergence argument for gene inevitabilism. Eventually, he suggests, a path of inquiry angled away from the gene becomes intolerably steep. Under Lysenkoism, the ignored genes wreaked their vengeance through Soviet agriculture, leaving it enfeebled compared with gene-savvy American agriculture. The message borne home to Khrushchev—that, in Graham's gloss, Western genetics had developed 'much more effective agricultural practices than Lysenko's genetics'—amounts, for Graham, 'to the intrusion of reality into Lysenko's socially constructed worldview.' No player of favourites, reality would, it seems, have intruded just as rudely in the Western market economies if Mendelian genetics had somehow failed to find its footing there in the early twentieth century. The greater success of American versus Soviet agriculture at mid-century thus appears to count against gene contingentism.[16]

Is the testimony of agriculture indeed so unequivocal? The legacies of the Cold War are such that, even now, one needs to consult the Marxists for a contrary view. The case for doubt has been put most effectively by the self-described 'dialectical biologist'

[15] Loren R. Graham, *What Have We Learned About Science and Technology from the Russian Experience?* (Stanford: Stanford University Press, 1998), 17–31, quotation on 31.

[16] Graham, op. cit. note 15, quotation on 25.

Richard Lewontin and his colleagues. Their arguments have not, to my knowledge, been answered. Graham does not even acknowledge them. Here are four of the most impressive in the Lewontonian brief. First, comparative data on annual crop yields from the 1920s to 1960s, far from showing the damaging effects of Lysenkoism, reveal roughly similar rates of gain in yield in the Soviet Union as in the United States—perhaps because better machinery and chemicals, common to farming in both nations, mattered much more than divergent theories of inheritance. Second, the rejection of Lysenkoism should be seen as part of a wider generational shift in the Soviet Union, as the idealist revolutionaries, willing to bear the costs of establishing a socialist alternative, gave way to pragmatic bureaucrats unwilling to bear those costs. Third, the famous Mendelian agricultural success story, hybrid corn, is not universally more productive. It does best under the conditions of soil and climate which characterize the American corn belt. Under other conditions, whether in the US or in the former USSR (which has a tiny corn belt), local corn varieties do better. Fourth, there is room to doubt that only Mendelism can guide the breeding of corn as productive (*ceteris paribus*) as hybrid corn. Horticulturalists might well have achieved as much using pre-Mendelian methods, selectively crossing the highest-yield individuals from the highest-yield variety, generation after generation. The attraction of Mendelism for American seedsmen was not its promise of otherwise unattainable yields, but the prospect of forcing farmers to return to the seedsmen year after year (since plants born of seeds produced through Mendel-style, intervarietal hybridization would not themselves breed true).[17]

Each of these points applies pressure to the presumption that theories of inheritance, correct or incorrect, on either side of the former Iron Curtain, have had much to do with the practice of agriculture. Here are historical and scientific grounds on which to hesitate before concluding, with Graham and others, that agricultural reality crushed a would-be rival to genic biology. Even so, there are other, conceptual grounds for distinguishing the actual fate of Lysenkoism from the possible fates of nongenic biologies. As we have seen, Lysenkoism was not defined solely by a negative doctrine, the non-existence of genes. There were a number of positive doctrines, most famously a belief in the 'Lamarckian' inheritance of acquired characters. There were also less well-

[17] See Levins and Lewontin, op. cit. note 13, esp. 171–4, 188–191, and Jean-Pierre Berlan and R. C. Lewontin, 'The Political Economy of Hybrid Corn', *Monthly Review* **38** (July-August 1986), 35–47.

defined but no less characteristic attitudes, such as the emphases on process over structure, on the environmental situation of the organism, and on the need to study problems which bore directly on agricultural concerns. None of these positive doctrines and attitudes are deductively entailed by scepticism about the existence of genes. Moreover, all of them, especially the Lamarckism, mark Lysenkoist biology off from current biology. For purposes of counterfactual testing of gene scepticism, at least at the first step, we need to do away as much as possible with such complications. What we require is something as much like Mendelian genetics as possible, except without the genes. One promising candidate is Weldonian biometry.

5. Weldonian biometry as a plausible competitor to Mendelian genetics

Born the same year as Mendel (1822), Francis Galton is now most often recalled, indeed reviled, as the begetter of the rational management of human breeding, or what he called 'eugenics'. But eugenics was just one facet of a remarkably creative, diverse and influential scientific enterprise, stretching from the 1850s into the 1900s. In his own lifetime, Galton's ideas about controlling heredity had less impact than his ideas about how to study it and how it worked. He inaugurated the analysis of human pedigree data and the study of twins as means for disentangling nature from nurture. He conducted careful experiments to test his cousin Charles Darwin's theory of inheritance, pangenesis. He developed his own theories on the physiology of inheritance.[18] But what most impressed the biologists and anthropologists who came of professional age in the 1890s was the programme, set out most fully in Galton's 1889 book *Natural Inheritance*, for the statistical study of inheritance at the level of the population. This was 'biometry'; and in the hands of its leading practitioners and propagandists, the mathematician Karl Pearson and, especially, the zoologist W. F. R. Weldon, it came to stand for a well-defined set of means, ends and objects of study.[19]

[18] An excellent study of Galton in the round is Nicholas Wright Gillham, *A Life of Sir Francis Galton: From African Exploration to the Birth of Eugenics* (Oxford: Oxford University Press, 2001). Like Mendel, Galton is well served on the web; an especially generous selection of Galtoniana is available at http://www.mugu.com/galton/ (accessed July 2004).

[19] Francis Galton, *Natural Inheritance* (London: Macmillan, 1889). On this book and its role in fostering biometry, see Gillham, op. cit. note 18, chs. 18 and 19.

A good number of these are visible in a collaborative paper of 1893, regarded as exemplary in its own day. (How far the exemplar was, in one or another of Kuhn's senses, paradigmatic, is a matter I shall consider below.) Under scrutiny were measurements of eleven anatomical characters in adult female shore crabs—carapace breadth and so on—from two different populations or 'races', one living in Plymouth Sound, the other in the Bay of Naples. The mathematical sifting of this data revealed what were, for Weldon and Pearson, three major prizes. First, the measurement sets almost all distributed themselves into bell-shaped curves. Second, the sole exception resolved itself, on further analysis, into two separate bell-shaped curves, revealing dimorphism for that character in that population. Third, variation in some features correlated with variation in other features in numerically precise ways. (The now-standard statistical concept of correlation was Galton's invention, as was the concept of regression.) Taken as a model, the paper thus commended attention, first and foremost, to statistical regularities among continuously varying characters in large natural populations.[20]

Biometry so construed was not so much a theory of inheritance as a cluster of methodological preferences. In the late 1890s, however, a theory of inheritance precipitated out as well, around what Pearson dubbed Galton's Law of Ancestral Heredity. Galton introduced the law formally in 1897, though its origins can be traced back much further in his writings.[21] Weldon later stated it thus: 'that the two parents contribute between themselves one-half of the total heritage of the offspring, that the four grandparents contribute one-quarter, the eight great-grandparents one-eighth, and so on. Thus the sum of the ancestral contributions is expressed by the series $(1/2 + 1/4 + 1/8 + 1/16 + \ldots\ldots)$, which, being equal to 1, expresses the whole heritage.'[22] What, precisely, was being added up here was

[20] W. F. R. Weldon, 'On Certain Correlated Variations in *Carcinus moenas*', *Proceedings of the Royal Society of London* **54** (1893), 318–29. On this paper, and Pearson's contribution to it, see Gillham, op. cit. note 18, 281–3, and Jean Gayon, *Darwinism's Struggle for Survival: Heredity and the Hypothesis of Natural Selection*, M. Cobb (trans.) (Cambridge: Cambridge University Press, 1998), 204–10.

[21] Francis Galton, 'The Average Contribution of Each Several Ancestor to the Total Heritage of the Offspring', *Proceedings of the Royal Society of London* **61** (1897), 401–13, and 'A Diagram of Heredity', *Nature* **57** (1898), 293. On the law as Galton conceived it, see the superb discussion in Gayon, op. cit. note 20, 132–46.

[22] [W. F. R. Weldon], 'Current Theories of the Hereditary Process' (eighth lecture), *The Lancet* (25 March 1905), 810.

never fully settled. Galton was happy for the formula to apply sometimes to a single individual, and at other times to a whole generation. Pearson judged these conceptions to be inconsistent, however, and introduced a series of modifications aimed at bolstering the law as a predictor of characters in the individual (the law's proper domain, he thought). Through all the debate, the core 'ancestrian' intuition nevertheless remained intact: the hereditary contribution of an ancestor to descendants suffers regular diminution with each generation, but, as a rule, is never extinguished.[23]

A thorough positivist, Pearson felt there was no need to make physiological sense of the law, so long as it successfully predicted what was observed; and this attenuated version of biometry has tended to be best remembered. But Galton's thinking was quite otherwise, as was Weldon's.[24] At the start of a series of lectures on inheritance, presented in London in 1904–5, Weldon—by far the most expert biologist at the biometrical vanguard—argued that while statistical facts were the proper data of a science of heredity, 'when an explanation was sought of the mechanism or *modus operandi* of heredity, one passed ... outside the domain of statistics and concrete facts and had to picture the invisible organic processes accompanying the growth and the reproduction of animals.'[25] Weldon's own picture of those processes remained

[23] Pearson reviewed the changes in Karl Pearson, 'A Mendelian's View of the Law of Ancestral Inheritance', *Biometrika* 3 (1904), 109–12. On Pearson's interpretations of Galton's law, see Michael Bulmer, 'Galton's Theory of Ancestral Inheritance', *A Century of Mendelism in Human Genetics*, M. Keynes, A. W. F. Edwards and R. Peel (eds.) (London: Galton Institute/CRC Press, 2004), 13–18, esp. 15–16, and, more extensively, Bernard J. Norton, *Karl Pearson and the Galtonian Tradition: Studies in the Rise of Quantitative Social Biology* (unpublished Ph.D. dissertation, UCL, 1979), ch. 6.

[24] Pearson was of course the author of that influential positivist breviary, *The Grammar of Science* (London: Scott, 1892). In Galton's 1897 paper introducing the law, he had argued that 'its close agreement with physiological phenomena'—in particular, the halving of the germinal material in the production of gametes—'ought to give a prejudice in *favour* of its truth.' Galton, op. cit. note 21, 403, emphasis in original. For Pearson, however, the law, as he wrote in 1903, 'is not a biological hypothesis at all, it is simply the statement of a fundamental theorem in the statistical theory of multiple correlation applied to a particular type of statistics.' Karl Pearson, 'The Law of Ancestral Heredity', *Biometrika* 2 (1903), 211–29, quotation on 226.

[25] The abstracts of Weldon's lectures on 'Current Theories of the Hereditary Process' appeared in *The Lancet* (1905), 42, 180, 307–8, 512, 584–5, 657, 732, 810. The quotation is from 42.

tragically incomplete: he died unexpectedly in 1906, at the age of forty-six, while at work on a book on inheritance. The outlines can nevertheless be made out clearly enough. Roughly, in Weldon's view, what an individual inherited was a set of 'determinants', themselves—in higher animals—constituents of the chromosomes. 'Determinant' sometimes went in quotes for Weldon, to indicate that this term was common among students of inheritance, but also perhaps because he emphatically did not think of germinal causes as acting independently of context. He insisted on the influence of the chemical and physical environments on the form of hereditary characters. He also envisaged a kind of contest among the chromosomal determinants. In general, the more active or vigorous an individual determinant, the greater its share in the character. At the extreme, one determinant could dominate wholly.[26]

Weldon's early death cut short the most promising interpretative effort on behalf of ancestrian biometry. It also, and rather more famously, brought to an end the most formidable resistance to Mendelian genetics in its early days. The shape of the 'biometrician-Mendelian' controversy, pitting Weldon, Pearson and their biometrical allies against Bateson and his Mendelian allies, is well known, as are some of the explanations historians have offered for its bitterness. These need not detain us here.[27] What matters for our purposes is that there were issues of substance in dispute—issues that might well have been decided in another way.

No less than ancestrian biometry, Mendelism was a theory of inheritance and a set of beliefs about how it ought to be studied. Aspects of both ran against the biometrical grain. Theoretically, a major point of contention concerned the gametes of hybrids in

[26] Weldon's 'Theory of Inheritance' and other unpublished writings are contained in the Pearson Papers, 264/2, UCL. For discussion of these and other sources, see Robert Olby, 'The Dimensions of Scientific Controversy: The Biometric-Mendelian Debate', *British Journal for the History of Science* **22** (1988), 299–320, esp. 314–7. See also Norton, op. cit. note 23, 190–3, 218–20. The fullest treatment of Weldon's life and thought remains Pearson's long obituary notice, in *Biometrika* **5** (1906), 1–52. For Pearson's reconstruction of Weldon's theory, see Karl Pearson, 'On a Mathematical Theory of Determinantal Inheritance, from Suggestions and Notes of the Late W. F. R. Weldon', *Biometrika* **6** (1908), 80–93.

[27] The historiography of this debate up to the mid-1980s is summarized in Olby, op. cit. note 26, 300–4. Notable contributions since then include Gayon, op. cit. note 20, ch. 8, and Eileen Magnello, 'The Reception of Mendelism by the Biometricians and the Early Mendelians (1899–1909)', in *A Century of Mendelism in Human Genetics*, op. cit. note 23, 19–32, which makes use of some of Weldon's unpublished letters.

Mendelian crosses. Mendelian theory predicted that hybrids produced equal numbers of gametes of two kinds. Half the gametes determined one form of a character—the form exhibited by one of the hybrid's pure-bred parents. The other half determined the form exhibited by the other parent. Individual gametes thus carried no legacy of the hybrid state of the organism issuing them, but were 'pure' in respect of the parental forms. Bateson and Weldon agreed both that this 'doctrine of gametic purity' was fundamental to Mendelian theory, and that it represented a departure from the Galtonian tradition, since it predicted that ancestral influence could go to zero very rapidly.[28] The difference was clearest in the predictions the two theories made about 'extracted recessives': the organisms comprising the 1 in the Mendelian 3:1 ratio—the green-seeded pea plants born to yellow-seeded hybrid plants. If inbred, extracted recessives should, on Mendelian theory, yield generation after generation of organisms showing the same, recessive character. The reappearance of the old dominant character—an atavism—has to be put down to accident (mutation) or initial impurity. In Weldonian theory, by contrast, the vast majority of individuals among the extracted recessives were expected to harbour the domi-nant-character determinant. Weldonian theory thus predicted the dominant form of the character to reappear if inbreeding were kept up in such a lineage.[29]

The accompanying differences in method, although less clear-cut than the differences in theory and prediction, are no less striking. The exemplary investigation in the Mendelian tradition was of

[28] Bateson presented gametic purity as the 'essence' of Mendelism in his polemical *Mendel's Principles of Heredity: A Defence* (Cambridge: Cambridge University Press, 1902), quotation on 115. On 'the Mendelian doctrine of gametic purity' as irreconcilable 'with the vast body of facts and data of heredity in human families and races collected and published by Francis Galton and Karl Pearson', see [Weldon], 'Current Theories of the Hereditary Process', op. cit. note 25, 732. Weldon took care to attribute the doctrine to the Mendelians, not to Mendel; see W. F. R. Weldon, 'Mr Bateson's Revisions of Mendel's Theory of Heredity', *Biometrika* **2** (1903), 286–98; esp. 288–9.

[29] For Weldon's derivation of the Mendelian ratio without the assump-tion of gametic purity, see Norton, op. cit. note 23, 190–3, which presents in more accessible form part of the discussion in Pearson, 'On a Mathematical Theory of Determinantal Inheritance', op. cit. note 26. As Pearson summarized (93): 'We see that Mendelian dominance and the Mendelian quarter may arise in cases where there is no pure gamete, and that the discovery of a latent character may need several generations of breeding.'

course Mendel's own: the experimental hybridizing of distinct varieties, carried through for several generations. The Weldon-Pearson biometrical exemplar offered at least three contrasts. First, the Mendelian began not with continuously varying characters, but with those characters that come in just two forms. Second, the Mendelian tracked those characters not in large, randomly inter-breeding populations, but in single lineages born of the selective mating of individuals themselves produced through selective mating. Third, the Mendelian was indifferent to the ancestry of the first, parental generation in a hybridization experiment. It did not matter whether a lineage had been breeding true for twelve generations or two generations. All that mattered was that it bred true. Here, Weldon argued, was a methodological upshot of the doctrine of gametic purity. 'The fundamental mistake which vitiates all work based upon Mendel's method is the neglect of ancestry', he wrote in a famous 1902 critique.[30] 'This neglect of ancestry, the tendency to regard offspring as resembling their parents rather than their race, accounts for much of the apparent inconsistency between the results obtained by different observers who have crossed plants or animals.'[31]

The success of Mendelism over biometry was not total, of course. From very early on, there were demonstrations showing the possibility of Mendelizing characters which varied continuously, so long as one assumed that lots of Mendelian genes of small effect governed a character.[32] Biometry was accordingly made Mendelism-friendly over the first decades of the twentieth century. There remained, and still remain, textbooks on biometry, journals of biometry, departments of biometry, learned people who identify themselves with pride as 'biometricians'. What did not survive the Mendelian revolution is the law of ancestral heredity as more than a merely statistical tool, associated with scepticism about gametic purity and doubts about the wisdom of founding a science of heredity on alternating characters and hybridization experiments. As a result, we live in world where scientific students of heredity organize their knowledge around qualified Mendelism, rather than qualified biometry. A recent and representative undergraduate

[30] W. F. R. Weldon, 'Mendel's Laws of Alternative Inheritance in Peas', *Biometrika* **1** (1902), 228–54, quotation on 252.
[31] Weldon, op. cit. note 30, 242.
[32] The subsumption of the ancestral law under Mendelism culminated in Ronald Fisher's famous paper, 'The Correlation Between Relatives on the Supposition of Mendelian Inheritance', *Transactions of the Royal Society of Edinburgh* **52** (1918), 399–433. For discussion, see Norton, op. cit. note 23, 220.

genetics textbook, for instance, introduces Mendelian phenomena, peas and all, in the second chapter, with biometric phenomena making an entrance only in chapter sixteen.[33]

Could the biometricians have triumphed over the Mendelians? Mendelian success has tended to obscure several points in biometry's favour. We have seen that biometry and Mendelism offered methods and theories of comparable reach. As Weldon practised it, moreover, biometry had experimental and physiological sides potentially as robust as Mendelism's. Weldon and Pearson, professors at Oxford and UCL respectively, commanded more institutional prestige and resources than Bateson, who for a long period held no university position at Cambridge.[34] On a couple of issues, furthermore—and here we adopt a 'Whiggish' stance for the moment—Weldon was much closer to current consensus than Bateson was. Where Bateson was famously reluctant to accept a role for the chromosomes as the locations of the hereditary determinants, Weldon had no such difficulty. Where Bateson was eager to show that the new understanding of heredity made nonsense of Darwinism, Weldon was a loyal Darwinian, held by some to have furnished the first demonstration of natural selection in the wild. A biometrical triumph, then, far from impeding progress, might have helped it along.[35]

6. Theory-laden data and theory incommensurability revisited[36]

Let us allow that, at Weldon's death, ancestrian biometry had more going for it than is sometimes appreciated, maybe even a lot more. Can we go any further in evaluating its counterfactual credentials?

[33] Daniel L. Hartl and Elizabeth W. Jones, *Genetics: Principles and Analysis*, fourth edition (Boston: Jones and Bartlett, 1998).

[34] As Olby has put it, within zoology, 'Weldon enjoyed *insider* status and Bateson *outsider* status.' Olby, op. cit. note 26, 313, emphasis in original.

[35] On Bateson and chromosomes, see William Coleman, 'Bateson and Chromosomes: Conservative Thought in Science', *Centaurus* **15** (1970), 228–314. On Weldon and chromosomes, see [Weldon], op. cit. note 25, 584–5, 810, and Pearson's remarks in Pearson, 'On a Mathematical Theory of Determinantal Inheritance', op. cit. note 26, 81–82. On Weldon and Bateson's divergent attitudes towards Darwinism and other topics, see Olby, op. cit. note 26.

[36] This section owes much to provocative questions from Jeff Ketland, then at Leeds, and from Richard Gray at TCD.

What other sorts of evidence, if any, might we use to judge whether this body of ideas and practices was capable of sustaining a successful, nongenic biology? One intuitively attractive answer suggests itself. If Weldon had lived, he would surely have continued his efforts at showing how well his own theory of inheritance explained the observations explained differently by Mendelian theory, and also how poorly Mendelian theory coped with observations his theory handled well. Since Weldon's day, of course, the stock of accumulated observations to do with inheritance has grown enormously. We know the successes and failures of Mendelian theory with these observations. Why not pick up where Weldon left off, and see how well Weldonian theory does with the same? The better it does, the better will be our reasons for believing the theory was a casualty of contingent history.

There is, however, a possibly fatal objection to such a strategy. The accumulated observations on inheritance, or anything else for that matter, are not pure reports of how the world really is. The observations are contaminated with the theories of the accumulators—'theory laden', in the jargon. Observers beholden to different theories might well have reported the same events quite differently, noticed different patterns, contrived different experiments, attended to quite different events. The same data would therefore likely not have accumulated under the watch of seriously alternative ideas and practices to the ones we have now. On this view, it is therefore pointless to show how well a failed theory could have dealt with the data as we have it now, since it would never have had to deal with those data. Borrowing from fashionable physics, we can picture rival theories as locked in to data sets which exist only in those histories where one or the other theory is dominant. Rival theories are thus, in a quite literal sense, incommensurable; so far as fit-with-the-data is a criterion for theory choice, there is no common metric to reckon the one against the other.[37]

In fact, some splendid examples of data laden with Mendelian theory lie to hand. The most celebrated instance, among historians of biology at least, comes from laboratory studies of the fruitfly. As Robert Kohler has shown, Morgan and his students did not simply investigate flies as they found them, adhering to decaying bananas in flasks around the lab. Rather, they painstakingly bred flies to

[37] On incommensurability in this sense, see Ian Hacking, 'The Self-Vindication of the Laboratory Sciences', *Science as Practice and Culture*, Andrew Pickering (ed.) (Chicago: University of Chicago Press, 1992), 29–64, see 56–7.

make them ever more suitable candidates for Mendelian studies, systematically eliminating whatever interfered with presumptively Mendelian processes. The results, the lab-standardized fly lineages, were theory-laden scientific objects if ever there were.[38] Another instance is less well known, but especially apposite here: Mendel's own observations of peas. In *Biometrika*, the journal Weldon founded with Pearson to carry their programme forward, Weldon published a remarkable colour plate. It shows the seeds of eighteen peas. We do not see two sorts: either yellow or green. What we see is a continuously varying scale, from green to yellowy-green through to greenish-yellow and then finally yellow. 'If Mendel's statements were universally valid, even among Peas', commented Weldon, 'the characters of the seeds in the numerous hybrid races now existing should fall into one or other of a few definite categories, which should not be connected by intermediate forms.'[39] But this was not what Weldon had found, as he explained:

In attempting to judge the results of other observers, including those of Mendel himself, I have constantly found it difficult to understand the statements made, because of the vagueness of the terms used to describe shape and colour. In order to make my own statements about colour as intelligible as may be, I selected from a sample of [one hybrid variety] a series of 18 peas, which show, after removal of the seed-coats, a fairly gradual series of transitional colours from a deep green to an orange yellow.[40]

Having called the witness of the peas, Weldon arraigned Mendel on charges of letting his theoretical preferences bias his observations. Of course Mendel had been able to see that some yellow seeds were more greenish than others and vice versa. But, according to Weldon, Mendel's prior ideas about inheritance and its study had precluded his appreciating such variation as at all meaningful. We have already encountered Weldon's diagnosis: Mendelian indifference to the ancestry of the parental peas in experimental crosses. As a result of

[38] See Robert E. Kohler, *Lords of the Fly: Drosophila Genetics and the Experimental Life* (Chicago: University of Chicago Press, 1994), esp. chs. 2 and 3. For discussion, see Gregory Radick, 'Cultures of Evolutionary Biology', *Studies in History and Philosophy of Biological and Biomedical Sciences* **34** (2003), 187–200, 197–8. Little in Kohler's analysis would have been news to the Lysenkoists; see Levins and Lewontin, op. cit. note 13, 181.

[39] Weldon, op. cit. note 30, 244.

[40] Weldon, op. cit. note 30, 245. The plate can be found facing 254.

this indifference, Mendel disregarded deviations in character from the parental types. The yellowy green seeds got categorized under 'green'; the greenish yellow seeds got categorized under 'yellow'; and anything really out of the ordinary probably got filed away under 'exceptional'.[41]

The possibility that Mendelian theory infects the accumulated data on inheritance cannot be brushed aside. Its Mendelism-ladenness need not, however, disqualify that data from a role in credentialing Weldonian theory. As we have seen, concerns to the contrary pivot on whether the ancestrian biometry which might have been would likely have answered to an altogether different data set than the one to which Mendelian genetics answers. If so, then the theories are incommensurable, and there is no using the data belonging to one in order to gauge the potential for success in the other.

Certainly the biometricians and the Mendelians held quite different sorts of investigation as exemplary. In their settled forms, moreover, their theories were mutually exclusive, in the sense that the leading practitioners sought to present what was exemplary for the other as a mere special case. A choice had to be made: either the Mendelian ratios were the results of non-Mendelian, gametically-impure processes which more generally conformed in their effects to the ancestral law, or the ancestral law arose from Mendelian, gametically-pure processes operating under specific conditions.[42] So there was exclusivity of a sort. But this exclusivity falls far short of incommensurability. Yes, Weldon gave Mendel rough treatment about the reality of alternative characters in peas. But Weldon did not assert that alternative characters were a fantasm, unintelligible within the biometrical worldview. Rather, he worked to derive Mendelian ratios from non-Mendelian assumptions. In certain

[41] For Weldon's remarks on Mendel's 'yellow' and 'green', see W. F. R. Weldon, 'On the Ambiguity of Mendel's Categories', *Biometrika* **2** (1902), 44–55. Weldon was the first person to point out that Mendel's published data fit his theories improbably well. See Weldon, op. cit. note 30, 233–5; and for discussion, see Magnello, op. cit. note 27, 22–3.

[42] While it is true, as the sociologist of science Barry Barnes has noted, that 'the biometry-Mendelism controversy' is 'itself a slightly problematic historical construct, with many scientists claiming both affiliations', it would be a mistake to conclude from this that there was no real intellectual conflict between biometry and Mendelism. All combinings of the biometrical and Mendelian perspectives called for choices, changes and/or partitionings of domain. See Barry Barnes, review of Kyung Man Kim's *Explaining Scientific Consensus: The Case of Mendelian Genetics* (1994), in *Isis* **87** (1996), 198–9, quotation on 198.

moods, he even described Mendelism and the ancestral law as complementary (though never in a way that suggested they were equals).[43] And Bateson, for his part—after a brief period where he treated the ancestral law and Mendelism as dividing the phenomena of inheritance between them—was among the first to sketch how a modified Mendelism could account for nature's bell curves.[44]

Earlier I raised the question of whether biometry and Mendelism were rival 'paradigms', in Thomas Kuhn's terms. We are now in a position to see that the answer, in time-honoured intellectual fashion, is yes and no. They were to the extent that they supplied different exemplars (Kuhn's own preferred meaning of 'paradigm'). But they were not to the extent that the theories were commensurable, with enough in common to permit efforts at making each the appendage of the other. Biometry and Mendelism confront us not with incommensurability—different theories answering to different data—but with another familiar epistemological condition, that of underdetermination—different theories answering to the same data. As such, the path is open to the counterfactualist historian to see how far Weldon's early efforts at biometrizing Mendelism can be extended.[45]

[43] 'Probably both views, the Galtonian and the Mendelian, will be reconciled in time in a wider generalisation of the facts of inheritance and descent—a larger theory of heredity', was how Weldon put it near the start of his seventh London lecture on inheritance. However, he devoted the rest of the lecture, and the final lecture too, to the problems plaguing Mendelism. [Weldon], op. cit. note 25, 732, 810, quotation on 732. In his unpublished book manuscript, Weldon expanded: 'Mendel's work and Galton's are ... in a sense complementary, the one dealing with the case in which selective mating is carried to its extreme limit among the ancestors of the stock observed, while the parents belong to distinct races, the other dealing with the stock produced by parents of a single race, in which selective mating is reduced to a minimum.' Quoted in Olby, op. cit. note 26, 316.

[44] See Robert Olby, 'William Bateson's Introduction of Mendelism to England: A Reassessment', *British Journal for the History of Science* **20** (1987), 399–420, esp. 412–5.

[45] For another reading of the controversy by Kuhnian lights, see Donald MacKenzie and Barry Barnes, 'Scientific Judgment: The Biometry-Mendelism Controversy', in *Natural Order: Historical Studies of Scientific Culture*, B. Barnes and S. Shapin (eds.) (Sage: London, 1979), 191–210, esp. 198–203. MacKenzie and Barnes also concluded that this was not an instance of paradigms clashing. For paradigms as exemplars, see Thomas S. Kuhn, *The Structure of Scientific Revolutions*, 2nd edition (Chicago: University of Chicago Press, 1970), 187–91, 198–204.

7. Conclusions

Might other histories have produced other, nongenic biologies? Here I have attempted less to answer the question than to dissolve some prejudices about taking it seriously, since 'no' looks so obvious. One issue considered is the too-quick joining of realism-to-inevitabilism and antirealism-to-contingentism. Another is the now-exploded idea that, around 1900, three men independently rediscovered a theory of inheritance propounded decades earlier by the forgotten Mendel. A third is the misguided temptation to count the abandonment of one nongenic biology in the actual past, Lysenkoism, against the prospects of other nongenic biologies in the possible past. A fourth is the forgetting of just how strong a position, conceptually and institutionally, the main competitor to Mendelism, ancestrian biometry, enjoyed before the death of its most able supporter, Raphael Weldon (and of course such deaths— so emblematic of contingency in history—have long been staple features of 'what if?' conjectures). A fifth is the suspicion that the post-1900 data on inheritance, laden with Mendelian preconceptions, cannot be used to test the potential for success in non-Mendelian alternatives.

Throughout I have emphasized questions of evidence, for biologists making sense of the world, and for historians making sense of biologists. In closing let me revisit two such questions, one resolved, one not. I noted that the issue on which the biometricians diverged most clearly from the Mendelians, of gametic purity ('the central dogma of Mendelism', as the historian Jean Gayon calls it), lent itself in principle to empirical checking.[46] To find out whether or not the gametes were pure, biologists could have gone ahead and examined the gametes, or—something much more tractable near the turn of the century—examined the self-fertilizing progeny of extracted recessives. Indeed, we can imagine a possible past in which the Mendelians won, and the biometricians lost, after years of patient, international toil vindicated the truth of the gametic purity of extracted recessives. But this is not what happened. After Weldon's death, doubts about gametic purity were not so much assuaged as abandoned.[47] Like all scientific programmes that

[46] Gayon, op. cit. note 20, 310.
[47] An exceptionally interesting and complex figure in this story is the Harvard geneticist William Castle. In the early days of Mendelism, he counted himself a Mendelian who doubted that gametes were pure. He was also uncomfortable with the mutationism then current among his fellow Mendelians. If Castle had not been rude about the ancestral law, the

acquire momentum, Mendelism grew to encompass all manner of exculpatory explanations. If some of the offspring of inbred extracted recessives displayed the dominant character, well, that showed that the parent organisms had not been true-breeding after all, or that there had been mutations, and so on. It did not show that Mendelism was false. By the 1940s, the only group that found these sorts of self-sealing manoeuvres remotely objectionable were the Lysenkoists.[48]

If evidence has constrained biologists so lightly, what hope is there for empirical rigour from the historian of the counterfactual biological past? More hope than one might think, as this paper has attempted to show.[49] But there are serious difficulties to be faced. Consider, for instance, the simple fact that most scientific theories change over time. In the course of change, parts of the theory can be modified and even, at the extreme, jettisoned. So there seems no reason in advance to bar the counterfactualist historian from allowing, say, the Weldonian biometricians that never were, or their successors, gradually to have cut away from the theory whatever was inadequate or inconsistent (as the Mendelians did for their theory). But if we permit that much, then it seems, in principle, that *any* unsuccessful theory from the past has to be regarded as a potentially successful theory.[50] What is needed is some criterion for

[48] See Levins and Lewontin, op. cit. note 13, 178–9.

[49] On methods and motives for engaging the counterfactual history of science, see Gregory Radick, 'The Scientific Pasts that Might Have Been, and Why They Matter', *New Scientist* (in press).

[50] A related worry is that every failed but potentially successful theory can be described as a variant—more and less extreme—of a successful theory. The upshot would be that, no matter what had happened in the science of heredity, there would be grounds for declaring the winning theory 'Mendelism'.

---

ancestrians might well have seen him as one of their own, though operating in a niche—selection experiments—that they regarded as marginal. Eventually Mendelian critics persuaded Castle that experimental results apparently showing gametic impurity could be explained if one postulated the existence in pure gametes of modifier genes. See Gayon, op. cit. note 20, 310-314, and, for Castle's hooded-rat experiments as a case study in scientific realism about entities, see Marga Vicedo, 'Experimentation in Early Genetics: The Implications of the Historical Character of Science for Scientific Realism', *Biology and Epistemology*, Richard Creath and Jane Maienschein (eds.) (Cambridge: Cambridge University Press, 2000), 215–43. For Castle on the ancestral law, see Pearson, op. cit. note 23 (the 'Mendelian' of Pearson's title is Castle). I am grateful to Steve French and Jon Hodge at Leeds for helpful discussion of Castle.

deciding how different two theories need to be before they count as different theories. Such a criterion would be of interest, of course, independently of its usefulness in disciplining counterfactual inquiries.

So there is distinctively philosophical work ahead. There may also be distinctively philosophical returns. I have suggested that realism goes with inevitabilism, and antirealism with contingentism, as a matter not of logic but of psychology. That association can be turned to advantage. A common predicament for scientific realists, as Peter Lipton has pointed out, is to find antirealism both hard to refute and hard to believe.[51] Anyone with remotely realist intuitions finds it well-nigh impossible to accept, for instance, that, though the world now contains goats engineered to produce milk containing spider silk, we have no warrant to believe that a spider gene for silk-making really exists, with properties much like those attributed to it in current genetic theory.[52] What these realists require is help in seeing how such achievements could have arisen in the absence of the ideas that in fact make them possible. A decent counterfactual historiography of science could be just the therapy needed, to enable either the surrendering of stubborn realist intuitions or, as it could well turn out, a surrendering to them.

[51] Peter Lipton, *Inference to the Best Explanation*, 2nd edition (London: Routledge, 2004), 206.

[52] On the transgenic silky goats, see Lawrence Osborne, 'Got Silk', *The Best American Science Writing 2003*, Oliver Sacks (ed.) (New York: HarperCollins, 2003), 186–93.

The Ontogenesis of Human Identity

GIOVANNI BONIOLO

"<<Es ist, als wären unsere Begriffe bedingt durch ein Gerüst
von Tatsachen>>.
Das hiess doch: Wenn du dir gewisse Tatsachen anders denkst,sie
anders beschreibst, als sie sind, dann kannst du die Anwendung
gewisser Begriffe dir nicht mehr vorstellen, weil die Regeln ihrer
Anwendung kein Analogon unter den neuen Umständen haben."[1]
(L. Wittgenstein, *Zettel*, § 350)

1. Introduction

Since the birth of western philosophy much time and energy have
been spent on identity. Is it worth saying more on the subject? Such
a question cannot have but a positive answer if philosophy is
considered as a contextualised unending research into fundamental
problems concerning human beings and their situation in history, in
nature, and in society. If philosophy is really an unending research,
its problems, its solutions, its arguments must depend on the
historical and cultural context in which they have been formulated.
A fortiori, this is true also for human identity.

In what follows, I will argue for a contextualised solution to the
problem of human identity. This means that I will use results of
contemporary disciplines that cannot be neglected if we want what
we affirm has a value beyond the philosophical domain in which it
has been formulated. In particular, I will resort to the biological
sciences. Why should we, philosophers, forget biology, and therefore science, in dealing with human identity? Are we sure we are
right in discussing the latter only from a purely philosophical point
of view, and without considering, and sometimes also contradicting,
what science teaches us? Are we sure that in this way we do not
display philosophical *hybris*. Are we sure that, from this point of
view, the scornful smile of the Thracian servant caused by the

---

[1] "<<It is as if our concepts involved a scaffolding of facts>>. That
would presumably mean: If you imagine certain facts otherwise, describe
them otherwise, than the way they are, then you can no longer imagine the
application of certain concepts, because the rules for their application have
no analogue in the new circumstances".

49

Giovanni Boniolo

proto-philosopher's tumble, magisterially discussed by Blumenberg (1987), must be really stigmatised?

If we glance at the history of modern discussions on human identity, we realise that Descartes, Locke, Hume, Leibniz, Kant were well-aware of the coeval science to which they sometimes actively contributed. Nevertheless if we run through the enormous contemporary philosophical literature on the same topic, we discover that science is totally on the sidelines, and its place is occupied by unreal and fictional thought-experiments, which are much used.

Let us think, for example, about the brain transplantation thought-experiment. Its first use may be dated back to Locke, and, given his scientific background, he was right in discussing it. But are we right in discussing it nowadays, more or less in the same terms and after almost four centuries of biological discoveries, in particular neurobiological ones?

If A's brain, or brain cortex, is transplanted into B, who is A? If half A's brain cortex is transplanted into B and half into C, who is A? If A's brain lay on a table in an anatomical theatre and if it is kept alive by artificial supports, where is A? If there is a tele-transporter ray that dissolves A here and now to reconstruct it in another place and in another time, what about A? If A's mental contents are totally transferred by means of a strange machine to B, who is A? Are we right in continuing discussing these cases?[2] Everyone is free to intellectually play as he prefers. I confess I prefer a different way of tackling human identity. I would rather ground my analyses in science than in science fiction.

Nevertheless, beyond a pure subjective preference, there are reasons that spur me to such a choice. The first concerns my belief that philosophy has to be useful also in non-philosophical domains, as has nearly always happened in its history. Nevertheless if we introduce fictional transplantations, fictional rays, fictional machinery, and so on, I do not believe that our conclusions are really interesting for others apart from ourselves.[3]

[2] On this discussion, cf. for example, Puccetti, 1969; Perry, 1972; Lewis, 1976; Parfit, 1984; Shoemaker, 1984; Robinson, 1985; Johnston, 1987; Wilkes, 1988; Noonan, 1989; Snowdon, 1991; Olson, 1997.

[3] For example, there is a lively debate inside biomedical sciences on the definition and criteria of death. This is an extremely important topic since, of course, it is preferable to perform organ transplantation when the donor is dead. But when is it dead? (cf. Boniolo, 2006). One of the seminal paper on this topic was written by Bernat et al., 1981. In it the authors, explicitly quoting some philosophers, write that they are totally disinterested in the "attempt to answer the speculation of science fiction, such as if the

50

The Ontogenesis of Human Identity

Some philosophers might reply they are doing metaphysics, not philosophy of science, or science. This is true. Metaphysics is a possibility, and personally I have nothing against it. It is on metaphysics that the castle of western thought was built a couple of thousand years ago. However, allow me to claim that to discuss certain topics physics and biology are more promising.

It is precisely from science that other reasons to discuss human identity without fictional machineries rise. What do you mean by brain transplantation? The entire brain transplantation, brain cortex transplantation, brain-stem transplantation, cerebellum transplantation, hippocampus transplantation? Are all of them technically possible? Just for the sake of discussion, let us suppose that even if they are not technically possible now, they could be technically possible in the future. Nevertheless there are still two problems.

The first one concerns our knowledge of the brain. Even if we know something about neurophysiology, we know almost nothing about how neurophysiology gives rise to concepts, judgments and reasonings, that is, the higher mental functions. It follows that any time we are discussing about them in correlation with human identity and brain (or a part of it) transplantation, we are discussing something we do not know enough about. That is, we are philosophing in a way that has been negatively stigmatised by many philosophers, for example by Locke: "I think not only, that it becomes the Modesty of Philosophy, not to pronounce Magisterially, where we want Evidence that can produce Knowledge; but also, that it is of use to us, to discern how far our Knowledge does reach" (Locke, 1690, Book IV, Ch. III, § 7, pp. 541–2).

The second problem springs from the fact that to discuss brain (or a part of it) transplantation forgetting the genetic or immunologic implications is rather bizarre and naive. Not only, those who discuss it usually forget the scholars who took these implications into consideration. Already since the first decades of the 20th century, in the biomedical field it has been extremely clear that when we examine human identity and organ transplantation we could not neglect the immunologic aspects of the matter. For example, in 1937 Loeb published his 'The Biological Basis of Individuality', where he wrote that rejection in the case of organ transplantation

brain continues to function independently of the rest of the organism" (p. 390). That is, most of the philosophical discussions on human identity grounded in fictional brain transplantation, or on some other fiction machineries, are simply put aside as non-interesting.

reveals the "differential of individuality", that is, what distinguishes an individual from another (cf. also Loeb, 1945). This means that to correctly face the problem of human identity we should discuss the problem of immunologic identity before talking of brain transplantation.

Moreover the mental contents we have, that is, what, according to some philosophers, is the main feature of personhood, are also due (even if we do not know how) to the brain we have. Yet we have the brain we have also because we have the genes we have. Therefore, before discussing identity from the point of view of the brain and its mental contents, we should face it from the genetic point of view, as some biologists already did in the 1930s (cf. Jennings, 1930).

2. The plan

After making the apologia of the discussion of human identity into a strong biological frame, it is time to unfold the plan oriented towards an argued solution to the question on stage.

First, I will survey some moments of the human ontogenesis particularly relevant to my purpose.[4] In specific, the endowment of genetic identity, the ontogenesis of both immunologic identity and neural identity. In this manner I will show that human identity is what results from an ontogenetic process during which genetically, epigenetically, and environmentally governed properties reveal themselves. By *genetically governed properties* I mean those phenotypic properties which appear only thanks to the genetic expression. It should be noted, with reference to this point, that a genetically governed property is totally different from the *property of having a particular genome*. The former concerns a possible phenotypic result of the latter. By *epigenetically governed properties* I mean those phenotypic properties which appear thanks to the expression of certain genes belonging to certain cells activated by their interactions with surrounding cell populations and with their peptidic products.[5] By *environmentally governed properties* I mean

---

[4] With reference to a more phylogenetic approach, even if it does not contain a philosophical analysis but a popular account, cf. Buss, 1987.

[5] There is a discussion on the definition of 'epigenetic process' and 'epigenetic property', cf. the seminal Waddington, 1957; also Jablonka and Lamb, 2002, pp. 310–11; West-Eberhard, 2003, p. 112.

those phenotypic properties which appear thanks to the interactions between cell populations, or even the entire human being, and the environment in which the latter lives.

Secondly, I will come back to philosophy to discuss more profoundly what developmental biology, immunology and neurobiology have taught. Therefore, I will try to offer a possible solution to the following problem:

"Given two human beings, B and B', which is the set of the sufficient properties $<PB_i>$ of B and $<PB'_i>$ of B', such that, at a certain time t, if $<PB_i>=<PB'_i>$ then B=B'?"

While tackling this question, I will also face another one:

"Given a human being B, which is the set of the sufficient properties $<PB_i>_t$ and $<PB_i>_{t'}$, where $t'>t$, such that if $<PB_i>_t=<PB_i>_{t'}$ then $B_t=B_{t'}$?"

This way of proceeding will clearly show that human identity has to do with something dynamic, something that concerns the genetic, epigenetic, and environmental appearance of necessary properties during the human being's development and life. Moreover, it allows me to implicitly present a different side of the problem of the correlation between human animal and person. This is a much discussed topic nowadays, also for its ethical implications, but almost always without resorting to real science.[6]

A last note to conclude these preliminaries. In the following, I will discuss an abstract (but not a fictional) living being from the time t_f, identifiable with the fusion between the pro-nucleus of its mother's ovule and the pro-nucleus of its father's spermatozoon, to a time $t<t_n$, where t_n is the time of the beginning of the necrotic processes.[7]

---

[6] Cf. Williams, 1970; van Inwagen, 1980; Parfit, 1984; Schoemaker, 1984; Lockwood, 1985; Johnston, 1987; Noonan, 1989; Unger, 1990; Lowe, 1991; Singer, 1995; Olson, 1997; Wiggins, 2001.

[7] The necrotic processes lead towards the entire organism's death, which is *a posteriori* recognisable by some associated changes such as *algor mortis*, *livor mortis*, *rigor mortis*, and *postmortem autolysis*. *Algor mortis* is the post-mortem decrease in body temperature; *livor mortis* is the purplish discoloration from settled blood in given body regions; *rigor mortis* is the muscle stiffening; and *postmortem autolysis* concerns the putrefactive changes. On the estimation of death time, cf. Hensshe *et al.*, 2002.

Giovanni Boniolo

3. Spacetime properties

In modern times, Locke (1690, Book II, Ch. XXVII, § 4) advanced the proposal that given two non-compound bodies, if they occupy the same spacetime region they are the same. As is well-known, this thesis was contested by Leibniz (1765, Book II, Ch. XXVII, §§ 1–2) who pointed out that two different light rays or two different shadows may occupy the same spacetime region without being the same ray or the same shadow.[8]

The Lockean idea was reformulated in more formal terms by Lewin (1922) who took from Special and General Relativity the notion of *worldline*, that is, the set of the spacetime points occupied by whatever being during its existence. It must be remarked that, in this way, all the 3-dimensional morphological spatial modifications of a living being that occur in time since its birth are considered.

Thus Lewin proposed the so-called *criterion of genidentity*, then reconsidered by Reichenbach (1927^1–1958^2): let **B** be the set of the living beings and **W** the set of the correlated worldlines,

$$\forall B,\ B' \in B \text{ and } \forall W,\ W' \in W,\ [B =_G B' \leftrightarrow (W \equiv W')],$$

where "$=_G$" is to be read as "... is genidentical to ...", and a) W and W' do not admit a solution of continuity; b) closed time-like curves in W and W' are not allowed. The continuity requirement (a) prohibits the "resurrection" of a living being.[9] Instead, the elimination of closed time-like curves (b) avoids strange meetings between a young and an old myself, i.e., the well-known "Grandfather paradox" (cf. Boniolo, 1999).[10]

Unfortunately Lewin's criterion has some problems, linked to the fact that it might be necessary but surely not sufficient. First, every living being loses some parts over its lifetime. Trivially, we lose some hair every day; more specifically there is the issue of the apoptosis, that is, the genetically programmed cellular death. Moreover, many times living beings split their worldlines into two

[8] It should be noted that if we wanted to tackle Locke's proposal and Leibniz' objections from the point of view of contemporary science, in particular Quantum Mechanics, the matter would profoundly change. In that case light should be considered also in its corpuscular nature. Moreover at a quantum level speaking of spatial regions for microscopic bodies means bumping into serious problems correlated with the quantum description (entanglement, uncertainty principle, etc.).

[9] For a debate about "resurrection", cf. Hughes, 2002.

[10] At this macroscopic level the problem of the striation of spacetime is not relevant.

or more branches, and it should be noted that any worldline of a human being continues in time and persists in space also after its death.[11]

However, for macroscopic bodies such as the human beings, that usually do not resurrect and do not bump into spacetime wormholes, Lewin's proposal can be turned into the first necessary property which makes up the set of the sufficient properties characterising human identity. That is, I can state the *spacetime necessary condition for human identity*:

> if ***B*** *is the set of human beings and* ***W*** *is the set of the correlated worldlines, then*
> $\forall B,\ B' {\in} \mathbf{B}$ *and* $\forall W,\ W' {\in} \mathbf{W},\ [B{\equiv}B'\ \rightarrow\ W{\equiv}W']$.

4. Life properties

I have just said that **B** is the set of human beings. I have also stated I consider the time interval from the fusion of the gametes to the beginning of the necrosis; that is, the time interval in which a human being is alive. How can we formulate the property of being alive?

We may start again with Locke, who in his 1690 masterpiece (Book II, Ch. XXVII, § 6) noticed that both the living beings and the non-living beings are organised beings, but with a really important difference: the organisation of a living being is such as to permit its life. More or less the same idea, even if with a totally different jargon and in a totally different philosophical context, is shared by Kant (1790) when in his *Kritik der Urteilskraft* he characterises living beings by their possessing a *Naturzweck* (or *Zweck der Natur*). That is, any living being has a *bildende Kraft*, which is correlated with what he calls *innere Zweckmässigkeit*. In other words, also Kant characterises living beings by means of a specific kind of organisation: the one which permits their life.

We may translate the particular kind of organisation that allows the human being to live, glimpsed at by Locke and Kant, into what nowadays we call metabolism. Therefore we may state that being alive means having functioning integrated metabolic processes.[12]

---

[11] On the biological body identity, cf. Boniolo and Carrara, 2004.

[12] Here metabolism has to be understood in a particular way: "[...It] refers to the use, and budgeting, of energy for bodily construction and maintenance, as well as for behaviour. Metabolism, in other words, is more than mere material self-organisation [...] Metabolism in this [...] sense,

Giovanni Boniolo

At this point we have another property that necessarily characterizes human identity: to be alive, that is, to have functioning integrated metabolic processes. Let us call L this property. Thus I may state the *metabolic necessary condition for the human identity*:

> *if **B** is the set of human beings and **L** is the set of properties permitting their being alive, that is, the set of certain functioning integrated metabolic processes, then*

$$\forall B,\ B' \in B\ and\ \forall L,\ L' \in L,\ [B \equiv B'\ \rightarrow\ L \equiv L'\,].$$

5. Genetic properties and the beginning of the ontogenesis

Around $3 \cdot 10^6$ spermatozoa are ejaculated and almost 200 of them arrive at the oviduct. Only one binds to the zona pellucida of the ovum. After about 24 hours the fertilisation is over: the two pro-nuclei of the human parents have concluded the fusion process; a zygote is formed, and the ontogenesis begins. This means that something new has appeared; something which has 23 couples of homologous chromosomes in its nucleus; something which has in it around $6 \cdot 10^9$ base pairs of nucleotides making up its DNA double helix. Here, in the DNA, there is most of what a human being was, most of what a human being is, and most of what a human being will be.

Given any two unrelated human beings' genomes, they differ for one base per thousand. This means that of the $6 \cdot 10^9$ base pairs, two human beings share the great part. In this part the phylogenetic story of each human being is contained. Instead in the remaining part, that is, in the $6 \cdot 10^6$ base pairs, its genetic individuality lies.[13]

[13] Of course, note that if two genomes differ at some 1/1000 of their bases, these are not necessarily the same ones for all the genomes. Moreover, beyond the differences in the nucleotide sequences, there are also differences in the number of nucleotides. Another remark is worth making here. Genetic human individuality can be expressed differently. We know that the coding part of the human DNA is around 3÷4% of the

both generates and maintains the distinction between the physical matter of the individual organism and that of other things, whether living or not. Metabolism, in this third sense, necessarily involves closely interlocking biochemical processes" (Boden, 1999, pp. 236-237). Boden (1999) offers a good and sharable argument to sustain that metabolism (in the sense just mentioned) is sufficient, at least *prima facie*, to consider a human being as a living one.

If our phylogenetic history is contained in ($6 \cdot 10^9$–$6 \cdot 10^6$) base pairs, it means that there, there are also the DNA sequences that characterize us as *Homo sapiens*. That is, there is what marks our species-specificity.[14] Therefore, I may enunciate the *species-specific necessary condition for human identity*:

if ***B*** *is the set of human beings and* ***S*** *is the set of the species-specific DNA sequences, then*

$$\forall B, B' \in B \text{ and } \forall S, S' \in S, [B \equiv B' \rightarrow S \equiv S'].$$

Once the condition of our belonging to the species *Homo sapiens* has been stated, that is, once our species-specific identity has been defined, we may turn to the genetic identity of each member of such a species.

In the long history of humankind more than one pattern has been proposed to grasp the differences among human beings. We started simply by estimating the more manifest phenotypic features (eyes, hair, skin, height, size, etc.). However with the rise of molecular genetics extremely more sophisticated patterns entered the field: from the differences in the protein sequences, to the differences in the

---

[14] It is well known that human genome has been sequenced (cf. Lander *et al.*, 2001; Craig Venter *et al.*, 2001). To actually identify the DNA sequences that are typically human, we should compare the human DNA with the DNA of the closest species, that seem to be *Pan troglodytes* (chimpanzee). Until the chimpanzee's genome has been sequenced, we cannot have the exact amount of the differences. However, it seems that *Homo sapiens* and *Pan troglodytes* share 94÷97% of the genome; cfr. Olson, 2000; Chen and Li, 2001; Marks, 2002. It should be noted that the forensic scientists have extremely sophisticated methods to identify a DNA as a human DNA; cf. Crouse and Schumm, 1995. Here above, I have implicitly talked about nuclear DNA, actually it is also possible to identify a living being as a human living being by resorting to the mitochondrial DNA, cf. Parson *et al.*, 2000.

---

total amount and that there are around $4 \cdot 10^4$ genes. It is supposed that the human average heterozygosity (the two correspondent loci in the two homologous chromosomes have two different alleles of the same gene) is around 6,7%. It means that a human being could be heterozygous in about 2680 loci. It follows that, in principle, it could produce 2^{2680} different germinal cells. If we take into account all of this and the fact that the zygote is given by two different germinal cells, we can say that two different zygotes have an extremely low (but nevertheless different from zero) possibility to possess the same alleles.

Giovanni Boniolo

Restriction Fragments Length Polymorphisms (RFLPs),[15] and to the differences of the so-called microsatellite DNA sequences.[16] Now a new pattern appears to be the best one to genetically grasp human individuality: the Single Nucleotide Polymorphism (SNP) based pattern.

Take a chromosome and a site containing a given nucleotide sequence, a SNP is a single nucleotide change in that sequence due to allelic polymorphisms. For example, if the sequence were TTAGGCTC, a SNP would be TTAAGCTC, where the fourth base G is changed into A.

In other words, given A and B, they have in common at least 99,9% of their genomes and their genetic individuality is given by the remaining 0,1%. Such individuality can be grasped by their SNPs. With some limitation and from the genetic point of view, A is A just because it has its own SNPs. And the same goes for B.

Is it, therefore, sufficient that two human beings have the same SNPs to conclude that they are the same human being? No, for at least two reasons.

The first concerns identical twins: they have the same SNPs, since they have the same genome, but, of course, they are not the same human being. The second has to do with the fact that the supposed number of different SNPs is rather great (approximately $10 \div 30 \cdot 10^6$) but not infinite. It follows that there should be an extremely low, but different from zero, probability that two different human beings have the same SNPs.[17]

---

[15] In the 1970s, enzymes called *restriction nucleases* were discovered. Each of them has the capacity to cut the DNA sequence at a specific site. Different restriction nucleases cut the DNA at different sites. In this manner DNA fragments can be obtained. Given the same DNA sequence of different individuals, each sequence, as a consequence of the diversity of the nucleotides making it up, will be fragmented in a different way by restriction nucleases of the same kind. On the RFLP, cf. Nathans and Smith, 1975; Danna, 1980; Kessler and Manta, 1990.

[16] Microsatellites are short repeated nucleotide sequences. Suitable chosen microsatellites on the same DNA sequence of two different individuals differ, and therefore the former permits us to distinguish the latter. Microsatellites can be used for the DNA fingerprint in forensic science, as well as the RFLP; cf. McElfresh *et al.*, 1993.

[17] By taking into account that in the human genome the SNP frequency is 1 per 1000 base pairs, it means that in the $6 \cdot 10^6$ base pairs that differentiate two individuals there should be about $6 \cdot 10^3$ SNPs. Therefore there should be an extremely low (but different from zero) probability that two different individuals have the same SNPs. With reference to the SNPs, cf. Hartl and Clark, 1997; Collins *et al.*, 1998; Przeworski *et al.*, 2000; The International SNP Map Working Group, 2001; Kruglyak and Nickerson, 2001.

It follows that we do not have a sufficient condition for human identity but a necessary one, and I may state the *genetic necessary condition for human identity*:[18]

> if **B** is the set of human beings and **G** is the set of the possible SNPs, then

> $\forall B,\ B' \in B$ and $\forall G,\ G' \in G,\ [B \equiv B' \rightarrow G \equiv G']$.

6. Immunologic properties

While I was criticising brain transplantation thought-experiments, I recalled the importance of the immunologic aspects as to the question of human individuality is concerned. Now we must discuss them.

Probably the first explicit distinction between what is called the *immunologic Self* and the *immunologic nonSelf*, that is, what marks immunologic identity, was introduced by Frank MacFarlane Burnet in the 1940s.[19] However, with reference to our aims, the best way to grasp why immunology is relevant to human individuality is to start from genetics. Indeed in each *Homo sapiens'* genome there are some genes that encode proteins strictly correlated with its individual immunologic responses. Beyond the interesting fact that it seems that such genes have a common evolutionary history (Hunkapiller and Hood, 1989; Williams and Barclay, 1988), two gene pools are particularly relevant here: the one coding for immunoglobulins and the one, called *Major Histocompatibility Complex* (*MHC*), coding for the Major Histocompatibility Complex (MHC) proteins.[20]

Let us start with the immunoglobulins, or antibodies. These proteins are produced by a particular kind of lymphocytes: the so-

[18] It should be clear that genome (or some of its sequences), if abstractly considered, may be though of as an *individualising necessary feature*. Nevertheless, if it is considered as an actual genome of an actual human being, it must be thought of as an *identifying necessary feature*. In this second way, it is used in forensic science, for example. Of course, the individualising feature and the identifying feature must be taken well separated; only the former interests our analysis.

[19] It was introduced in the second edition of his *The Production of Antibodies*, that he cowrote with E. Fenner; cf. Burnet and Fenner, 1949. On the history of immunology and its philosophical relevance, cf. Tauber, 1991; Tauber, 1997; Tauber and Podolsky, 1997.

[20] Usually the genes are written in italic and the encoded proteins in plain style. Note that in humans, *MHC* is called *Human Leukocyte Antigen* (*HLA*).

called B cells.[21] It is estimated that there are 10^{15} different kinds of antibodies and each kind is expressed by a specific kind of B cells. This means, on the one hand, that all the B cells expressing the same antibody can be thought of as clones of the B cell that first expressed that antibody. On the other hand, it means that there has to be a particular genetic mechanism capable of producing an enormous number of kinds of antibodies with comparatively few genes.[22]

Let us suppose that an antigen, that is, any substance capable of eliciting an immune response, enters a human body and suppose that it is the first time for that kind of antigen.[23] It happens that it is *de facto* impossible, because of the extremely high number of kinds of antibodies, that the antigen does not encounter its specific antibody. When this happens (we are in the case of the *primary immunologic response*) the antigen, or a part of it—the so-called epitope—, binds to the antibody which is on the surface of the B cell which has expressed it.[24] In this way, the B cell is activated and begins its proliferation and maturation. Such processes involve both the generation of clones—and therefore there will be always more and more B cells expressing the same kind of antibodies—and the secretion in the blood of the expressed antibodies. A part of these clones matures into memory B cells, which live in a sort of stand-by state. If the same kind of antigens, or an antigen with the same epitope, enters, the *secondary immune response* occurs and this is quicker and stronger than the first one. Now the antigen swiftly encounters the specific antibody and the immune response can be activated in a shorter time thanks to the memory B cells ready to express the right antibody.

[21] They are called B cells from *Bursa fabrici*: a bird limphoyd organ. In a human adult, they mature in the bone marrow, while in the foetal stage they mature in the liver.

[22] This is possible since each antibody is composed of two peptidic chains: the heavy chain (there are five classes of heavy chains) and the light chain (there are two classes of light chains). It happens that the two light chains and all the three heavy chains are encoded by three different pools of gene segments, and each segment encodes for a particular part of the corresponding light or heavy chain. The rearrangement of the gene segments and other genetic events, like somatic mutations, allow the incredible number of different antibodies.

[23] That is, let us suppose that it overcomes the other innate non-specific parts of the immune system, such as skin, mucous membrane, serum factors, phagocytic cells.

[24] It is estimated that a non-activated B cell has approximately 10^5 antibody molecules in its plasma membrane.

Two remarks are worth making here. The first concerns the fact that the aforementioned explanation of the B cell response is based on the clonal selection theory proposed by Burnet.[25] The second concerns the fact that each human being, before being exposed to any antigen, has a given repertoire of antibodies. This repertoire and the levels of different antibodies are innate, and therefore they may be thought of as genetically governed properties. Of course they are equal to those possessed by any other human being having the same genome, or at least the same antibody-gene pools, as it happens in the case of twins. However as soon as the B cells encounter the first antigens, the level of the different kinds of antibodies, and B cells as well, begins to change. So, the more the human being develops and grows, the more the B cell-governed response and the level of the antibody repertoire become individual. Since such an individualisation of the B cell-governed response is strictly correlated with the foreign microorganisms encountered by the B cells, for the first time we have come across an aspect of individualisation due to the environment in which the human being lives. That is, human individualisation linked to the B cell-governed immune response is partly due to the genetically governed properties, partly to epigenetically governed properties[26] (and therefore they are innate), and partly to environmentally governed properties due to the interactions with the environment (and therefore they are acquired and adaptative).[27]

Let us turn to the MHC proteins. They are expressed by the *MHC* genes that occupy a region of the sixth chromosome, and are characterised by one of the strongest polymorphisms of our genome. It means that any locus encoding for a MHC protein can be occupied by so many alleles that it has been estimated there are at least 10^{12} different possible MHC proteins. As a consequence, *de facto* any human being has its own MHC proteins. That is, it is

[25] The clonal selection theory is based on the assumption that any human being randomly produces an enormous number of antibodies before being exposed to any antigen. The binding of the antigen to its specific antibody activates the B cell which has expressed it, and such a B cell both proliferates and matures; cf. Burnet, 1959.

[26] I have not spoken yet about the fact that the B cell immune response is not only connected to the encountered antigens but also to the interaction with different cell populations, for example the so called T Helper cells.

[27] Note that the instantiation at a given time of the immunologic phenotype is not so different from any other phenotypic instantiation, at least from the point of view of the relation genotype/phenotype.

Giovanni Boniolo

individualised in a precise way by its *MHC*. Of course, there is always both the case of the twins who have the same genome, and *a fortiori* the same *MHC* genes, and the extremely rare case of two different human beings possessing the same *MHC*. However we are allowed to affirm that the MHC proteins give strong individual character to our immunologic response.[28]

There are two types of MHC proteins, the Class I MHC proteins, which are expressed in almost all the human cells, and the Class II MHC proteins, which are expressed in certain B cells, in the macrophages (a kind of white blood cells) and in the so-called antigen-presenting cells.

At this point I should recall that beyond the B cells there is another kind of lymphocytes: the T cells.[29] The T cells, differently from the B cells, neither present antibodies on their surface nor secrete them. Instead their surface has antigen-receptor proteins that recognise foreign antigens. As there are two classes of MHC proteins so there are two classes of T cells: the Cytotoxic T cells, whose antigen receptors recognise the Class I MHC, and the Helper T cells, whose antigen receptors recognise the Class II MHC.[30]

With reference to our aims, what happens in the thymus is extremely relevant. Here the T cells "learn" to distinguish the immunologic Self from the immunologic nonSelf. Indeed it happens that about 90% of the T cells die before maturing. This is a consequence of the fact that in the thymus a *positive selection* of

[28] The *MHC*, due to its great polymorphism, can be used also to reconstruct the phylogenetic history of the species; cf. Klein, 1986; Takahata, 1990.

[29] The T cells are called in this way since they develop in the Thymus.

[30] The T_c cells defend us against microorganisms that are inside our cells. The foreign proteins of such microorganisms are degradated by the host cell and then carried and presented at its surface by the Class I MHC proteins. The T_c cells recognise the complex (foreign peptide)–(Class I MHC) with their antigen receptors, and then their immune response begins by killing the infected cells. The T_H cells help us in defending from antigen in a different way. They recognise, by means of their antigen receptors, the foreign antigen when it is bound to the Class II MHC on the surface of the antigen-presenting cells, which before have ingested the foreign microorganism, degradated it and presented at their surface by means of the Class II MHC proteins. The activated T_H cells do not kill directly the antigen-presenting cells, but both stimulate macrophages to do it and help the right B cells to secrete their antibodies. It should be noted that also the T cell antigen receptors are specific, and therefore also the process concerning the level of different kinds of antigen-receptor T cells is explainable by means of the clonal selection theory.

the T cells happens. That is, only those T cells capable of recognising foreign peptides bound to the self-MHC, survive. This result, called MHC *restriction*, is therefore an acquired property of the immune system. Nevertheless, the T cells "must learn" also another important fact: they must tolerate the self-MHC and the self-peptides, otherwise, as happens in the autoimmune diseases, the consequences would be lethal for human beings. Also this process of *negative selection*, which leads to the acquired immunologic self-tolerance, takes place in the thymus by means of the elimination of the self-reactive T cells.

By taking into account what has been said both about the B cells and the T cells, when a human being is exposed to foreign microorganisms, that human being develops its own individual immunity. This process, which can be artificially induced (for example, by vaccination), or naturally induced (as happens, for example, when a human being is non-voluntarily exposed to infective microorganisms such as viruses or bacteria), leads to the so-called *actively acquired immunity*. Instead if the immunity is transferred to the human being by transferring the specific immune cells and/or antibodies from an immune host to it (as it happens in the transmission of maternal antibodies across the placenta to the foetus, or in the transmission of maternal secretory antibodies to the newborn *via* colostrum and milk), we speak about *passively acquired immunity*.

In both cases the immunity of a given human being and its immunologic individuation are a) grounded in its genome (in particular in the gene pools encoding the proteins related to the immune response), b) epigenetically developed (with reference to the interactions among the different cell populations of the immune system), and c) environmentally fixed by its interaction with foreign microorganisms (as to the particular level of the different kinds of T and B lymphocytes is concerned).

It is relevant to note that on a genetic basis, which is already individualising, a new process of individualisation takes place during the ontogenesis and it persists all through life. Another remarkable aspect concerns the fact that on a genetic basis, the immune system of any human being individualises itself by means of the interaction with the environment in which that human being lives. Therefore, we may speak of *plasticity of the immune system* that, during the ontogenesis and then during the whole life, can be instantiated in a particular way. With regard to the question at issue, we should clearly distinguish the particular manner in which the immunologic plasticity is really instantiated in that particular real

Giovanni Boniolo

human being (a topic involving the *identification* of that real human being, as is well-known in the forensic medicine), and the abstract possible instantiations of the immunologic plasticity in an abstract human being (a topic concerning the *individualisation* of that abstract human being *qua* that abstract human being).

Of course we are interested in the individualisation and therefore, I may state the *immunologic necessary condition for human identity*:

*if **B** is the set of human beings and **I** is the set of the possible instantiations of the immunologic plasticity, given by possible ensembles of MHC proteins and antibodies, then*

$$\forall B,\ B' \in \boldsymbol{B} \text{ and } \forall I,\ I' \in \boldsymbol{I},\ [\,B \equiv B' \rightarrow I \equiv I'\,]$$

7. Brain properties

More or less at the beginning of the third week from fecundation, gastrulation starts. There is a reorganisation of the embryonic cell mass and the formation of three cell layers: the germinal layers. The outer layer, the *ectoderm*, will give rise, beyond the skin covering and the sense organs, to the nervous system.[31] Since that moment on the process which will lead to the cerebral cortex takes place. We may summarize it in a few steps:

1) *Neural induction* that starts with the formation of the neural plate, the future nervous system, from a cell population of the ectoderm. Moreover around the fourth week, neurulation, that is, the development of the neural tube (i.e., the precursor of both the encephalon and the spinal marrow) begins.
2) *Neurogenesis*, that is, the neuron formation and proliferation from a layer of the neural tube. It is worth noting that each neural cell precursor, the neuroblast, gives rise to a finite number of neurons and that after a certain period the neurogenesis decreases drastically.[32]
3) *Neuron migration*. The new neurons are not in their position and therefore they migrate towards their final destination to form the six layers of the cerebral cortex.

[31] The other two layers are the *mesoderm* (the central one) which will give rise to muscles, excretory organs, circulatory organs, sex organs, and skeleton; and the *endoderm* (the inner one) which will give rise to the alimentary canal, the organs associated with digestion and breathing.

[32] It was thought that the neurogenesis stops at a certain moment of the foetal development. Yet it has been found that it continues in certain brain areas all life long, cf. Kempermann *et al.*, 1997; Gould *et al.*, 1999.

4) *Neuron programmed death and differentiation.* In order to give form and function to the developing cerebral cortex some neurons die, as happens for many other cells during the ontogenesis.[33] The remaining neurons begin differentiating and maturing. This means that dendrites and axons sprout from each neuron, arborising it. Then the axons begin stretching to arrive at the right target to form the right connection. Once they have arrived at their destination, they form a synapsis with a dendrite of the target neuron.

5) *Synaptogenesis.* The process of the genesis of the synaptic connections among neurons is the most important fact concerning the brain cognitive functionality. It begins around the seventh week after fecundation. It has its peak at approximately 24 months of age, and it stabilizes after about 9 years of age. It continues all through life, of course at a different rate.[34]

6) *Neural plasticity.*[35] Beyond the genetically and epigenetically governed processes of neuron proliferation and production of axons, dendrites and synapses, brain development is strongly characterised by plasticity, that is, by the fact that some synaptic connections are pruned, some are reinforced and some are created. The important aspect is that such *plasticity*, which continues throughout childhood and adulthood,[36] even if at different levels, is environmentally modulated. It seems that such environmentally governed plasticity may be explained by a neo-Darwinian selectionist model integrated with an instructionist model (Cf. Crair, 1999). According to the selectionist model (cf. Changeux *et al.*, 1973; Changeux, 1985; Changeux and Dehaene 1989; Edelman, 1987), the environmental selection acts on the overproduced synaptic connections by both reinforcing those which are used and pruning the other ones. Instead, according to the instructionist model, the environmental inputs lead to both the

[33] It is the so called programmed cell death, or apoptosis, which gives rise to the form and function of the embryo and of its organs and parts. On the cellular apoptosis, cf. Ameisen, 1994.

[34] On the brain development, cf. Huttenlocher, 1979 and 1990; O'Leary, 1992; Quartz and Seinowsky, 1997; Rakic, 1988 and 2000; Rakic and Zecevic, 2000; Zecevic, 1998; Marin-Padilla, 1990.

[35] On the historical bases of brain plasticity, cf. Konorski, 1948; Hebb, 1949.

[36] The adult's plasticity is limited and no longer arrives at deep structural changes of the synaptic connections; cf. Singer, 1987 and 1995; Tucker, 1992.

formation of new synapses (Quartz and Seinowsky, 1997) and the separation of the cortical areas (cf. Neville, 1990; Neville and Lawson, 1980).[37] These two models together seem to well-cohere with two periods of the environmentally governed development of the brain (Greenough and Black, 1992).

a) The *experience-expectant period*, during which particular synaptic connections are expected to be reinforced and stabilized by particular environmental inputs. It is supposed that such particular synaptic connections are the evolutionary outcome of environmental selections connected with species-specific inputs. Therefore the neglect and the failure of such environmental inputs may lead to a permanent deficit in the brain structure, and thus in the cognitive abilities.[38]

b) The *experience-dependent period* during which particular synaptic connections are reinforced or produced in response to unexpected environmental inputs.

At this point, before tackling the role of the synaptic connections and therefore of the cognitive functions, it is necessary to underline the role of the genes during the ontogenesis. Ontogenesis is an extremely complex process of cell proliferation, cell differentiation and cell death. It does not begin thanks to the self-expression of the genes contained in the zygote nucleus, but by means of their expression due to the proteins contained in the zygote's cytoplasm. Since the zygote's cytoplasm is nothing but the maternal ovum's cytoplasm, the early ontogenetic events are governed by the maternal genes that have encoded the zygotic cytoplasm's proteins.[39]

---

[37] Therefore, even if the first two, three years of the infant's life seem extremely important, they are not important because what it learns in those years is what it can learn, but because what it learns is the basis of what it can learn in the future. That is, it was thought that during the first two, three years the infant's synaptic connections were determined, with small changes, once and for ever. Instead it has been found that the infant's synaptic connections, which have been mostly epigenetically produced, are the basis on which, and from which, life long plasticity starts; cf. Bruer, 1999; Gopnik *et al.*, 1997.

[38] It is extremely well known the case of the blocking of the visual input of a cat's eye during the first period of its development. This blocking, even if it is later removed, produced an irreversible change in the visual cortex that led to vision damages. Cf. Wiesel, 1982; Hubel and Wiesel, 1979; Scarr, 1993; Taylor and Taylor, 1979.

[39] Note that other maternal "information" is organised as mRNA. On the misuse of the term "information", cf. Boniolo, 2003.

Not only are the zygotic cytoplasm's proteins important in themselves, but also the concentration of some of them is relevant. It is such concentration, indeed, that permits the correct embryo's morphogenesis. Of course, at that point also the new nucleus genes move into action. In particular the so-called homeotic genes are important. These contain a 180 base pair long nucleotide sequence (the homeobox) that encodes for 60 amino acids, which concur to form transcriptional factors, that is, proteins controlling the expression of other genes relevant to the development. In such a way these homeogenes control human development, in particular brain development (cf. Boncinelli, 1999; Reichert and Simeone, 1999).

It must be pointed out that the ontogenetic process, even if genetically based on the aforementioned developmental genes, is not a pure succession of genetic events. Instead it must be considered both as a process in which first the genes of a given nucleus and the biochemical elements of its cytoplasm interact, and, then, as a process in which a given cell expresses some of its genes thanks to the inter-action with surrounding cell populations. That is, the ontogenetic process is partly a genetic process, partly an epigenetic process.[40]

So far I have briefly sketched how brain development occurs by means of genetically, epigenetically, and environmentally governed processes. It should be already clear that these processes lead to the formation of a brain structure unique for each individual. Nevertheless another step is worth making, and it deals with one of the functions of such a brain structure: memory.

Since Augustine, a lot of philosophers have considered memory as one of the main, if not the unique, features of human identity, even personal identity. But very few of them have inquired about what memory is from a neurobiological point of view. This will be exactly our next step.

With a motto, we may affirm that *memory is nothing but synaptic connections*. We have said that each human being's synaptic connections are the result of genetically, epigenetically, and environmentally governed series of processes that are unique for each human being. Therefore each human being's memory is the result of genetically, epigenetically, and environmentally governed series of processes that are unique for each human being.[41]

[40] On the genetic and epigenetic bases of ontogenesis, cf. Le Douarin, 2000; Minelli, 2003. On the genetic and epigenetic bases of brain development, cf. Schlaggar and O'Leary, 1991; Chan and Jan, 1999.

[41] From this point of view, the position of those stating that we are our synaptic connections is understandable (cf. Le Doux, 2002), if not totally sharable since it takes into account only one of the individualising features.

Giovanni Boniolo

As far as we know, thanks to Brenda Milner's seminal works in the 1960s, human memory is thought of as a set of mnestic systems (cf. Cohen and Squire, 1980; Squire, 1987; Sherry and Schacter, 1987):

1) *implicit memories* (or *non-declarative memories*), connected with motor, visual, and cognitive capacities which may be activated unconsciously. There are three subsystems: a) *procedural learning memory* (tentatively located in the striatum and in specific cortical areas); it has to do with the knowledge acquisition of the structural properties of the relations among objects and among events; b) *conditioning paradigm memory* (tentatively located in the cerebellum); it is connected with the conditional learning that allows the individual to anticipate an event by detecting its precursor signal; c) *priming paradigm memory* (tentatively located in specific cortical areas); it concerns the detection, and the improvement of the detection, of an object recently experienced.

2) *explicit memories* (or *declarative memories*) are the memories you can declare since they refer to something that can be brought to mind, that is, something we are conscious of. They may be subdivided into: a) *pre-explicit memory* (tentatively situated in the hippocampus); it is related to the novelty detection; b) *semantic memory* (tentatively located in particular cortical areas); it is connected with what we can know without having direct experience; c) *episodic memory* (tentatively placed in certain cortical areas); it concerns the knowledge of what is directly experienced.

All the processes leading to the development of the different memory systems are not well understood yet (cf. Nelson, 1995, 1997 and 2000). Nevertheless it seems quite clear that these processes are epigenetically and environmentally governed, and that they can be thought of as mechanisms concerning the acquisition, the retention, and the retrieval of knowledge. Moreover, thanks to Eric Kandel (cf. Kandel and Spencer, 1968; Kandel, 1976), we know that these mechanisms are strictly connected with changes in the synaptic connections. Therefore they can be studied on genetic bases (cf. Alberini, 1999; Mayford and Kandel, 1999; Laroche, 2000). Indeed, both explicit and implicit memories are long-term memories, that is, memories whose acquisition, retention, and retrieval mechanisms are due to changes in the number and in the organization of the synaptic connections by means of the activation of certain genes, and therefore by means of the encoded proteins.[42]

[42] Also the short-term memory concerns synaptic modifications; however such modifications have to do with the synaptic activity thanks to modification of already existing proteins.

Some interesting conclusions may be drawn from what has been said above. First of all during the epigenetically governed part of the brain development it seems that the so-called species-specific mnestic mechanisms are located in the deeper cortical areas (cf. Fuster, 1995 and 1997). They should concern the experience-expectant mechanisms and, it seems, the implicit memory (Reber, 1992). Secondly, I have outlined that the memory systems are the complex outcome of our phylogenesis and ontogenesis. Moreover each different system seems to be located in a different part of our brain, and therefore to have a different developmental history. It is supposed that the thalamus and the hippocampus begin differentiating around the end of the fifth week from fecundation; the cerebellum starts developing around the end of the sixth week from fecundation; and the first synapses form approximately in the seventh week from fecundation. If this holds and if the brain location of memory systems holds, a human being can begin developing its own (both implicit and explicit) memory only after a certain time from fecundation and thus before its birth.[43] Finally, all the mnestic mechanisms are synaptically based and those concerning long-term memory have also a genetic substrate (even if, of course, they are not genetically determined, but epigenetically and environmentally governed).

If long-term memory is a particular stable synaptic organisation, therefore anytime we intervene to retrieve memories, our mnestic action is performed by a brain different from the brain that stored them. Anytime we reorganise our memories, we change the synaptic connections, also by creating new ones, as, unfortunately, it sometimes occurs when we are the object of bad psychotherapy (cf. Loftus and Ketcham, 1994; Kassin and Kiechel, 1996; Rubin, 1996; David, 1996).[44]

By taking all this into account, it is extremely hard to understand what the real bases of the brain transplantation thought-experiments are. Actually, scientifically, and not science fictionally, we may state that each human being has its own way in which its species-specific neural plasticity is instantiated all through its life by means of individual epigenetic interactions and individual environmental inputs grounded in an individual genome.

---

[43] Of course to control the actual foetus' mental contents is extremely difficult. However, it has been found that there are memories in the new-born due to input during the foetal period.

[44] It is nice to recall that also Leibniz discussed the topic of false memories, cf. Leibniz, 1765, Book II, Ch. XXVII, § 9.

Therefore, I can state the *neural plasticity necessary condition for human identity*:

*if **B** is the set of human beings and **N** is the set of possible instantiations of the neural plasticity, then*

$\forall B,\ B' \in \boldsymbol{B}$ and $\forall N,\ N' \in \boldsymbol{N},\ [B \equiv B' \rightarrow N \equiv N']$.

8. Human identity

At this point we may put together what has been found. We have seen that any human being is necessarily characterised a) by a partially individualizing worldline W describing its position in space and time during all its life (and not only); b) by a partially individualizing integrate metabolism L; c) by species-specific nucleotide sequences S; d) by partially individualizing nucleotide sequences G; e) by a partially individualizing instantiation of its immunologic plasticity I; and f) by a partially individualizing instantiation of its neural plasticity N. That is, given two human beings B and B', we have

$\forall B,\ B' \in \boldsymbol{B}$ and $\forall W,\ W' \in \boldsymbol{W},\ [B \equiv B' \rightarrow W \equiv W']$,
$\forall B,\ B' \in \boldsymbol{B}$ and $\forall L,\ L' \in \boldsymbol{L},\ [B \equiv B' \rightarrow L \equiv L']$,
$\forall B,\ B' \in \boldsymbol{B}$ and $\forall S,\ S' \in \boldsymbol{S},\ [B \equiv B' \rightarrow S \equiv S']$,
$\forall B,\ B' \in \boldsymbol{B}$ and $\forall G,\ G' \in \boldsymbol{G},\ [B \equiv B' \rightarrow G \equiv G']$,
$\forall B,\ B' \in \boldsymbol{B}$ and $\forall I,\ I' \in \boldsymbol{I},\ [B \equiv B' \rightarrow I \equiv I']$,
$\forall B,\ B' \in \boldsymbol{B}$ and $\forall N,\ N' \in \boldsymbol{N},\ [B \equiv B' \rightarrow N \equiv N']$.

My proposal about human identity concerns exactly the above mentioned six necessary conditions. That is, I am suggesting that all of them make up a sufficient condition for human identity. Thus

$\forall B,\ B' \in \boldsymbol{B},\ \forall W,\ W' \in \boldsymbol{W},\ \forall L,\ L' \in \boldsymbol{L},\ \forall S,\ S' \in \boldsymbol{S},\ \forall G,\ G' \in \boldsymbol{G},\ \forall I,$
$I' \in \boldsymbol{I},\ \forall N,\ N' \in \boldsymbol{N},$
$[(W \equiv W'\ \&\ L \equiv L'\ \&\ S \equiv S'\ \&\ G \equiv G'\ \&\ I \equiv I'\ \&\ N \equiv N') \rightarrow B \equiv B'].$ [45]

Therefore, let us come back to the first initial questions:

[45] With reference to this statement, it should be noted that each element of the 6-pla is not totally independent from the other ones; for example, both the immunologic and the neural element are connected to the genetic element, and there is a connection between the immunologic element and the neural one. Not to consider all the 6 elements in their complex relations would be a mistake and it is just for the sake of exposition that I have considered them one by one.

"Given two human beings, B and B', which is the set of the sufficient properties $<PB_i>$ of B and $<PB'_i>$ of B', such that, at a certain time t, if $<PB_i> \equiv <PB'_i>$ then B≡B'?".

Now I would suggest answering as follows:

"Given two human beings, B and B', and given, at a certain time t, two sets $<W, L, S, G, I, N>$ of properties of B and $<W', L', S', G', I', N'>$ of properties of B', it is sufficient that $<W, L, S, G, I, N> \equiv <W', L', S', G', I', N'>$ so that B≡B' ".

Now, we must come to the time dependent question:

"Given a human being B, which is the set of the sufficient properties $<PB_i>_t$ and $<PB_i>_{t'}$, where $t'>t$, such that if $<PB_i>_t \equiv <PB_i>_{t'}$ then $B_t \equiv B_{t'}$?"

Here we should pay attention because among the elements of the set $<W, L, S, G, I, N>$ there are properties which are time dependent and properties which are time independent. Of course we are looking for something which is time invariant, something which persists during human beings' life. Let us consider the elements of the just mentioned set one by one:

1) W is the property of having a possible worldline, which, as said, has to be continuous and without time loops. Let us call 3_t the 3-dimensional space section of W at t. If at t B occupies 3_t and at t' B occupies $3_{t'}$, and if between 3_t and $3_{t'}$ there is no solution of continuity, then at t and t' B occupies two different space sections of the same worldline W.

2) L is the property of possessing certain functioning integrated metabolic processes; that is, to be alive. This is a time independent property.

3) S is the property of having a given species-specific DNA sequence. This is a time independent property.

4) G is the property of having a given SNP. Also this is a time independent property.

5) I is the property of having a particular instantiation of the immunologic plasticity. This is a time dependent property, and it is useless for our aims. Actually we have a time invariant, that is, immunologic plasticity *qua* immunologic plasticity. Let us call it P^I.

6) N is the property of having a particular instantiation of the neural plasticity. Also this is a time dependent property, and it is useless for our aims. However we have a time invariant, that is, neural plasticity *qua* neural plasticity. Let us call it P^N.

Giovanni Boniolo

At this point I can answer the last question:

"Given a living (that is, possessing the property L) human being B at a time t and at a time t', so that $B_t \equiv B_{t'}$ it suffices that $<S, G, P^I, P^N>_t \equiv <S, G, P^I, P^N>_{t'}$, of course if B_t and $B_{t'}$ occupy different space sections of the same worldline."

Some may object I have not argued that the six necessary conditions truly make up a sufficient condition. If we were looking for an *a priori* justification, the objection would be sound. But if we wish to follow Locke's indication for "Modesty of Philosophy" and therefore "not to pronounce Magisterially, where we want [...] Evidence", I believe that we have not many other possibilities. This is what biological evidence teaches us, and we must be contented. However, we may pour the argument on the critics and ask them: "Please, find a case showing that the six necessary conditions together do not make up a sufficient condition".

9. Some philosophical consequences

From what has been said, we may draw some interesting philosophical remarks. First of all, we may inquire if it is really sound to claim that we are an animal plus a person, as many philosophers suggest (cf. Shoemaker, 1984). *We know that to define what a person is, is not so easy and unproblematic*: 'person' is one of the many philosophical terms which have a really long history of different definitions. However, for the sake of discussion let us assume that a person is identifiable by its mental contents, even though *we do not exactly know even what the mental contents are.*

That we are animals is sure, and, beyond some religious fundamentalist, nobody questions this statement. Actually, to claim that we are animals is not totally correct. It would be more correct to state that we, *Homo sapiens*, belong to genus *Homo*, family Hominidae, order Primates, class Mammalia, phylum Chordata, kingdom Animalia. If we like to speak in terms of kingdoms, we are animals. However, is to affirm that we are animals plus a person right? From what has been said and from what a phylogenetic and an ontogenetic analysis teaches us, that is, from the evolutionary and the developmental point of views (i.e., from the so called *evo-devo point of view*; cf. Minelli, 2003), this is simply false. We have the mental contents we have, also because we have the brain we have. And we have the brain we have also because we had both the phylogenesis we had and the ontogenesis we had. This is what biology teaches us and it is incorrect and misleading to forget it, especially if we believe that the (neo)Darwinian point of view has to be taken seriously into account (cf. Ruse, 1998).

It was our phylogenetic history that accidentally brought us to have a particular neural phenotype that allows us to have particular mental contents. If we like to state that we are persons just because we have mental contents nothing hinders. But 'person' is simply a name that we, *Homo sapiens* (better, a particular subset of *Homo sapiens* called 'philosophers'), give to a specific property that we may possess thanks to our evo-devo history.

Some people may affirm, by resorting to Wiggins' distinction between substantial sortal concepts and phased sortal concept, that 'person' is a phased sortal while 'human being' is a substantial concept.[46] Here, it is worth recalling Wiggins' objection according to which "all phased concepts are either latently or manifestly restrictions of underlying more general sortal concepts" (fn. 3, p. 63). *Prima facie*, I might agree that 'person' is a phased sortal which may be thought of as a restriction of a more fundamental sortal, that of '*Homo sapiens*'. But there are two problems.

The first one concerns the fact that not only may 'person' be thought of as an emerging property of *Homo sapiens*, but also that not each philosopher agrees that any *Homo sapiens* is a person. Actually I would prefer not to speak in terms of emerging properties. If 'person' is defined by resorting to mental contents and these have to do with the memory systems, I would prefer to affirm that it is the result of epigenetically and environmentally governed properties. However, this is not so relevant, it is just a matter of jargon, and evidently I have a preference for a jargon strictly linked with the biological terminology.

Let us come to the real question: "Is each *Homo sapiens* a person"? Of course this problem presupposes that we define a person by its mental contents.[47] But it can happen that *Homo sapiens* grows without having the right neural phenotype to possess mental contents, or that *Homo sapiens*, due to accidents, loses the right neural phenotype to continue having mental contents.

Let us analyse the first possibility by considering the case of

[46] For example, Olson (1997) seems to support this position; cf. Wiggins, 2001.

[47] It is worth noting that here we should indicate which set of mental contents we are considering: only the explicit ones, only the implicit ones, both of them?

anencephalic infants.[48] Even if anencephaly is a time-specific disease,[49] it is not a stimulus-specific one. This means that there could be more than one cause: genetic, infective, metabolic, chemical, radioactive noxae are possible. Let us dwell on the genetic cause. In this situation we cannot say anything but the anencephalic infant is a particular *Homo sapiens* with a particular genome that permits it to be anencephalic (or, if you like, that does not permit it to be non-anencephalic). *If we consider many diseases from an evolutionary point of view, their social interpretation changes enormously.* Therefore, if we accept this point of view, we may affirm that, due to human polymorphisms, anencephaly is one of the many possible phenotypic traits. Of course, we cannot say, from the biological point of view, that an anencephalic infant is less human than a non-anencephalic one. Both are humans, they have only different phenotypic traits, which derive also from an allelic difference between them.

The same conclusion may be reached by considering the non-genetic causes of anencephaly. It is sufficient to take into account what has been said about the fact that our neural structure is the result of both epigenetically and environmentally governed properties. From a certain point of view, we are not wrong in saying that anencephaly and non-anencephaly are two different ways in which neural plasticity can phenotipically reveal itself.

Let us now consider the loss of mental contents. This is a consequence of a loss of the neural phenotypic traits permitting us to have mental contents. In this case, must a human being without the latter be considered no longer as a person? If you like. As said 'person' is simply a word constructed by certain humans to refer to a particular (even if not well-defined) mental status connected with a particular (even if not well-identified) neural plasticity. However, this is not extremely relevant from a biological point of view; a

---

[48] Anencephaly is a malformation concerning the absence of brain, skull, and overlying scalp. It is thought to result from a failure of the anterior neuropore to close (in normal case, it should close after 25 days from the fecundation). Because these infants lack a functioning cerebral cortex, they are permanently unconscious. Brainstem function is present in varying degree, yet they exhibit many behaviours indicating their brainstem origin: responses to painful stimuli, feeding reflexes (rooting, sucking, swallowing,) respiratory reflexes, interactions involving eye movements, some facial expressions.

[49] It may arise between the XVI day from fecundation, that is, after the beginning of the development of the neural fold, and the XXV day, that is, before the closure of the anterior neuropore.

human being is always a human being, it always belongs to the species *Homo sapiens*. This is all we can state with extreme precision, in a non-ambiguous and empirically grounded way.

Note that what has just been discussed at the neural level is strictly analogous to what happens at the immune system level, that is, at the level of another constituent of human identity. There are situations in which our genome expresses the bases for "different" immune systems. Let us consider the case of the Severe Combined Immune Deficiency (SCID) (cf. Villa *et al.*, 2001). In this case we have a family of diseases characterised by the fact that certain mutant genes prevent the usual lymphocyte differentiation, and therefore they prevent the usual functioning of the immune system. Also in this case we cannot affirm that a human suffering from one of the SCID diseases is less human than one who does not. Both are humans, they differ only in their genome in the sense that they have two different alleles of the same gene and one allele permits the "correct" lymphocyte differentiation, while the other does not.

Analogously to the loss of certain mental contents due to the loss of certain neural traits, there is the possibility of losing the usual functioning of the immune system due to accidents, as happens in the case of Acquired Immunodeficiency Syndrome (AIDS).

Therefore, we can conclude that both immunologic and neural plasticity can be instantiated in many ways, due to genetic, epigenetic, and environmental situations. The particular way in which instantiation occurs concerns the identification of that particular real *Homo sapiens*, but the plasticity *qua* plasticity concerns its individuation, that is, what is relevant for us. The way in which the identification occurs is irrelevant as to human identity is concerned. It is irrelevant that there is a particular neural phenotype permitting or not permitting mental contents. It is irrelevant that there is a particular immunologic phenotype permitting or not permitting the usual defence from antibodies. Of course it is irrelevant with reference to the problem of human identity, and not as to health care! We can acquire or lose some identifying properties linked with a specific real instantiation of immunologic and neural plasticity, but this has nothing to do with our individualising properties given by our spacetime history, our genome, and our immunologic and neural plasticity.[50]

The second problem arising from the idea that 'person' is a restriction of a more fundamental sortal concerns the fact that we

---

[50] This approach has relevant ethical consequences that here I cannot discuss.

should stop considering all the human properties simply as human properties. What Charles Darwin and his followers taught us and continue teaching us is that any biological property has to be seen in the light of evolution. In our case this means that what appears to be strongly ontologically grounded as human property actually is a result of at least $3,5 \cdot 10^9$ years long evolutionary history which has led to that property, but that could have led to a different property. From this point of view not only does each human phased sortal appears to be a restriction of a human substantial sortal, but in turn each human substantial sortal appears to be a biological phased sortal. That is, 'person' may be considered as a restriction of a more fundamental sortal concept: that one of '*Homo sapiens*'. '*Homo sapiens*' may be considered as a restriction of a more fundamental sortal concept: that one of 'Animalia'. 'Animalia' of 'living being'. 'Living being' of 'organised system of cells'. Eventually 'organised system of cells' of 'organised system of molecules and atoms'. In this way we arrive at $3,5 \cdot 10^9$ years ago and, from a biological point of view, nothing more can be seriously claimed.

This simple evolutionary consideration should suggest to us either to abandon any possibility of speaking in terms of human substantial properties, or to interpret "substantial" not in an Aristotelian way but in a purely evolutionary way, as something which characterises a given species, in particular, *Homo sapiens*, but which, at the same time, has to be considered as an accidental evolutionary outcome.[51]

10. Conclusion

The position on human identity just proposed is evidently non-Aristotelian both from the ontological and the metaphysical point of view. Yet this is what we may safely and modestly state, if we want to take biology seriously. However it should be noted that Aristotle gave great importance to coeval biology. Why cannot we do the same? Why, in discussing human identity, cannot we be Aristotelian in this way and therefore forget the brain transplantation thought-experiments, or, more general, science fiction?

---

[51] Here general ontological and epistemological remarks related to the topic of essentialism can be drawn. In particular it seems clear that it is not so easy to be an essentialist if the evolutionary theory is taken seriously.

11. Acknowledgment

I would like to express my sincere thanks to the friends with whom I have discussed the content of the paper: Antonio Amoroso, Aldo Fasolo, Alessandro Minelli, William Shea, Paolo Vezzoni.

References

Alberini, C. M. 1999. 'Genes to Remember', *Journal of Experimental Biology*, **202**, pp. 2887–91.

Ameisen, J. C. 1994. *Le sculptur du vivant. Le suicide cellulaire ou la Mort créatrice* (Paris: Ed. du Seuil).

Bernat, J. L., Culver, C. M. and Bernard, G. 1981. 'On The Definition And Criterion Of Death', *Ann. Intern. Med.*, **94**, pp. 389–94.

Blumenberg, H. 1987. *Das Lachen der Thrakerin* (Frankfurt am Main: Suhrkamp).

Boden, M. A. 1999. 'Is Metabolism Necessary', *The British Journal for the Philosophy of Science*, **50**, 231–48.

Boncinelli, E. 1999. '*Otx* and *Emx* Homeobox Genes in Brain Development', *The Neuroscientist*, **5**, 164–72.

Boniolo, G. 1999. 'Wormholes and Timelike Curves: Is there Room for the Grand-father Paradox?', in M. Dalla Chiara, R. Giuntini, F. Laudisa (eds.), *Language, Quantum, Music* (Dordrecht: Kluwer), 143–57.

Boniolo, G. 2003. 'Biology without Information', *History and Philosophy of the Life Sciences*, **25**, 257–75

Boniolo, G. 2006. 'Death and Transplantation: Let's Try to Get Things Methodologically Straight', *Bioethics*, forthcoming.

Boniolo, G. and Carrara, M. 2004. 'On Biological Identity', *Biology and Philosophy*, **19**, 443–457

Bruer, J. 1999. *The Myth of the First Three Years* (New York: Free Press).

Burnet, F. M. 1959. *The Clonal Selection Theory of Acquired Immunity* (Nashville (TN):Vanderbilt University Press).

Burnet, F. M. and Fenner, F. 1949. *The Production of Antibodies* (London: Macmillan), II ed.

Buss, L.W. 1987. *The Evolution of Individuality* (Princeton: Princeton University Press).

Chan, Y. M. and Jan, Y. N. 1999. 'Observation of Neurogenic Genes and Mechanisms', *Curr. Opin. Neurobiol.*, **9**, 582–8.

Changeux, J. P., Courrege, P. and Danchin, A. 1973. 'A Theory of the Epigenesis of Neuronal Networks by Selective Stabilisation of Synapses', *Proceedings of the National Academy of Sciences U.S.A.*, **70**, 2974–8.

Changeux, J. P. and Danchin, A. 1976. 'Selective Stabilisation of Developing Synapses as a Mechanism for the Specification of Neuronal Networks', *Nature*, **264**, 705-712.

Changeux, J. P. and Dehaene, S. 1989. 'Neuronal Models of Cognitive Functions', *Cognition*, **33**, 63–109.

Chen, F. C. and Li, W. H. 2001. 'Genomic Divergences Between Humans and Other Hominoids and the Effective Population Size of the Common Ancestor of Humans and Chimpanzees', *American Journal of Human Genetics*, **68**, 444–56.

Cohen, N. J. and Squire, L. 1980. 'Preserved Learning and Retention of Pattern-analysis Skill in Amnesia: Dissociation of Knowing How and Knowing That', *Science*, **210**, 207–9.

Collins, F. S., *et al*. 1998. 'A DNA Polymorphism Discovery Resource for Research on Human Genetic Variation', *Genome Res.*, **8**, 1129–1231.

Craig Venter, J. *et al*. 2001. 'The Sequence of the Human Genome', *Science*, **291**, 1304–51.

Crair, M. C. 1999. 'Neuronal Activity During Development: Permissive Or Costructive?', *Curr. Opin. Neurobiol.*, **9**, 88-93.

Crouse, C. A. and Schumm, J. 1995. 'Investigation of Species Specificity Using Nine PCR-Based Human STR System', *Journal of Forensic Science*, **40**, 952–6.

Danna, K. J. 1980. 'Determination of Fragment Order Through Partial Digests and Multiple Enzyme Digests', *Methods Enzymol.*, **65**, 449–67.

David, C. R. (ed.) 1996. *Rememberuing Our Past. Studies in Autobiographical Memory* (Cambridge: Cambridge University Press.

Edelman, G. 1987. *Neural Darwinism* (New York: Basic Books).

Fuster, J. 1995. *Memory in the Cerebral Cortex. An Empirical Networks in Human and Nonhuman Primates* (Cambridge (Mass.): The MIT Press).

Fuster, J. 1997. *The Prefrontal Cortex* (Philadelphia: Lippincott-Raven Press).

Gopnik, M. *et al*. 1997. *The Scientist in the Crib* (New York: Morrow).

Gould, E. *et al*. 1999. 'Learning Enhances Adult Neurogenesis in the Hippocampal Formation', *Nature Neuroscience*, **2**, 260–5.

Greenough, W. and Black, J. 1992. 'Induction of Brain Structure by Experience: Substrate for Cognitive Development', in M. R.Gunnar, C. A. Nelson (eds.), *Developmental Behavioral Neuroscience. Minnesota Symposia on Child Psychology*, 24 (Hillsdale (NJ): Lawrence Erlbaum), 155–200.

Hartl, D. L. and Clark, A. G. 1997. *Principles of Population Genetics* (Sunderland (Mass): Sinauer Associates Inc.), 3rd ed.

Hebb, D. O. 1949. *The Organisation of Behavior. A Neuropsychological Theory* (New York: Wiley).

Hensshe, C. *et al*. 2002. *The Estimation of the Time Since Death in the Early Postmortem Period* (London: Arnold).

Hubel, D. and Wiesel, T. 1979. 'Brain Mechanism of Vision', *Scientific American*, **241**, 150–62.

Hughes, C. 2002. 'Starting over', in A. Bottani, M. Carrara and P. Giaretta (eds.), *Individuals, Essence and Identity.Themes of Analytic Metaphysics* (Dordrecht: Kluwer), 451–75.

Hunkapiller, T. and Hood, L. 1989. 'Diversity of the Immunoglobulin Gene Superfamily', *Adv. Immunol.*, **44**, 1–63.

Huttenlocher, P. R. 1979. 'Synaptic Density in Human Frontal Cortex. Developmental Changes and Effects of Aging', *Brain Research*, **163**, 195–205.

Huttenlocher, P. R. 1990. 'Morphometric Study of Human Cerebral Cortex Development', *Neuropsychologia*, **28**, 517–27.

Jablonka, E. and Lamb, M. J. 2002. *Epigenetics*, in M. Pagel (ed.), *Encyclopedia of Evolution* (Oxford: Oxford University Press).

Jennings, H. S. 1930. *The Biological Basis of Human Nature* (New York: W. W. Norton & Co.).

Johnston, M. 1987. 'Human Beings', *Journal of Philosophy*, **84**, 59–83.

Kandel, E. R. and Spencer, W.A. 1968. *Physiological Review*, **48**, 65–134.

Kandel, E. R. 1976. *Cellular Basis of Behavior* (San Francisco: W.H. Freeman).

Kant, I. 1790. *Kritik der Urteilskraft*. Engl. transl. *Kant's Critique of Judgement* (Mamillan: Londra, 1914).

Kassin, S. M. and Kiechel, K. 1996. 'The Social Psychology of False Confessions: Compliance, Internalisation, and Confabulatio', *Psychological Sciences*, **7**.

Kempermann, G. *et al.* 1997. 'More Hippocampal Neuron in Adult Mice Living in an Enriched Environment', *Nature*, **386**, 493–5.

Kessler, C. and Manta, V. 1990. 'Specificity of Restriction Endonucleases and Dna Modification Methyltransferases: A Review', *Gene*, **92**, 1–248.

Klein, J. 1986. *Natural History of the Major Histocompatibility Complex* (New York: Wiley).

Konorski, J. 1948. *Conditioned Reflexes and Neuron Organisation* (Cambridge: Cambridge University Press).

Kruglyak, L. and Nickerson, D. A. 2001. 'Variation Is the Spice of Life', *Nat. Genet.*, **27**, 234–6.

Lander, E. S. *et al.* 2001. 'Initial Sequencing and Analysis of The Human Genome', *Nature*, **409**, 860–921.

Laroche, C. 2000. 'Cellular and Molecular Approaches to Memory Storage', *Therapy*, **55**, 461–6.

Le Douarin, N. 2000. *Des chimère, des clones at des gènes* (Paris : Ed. Odile Jacob).

Le Doux, J. 2002. *Synaptic Self. Our Brains Become Who We Are* (New York: Viking Penguin).

Leibniz, G. W. 1765. *Nouveau essais sur l'entendement humain*. Engl. transl. *New Essays on Human Understanding* (Cambridge: Cambridge University Press, 1996).

Lewin, K. 1922. *Der Begriff der Genese* (Berlin).

Lewis, D. 1976. 'Survival and Identity', in A. Rorty (ed.), *The Identities of Persons* (Berkeley: University of California Press).

Locke, J. 1690. *An Essay Concerning Human Understanding* (Oxford: Clarendon Press, 1975).

Lockwood, M. 1985. 'When does a Life Begin?', in M. Lockwood (ed.), *Moral Dilemmas in Modern Medicine* (Oxford: Oxford University Press).

Loeb, L. 1937. 'The Biological Basis of Individuality', *Science*, **86**, 1–5.

Giovanni Boniolo

Loeb, L. 1945. *The Biological Basis of Individuality* (Springfield: Thomas).

Loftus, E. F. and Ketcham, K. 1994. *The Myth of Repressed Memory. False Memories and Allegations of Sexual Abuse* (New York: St.Martin Press).

Lowe, E. J. 1991. 'Real Selves: Persons and Substantial Kinds', in D. Cockburn (ed.), *Human Beings* (Cambridge: Cambridge University Press).

Marin-Padilla, M. 1990. 'Origin, Formation and Prenatal Maturation of the Human Cerebral Cortex: An Overview', *Journal of Craniofacial Genetics and Developmental Biology*, **10**, 137–46.

Marks, J. 2002. *What It Means to Be 98% Chimpanzee*, University of California Press, Berkeley.

Mayford, M. and Kandel, E. R. 1999. 'Genetic Approaches to Memory Storage', *Trends in Genetics*, **15**, 463–70.

McElfresh, K. C. *et al.* 1993. 'DNA-Based Identity Testing in Forensic Science', *BioScience*, **43**, p. 149 ff.

Minelli, A. 2003. *The Development of Animal Form* (Cambridge: Cambridge University Press).

Nathans, D. and Smith, H. O. 1975. 'Restriction Endonucleases in the Analysis and Restructuring of Dna Molecules', *Ann. Rev. Biochem.*, **44**, 273–93.

Nelson, C. A. 1995. 'The Ontogeny of Human Memory. A Cognitive Neuroscience Perspective', *Developmental Psychology*, **31**, 723–35.

Nelson, C. A. 1997. 'The Neurobiological Basis of Early Memory Development', in N.Cowan (ed.), *The Development of Memory in Children*, Psychology Press, Hove, 41–82.

Nelson, C. A. 2000. 'Neural Plasticity and Human Development. The Role of Early Experience in Sculpting Memory Systems', *Developmental Science*, **3**, 115–30.

Neville, H.J. 1990. 'Intermodal Competition and Compensation in Development. Evidence from Studies of the Visual System in Congenitally Deaf Adults', *Ann. NY Acad. Sci.*, **608**, 71–87.

Neville, H.J. and Lawson, D. 1987. 'Attention to Central and Peripheral Visual Space in a Movement Detection Task. II. Congenitally Deaf Adults', *Brain Res.*, **405**, 268–83.

Noonan, H. 1989. *Personal Identity* (London: Routledge).

O'Leary, D. D. 1992. 'Development of Connectional Diversity and Specificity in the Mammalian Brain by the Pruning of Collateral Projection', *Curr. Opin. Neurobiol.*, **2**, 70–7.

Olson, E. T. 1997. *The Human Animal. Personal Identity without Psychology* (Oxford: Oxford University Press).

Olson, S. 2000. *Mapping Human History* (New York: Houghton Mifflin Co.).

Parfit, D. 1984. *Reasons and Persons* (Oxford: Clarendon Press).

Parson, W. *et al.* 2000. 'Species Identification by means of the Cytochrome b Gene', *International Journal of Legal Medecine*, **114**, 23–8.

Perry, J. 1972. 'Can the Self Divide?', *Journal of Philosophy*, **69**, 463–88.

Przeworski, M. *et al*. 2000. 'Adjusting the Focus on Human Variation', *Trends Genet*., **16**, 296–302.

Puccetti, R. 1969. 'Brain Transplantation and Personal Identity', *Analysis*, **29**, 65–77.

Quartz, S. R. and Seinowski, T. J. 1997. 'The Neural Basis of Cognitive Development: a Constructive Manifesto', *Behav. Brain Sci*., **20**, 537–56.

Rakic, P. 1988. 'Specification of Cerebral Cortical Areas', *Science*, **241**, 170–6.

Rakic, P. 2000. 'Radial Unit Hypothesis of Neocortical Expansion', *Novartis Foundation Symposium*, **228**, 30–42.

Rakic, S. and Zecevic, N. 2000. 'Programmed Cell Death in the Developing Human Telencephalon', *European Journal of Neuroscience*, **12**, 2721–34.

Reber, M. 1992. 'Mental Retardation', *Psychiatr. Clin. North Am*., **15**, 511–22.

Reichenbach, H. 1927[1], 1958[2]. *The Philosophy of Space and Time*, Dover, New York.

Reichert, H. and Simeone, A. 1999. 'Conserved Usage of Gap and Homeotic Genes on Pattering the CNS', *Curr. Opin. Neurobiol*., **9**, 589–95.

Robinson, J. 1985. 'Personal Identity and Survival', *Journal of Philosophy*, **85**, 319–28.

Rubin, J. B. 1996. 'Psychoanalysis is Self-centred', *J. Am. Acad. Psychoanal*., **24**, 633–48.

Ruse, M. 1998. *Taking Darwin Seriously* (Amherst (N.Y): Prometheus Book).

Scarr, S. 1993. 'Biological and Cultural Diversity: The Legacy of Darwin for Development', *Child Development*, **64**, 1333–53.

Schlaggar, B. L. and O'Leary, D. D. 1991. 'Potential of Visual Cortex to Develop an Array of Functional Units Unique to Somatosensory Cortex', *Science*, **252**, 1556–60.

Sherry, D. and Shacter, D. 1987. 'The Evolution of Multiple Memory Systems', *Psychological Review*, **94**, 439–54.

Shoemaker, S. 1984. 'Personal Identity: A Materialist's Account', in S.Shoemaker, R.Swinburne (eds.), *Personal Identity* (Oxford: Basil Blackwell).

Singer, P. 1995. *Rethinking Life and Death: The Collapse of our Traditional Ethics* (Oxford: Oxford University Press).

Singer, W. 1987. 'Activity-dependent Self-organisation of Synaptic Connections as a Substrate of Learning', in J. Changeux, M. Konishi (eds.), *The Neural and Molecular Basis of Learning*, Wiley, New York, 301–36.

Singer, W. 1995. 'Development and Plasticity of Cortical Processing Architectures', *Science*, **270**, 758-764.

Snowdon, P. F. 1991. 'Personal Identity and Brain Transplants', in D. Cockburn (ed.), *Human Beings* (Cambridge: Cambridge University Press).

Squire, L. 1987. *Memory and the Brain* (Oxford: Oxford University Press).

Takahata, N. 1990. 'A Simple Genealogical Structure of Strongly Balaced Allelic Lines and Trans-species Evolution of Polymorphism', **87**.

Tauber, A. I. 1997. *The Immune Self: Theory and Metaphor* (Cambridge: Cambridge University Press).

Tauber, A. I. (ed.) 1991. *Organism and the Origins of Self* (Dordrecht: Kluwer).

Tauber, A. I. and Podolsky, S. H. 1997. *The Generation of Diversity. Clonal Selection Theory and the Rise of Molecular Immunology* (Cambridge (Mass.): Harvard University Press).

Taylor, V. and Taylor, D. 1979. 'Critical Period for Deprivation Amblyopia in Children', *Transactions of the Ophthalmological Societies of the UK*, **99**, 432–9.

The International SNP Map Working Group 2001. 'A Map of Human Genome Sequence Variation Containing 1.42 Million Single Nucleotide Polymorphisms', *Nature*, **409**, 928–33.

Tucker, D. 1992. 'Developing Emotions and Cortical Networks', in M. R. Gunnar, C. A. Nelson (eds.), *Developmental Behavioral Neuroscience. Minnesota Symposia on Child Psychology* (Hillsdale (NJ): Lawrence Erlbaum), 75–128.

Unger, P. 1990. *Identity, Consciousness and Value* (Oxford: Oxford University Press).

van Inwagen, P. 1980. 'Philosophers and the Word 'Human body'', in P. van Inwagen (ed.), *Time and Cause* (Dordrecht: Reidel).

Villa, A., Sobacchi, C. and Vezzoni, P. 2001. 'Recombination Activating Gene and Its Defects', *Current Opinion in Allergy and Clinical Immunology*, **1**.

Waddington, C. H. 1957. *The Strategy of the Genes* (London: Allen & Unwin).

West-Eberhard, M. J. 2003. *Developmental Plasticity and Evolution* (Oxford: Oxford University Press).

Wiesel, T. 1982. 'Postnatal Development of the Visual Cortex and the Influences of Environment', *Nature*, **299**, 583–91.

Wiggins, D. 2001. *Sameness and Substance Renewed* (Cambridge: Cambridge University Press).

Wilkes, K. 1988. *Real People: Personal Identity without Thought-experiments* (Oxford: Clarendon Press).

Williams, A. F. and Barclay, A. N. 1988. 'The Imunoglobulin Superfamily-Domains for Cell Surface Recognition', *Ann. Rev. Immunol.*, **6**, 381–406.

Williams, B. 1970. 'Are Persons Bodies?', now in B. Williams, *Problems of the Self*, (Cambridge: Cambridge University Press, 1973).

Wittgenstein, L. 1967. *Zettel*, eds. by G. E. M. Anscombe, G. H. von Wright (Oxford: Basil Blackwell).

Zecevic, N. 1998. 'Synaptogenesis in Layer 1 of the Human Cerebral Cortex in the First Half of Gestation', *Cerebral Cortex*, **8**, 245–52.

Souls, Minds, Bodies and Planets[1]

MARY MIDGLEY

Separate Substances?

What does it mean to say that we have got a mind-body problem?
Do we need to think of our inner and outer lives as two separate
items between which business must somehow be transacted, rather
than as aspects of a whole person?

Dualist talk assumes that we already have before us two separate
things which we don't see how to connect. This is a seventeenth-
century way of seeing the problem. It is tied to views in physics and
many other topics that we no longer hold.

'Mind' and 'matter', conceived as separate in this way, are
extreme abstractions. These are terms that were deliberately
designed by thinkers like Descartes to be mutually exclusive and
incompatible, which is why they are so hard to bring together now.
In Descartes' time, their separation was intended as quarantine to
separate the new, burgeoning science of physics from views on other
matters with which it might clash. It was also part of a much older,
more general attempt to separate Reason from Feeling and
establish Reason as the dominant partner, Feeling being essentially
just part of the body. That is why, during the Enlightenment, the
word 'soul' has been gradually replaced by 'mind', and the word
'mind' has been narrowed from its ordinary use ('I don't mind' ...
'I've a good mind to do it') to a strictly cognitive meaning.

That was the background against which philosophers designed
the separation of soul and body. And they saw it as an answer to a
vast metaphysical question of a kind which we would surely now
consider ill-framed. This was still the question that the pre-Socratic
thinkers had originally asked; 'What basic stuff is the whole world
made of?' The dualist reply was that there was not just one such
stuff but two—mind and body.

In the seventeenth century, hugely ambitious questions like this
were much in favour. Perhaps because of the appalling political
confusions of that age, seventeenth-century thinkers were peculiarly

[1] Another version of this article appears in *Science, Consciousness and Ultimate Reality*, edited by David Lorimer and published by Imprint Academic in July 2004.

determined to impose order by finding simple, final answers to vast questions through pure logic, before examining the complexity of the facts. In philosophy, as in politics, they liked rulings to be absolute. The grand rationalist structures that they built—including this one— supplied essential elements of our tradition. But there are limits to their usefulness. We do not have to start our enquiries from this remote distance. When we find the rationalist approach unhelpful we can ago away and try something else.

How Consciousness Became a Problem

Officially, we English-speaking philosophers are supposed to have done this already over mind-body questions. Half-a-century back we agreed that we should stop talking in terms of a Ghost in a Machine. But our whole culture was much more deeply committed to that way of thinking than we realized. Existing habits made it seem that our next move would be quite simple. We could at last triumphantly answer that ancient, pre-Socratic question—which was still seen as a necessary one—by once more finding a single solution for it. We could rule that everything was really matter. We could keep the material machine and get rid of the mental ghost.

So behaviourist psychologists tried this. They tabooed all talk of the inner life, with the effect that, through much of the twentieth century, people who wanted to seem scientific were forbidden to mention consciousness or subjectivity at all. But this turned out not to work very well. A world of machines without users or designers —a world of objects without subjects—could not be made convincing. Gradually it became clear that the concept of the Machine had been devised in the first place to fit its Ghost and could not really function without it. Attempts to use it on its own turned out so artificial and unreal that the learned population eventually rebelled. Some thirty years back, scientists suddenly rediscovered consciousness and decided that it constitutes a crucial Problem. But the concepts that we now have for dealing with it are still the ones that were devised to make it unspeakable in the first place.

Colin McGinn has stated this difficulty with admirable force in his recent book *The Mysterious Flame; Conscious Minds In A Material World* (New York, Basic Books, 1999)—

The problem is how any collection of cells ... could generate a conscious being. The problem is in the raw materials. It looks as if, with consciousness, a new kind of reality has been injected into the universe. ... How can mere matter generate consciousness? ... If the brain is spatial, being a hunk of matter in space, how on earth could the mind *arise* from the brain? ... This seems like a miracle, a rupture in the natural order. (pp. 13–115)

McGinn's drastic answer is that this state of affairs is indeed a real mystery—a puzzle that our minds simply cannot fathom because it lies outside the area that they are adapted to deal with. His suggestion is that there must be an unknown physical property, which he calls C*, that makes consciousness possible. This property is present in the stuff of brains, but it may be something which it is altogether beyond us to understand.

It is surely good news to find a respected analytic philosopher recognising mysteries—insisting that there are limits to our power of understanding. But I shall suggest that we don't need to fall back on his rather desperate solution. This particular difficulty arises from a more ordinary source. Our tradition is leading us to state the problem wrongly. We really do have to start again somewhere else.

I will suggest that a better starting-point might be to consider directly the relation between our inner and outer lives—between our subjective experience and the world that we know exists around us—in our experience as a whole, rather than trying to add consciousness as an afterthought to a physical world conceived on principles that don't leave room for it. The unit should not be an abstracted body or brain but the whole living person. In order to show why this is necessary it will be best to glance back first at the tradition to see just how and where things have gone wrong.

Rationalist Wars

This takes us back to Descartes. But of course he is not personally to blame for our troubles. If he had never written, sooner or later someone else would certainly have made the dualist move. And it is most unlikely that they would have done it any better than he did.

As I have suggested, one factor calling for dualism was the general, lasting wish to establish Reason as a supreme ruler, a separate force able to arbitrate the confusion caused by disputes between warring authorities in the world. But the special factor that made this need pressing at that time was the advent of a new form of Reason, one that seemed likely to compete with old forms of knowledge—namely, modern physics.

Mary Midgley

Once that discipline was launched into an intellectual world that had been shaped entirely round theology—a world, too, where theological opinions were dangerously linked to international politics—some device for separating these spheres had to be invented. That device ought to have been one that led on to Pluralism—meaning, of course, not a belief that there are many basic stuffs but a recognition that there are many different legitimate ways of thinking. Different conceptual schemes can quite properly be used to trace the different patterns in the world without conflicting. But, instead, the train of thought stopped at the first station—dualism—leaving its passengers still there today.

We see signs of this trouble whenever people raise this kind of question—for instance over the problem of Personal Identity. When we talk about relations between mind and body, we are asking what a person essentially is. Modern analytic philosophers have puzzled a great deal about this, usually setting out from John Locke's discussion of it and concentrating on just one point in that discussion—his famous example of the Prince and the Cobbler.[2]

Locke argued that, if we ask whether someone is 'the same person' as he was in the past, the answer must depend on the continuity of his memory, not on continuity of substance, 'For', (says Locke) 'should the soul of a prince, carrying with it the consciousness of the prince's past life, enter and inform the body of a cobbler ... everyone sees he would be the same person with the prince, accountable only for the prince's actions'. So the 'person' must be the memory lodged in the soul, not the body.

Starting from this little example philosophers have produced a striking monoculture of science-fiction stories. They have repeatedly asked whether various kinds of extraordinary beings would count as 'the same person' after they had undergone equally extraordinary kinds of metamorphosis. Their answers tend not to be very helpful because, when we go beyond a certain distance from normal life, we really don't have a context that might make sense of the question. And—as students often complain—these speculations seem fairly remote from the kind of problems that actually make people worry about personal identity in real life, which are mostly problems that arise over internal conflicts and clashes of loyalty to different groups around us. We will come back to these conflicts presently.

The difficulty of talking sense about detachable souls afflicts real,

[2] John Locke, *Essay Concerning Human Understanding*, Bk. 2, Ch. 27, Section 15.

professional science-fiction writers too, for their art is deeply committed to dualism. They often produce transmigrational stories in which characters in a wide range of situations keep jumping into other people's bodies, or having their own bodies taken over by an alien consciousness. It even happens in *Star Trek*, which shows how natural the thought still is today. But, in order to be convincing, the authors have to fill in a rich imaginative background that links this situation to normal life. And these stories are still strangely limited because they proceed on such an odd assumption.

They treat soul or consciousness as an alien package radically separate from the body. They go on as if one person's inner life could be lifted out at any time and slotted neatly into the outer life of someone else, much as a battery goes into a torch or a new cartridge into a printer. But our inner lives aren't actually standard articles designed to fit just any outer one in this way. The cobbler's mind needs the cobbler's body. It is not likely that two people with different nerves and different sense organs would perceive the world in the same way, let alone have the same feelings about it, or that their memories could be transferred wholesale to a different brain. Trying to exchange their bodies is not really at all like putting a new cartridge in the printer. It is more like trying to fit the inside of one teapot into the outside of another. And this is something that few of us would attempt.

Ships and Pilots; Batteries and Torches

It is surely very interesting that so many writers of science-fiction have signed up for this strange metaphysic. Of course there is nothing odd about their dealing in metaphysics in the first place. Sci-fi arises out of metaphysical problems quite as often as it does from those in the physical sciences, and good sci-fi stories can often be metaphysically helpful. But reliance on this particular metaphysic seems to be part of a rather unfortunate recent attempt to simplify the relation between our inner and outer lives by talking as if they were indeed completely separate items. This has the unlucky effect of making it even harder to connect them sensibly— even harder to see ourselves as a whole—than Descartes' separation of mind and body had already made it. Since his time, dualism has persisted. In fact it has grown a good deal cruder.

It is interesting that Descartes himself did not actually show souls as totally irrelevant to their bodies. Though he ruled that they were substances of different kinds, he placed them both firmly within the wider system of God's providence. He thought God must have good reasons for connecting them, even though those reasons were obscure to us. In fact, Descartes surprises his reader by saying twice explicitly that the soul or self is NOT actually a loose extra added to the body. He writes;

> *I am not only lodged in my body as a pilot in a vessel* ... I am besides so intimately conjoined, and as it were intermixed with it, that my mind and body compose a certain unity. For if this were not the case, I should not feel pain when my body is hurt.[3]

Descartes actually knew quite a lot about nerves. He saw that treating the soul as an alien, arbitrary item raised great difficulties about action and perception, so he assumed some underlying connection. And in this he was in tune with Christian thinking, which insisted on the Resurrection of the Body. Souls needed bodies, so God would restore the bodies at the Resurrection.

But unfortunately Descartes' occasional statements of this link don't stop him arguing all the rest of the time that the separation is absolute. He identifies his self, his 'I' entirely with the soul, the pure spark of consciousness. He speaks of the body as something outside it, something foreign which the soul discovers when it starts to look around it. (The pilot wakes up, so to speak, and finds himself mysteriously locked into his ship). Descartes rules that, 'the natures of these two substances are to be held, not only as diverse, but even in some measure as contraries'[4] They have no intelligible relation. Only God's mysterious plan can hold them together.

A soul conceived in this way is, of course, well-fitted to survive on its own after death, which is something that concerned Descartes. It could travel well. *But immortality is not the first thing we need to consider when we form our conception of ourselves.* Before we fit our minds out for the afterlife we need, first and foremost to have a view of them that makes good sense for the life that we have to live now. By making them so thin and detachable as to be thus independent, Descartes put our inner lives in danger of looking unnecessary.

As the Enlightenment marched on and God gradually faded into the background, the enclosing framework of providence was lost, while the conviction of a gap between soul and body remained and

---

[3] René Descartes, *Meditations On The First Philosophy*, (tr. John Veitch, Everyman's Library, Dent & Dutton, London 1937) Meditation 6, 'Of The Existence of Material Things', p. 135.

[4] Ibid, Synopsis of the Meditations, p. 76.

hardened. Increasingly, the advance of physical science made matter seem intelligible on its own. Mind and body did indeed start to look more like ship and pilot. And then, starting from that picture, people began to wonder whether the pilot was actually needed at all. If perception and action were physical processes that could go on without him, had he any function?

These were the thoughts that led the behaviourist psychologists to drop him overboard, leaving a strictly material world of self-directing ships—uninhabited bodies. Descartes' theistic dualism turned into materialistic monism. Subjective experience was dismissed as an ineffective extra, a mere by-product, irrelevant froth on the surface of physical reality. That is why, for a time, people who wanted to seem scientific were not allowed to mention their own or anybody else's inner experience.

But it is very hard to discuss human life intelligibly if you have to ignore most of its more pressing characteristics. Even the most docile of academics don't obey these vetoes for ever. So, as we have seen, eventually some bold people who had noticed that they had inner lives suggested that there was after all this 'problem of consciousness'. (Apparently, it was just one problem...) And now everybody wants to talk about it. But it is notably hard to do so.

One thing that makes the difficulty worse is that scientifically-minded people tend to see this problem of consciousness as a problem of how to insert a single extra term—consciousness—into the existing pattern of the physical sciences and handle it with methods that are already recognized there as scientific. Thus, the famous Tucson conferences on the subject set themselves the goal of producing, not an understanding of consciousness but a 'science of consciousness', which it is presumably hoped would be just one more scientific speciality, perhaps something comparable with the sciences of particular kinds of material?

This project is an attempt to revive Descartes' highly abstract soul—his pure spark of consciousness—and to fit it in somehow within the study of the physical world. Since the whole point of separating off this soul-concept in the first place was that it couldn't be handled by the methods used on the physical world, this can't work. Descartes was right about that and McGinn is right to follow him here. What we need now instead is to stand back and consider human beings quite differently—not as loose combinations of two incompatible parts but as whole complex creatures with many aspects that have to be thought about in different ways. Mind and body are more like shape and size than they are like ice and fire, or oil and water. Being conscious is not, as Descartes thought, a queer extra kind of stuff in the world. It is just one of the things that we do. Verbs are needed here, not nouns.

To grasp this, we need to start by abandoning both the extreme abstractions that have reigned on the two sides of the divide so far.

Inner Lives Are Neither Simple Nor Solitary

At the mental end, we need to get right away from Descartes' idea that the inner life is essentially a simple thing, a single, unchanging entity, an abstract point of consciousness. He put this point strongly. Unlike body, which is always divisible, mind, he says—

> cannot be conceived except as indivisible. For we are not able to conceive the half of a mind, as we can of any body, however small ... When I consider myself as a mind, that is, when I consider myself only in so far as I am a thinking thing, I can distinguish in myself no parts, but I very clearly discern that *I am somewhat absolutely one and entire.*
>
> ... although all the accidents of the mind be changed,— although, for example, it think certain things, will others and perceive others, *the mind itself does not vary* with these changes.[5]

This story abstracts entirely from the inner complexity, conflict and change that are primary elements in all subjective experience. Locke's discussion shows well how misleading this abstraction is. Locke did not dismiss the idea of a separable self or soul, but he asked what it would have to be like if it did exist. He was intrigued by the idea of reincarnation because he had (it seems) a friend who claimed to have been Socrates in a former life. So he asked what we would say if we did come across a case like this where the familiar whole seemed to be divided.

Is the transmogrified prince still the same person? Yes he is, said Locke, provided that he keeps his memories. The word *person* is, he says, essentially 'a forensic term', one centring on responsibility, and we are only responsible for what we can remember doing. With continuity of memory you can still be called 'the same person'. But if you now have a different body, you can't be called 'the same man'.

This suggestion notoriously led to further muddles. But Locke was surely right that any usable idea of a self or person does have to be the idea of something complex and therefore of something socially connected with the surrounding world. It must be an entity

[5] Ibid, pp. 76, 139, 77.

that incorporates the whole content of a life, the richness of a highly contingent individual experience. The cobbler would not be who he is without the connections established by his cobbling. Even within the restricted forensic context, Locke sees this need for complexity because of its bearing on justice. What (he asks) is to happen if an offender really has no continuity of memory? In that case, he says—

> the same man would at different times make different persons; which, we see, is the sense of mankind in the solemnest declaration of their opinion, human laws not punishing the mad man for the sober man's actions, nor the sober man for what the mad man did, thereby making them two persons; which is somewhat explained by our way of speaking in English, when *we say, such an one was 'not himself' or is 'beside himself'*[6]

If this defendant was not himself, then who was he?

It seems that after all people are not simple unities, they are highly complex items often riven by inner conflict. Even the law, which usually ignores these complications, cannot always do so and in ordinary life they are matters of the first importance. We often have to consider, not just 'is this man in the dock the same person?' but 'am I myself altogether the same person? Am I (for instance) really committed to my present project?' or again 'which of us within here should take over now?' There are law-courts inside us as well as out in the world. A friend of mine used to say that he unfortunately contained a committee. The trouble was not just that the members didn't always agree but that, when they disagreed, all too often the wrong person got up and spoke all the same

The truth is that the unity of a human being is not something simple and given. We could easily go to pieces and that would be our final disaster. Harmonizing out inner life is a project central to our existence, a difficult, continuous ongoing enterprise, an aim that has to be continuously struggled for and is never fully attained. Carl Jung called it 'the integration of the personality' and thought it was the central business of our lives.

The Importance of Conflict

Plato, who was a very different kind of dualist from Descartes, thought so too and gave conflicts of this sort a central place in his theory. These conflicts take place (he said) within the soul itself and

[6] *Essay On Human Understanding*, p. 196, Emphasis mine.

91

they are a torment to it. The soul is by no means a unity. It is divided into three parts—good desires, bad desires and Reason, which is the unlucky charioteer trying desperately to drive this mixed team of horses.[7] This is, of course, primarily a moral doctrine. But it is also an integral part of Plato's metaphysic and its psychological acuteness has been widely recognized.

Its difference from Descartes' scheme shows plainly that *there is not just one way of dividing up a human being.* There is no single perforated line marking off soul from body, no fixed point at which we should tear if we want to separate them. Many ways of thinking about this are possible. None of them is specially 'scientific'. Each is designed to bring out the importance of some particular aspect of our life. Plato's main concern was with emotional conflicts within the self, notably those that surround sex. Descartes, by contrast, was most disturbed about an intellectual conflict, one that arose between two different styles of thinking. It is not surprising that these different biases led them to different views about what a person essentially is. But something that they have in common, and which we may want to question, is that they both wanted to settle the matter by finding one ultimate arbitrator—by crowning one part of the personality as an absolute ruler and calling it Reason.

Just as Hobbes, in trying to end political feuds, put all his trust in a single absolute sovereign, so these moralists, in discussing the feuds within us, want to appoint an inner monarch against whom there is no appeal. They aren't prepared to leave decisions in the hands of a committee. And plenty of people have tried to find that monarch. But their efforts have never been altogether satisfactory. Today, we may well think that, although the committee system gives us a lot of trouble, it is perhaps the least bad alternative that is available to us.

Once we notice this inner complexity we begin to see that it makes the solipsistic isolation of the simple 'thinking thing' impossible too. Inner complexity echoes, and is linked to, a corresponding complexity in the world around us. The divided self is not an independent unit, quarantined from outside interference. Wider patterns outside affect its structure. As Locke saw, a person who has a memory must be an active social being, one capable of being involved in responsibility. Our personal identity is shaped by the surrounding world, depending radically on the attitudes of others.

Thus, when King Lear's daughters begin to treat him rudely, he first says to Goneril 'Are you our daughter?' and then

[7] See Plato, *Phaedrus*, sections 246–57.

Doth any here know me? Why, this is not Lear;
Doth Lear walk thus? speak thus? Where are his eyes?
Either his notion weakens, his discernings
Are lethargied—Ha, waking?—'tis not so.
Who is it that can tell me who I am?[8]

To which the Fool replies, 'Lear's shadow'.

At this point Lear is speaking somewhat sarcastically. But he soon
has to confront these questions literally. The whole point of the play
is that his identity has so far centred on being treated as a king. He
can't see how to exist without it. And though his case is a specially
dramatic one, this point about the crucial importance of social
context holds for all of us. The role that we play in the social drama
has huge force in shaping who we are. No human being exists in the
artificial isolation of the Cartesian pure thinker. When Lear asks
who he is, it would not help him to be told that he is a thinking
thing.

The Price and the Rewards of Dualism

Descartes supposed himself to be abstracting from all social
influences. He thought he had withdrawn into a realm of pure
intellect, designing *a priori* an impartial picture of human knowledge. But the most withdrawn thinkers still take the premises of
their reasoning into their study with them. Descartes was in fact
responding to certain quite particular pressures of his own time,
trying to resolve the doubts and debates that fuelled the fierce
religious wars of his day. He hoped to find a system of thought so
universal, so compelling that it could accommodate conflicting
theological views and also take in physical science, which might
soon begin to rival them.

He devised his dualism as a way of fitting that new science into
European culture without harming its Christian background. And,
because he wanted above all to unify the system—to avoid doubts
and divisions within it—he concentrated intensely on the problem
of knowledge. He made the assumption, which has turned out not
to be a workable one, that by reasoning we can get absolute,
infallible certainty for our beliefs. That is why the soul that he
pictured turns out to be essentially an intellect, a reasoning and
knowing subject rather than an acting or a feeling one. For him the
centre of our beings is the scientist within.

[8] Act 1. Scene iv, lines 215 and 223–8.

Mary Midgley

For a time this ingenious division of intellectual life did succeed. It suited Newton well enough. For a great part of the eighteenth century, scientists managed to divide themselves internally to suit the two permitted viewpoints. In their work, they could function as pure thinking beings—that is, essentially as mathematicians. They could view the world around them as an abstract moving pattern, a mass of lifeless, inert particles driven ceaselessly here and there by a few simple natural forces. The rest of the time they could respond to it normally as a familiar rich, complex jumble full of living beings who supplied the meaning for each other's lives. A benign God still regulated the relation between the two spheres.

But as time went on and technology advanced, the more abstract, scientific way of thinking gained strength and pervaded people's lives. Inevitably, conflicts between these two approaches were noticed. As the gap between them widened and became more disturbing, it grew hard to treat them as having equal importance— hard not to ask 'but which of these stories is actually the true one? Which tells us what the world is really like?' People felt that this question had to be answered—that one realm must be accepted as genuine and the other demoted to an illusion. They felt this because it seemed that, if both were equally real, there was no intelligible way of connecting them and reality was irremediably split. Hence McGinn's worry about 'a new kind of reality'. Hence the question that disturbs him and many other people—

> If the brain is spatial, being a hunk of matter in space, and the mind is non-spatial, how on earth can the mind arise from the brain? ... This seems like a miracle, a rupture in the natural order.[9]

Or, as he puts it after citing a lively sci-fi illustration, 'The point of this parable is to bring out how surprising it is that the squishy gray matter in our heads—our brain-meat—can be the basis and cause of a rich mental life'[10].

But this is an extraordinary abstraction from reality. Brains do not go about being conscious on their own. Meat is, by definition, dead and these brains belong to conscious, living creatures. Conscious pieces of matter are never just consignments of squishy grey matter, sitting on plates in a lab like porridge. They are live, moving, well-guided bodies of animals, going about their business in a biosphere to which they are naturally adapted. And the

[9] p. 115.
[10] p. 8.

question about them is simply whether it makes sense to diagnose *consciousness* as an integral, necessary, appropriate, organic part of the behaviour of such entities—including ourselves—or whether it is more reasonable to suppose that they might all just as well actually be unconscious.

What Sort of Explanation?

It is important to notice exactly what we are trying to do here if we want to 'explain consciousness' in a way that resolves McGinn's metaphysical difficulty. The point is not, of course, just to find some physical condition that is always causally conjoined with it. We want to make that junction intelligible— to show that the one item is in some way suitable to the other.

When one is trying to find the connection between two things in this way— for instance the connection between roots and leaves or between eyes and feet—the best approach is not usually to consider these two on their own in isolation. It is to step back and look at the wider context that encloses them. In the case of consciousness that context is, in the first place, organic life and, in the second, the power of movement.

Any being that lives and moves independently, as animals do, clearly needs to guide its own movements. And the more complex the lives of such beings become, the more subtle and varied must be their power of responding to changes that are going on around them, so that they are able to respond flexibly. That increasing power of responding calls for an ever-increasing power to perceive, think and feel. So it necessarily calls for consciousness, which is not an intrusive supernatural extra but as natural and appropriate a response to the challenges that confront active life as the power of flying or swimming. Plants can get on without such a power but animals could not because they are confronted with problems of choice. We ourselves do a lot of things unconsciously—that is, without attention. But when a difficulty crops up and a choice is needed, we rouse ourselves and become conscious of it.

There is no miracle here. The really startling factor in this scene is something which is usually ignored in these discussions, namely the introduction of life itself. Indeed, one might be tempted to say that consciousness is merely the superlative of life—just one more increase in the astonishing power of spontaneous development and adaptation which distinguishes living things from stones. Once life is present, the move from inactive creatures to highly-organized

95

moving animals is simply one more stage in the long, dazzling creative process which is already a kind of miracle on its own, but one which is not usually treated as a scandalous anomaly.

Discontinuities Within

Can it be true that there is not really an alarming gap here? If so, what is it that has made this particular transition seem so strange?

The answer is, I think, that the sense of strangeness arises simply from *the shift that we have to make in our own point of view when we consider it*. When we are confronted with a conscious being such as a human, all our social faculties at once leap into action. We cannot doubt that it has an inner life. Questions about its thoughts and feelings at once strike us. We bring to bear a whole framework of social concepts, a highly sophisticated apparatus that works on quite different principles from the one we would use if we were thinking about squishy grey matter in the lab.

This shift of methods can raise great difficulties, particularly on the many occasions when we need to use both these ways of thinking together. To use an image that I have suggested elsewhere, it is as if we are looking into a large aquarium through two opposite windows—trying to harmonize views of the same thing from quite different aspects. This trouble arises for instance over mental illness. We find it very hard to bring together our thoughts about the inner and the outer life of disturbed people—again, perhaps including ourselves. We often run into painful confusions. *But the clash in these cases is not a cosmic clash between different forms of reality. It is not a clash between ontological categories in the world, not a clash between natural and supernatural entities. It is a clash between two distinct mental faculties within ourselves, two distinct ways of thinking, along with the various emotional attitudes that underly them. It constantly raises moral questions about how we should act in the world, questions about what is most important in it.*

This discontinuity does not, then, actually raise metaphysical questions about what is real. But of course that does not mean that it is trivial— quite the contrary. The difficulty of bringing together the different parts of our own nature so as to act harmoniously is a crucial one that pervades our lives. The reason why we are so highly conscious is that we are complex social beings and this means that our choices are never likely to become simple.

Matter is not Simple Either

As I suggested earlier, the sense of bizarreness infesting the mind-body conjunction is made worse by the extreme abstraction to which both these terms have been subjected. Here I think the parallel with apartheid is actually quite illuminating. 'Black' and 'white' are extremes of the colour-range. If they are colours at all they are colours that are never actually seen on any human skin. The use of this dramatic contrast to categorize the vast range of people found in South Africa or anywhere else imposes a quite irrelevant artificial way of thinking, an approach which distorts all perceptions of these populations and makes it impossible to understand their diversity realistically. In the same sort of way, the sharp contrast between extreme conceptions of mind and body has obscured our thinking when we try to meditate on the complexities of our nature.

We have seen how, at the mental end of this mind-body axis, the idea of soul or mind became narrowed to a bare point of consciousness. But at the other end of it too the idea of matter has also been narrowed. Indeed, muddles about matter have probably been even more disastrous than muddles about mind.

Under a blindly reductive approach, the conscious animal that we ought to be asking about is reduced to a brain and even the brain loses its structure, becoming just a standard consignment of chemicals—inert porridge, squishy grey matter-as-such. It was indeed a central doctrine of seventeenth-century dualism that matter-as-such is inert and can do nothing, all activity being due to spirit. That is surely the conviction that still makes people like McGinn feel that a miracle must be involved if something material takes the enterprising step of becoming conscious.

This thesis of the inertness of matter is not often stated explicitly today, but it is often implied. Peter Atkins expressed it strongly in his book *The Creation* when he made the startling remark, 'Inanimate things are innately simple. That is one more step along the path to the view that *animate things, being innately inanimate, are innately simple too*'.[11]

Animate life, Atkins suggests, is not a serious factor in the world. It is just a misleading surface froth that obscures the grand, ultimate simplicity revealed by physics. Life has no bearing on consciousness, which (he explains) appears in the universe independently of it:

[11] Peter Atkins, *The Creation* (W. H. Freeman, Oxford & San Francisco 1987) p. 53.

> Consciousness is a property of minute patches in the warm surfaces of mild planets.... Here now (and presumably cosmically elsewhere at other times) the patches are merging through the development of communication into a global film of consciousness which may in due course pervade the galaxy and beyond... Consciousness is simply complexity. ... Space itself is self-conscious. ... Consciousness is three-dimensional.[12]

This is scandalously muddled talk. Consciousness is not a property of such patches but a property that (as far as we know) is found nowhere in the universe except in certain rather complex living beings—in fact in animals. And that is the only context in which its presence makes sense.

This kind of attempt to make consciousness respectable as an isolated phenomenon, without mentioning biological considerations, by inserting it directly into physics and treating it mainly as a basis for cybernetics, the IT revolution and the colonization of space is rather prevalent at present. Similarly David Chalmers suggested that, in order to avoid reducing mind to body, we should take 'experience itself as a fundamental feature of the world, *alongside mass, charge and space-time*'.[13] This list shows his conviction that, in order to be fundamental, a feature must belong to physics. He does not name life as one of these fundamental features, and he goes on to remark with satisfaction that, if this view is right—

> then in some ways a theory of consciousness will have more in common with a theory in physics than a theory in biology. Biological theories involve no principles that are fundamental in this way, so *biological theory has a certain complexity and messiness about it* but theories in physics, insofar as they deal with fundamental principles, aspire to simplicity and elegance.

In talk like this, the desire to keep one's theories clean of messy complications takes precedence over any wish to get a useful explanation. Such physics-envy is one more consequence of the unlucky fact that, in the seventeenth century, modern physics gained huge status because it was invented before the other sciences. This gave the Newtonian vision of the physical world an absolute standing as the final representation of reality, which is why that vision is still the background of much thinking today. It is surely the source of

[12] Ibid, pp. 71, 73, 83, & 85.
[13] D. Chalmers. 'Facing Up To The Problem of Consciousness', *Journal of Consciousness Studies*. Vol. 2, No. 3, 1995.

Atkins's amazing contention that all the things in the world are innately (whatever that may mean) simple.

That drastic assumption of simplicity was a central part of the seventeenth century's determination to get final, authoritative answers to all its questions. Physicists today have learnt better; they do not make this assumption. Like other scientists, they still look for simplicity, but they know they have no right to expect it. And they have, of course, altogether abandoned the simplistic doctrine of inert matter. Solid, billiard-ball like atoms have vanished entirely. As Heisenberg pointed out long ago,

> Since mass and energy are, according to the theory of relativity, essentially the same concepts, we may say that all elementary particles consist of energy. This could be interpreted as defining energy as the primary substance of the world ... With regard to this question *modern physics takes a definite stand against the materialism of Democritus* and for Plato and the Pythagoreans. The elementary particles are certainly not eternal and indestructible units of matter, they can actually be transformed into each other.[14]

In fact, when physicists abandoned the notion of solid particles the word 'materialism' lost its old meaning. Though this word is still used as a war-cry it is by no means clear what significance it ought to have today. That change in the ontology of physics is one scientific reason why it is now clear that the notion of matter as essentially dead stuff—hopelessly alien to conscious life—is mistaken. But an even more obvious reason is, of course, the Darwinian view of evolution.

We now know that matter, the physical stuff that originally formed our planet, did in fact develop into the system of living things that now inhabit its surface, including us and many other conscious creatures. So, if we are still using a notion of physical matter that makes it seem incapable of giving rise to consciousness, we need to change it. That notion has proved unworkable. We have to see that the potentiality for the full richness of life must have been present right from the start—from the first outpouring of hydrogen atoms at the big bang. This was not simple stuff doomed for ever to unchanging inertness. It was able to combine in myriad subtle ways that shaped fully active living things. And if it could perform that startling feat, why should it be surprising if some of those living things then went on to the further activity of becoming conscious?

[14] Werner Heisenberg, *Physics and Philosophy* (New York, Harper & Row 1962) pp. 58–9.

Mary Midgley

Disowning the Earth

Many people have pointed out that Descartes' notion of the secluded soul played a part in the rise of individualism by cutting us off from our fellow-humans. But until lately less attention has been paid to the way in which it cuts us off from the living world around us. Descartes viewed all non-human animals, equally with plants, as literally unconscious automata. An animal, he said, does not *act*. It is driven. Human bodies too were automata; their only difference from the rest of the machinery was that they were driven by the alien soul set within them. All organisms, along with the planet they inhabited, were merely arrangements of inert matter. Life belonged only to spirit. And though views about consciousness have softened somewhat since his time, the more general idea that the rest of the biosphere is something foreign and decidedly beneath us has not shifted half as far as it should have done.

This idea still centres on the old notion of physical matter as inert and alien to us. It is worth while to notice here where this notion came from. Though Descartes used it for his purpose of isolating physics, it is not an objective conception demanded by science. It is part of an ideology that was long encouraged by Christian thinking, an ideology that centred on fear and contempt for the earth, which was seen primarily as the opposite of Heaven. Human souls were conceived as having their real home in a remote spiritual paradise. Earth was at best a transit-camp, a place of trial through which they must pass. All sorts of nuances in our language still reflect this drama. Thus, the Oxford dictionary gives as the meaning of *earthy* —'Heavy, gross, material, dull, unrefined ... characteristic of earthly as opposed to heavenly existence.'

Pre-Copernican cosmology set this heaven literally in the sky, beyond the concentric spheres that bore the sun, moon, stars and planets. The earth was held to be merely the dead point in the middle of the system, the midden to which worthless matter that could not move upwards eventually drained. That central position was not seen as a sign of importance, as is often said, but as a mark of worthlessness, of distance from the celestial heights that held everything of real value. After all, what lay at the centre of Earth itself was Hell.

Accordingly, when Copernicus displaced our planet from its central position, Christian people did *not* feel the humiliation that is often said to have followed that move. Of course there was a sense of confusion and insecurity. But human souls still had their celestial citizenship. Their salvation was still essential cosmic business.

This sense of complacent independence from the earth did not die away, as might have been expected, when confidence in the Christian vision declined. Secular Westerners who stopped seeing themselves as Christian souls subject to judgment did stop expecting their previous welcome in the sky. But this did not lead them—as one would think it might have done—to conclude that they might be only rather gifted earthly animals. Instead, they still managed to see themselves in the terms that Descartes had suggested as pure intellects—detached observers, set above the rest of the physical world to observe and control it. When they stopped venerating God, they began instead to venerate themselves as in some sense the supreme beings in the universe—intellectual marvels whose production must have been the real purpose of evolution. This rather surprising position is expressed fully today in the Strong Anthropic Principle, and to some extent by other manifestoes of what is now called Human Exceptionalism.

Human intellect, in fact, now shone out as supreme in isolation from the whole animal background that might have helped to explain it, and from the rest of the biosphere on which it depended. 'The mind' did indeed begin to look like a miracle, a self-supporting phenomenon without a context. As Roy Porter says, 'In a single intrepid stroke, Descartes had disinherited almost the whole of Creation—all, that is, except the human mind—of the attributes of life, soul and purpose which had infused it since the speculation of Pythagoras and Plato, Aristotle and Galen'.[15] (pp. 65–6). The physical universe no longer seemed to be what Plato had called it, a mighty living creature. It was simply a more or less infinite pile of raw material provided for humans to exploit.

That exploitation accordingly went on without much check throughout the Industrial Revolution. The pile of resources did indeed seem infinite. Doubts about this are, of course, beginning to be felt now. But the sense of humans as essentially independent, powerful super-terrestrial beings is still extraordinarily strong.

Some people—apparently quite a lot in the United States—still ground this confidence in the Christian heaven, expecting to be carried off there in chariots when disaster strikes. Others use the sky differently, advertising future desirable residences in outer space rather than in the traditional heaven. And even among people who don't go for either of these scenarios, many are still confident that scientific ingenuity will always resolve our difficulties somehow. The vision of ourselves as essentially invulnerable minds

[15] Roy Porter, *Flesh In The Age Of Reason* (London, Penguin 2003) pp. 65–6.

independent of earthly support, colonists whose intellects will get them out of trouble whatever may go wrong, is still amazingly strong.

Life and Its Effects

This flattering illusion of human separateness and self-sufficiency is surely the really disastrous legacy still left over from Cartesian dualism. It is closely linked to the idea that physical matter is inert. That idea makes our planet appear as a mere jumble of blindly interacting particles senselessly forming themselves into handy products for us to consume. If we want to move to a more realistic notion of ourselves, we need to have a more realistic conception of what the earth itself is—namely a living, working system.[16]

That is why we now need James Lovelock's concept of Gaia. This idea is not just some idle Californian fancy, a futile substitute for traditional religion. It is the world-view that fills in the appropriate background to our new, more realistic idea of ourselves as working parts of the biosphere.

The point is that this biosphere does not consist of two separate parts any more than we ourselves do. It is not an inorganic machine that has accidentally got infested by some irrelevant life. Instead it is a working whole—an organic system, whose living components continuously affect the rest in a way that determines the fate of the whole. There is now plenty of evidence that the reason why our planet has not become a dead one—one unable to support life, like Mars and Venus—is that the biota on it have continuously modified its soil and atmosphere in a way that has made possible their own survival and development. Without this work, they would not be here and neither would we. We are not the owners and engineers of this system. We are a tiny dependent part of it.

Today, this idea of the self-preservative function of life is no longer dismissed as bad science. It is widely accepted. There are now many Departments of Earth Science where the interdependence of living things with non-living is taken for granted. In these departments geologists and biologists work together, in a way that they never used to do, to investigate the details of this process.

But of course these scientists are not required to look at the wider implications of that interdependence. It is not their business to consider how this new view of the earth ought to affect our

[16] I cannot discuss this topic at length here but I have done so in the end section of my book *Science and Poetry*.

conception of ourselves. In fact they usually manage not to notice how far-reaching those implications are, how many questions they raise about the notoriously puzzling concept of *life* itself. And they are helped in this inattention by avoiding the actual name Gaia. Indeed, in order to make it easier for them to accept his scientific message Lovelock himself at one time considered dropping the name Gaia and substituting 'geophysiology'.

But in the end he decided that the wider problems are too important to allow this kind of evasion. The change needed cannot be encapsulated in this way. It is not one internal to the physical sciences; it affects the whole shape of our thought.

The Mystery Is Within

After the enquiry that we have been making, two questions may well occur to us. One is, 'Why has the unworkable mind-body dualism that we have been examining lasted so long?' The other is, 'Why did scientists studying the earth not notice earlier that organisms might have causally affected the planet, as well as vice versa? Why did they take it for granted that life was merely an inconsequential by-product of inorganic phenomena? Why, in fact, did biologists and geologists not talk to each other on these matters until the last few decades, when, to their own surprise, they have suddenly brought themselves together in departments of Earth Science?'

I think the answers to these two questions are related. The delay on both points springs from the difficulty that we have in bringing together two very different ways of thinking—two sides of our personality—two distinct approaches. When we are dealing with conscious subjects we think socially. When we deal with lifeless things we treat them as objects. These two approaches call out different faculties within us.

The relations between these faculties are not at all simple. It is often hard to see which of them to use. We see cases (such as trees) that seem intermediate. We also see others (such as mentally ill people) for which we are sure that both methods are needed. In fact, because our social life is so pervasive, it is probable that both play some part in most of our transactions with the world around us. The art of combining these two approaches—of making them work together in our lives—is as necessary as the art of using our two eyes together, or as using sight together with touch. The idea that it is always scientific to avoid the personal approach—that we should be always 'objective' in the sense of treating everything as an inert object—is an unworkable fantasy. It can only produce a terrible mental squint.

McGinn is quite right to say that there are real mysteries in the world, matters that we are not at all well-equipped to understand. Foremost among these mysteries are those that concern the inner structure of our own minds, the relation between different parts of our lives. We are not totally helpless here. We can make some sense of this structure if we attend to it carefully. But if, instead of attending to it, we simply project its conflicts onto the outer world and try to deal with them there by metaphysical conjuring, we shall get nowhere.

Evo-devo: A New Evolutionary Paradigm?[1]

MICHAEL RUSE

> The homologies of process within morphogenetic fields provide some of the best evidence for evolution—just as skeletal and organ homologies did earlier. Thus, the evidence for evolution is better than ever. The role of natural selection in evolution, however, is seen to play less an important role. It is merely a filter for unsuccessful morphologies generated by development. Population genetics is destined to change if it is not to become as irrelevant to evolution as Newtonian mechanics is to contemporary physics. (Gilbert, Opitz, and Raff 1996, 368)

These are exciting days for evolutionary biology. In the past twenty years or so, the molecular approach to biology—evolutionary development or more familiarly 'evo-devo'—has swept all before it. Now we can trace development from the gene to the finished organism. Along the way, some magnificent discoveries have been made, most significantly that organisms as different as the fruitfly and the human share hugely important genes for development. We humans are put together in the same way as are those little insects that hang around compost heaps and rotting vegetables in garbage cans. This has led some enthusiasts to think that we are on the verge of—certainly in need of—a whole new theory of evolution. A new paradigm, that rejects Darwinian natural selection, or that at least reduces it to an unimportant role in cleaning up after the real work has been done. Now we have or are after a new theory—perhaps one that makes the really creative work appear in the course of development. Nature unfurls according to its molecularly based developmental laws, and that is where the real sources of change should be sought. It is true that the fittest survive, but this is little more than a truism with no real evolutionary import.

I am not sure that this is so. I applaud the new work in evo-devo—I think it is some of the most exciting that has ever been done by evolutionists. But whether this spells the demise of natural selection—the end of Darwinian evolutionary theory as we know

---

[1] Much of the discussion in this essay is based on the relevant parts of my recent book, *Darwin and Design: Does Evolution have a Purpose?*

Michael Ruse

it—is altogether another matter. I think, in fact, we are seeing an ongoing debate that dates back to Aristotle, between what biologists have labelled 'form' and 'function.' The debate predates the coming of evolution, and it postdates it also (Russell 1916; Ruse 1989). Which, has interesting consequences for those of us trying, as philosophers, to understand the nature of science. In a way, I do think we have different paradigms, but unlike the normal understanding of 'paradigm,' I am not sure that one is replacing—will ever replace—the other. This is something that biologists should realize and philosophers should try to understand. Which is why I am writing this essay.

Form and function

We have two ways of looking at organisms. It is useful and illuminating to speak of them as two different paradigms, because there is overlap with what is going on in biology with the usage of that term by Thomas Kuhn in his *Structure of Scientific Revolutions* (1962), although I admit fully that there are differences from his usage. For Kuhn, a paradigm is a way of looking at things—now you see it one way, now you see it another. Now you see the earth stationary and everything going around it; now you see the sun stationary and everything going around it. This is not just a question of reason but more a question of attitude. From taking one or the other position, a whole discipline can be founded, with its own research problems or puzzles and its own techniques and much more.

It is in this sense, in this essay, that I use the word 'paradigm.' In the world of organisms, you either see function as dominant—as all-pervasive—and everything else as secondary, or you do not. If you do not, then various formal structures and so forth are what dominate your thinking. If you are a functionalist, then your job is to find function and explain it. If you are a formalist, then your job is to find structure and explain it. Differing from a Kuhnian paradigm, no one is exactly and exclusively a subscriber to the one position and not to the other—although some people get pretty close to the extremes—and these positions and commitments are ongoing. As noted, the psychological picture—the way of seeing—is what is central to a Kuhnian paradigm, and it is this which is central to the way in which I am using 'paradigm' here. Some see function, and form is secondary and virtually a nuisance, and some see form, and function is secondary and virtually a nascence.

Aristotle, a first-class biologist, spotted both senses or ways of viewing organisms. On the one hand we have function, or what today is often called teleology. What Aristotle called final cause.

106

[We have cause] in the sense of end or that for the sake of which a thing is done, e.g. health is the cause of walking about. ('Why is he walking about?' We say: 'To be healthy', and, having said that, we think we have assigned the cause.) The same is true also of all the intermediate steps which are brought about through the action of something else as means towards the end, e.g. reduction of flesh, purging, drugs, or surgical instruments are means towards health. All these things are for the sake of the end, though they differ from one another in that some are activities, others instruments. (*Physics* 194b 30–195a 1, in Barnes 1984, 1)

Aristotle chided: 'What are the forces by which the hand or the body was fashioned into its shape?' A woodcarver (speaking of a model) might say that it was made as it is by tools like an axe or an auger. But note that simply referring to the tools and their effects is not enough. One must bring in ends. The woodcarver 'must state the reasons why he struck his blow in such a way as to effect this, and for the sake of what he did so; namely, that the piece of wood should develop eventually into this or that shape.' Likewise against the physiologists, 'the true method is to state what the characters are that distinguish the animal—to explain what it is and what are its qualities—and to deal after the same fashion with its several parts; in fact, to proceed in exactly the same way as we should do, were we dealing with the form of a couch' (*Parts of Animals*, 641a 7–17, in Barnes 1984, 1, 997).

On the other hand there is form. 'Whatever parts men have in front, these parts quadrupeds have below, on the belly; and whatever parts men have behind, these parts quadrupeds have on their back' (*History of Animals*, Barnes 1984, 1, 793). In the case of organisms, the similarities or isomorphisms between the parts of very different animals—isomorphisms between parts with very different functions. Traditionally, one refers here to the forelimbs of vertebrates being the favourite example. The arm of man, the wing of bird, the front leg of horse, the flipper of whale, the paw of mole—all used for very different purposes but with similarities in their structures. There seems to be no final cause at work here. Homologies do not exist for the sake of some end. (We today use the word 'homology,' meaning similarity due to common descent. Aristotle was not an evolutionist. But, although the word was not first applied until the 1840s, for clarity we can use the term without undue anachronism.)

Michael Ruse

Function across the evolutionary divide

The important point from our perspective is that these two ways of looking at organisms go across the evolutionary divide. There are pre-evolutionary functionalists. There are post-evolutionary functionalists. There are pre-evolutionary formalists. There are post-evolutionary formalists. To take the former, consider the famous arguments of the clergyman-naturalist John Ray (1628–1705), especially in his *Wisdom of God, Manifested in the Words of Creation* (1691, fifth edition 1709). His way of thinking is functional through and through. 'Whatever is natural, beheld through [the microscope] appears exquisitely formed, and adorned with all imaginable Elegancy and Beauty. There are such inimitable gildings in the smallest Seeds of Plants, but especially in the parts of Animals, in the Lead or Eye of a small Fry; Such accuracy, Order and Symmetry in the frame of the most minute Creatures, a Louse, for example, or a Mite, as no man were able to conceive without seeming of them.'

Everything that we humans do and produce is just crude and amateurish compared to what we find in nature. But this is not a conclusion that is then used to prove evolution. The very opposite. It is used for the argument to design. The living world was likened to a product of design. A machine implies an architect or an engineer, and so likewise inasmuch as the world of life is machine-like, it too implies a being, as much above us as the world of life is above our artifacts and creations. 'There is no greater, at least no more palpable and convincing argument of the Existence of a Deity, than the admirable Art and Wisdom that discovers itself in the Make and Constitution, the Order and Disposition, the Ends and uses of all the parts and members of this stately fabric of Heaven and Earth' (Ray 1709, 32–3).

A neat package, as the teleological way of thought in biology was tied back into the proof of the divine: the classic argument for design. 'That under one skin there should be such infinite variety of parts, variously mingled, hard with soft, fluid with fixt, solid with hollow, those in rest with those in motion:—all these so packed and thrust so close together, that there is no unnecessary vacuity in the whole body, and yet so far from clashing or interfering with one another, or hindering each others motions, that they do all help and assist mutually on the other, all concur in one general end and design' (Ray 1709, 335–6). Moreover, this is design which is of absolutely the top quality and so the same must be said of the intelligence behind it. This points to a being worthy of worship, not to some ethereal, local spirit before which the heathen humble themselves.

Then, on the other side of the evolutionary divide, we have Charles Darwin himself. Function is the starting point of his thinking about organisms. Take the little book on orchids, that Darwin published just after the *Origin*. There Darwin was laying out evolutionary biology as he hoped it would be done. 'I think this little book will do good to the Origin, as it will show that I have worked hard at details, and it will perhaps, serve [to] illustrate how natural History may be worked under the belief of the modification of species' (Letter to his publisher, John Murray, September 24, 1861, in Darwin 1985–, 9, 279). It is teleological through and through. The very title flags you to this fact: *On the Various Contrivances by which British and Foreign Orchids are Fertilized by Insects, and on the Good Effects of Intercrossing* (1862). It flags you also to the fact that, as with Paley, Darwin was looking at the organic world as if it were an object of design: he was taking organized end-directed complexity as the absolutely crucial key to unlocking the secrets of the living world and its attributes. Contrivances are human-made objects, which are created with an end in view. As in: 'I have invented a remarkable contrivance for shelling hot chestnuts without burning your fingers.' This was Darwin's perspective on the living world, just as it had been for Paley.

Then, when we get into the text of the orchids book, the natural theological perspective—the argument to complexity, that is—was used constantly, with great effect. Thus right at the beginning, speaking of how an orchid is fertilized, Darwin described in detail the 'complex mechanism' which causes this to happen. There are little sacks of pollen which are brushed by an insect as it pushes its way in, in search of nectar. But not just little sacks. Rather little sacks (or balls) which are going to go travelling. 'So viscid are these balls that whatever they touch they firmly stick to. Moreover the viscid matter has the peculiar chemical quality of setting, like a cement, hard and dry in a few minutes' time. As the anther-cells are open in front, when the insect withdraws its head,... one pollinium, or both, will be withdrawn, firmly cemented to the object, projecting up like horns' (Darwin 1862, 15). Then when the insect visits another plant, the pollen is transferred. But not just by chance. 'How then can the flower be fertilised? This is effected by a beautiful contrivance: though the viscid surface remains immoveably affixed, the apparently insignificant and minute disc of membrane to which the caudicle adheres is endowed with a remarkable power of contraction..., which causes the pollinium to sweep through about 90 degrees, always in one direction, viz., towards the apex of the proboscis..., in the course, on an average, of thirty seconds' (Darwin 1862, 16).

And so on and so forth. Right through the book, the picture was one of complexity, of adaptation, of function, of purpose. 'When we consider the unusual and perfectly-adapted length, as well as the remarkable thinness, of the caudicles of the pollinia; when we see that the anther-cells naturally open, and that the masses of pollen, from their weight, slowly fall down to the exact level of the stigmatic surface, and are there made to vibrate to and fro by the slightest breath of wind till the stigma is struck; it is impossible to doubt that these points of structure and function, which occur in no other British Orchid, are specially adapted for self-fertilisation' (Darwin 1862, 65). And: 'In many Vandeæ the caudicles are easily ruptured, and the fertilisation of the flower, as far as this point is concerned, is a simple affair; but in other cases the strength of the caudicles and the length to which they can be stretched before they break is surprising. I was at first perplexed to understand what good purpose the great strength of the caudicles and their capacity of extension could serve' (Darwin 1862, 182).

And of course, this functional perspective on nature was just what natural selection was supposed to address. Selection implies not just change but change towards adaptation, contrivance, function.

A struggle for existence inevitably follows from the high rate at which all organic beings tend to increase. Every being, which during its natural lifetime produces several eggs or seeds, must suffer destruction during some period of its life, and during some season or occasional year, otherwise, on the principle of geometrical increase, its numbers would quickly become so inordinately great that no country could support the product. Hence, as more individuals are produced than can possibly survive, there must in every case be a struggle for existence, either one individual with another of the same species, or with the individuals of distinct species, or with the physical conditions of life. It is the doctrine of Malthus applied with manifold force to the whole animal and vegetable kingdoms; for in this case there can be no artificial increase of food, and no prudential restraint from marriage. (Darwin 1859, 63)

And then on to natural selection:

Evo-devo: A New Evolutionary Paradigm?

Let it be borne in mind in what an endless number of strange peculiarities our domestic productions, and, in a lesser degree, those under nature, vary; and how strong the hereditary tendency is. Under domestication, it may be truly said that the whole organization becomes in some degree plastic. Let it be borne in mind how infinitely complex and close-fitting are the mutual relations of all organic beings to each other and to their physical conditions of life. Can it, then, be thought improbable, seeing that variations useful to man have undoubtedly occurred, that other variations useful in some way to each being in the great and complex battle of life, should sometimes occur in the course of thousands of generations? If such do occur, can we doubt (remembering that many more individuals are born than can possibly survive) that individuals having any advantage, however slight, over others, would have the best chance of surviving and of procreating their kind? On the other hand we may feel sure that any variation in the least degree injurious would be rigidly destroyed. This preservation of favourable variations and the rejection of injurious variations, I call Natural Selection. (pp. 80–81)

Form across the evolutionary divide

Turn to the other side, that of formalism. Pre-evolutionary formalists included German thinkers like Johann Wolfgang von Goethe, the great poet; French morphologists like Étienne Geoffroy Saint-Hilaire; as well as British thinkers (Richards 2003; Appel 1987; Ruse 1996). The classic case was Richard Owen who saw all organisms as being based on one fundamental archetype. 'What Plato would have called the 'Divine idea' on which the osseus frame of all vertebrate animals ... has been constructed' (Owen 1894, 1, 388). Post-evolutionary formalists abounded at the time of Darwin. In fact, it was the author of the *Origin* who was the odd man out. For all that he was a great critic of Richard Owen, Thomas Henry Huxley worked exclusively in terms of types. In the text book he coauthored with his student H. N. Martin, Huxley appealed to the type as he led the students through the living world group by group: mussels, snails, lobsters, frogs, and so forth (Huxley and Martin 1875). The same was true of others in Britain. The brilliant embryologist Frank Balfour (1880–1881) wrote that, with respect to the rabbit, 'there are grounds for thinking that not inconsiderable variations are likely to be met with in other species' (2, 214), but this did not stop him from using that very animal as the model when he discussed the mammals, saying indeed that for 'the early stages the rabbit necessarily serves as type'.

Likewise in Germany, notwithstanding his leadership of the 'Darwinismus' movement, Ernst Haeckel (1866) owed far more to Goethe and other transcendentalists than to anything in England. The same was true also of his some-time co-worker, the morphologist Carl Gegenbaur (1878). The latter wrote explicitly of 'the subordinate importance we must assign to the physiological duties [ie functions] of an organ when we are engaged in an investigation in Comparative Anatomy' (p. 4). He was open in his judgment that 'physiological value' was secondary and only to be used to avoid mistakes in comparisons. And in America we find that Louis Agassiz, student of the *Naturphilosophen* Lorenz Oken and Friedrich Schelling, arguing that 'one single idea has presided over the development of the whole class, and that all the deviations lead back to a primary plan' (Agassiz 1885, 1, 241). Unlike the teacher, Agassiz's most brilliant student, the invertebrate paleontologist Alpheus Hyatt, became an evolutionist at some point in the 1860s, a Lamarckian of some kind. Yet, so much had he absorbed his master's teachings, that from his papers no one can quite tell when Hyatt made the transition! At some important level, evolution really did not matter. And function was a positive handicap to the real work at hand (Ruse 1996).

Hyatt was not alone. Even when people thought about change, adaptation and function were downplayed. Although *Naturphilosophie* and its legacy was developmental through and through, it generated an attitude where the type rather than the end was the fundamental organizing concept. The model here, of course, is the individual organism—the very idea of evolution itself is linked to individual growth. Hence, there was a long tradition of drawing an analogy between the order in which organisms appear in the fossil record and the order of the various changes in the embryonic development of the single organism (Richards 1992). Agassiz indeed drew a three-fold parallelism, between the history of life, the history of the individual, and the order of complexity to be found across today's organisms. 'One may consider it as henceforth proved that the embryo of the fish during its development, the class of fishes as it at present exists in its numerous families, and the type of fish in its planetary history, exhibit analogous phases through which one may follow the same creative thought like a guiding thread in the study of the connection between organized beings' (Agassiz 1885, 1, 369–70).

With the coming of evolution, Haeckel (1866) converted the

history into phylogeny—the history of the developing class—and thus he had his so-called 'biogenetic law,' that the history of life can be found in the history of the organism. 'Ontogeny recapitulates phylogeny.' In fact, morphologists themselves grew increasingly critical of this law in its crude form—there are far too many exceptions—but generally speaking, however people drew the connections between paleontology and embryology, there was little or no interest in seeing the development of the type through time as being selection-driven. Other forces, internal forces akin to the forces that lead to individual growth, were thought the key to organic history.

Constraint

As is well known, in the 1930s the world of evolution took a dramatic turn to Darwinism and function. Thanks to the work of the population geneticists like R. A. Fisher and J. B. S. Haldane in Britain and Sewall Wright in America, and then the experimentalists and empiricists like E. B. Ford in Britain and Theodosius Dobzhansky in America, natural selection was recognized as the dominant mechanism of evolutionary change and function was seen to be the dominant feature of living beings (Ruse 1996, 1999). Entirely typical of this ultra-Darwinian attitude today—ultra-functionalist attitude today—is the British biologist and popular science writer Richard Dawkins. He asks what job we expect an evolutionary theory to perform.

> The answer may be different for different people. Some biologists, for instance, get excited about 'the species problem,' while I have never mustered much enthusiasm for it as a 'mystery of mysteries.' For some, the main thing that any theory of evolution has to explain is the diversity of life-cladogenesis [branching like a tree]. Others may require of their theory an explanation of the observed changes in the molecular constitution of the genome. I would not presume to try to convert any of these people to my point of view. All I can do is to make my point of view clear, so that the rest of my argument is clear. (Dawkins 1983, 404)

Dawkins goes on to agree with John Maynard Smith (1968) that 'The main task of any theory of evolution is to explain adaptive complexity, i.e. to explain the same set of facts which Paley used as evidence of a Creator.' Jokingly he refers to himself as a 'neo-Paleyist,' concurring with the natural theologian 'that adaptive complexity demands a very special kind of explanation: either a Designer as Paley taught, or something such as natural selection that does the job of a designer. Indeed, adaptive complexity is probably the best diagnostic of the presence of life itself' (Dawkins 1983, 404).

But now we have this position challenged. The mantra seems to be 'constraint.' Because of constraints, supposedly natural selection cannot do its job and function is not realized. John Maynard Smith (writing with a group of co-authors) tells us what is at issue: 'Organisms are capable of an enormous range of adaptive responses to environmental challenge. One factor influencing the pathway actually taken is the relative ease of achieving the available alternatives. By biasing the likelihood of entering onto one pathway rather than another, a developmental constraint can affect the evolutionary outcome even when it does not strictly preclude an alternative outcome' (Maynard Smith et al. 1985, 269). And, we are told, the study of evolutionary development, reveals many constraints. Hence we cannot rely on natural selection, function is to be downgraded, and other more formal factors are to come to the fore.

Genetic constraints

What about some examples of constraints in action? One much-cited set of examples focuses on so-called 'genetic constraints.' The developmental morphologist Rudolf Raff (1996) invites us to look at the issue of genome size. 'Having a large genome has consequences outside of the properties of the genome per se. Larger genomes result in larger cells. Because cells containing large genomes replicate their DNA more slowly that cells with a lower DNA content, large genomes might constrain organismal growth rates. Cell size will also determine the cell surface-to-volume ratio, which can affect metabolic rates' (p. 304). Salamanders are one kind of organism that often have large genome sizes. Hence, they seem to be good organisms on which to test hypotheses about constraints, and it seems that the formalists do have a point. 'Roth and co-workers have observed that in both frogs and salamanders, larger genome size results in larger cells. In turn, larger cells result in a simplification of brain morphology. Thus, quite independently of the demands of function, internal features such as genome size can affect the morphology and organization of complex animals. Plethodontid salamanders share the basis vertebrate nervous system and brain, but they have very little space in their small skulls and spinal chords' (p. 305, referring to Roth et al (1994)).

The problem is, however, that none of this really excludes a functionalist type of explanation. Raff has to admit that if there are constraints at work, they apparently do not make much difference. The salamanders can do some pretty remarkable things—remarkable salamander things, that is—seeming not at all to be functionally constrained. 'These salamanders occupy a variety of caverniculous, aquatic, terrestrial, and arboreal habitats. They possess a full range of sense organs, and most remarkably, a spectacular insect-catching mechanism consisting of a projectile tongue that can reach out in ten milliseconds to half the animal's trunk length (snout to vent is the way herpetologists express it).'

They have pretty good depth perception too. And indeed, their slow metabolic rate brought on by large genome size may even be of adaptive advantage. 'Plethodontids are sluggish, and the low metabolic rates introduced by large cell volume may be advantageous to sit-patiently-and-wait hunters that can afford long fasts. Vision at a distance is reduced to two handbreadths, but since these animals are ambush hunters that strike at short range, that probably doesn't affect their efficiency much' (p. 306). All in all, there is not much for an ardent selectionist to worry about here, and apparently, if need be, the salamanders can start to bring down their genome sizes. The constraints are just not that strong.

Developmental constraints

This kind of pattern—constraints; need to take seriously formal issues; but not excluding functionalist interpretations—plays itself out over and over again. Consider developmental constraints, and to do this, take the stunning new discoveries in science mentioned at the beginning of this essay. As Darwin pointed out, especially in his little book on orchids, organisms often do not start from scratch. They use what they have at hand and adapt from there. They recycle, in other words. Apparently, at the molecular level, organisms are even greater recyclers of already-available material than they are at the physical level (Carroll 1995; Carroll, Grenier, and Weatherbee 2001). Most remarkable of all are certain so-called 'homeotic genes.' These are not structural genes, that is genes that are coded to make the actual bodily products, but developmental genes that are coded to process the production of bodily products by structural genes. The homeotic genes are those that regulate the identity and order of the parts of the body—a mutation in one perhaps moving an eye to where a leg might normally appear, or vice versa. A subclass of such homeotic genes contains '*Hox* genes,' a group of genes to be found in bilaterans (organisms the same on both sides), that order the appearance of various bodily parts, and that seem to work in the sequence as they are found on the chromosomes. In *Drosophila*, the *Hox* genes start up at the head, work down through the thorax, and so on to the end of the abdomen. Within these genes, one finds lengths of DNA, of 180 base pairs, that are used to bind the genes to other DNA segments that are part of structural genes. In other words, these 'homeoboxes' make a protein (of sixty amino acids)—the 'homeodomain'—that is the key to the *Hox* genes actually functioning in regulating the structural genes.

What was absolutely staggering was the discovery of a homology between the homeodomains of *Drosophila* (fruitflies) and other bilaterans, from frogs through fish and mice to humans. Although it has been hundreds of millions of years since humans and fruitflies shared a common ancestor, it is still the case that we use essentially the same chemical mechanisms to order the production of our various bodily parts. The flies' legs and the humans' legs go back to the same processes. The identities are just too great to be chance or even convergence on a common solution. They are homologous. A consequence that leaves some entirely to downplay the significance of selection. The late Stephen Jay Gould (2002), for one, took all of this to be a clear case of the need for a new perspective. Instead of selection, one has certain basic ground plans or archetypes—*Baupläne*—and it is these that really count in evolution, constraining its course and nature. Organisms get certain basic patterns in place, and from then on they cannot escape or do anything outside the constraints set by these unmovable patterns.

Functionalists strike back

But is this well taken? Could it not simply be a case of: 'if it ain't broke, don't fix it'? In other words, could it not be the case that the way that these genes work is adaptive, and that they are kept in place by selection? It works for fruitflies, it works for humans. End of story. Talk of selection not operating because of 'phylogenetic inertia,' or some such thing, is simply unwarranted. For all that Rudolf Raff was one of those quoted above about the triumph of the developmental way, it is he who points out that the genetic homologies may in fact not be all that rigid—suggesting that if selection wants to move things functionally, it can. It is not simply a case of being locked in and unable to do anything else.

Raff discusses a certain *Hox* gene (the Antennapedia complex) that occurs in two species of *Drosophila*, *D melanogaster* and *D pseudoobscura*, species that (measured by molecular clocks) parted about 46 million years ago, not that long in the history of life. 'As expected, the clusters of two *Drosophila* species are highly similar in gene composition, arrangement, and conservation of the very long transcription units characteristic of the *D. melanogaster* Antennapedia complex. However, some revealing differences were found. The *Deformed* locus of *D. pseudoobscura* is inverted with respect to the *Deformed* gene in the *D. melanogaster* cluster. The *D. pseudoobscura* orientation of this gene is the primitive one shared with mammals (all Hox genes transcribed in the same order). It was inverted sometime during the 46 million years that separates the *D. melanogaster* lineage from its congeners' (Raff 1996, 309). There are other differences of a like kind, adding up to the conclusion that 'the Hox complex can tolerate substantial change over moderate periods of evolutionary time and within a common body plan.'

In short, no one will deny that homologies—including molecular homologies—exist and are obviously important. A clear sign of evolution and a significant aspect of organic form. But do they—or any like instances of 'phylogenetic inertia'—constrain evolution in any significant way? By analogy, could it not be that 'the fact that all tyres are round more likely means that round wheels are optimally functional than that tyre companies are somehow constrained by the round shape of their existing molds. Thus phylogenetic inertia is not an alternative to natural selection as a mechanism of persistence, and evidence of the former is not evidence against the latter' (Reeve and Sherman 1993, 18)? One needs evidence of more than homology to argue against adaptation. One needs evidence that homology is preventing adaptation.

To be frank, Darwinians suspect that there is something of a slight of hand at work here. The new formalists, people like Stephen Jay Gould, focus on things like the four-limbedness of vertebrates—things that have no obvious adaptive function today. But rather than at once plunging back into a quest for adaptation in the past, when such features first appeared, the formalist focus remains on the present and—thanks to somewhat idiosyncratic (and self-serving) definitions of adaptation, that refuse to apply the term to subsequent uses after the initial use—all that occurs is the labeling of four-limbedness today as 'non-adaptive.' And from there it is all-too-easy to slip into calling it 'non-adaptive' period. A final move is to think up some fancy name like 'archetype' or '*Bauplan*,' giving ontological status to what you are promoting, and the dish is complete. Function is relegated to the sidelines.

Michael Ruse

Structural constraints

There are other kinds of putative constraint, including structural constraints—the prime examples of which (in the human world) are the structural constraints of the pillars in mediaeval churches leading (at the points where pillar meets roof) to areas of no function, the much-discussed (in the opinion of some, the overly much-discussed) 'spandrels' of which Gould made so much. Although such spandrels seem adaptive—areas for creative outpourings—in fact they are just by products of the builders' methods of keeping the roof in place. 'The design is so elaborate, harmonious, and purposeful that we are tempted to view it as the starting point of any analysis, as the cause in some sense of the surrounding architecture.' This, however, is to put the cart before the horse. 'The system begins with an architectural constraint: the necessary four spandrels and their tapering triangular form. They provide a space in which the mosaicist worked; they set the quadripartite symmetry of the dome above' (Gould and Lewontin 1979, 148). Perhaps, argues Gould, we have a similar situation in the living world. Much that we think adaptive is merely a spandrel, and such things as constraints on development prevent anything like an optimally designed world. Perhaps things are much more random and haphazard—non-functional—than the Darwinian thinks possible.

To which the functionalist replies: Who ever thought otherwise? No one since Darwin has ever claimed that everything works just right. It is more the case that one should look first for function, and recognize that sometimes it is more complex than simply one thing or another. After all, things like allometry (where body parts are a logarithmic function of the overall body and hence these parts can grow at a much greater rate than the whole) have long been known and acknowledged, and they are the prime example of trying to put a functioning organism together properly and of having trouble optimizing every last feature. The adult, male Irish Elk had a huge set of antlers that may well have been non-adaptive—but this could have come from extreme sexual selection among young males (the Elks were cervine deer, a group where the successful male uniquely keeps and impregnates a whole harem), with much pressure to produce antlers when young, even though when fully adult the antlers proved counter-productive. This would be a case where function worked but then back-fired into non-functionality.

It has also always been agreed that redundant or unwanted characteristics, produced as part of the process of putting things together, might later be picked up by selection and used in their own right—as of course are the spandrels of San Marco. Pumping testosterone through the bodies of male humans has all sorts of adaptive virtues—penises and testicles for a start. Perhaps it is indeed the case that a secondary effect is hair on the male face, but despite the best advertizing efforts of the Gillette razor company, it is not obvious that beards are without their adaptative advantages. Or to use Gould's (2002) own favourite example, that the much enlarged clitoris of the female hyena has no present adaptive virtues. It may be that such a pseudo penis came by chance, but this does not deny its value today in mating rituals.

In fact, it has always been a key part of Darwinism that side effects can be a crucial part of the evolutionary story. A big question is about how new characteristics ever get started. As Gould forever asks, could a tenth of an eye be of any great value? Well, as Dawkins (1986) responds, perhaps it could, but there is no need to suppose immediate value in every new feature. Feathers today obviously have the adaptive edge when it comes to flying, and no one would say that flight is without its purposes. Increasingly, however, the evidence is that feathers first appeared on the dinosaurs, not for flight, but for other ends, most likely insulation and heat control. Only later were they used to invade the air.

Physical constraints

There are other potential types of constraint. Particularly interesting are physical constraints. Why do we never get a cat as big as an elephant? Because size and consequent weight goes up rapidly, according to the cube power of length or height. Suppose you have two identically shaped mammals, one twice the height of the other. It is going to be eight times as heavy. This means that from, a structural perspective, it has got eight times the weight problem. You simply cannot build elephants as agile as cats. They need far more support, which in turn means bigger and more stocky bones (Vogel 1988).

Another interesting calculation concerns what has irreverently been called the 'Jesus number.' What are the constraints on walking on water? In fact, a fairly simple formula governs the activity. Pushing up is the surface tension, γ, times the perimeter of the feet or area that is touching, l. Pushing down is gravity, which is a function of the mass, m, times the gravitational attraction, g ($F = mg$), or restating in terms of density, ρ, times the volume, which is a function of l cubed. In other words: $Je = \gamma l/\rho l^3 g = \gamma/\rho l^2 g$. Since the surface tension, the density, and the gravitational constant remain the same, this means that the ability to walk on water is essentially a function of the perimeter squared. In other words, the smaller you are the better off you are, and conversely the bigger you are the more likely you are to sink. This is no problem for insects, especially given that they have six legs and so have a lot of perimeter for the body size. Humans however are another matter. 'What would be the maximum weight of a human who could walk on water? My size-9 sandals have a perimeter of 0·62 meters each; that length times the surface tension of water gives 0·045 newtons of force, or 4·6 grams (less than half an ounce) of weight—9·2 grams to stand (two feet in contact) or half that to walk. The theological implications are beyond the scope of the present book' (Vogel 1988, 100). This essay too!

However the philosophical implications are clear. There is more to life than simple function, but even in a case like this the functionalist will see selection at work. The point is that organisms exploit physical constraints for their own ends. John Maynard Smith and his co-authors have explored in depth the example of the coiling of shells in such organisms as molluscs and brachiopods. The coiling itself is fairly readily reduced to a simple logarithmic equation and it is possible to draw a plain that maps the coiling as a function of the vital causal factors, particularly the rate of coiling and the size of the generating curve. Given such a map, one feature stands right out for comment: whereas for most shells the coils touch all the way from the centre to the perimeter, some such shells coil without touching. There is a gap between the coils. Now, map the actual shells of a group of organisms, for instance, the genera of extinct ammonoids (cephalopod molluscs), including the theoretical line dividing touching coils from non-touching coils. The isomorphism between the theoretical and the actual is outstanding.

[N]early all ammonoids fall on the left side of the [theoretical] curved line and thus display overlap between successive whorls. This is clearly a constraint in the evolution of the group but what kind of constraint? In this particular case, the answer is apparently straightforward... Evolving lineages can and occasionally do cross the line so there is no reason to believe that open coiling violates any strict genetic or developmental constraint. Rather, the reason for not crossing the line appear to be biomechanical. Other things being equal, an open coiled shell is much weaker than its involute counterpart. Also, open coiling requires more shell material because the animal cannot use the outer surface of the previous whorl as the inner surface of the new whorl. (Maynard Smith *et al.* 1985, 280)

Even the exceptions prove the point. The shell of the living pelagic cephalopod Spirula has a shell that coils but does not touch. Exceptionally, this organism carries the shell internally, using it for buoyancy. There is no need for strength.

Maynard Smith and co-authors conclude 'that the constraint against open coiling is an adaptive one brought about by simple directional selection.' A conclusion which surely brings us full circle, for if constraints can be *adaptive*, brought on by selection, the distinction between form and function has truly collapsed. Indeed, theoretical biologist Gunter Wagner (1988) goes so far as to argue that constraints may be necessary for the action of selection, else variation will be all over the place with any positive changes being outweighed by other moves in a wrong direction.

Conclusion

Enough has been said. Around about 1959, the centenary of the publication of the *Origin*, functionalism was just about the only game in town. Apart from a few despised German morphologists and one or two idiosyncratic philosophers, no one had any time for a formalist approach to nature. Now things have swung the other way, and in some evolutionary circles, formalism rules triumphant. However, pulling back and looking at biology as an outsider—as a philosopher that is—one can see that things are not quite this simple. As the above discussion shows, a case can be made for formalism. But equally, as the above discussion shows, a case can still be made for functionalism.

In this sense, one should probably not speak of rival paradigms, but rather of different elements that go to make up the overall complete picture. But one senses that, historically and philosophically, there is more to be said than this. Historically, the form-function dichotomy—form-function tension rather—goes back to Aristotle and forward to today, right across the coming of evolution. And philosophically one does see some of the features of a paradigm, inasmuch as—rather like the Gilbert and Sullivan operetta, where every little child that is born into this world alive, is either a little Liberal or a little Conservative—biologists do seem to split over whether one should think form first and function second (and reluctantly at that), or function first and form second (and reluctantly at that).

Darwin, to take one example, was an out-and-out functionalist. He recognized form—he spoke of homology as Unity of Type—but saw it as coming from function. Gould, to take the other extreme,

Michael Ruse

was an out-and-out formalist, and he saw function as coming a distant second. His hero was the early twentieth century Scottish morphologist, D'Arcy Thompson, who had no sympathy with the Darwinian's focus on final cause, and who argued strenuously that material and formal causes are prior and more important. 'To seek not for ends but for antecedents is the way of the physicist, who finds "causes" in what he has learned to recognise as fundamental properties, or inseparable concomitants, or unchanging laws, of matter and of energy. In Aristotle's parable, the house is there that men may live in it; but it is also there because the builders have laid one stone upon another' (Thompson 1948, 6). Continuing: 'Cell and tissue, shell and bone, leaf and flower, are so many portions of matter, and it is in obedience to the laws of physics that their particles have been moved, moulded and conformed. ... Their problems of form are in the first instance mathematical problems, their problems of growth are essentially physical problems, and the morphologist is, *ipso facto*, a student of physical science' (p. 10). Thus: 'We want to see how, in some cases at least, the forms of living things, and of the parts of living things, can be explained by physical considerations, and to realise that in general no organic forms exist save such as are in conformity with physical and mathematical laws' (p. 15).

We have different perspectives, different visions. In this sense, we do have different paradigms. And, let me stress, in case you think I am ambiguous or disapproving, this is no bad thing. I do not see this as a sign of weakness in biology or of immaturity. If a division has been around for 2500 years, and is thriving today as never before, I doubt it is going to go away in a hurry. But the point I would make is that because biologists are motivated to go out and make their case—form or function—some terrific science gets done. The division is incredibly creative. So let us not regret it, but rejoice in it. The task now for philosophers is to try to understand it. What is this modified notion of 'paradigm' with which I am playing? Is it unique to biology or can it be found elsewhere in science? And what does this tell us about such issues as objectivity and subjectivity? These are the questions to which we philosophers should turn now.[2]

[2] I do not pretend that I am the first to discover the kind of entity that I am calling a 'paradigm.' In a way, it seems to me to be much like what Karl Popper (1974) called a 'metaphysical research programme.' I am not, of course, claiming that Popper would agree that form and function are exemplars of such a notion. One thing that does seem important to this notion as I am using it is the idea of metaphor. We are seeing the world as if it were an object of design—utilitarian or formal. I explore this kind of

References

Agassiz, E. C., Editor. 1885. *Louis Agassiz: His Life and Correspondence.* Boston: Houghton Mifflin.

Appel, T. 1987. *The Cuvier-Geoffroy Debate: French Biology in the Decades Before Darwin.* New York: Oxford University Press.

Balfour, F. M. 1880–1881. *A Treatise on Comparative Embryology.* London.

Barnes, J, editor. 1984. *The Complete Works of Aristotle.* Princeton: Princeton University Press.

Carroll, S. B. 1995. Homeotic genes and the evolution of arthropods. *Nature* 376: 479–85.

Carroll, S. B., J. K. Grenier, and S. D. Weatherbee. 2001. *From DNA to Diversity: Molecular Genetics and the Evolution of Animal Design.* Oxford: Blackwell.

Darwin, C. 1859. *On the Origin of Species.* London: John Murray.

———. 1862. *On the Various Contrivances by which British and Foreign Orchids are Fertilized by Insects, and On the Good Effects of Intercrossing.* London: John Murray.

———. 1985-. *The Correspondence of Charles Darwin.* Cambridge: Cambridge University Press.

Dawkins, R. 1983. Universal Darwinism. *Molecules to Men.* editor D. S. Bendall. Cambridge: University of Cambridge Press.

———. 1986. *The Blind Watchmaker.* New York, N.Y.: Norton.

Gegenbaur, C. 1878. *Elements of Comparative Anatomy.* London: Macmillan.

Gilbert, S. F., J. M. Opitz, and R. A. Raff. 1996. Resynthesizing evolutionary and developmental biology. *Developmental Biology* 173: 357–72.

Gould, S. J. 2002. *The Structure of Evolutionary Theory.* Cambridge, Mass.: Harvard University Press.

Gould, S. J., and R. C. Lewontin. 1979. The spandrels of San Marco and the Panglossian paradigm: a critique of the adaptationist program . *Proceedings of the Royal Society of London, Series B: Biological Sciences* 205: 581–98.

Haeckel E. 1866. *Generelle Morphologie der Organismen.* Berlin: Georg Reimer.

Huxley, T. H., and H. N. Martin. 1875. *A Course of Practical Instruction in Elementary Biology.* London: Macmillan.

Kuhn, T. 1962. *The Structure of Scientific Revolutions.* Chicago: University of Chicago Press.

———. 1993. Metaphor in science. In *Metaphor and Thought.* 2nd ed., Editor Andrew Ortony, pp. 533–42. Cambridge: Cambridge University Press.

thought in my *Mystery of Mysteries: Is Evolution a Social Construction?* I note with some interest that Kuhn (1993) himself tied in paradigm thinking with metaphor.

Michael Ruse

Maynard Smith, J. 1968. *Mathematical Ideas in Biology*. Cambridge: Cambridge University Press.

Maynard Smith, J., R. Burian, S. Kauffman, P. Alberch, J. Campbell, B. Goodwin, R. Lande, D. Raup, and L. Wolpert. 1985. Developmental constraints and evolution. *Quarterly Review of Biology* 60: 265–87.

Owen, Rev. R. 1894. *The Life of Richard Owen*. London: Murray.

Popper, K. R. 1974. Darwinism as a metaphysical research programme. In *The Philosophy of Karl Popper*. Editor P. A. Schilpp, 133–43. Vol. 1. LaSalle, Ill.: Open Court.

Raff, R. 1996. *The Shape of Life: Genes, Development, and the Evolution of Animal Form*. Chicago: University of Chicago Press.

Ray, J. 1709. *The Wisdom of God, Manifested in the Words of Creation*. Fifth ed. London: Samuel Smith.

Reeve, H. K., and P. W. Sherman. 1993. Adaptation and the goals of evolutionary research. *Quarterly Review of Biology* 68: 1–32.

Richards, R. J. 1992. *The Meaning of Evolution: The Morphological Construction and Ideological Reconstruction of Darwin's Theory*. Chicago: University of Chicago Press.

———. 2003. *The Romantic Conception of Life: Science and Philosophy in the Age of Goethe*. Chicago: University of Chicago Press.

Roth, G., J. Blanke, and D. B. Wake. 1994. Cell size predicts morphological complexity in the brains of frogs and salamanders. *Proceedings of the National Academy of the Sciences, USA* 91: 4796–800.

Ruse, M. 1989. Is the theory of punctuated equilibria a new paradigm? *Journal of Social and Biological Structures* 12: 195–212.

———. 1996. *Monad to Man: The Concept of Progress in Evolutionary Biology*. Cambridge, Mass.: Harvard University Press.

———. 1999. *Mystery of Mysteries: Is Evolution a Social Construction?* Cambridge, Mass.: Harvard University Press.

———. 2003. *Darwin and Design: Does Evolution have a Purpose?* Cambridge, Mass.: Harvard University Press.

Russell, E. S. 1916. *Form and Function: A Contribution to the History of Animal Morphology*. London: John Murray.

Thompson, D. W. 1948. *On Growth and Form, Second Edition*. Cambridge: Cambridge University Press.

Vogel, S. 1988. *Life's Devices: The Physical World of Animals and Plants*. Princeton, N J: Princeton University Press.

Wagner, G. P. 1988. The influence of variation and of developmental constraints on the rate of multivariate phenotypic evolution. *Journal of Evolutionary Biology* 1: 45–66.

Is Drift a Serious Alternative to Natural Selection as an Explanation of Complex Adaptive Traits?

ELLIOTT SOBER

> 'There are known knowns; there are things we know we know. We also know there are known unknowns; that is to say we know there are some things we do not know. But there are also unknown unknowns—the ones we don't know we don't know.'
> —Donald Rumsfeld, 2003, President George W. Bush's Secretary of Defense, on the subject of the U.S. government's failure to discover weapons of mass destruction in Iraq

Gould and Lewontin's (1978) essay, 'The Spandrels of San Marco' is famous for faulting adaptationists for not considering alternatives to natural selection as possible evolutionary explanations. One of the alternatives that Gould and Lewontin say has been unfairly neglected is random genetic drift. Yet, in spite of the article's wide influence, this particular suggestion has not produced an avalanche of papers in which drift is considered as an explanation of complex adaptive features such as the vertebrate eye. The reason is not far to seek. Biologists whose adaptationism remained undented by the Spandrels paper continued to dismiss drift as an egregious non-starter. And even biologists sympathetic with Gould and Lewontin's take-home message—that adaptationists need to pull up their socks and test hypotheses about natural selection more rigorously—have had trouble taking drift seriously. Both critics and defenders of adaptationism have tended to set drift to one side because they are convinced that complex adaptive traits have only a tiny probability of evolving under that process. The probability is not zero, but the consensus seems to be that the probability is sufficiently small that drift can safely be ignored.

There is a statistical philosophy behind this line of reasoning that I think is mistaken. Once the mistake is identified, drift becomes an interesting alternative to natural selection, but not because I or any-one else thinks it is a plausible explanation of complex adaptive traits. Rather, the hypothesis is interesting because it provides a *foil*;

considering drift as an alternative to natural selection forces one to identify the information that is needed if one wishes to say that an adaptive feature is better explained by one hypothesis or the other. I'll examine two relatively simple phenotypic models of selection and drift with the goal of identifying these informational requirements. It is interesting that the requirements are not trivial.

1. There is no Probabilistic *Modus Tollens*—Against Fisherian Significance Tests

Modus tollens is familiar to philosophers and scientists; it is the centrepiece of Karl Popper's views on falsifiability:

(MT)   If H, then O
                  not-O
               _____

                  not-H

Modus tollens says that if the hypothesis H entails the observation statement O, and O turns out to be false, then H should be rejected. Since *modus tollens* is a deductively valid rule of inference (hence my use of a single line to separate premises from conclusion), perhaps the following probabilistic extension of the rule constitutes a sensible principle of nondeductive reasoning:

(Prob-MT) $Pr(O|H)$ is very high.
                  Not-O.
               ═══════════

                  not-H

According to *probabilistic modus tollens*, if the hypothesis H says that O will *very probably* be true, and O turns out to be false, then H should be rejected. Equivalently, the suggestion is that if H says that some observational outcome (not-O) has a very low probability, and that outcome nonetheless occurs, then we should regard H as false. I draw a double line between premises and conclusion in (Prob-MT) to indicate that the argument form is not supposed to be deductively valid.

Probabilistic *modus tollens* is Fisher's (1925) test of significance. Fisher describes his test as leading to a disjunctive conclusion— either the hypothesis H is false, or something very improbable has occurred. Even if this disjunction followed from the premises[1], that would not mean that the first disjunct also follows, either deductively or nondeductively. I agree with Hacking (1965), Edwards (1973), and Royall (1997) that probabilistic modus tollens is an incorrect principle. As these authors make clear, lots of perfectly reasonable hypotheses say that the observations are very improbable; in particular, this is something we should expect when the observations are numerous and are conditionally independent of each other, given a *probabilistic* hypothesis. Consider, for example, the hypothesis that a coin is fair. If the coin is tossed a million times, the exact sequence of heads and tails that results will have a probability of $(1/2)^{1,000,000}$. However, that hardly shows that the hypothesis should be rejected. Indeed, every sequence of heads and tails has the same small probability of occurring; probabilistic *modus tollens* therefore claims that the hypothesis should be rejected *a priori*—no matter what the outcome of the experiment turns out to be—but surely that makes no sense.

It may seem that the kernel of truth in (Prob-MT) can be rescued by modifying the argument's conclusion. If it is too much to conclude that H is false, perhaps we may conclude that the observations constitute evidence against H:

(Evidential Prob-MT) $Pr(O|H)$ is very high.

not-O
$$\overline{}$$

not-O is evidence against H.

This principle is also unsatisfactory, as Royall (1997, p. 67) nicely illustrates via the following story: Suppose I send my valet to bring me one of my urns. I want to test the hypothesis (H) that the urn he returns with contains 0.2% white balls. I draw a ball from the urn and find that it is white. Is this evidence against the hypothesis? It may not be. Suppose I have only two urns—one of them contains 0.2% white balls, while the other contains 0.0001% white balls. In this instance, drawing a white ball is evidence *in favour* of H, not evidence *against* it.[2,3]

[1] Even if H and not-O are true, and $Pr(not-O|H)$ is very low, it does not follow that not-O is 'intrinsically' improbable. It is perfectly possible for there to be another true hypothesis that confers a high probability on not-O.

[2] Forensic identity tests using DNA data provide further illustrations of Royall's point. For example, Crow (2000, pp. 65–67) computed the probability of a DNA match at 13 loci, based on known allele frequencies. If

Elliott Sober

Royall's story brings out the fact that judgments about evidential meaning are essentially *comparative*. To decide whether an observation is evidence against H, we usually need to know what alternatives there are to H. In typical cases, *to test a hypothesis requires testing it against alternatives*.[4] In the story about the valet, observing a white ball is very improbable according to H, but in fact that outcome is evidence in favour of H, not evidence against it. The reason is that O is even more improbable according to the alternative hypothesis. Probabilistic *modus tollens*, in both its vanilla and evidential versions, needs to be replaced by the *Law of Likelihood*:

Observation O favours hypothesis H_1 over hypothesis H_2 if and only if $\Pr(O|H_1) > \Pr(O|H_2)$.

The term 'favouring' is meant to indicate *differential support*; the evidence points away from the hypothesis that says it is less probable and towards the hypothesis that says it is more probable.

This is not the place to undertake a defence of the Law of Likelihood (on which see Hacking 1965, Edwards 1972, Royall 1997) or to consider its limitations (Forster and Sober 2004), but a comment about its intended scope is in order. The Law of Likelihood should be restricted to cases in which the probabilities of hypotheses are not under consideration (perhaps because they are not known or are not even 'well-defined') and one is limited to information about the probability of the observations given different hypotheses. To see why this restriction is needed, consider an example presented in Leeds (2000). One observes that an ace has just been drawn from a standard deck of cards (O) and

---

[4] I say that this is 'usually' true because the thesis that testing a hypothesis H is *always* contrastive is false. For example, if a set of true observational claims entails H, there is no need to consider alternatives to H; one can conclude without further ado that H is true. And, as we know from *modus tollens*, if H entails O and O turns out to be false, one can conclude that H is false without needing to contemplate alternatives.

the individuals are sibs, the probability is 7.7×10^{-32}. The observations are very improbable under the sib hypothesis, but that hardly shows that they are evidence against it. In fact, the data favour the sib hypothesis over the hypothesis that the two individuals are unrelated. If they are unrelated, the probability is 6.5×10^{-38}.

[3] A third formulation of probabilistic *modus tollens* is no better than the other two. Can one conclude that *H* is *probably* false, given that H says that O is highly probable, and O fails to be true? The answer is no; inspection of Bayes' theorem shows that $\Pr(\text{not-}O|H)$ can be low without $\Pr(H|\text{not-}O)$ being low.

the hypotheses under evaluation are H_1 = 'the card is the ace of hearts' and H_2 = 'the card is the ace of spades or the ace of clubs.' It follows that $Pr(H_1|O) = {}^1/_4$ and $Pr(H_2|O) = {}^1/_2$, while $Pr(O|H_1)$ = $Pr(O|H_2)$ = 1.0. It would be odd to maintain that O does not favour H_2 over H_1; in this case, the favouring relation is mediated by the probabilities of hypotheses, not their likelihoods.[5] Since scientists are often disinclined to discuss the probabilities of hypotheses (when these probabilities can't be conceptualized as objective quantities), this restriction of the Law of Likelihood accords well with much scientific practice.

I hope it is clear how Royall's story and the Law of Likelihood apply to the task of evaluating drift as a possible explanation of a complex adaptive trait. The fact that $Pr(Data|Drift)$ is very low does not show that the drift hypothesis should be rejected. It does not even show that the data are evidence against the drift hypothesis. What we need to know is how probable the data are under alternative hypotheses. In particular, we need to consider $Pr(Data|Selection)$. If the data favour Selection over Drift, this isn't because $Pr(Data|Drift)$ is *low*, but because $Pr(Data|Drift)$ is *lower* than $Pr(Data|Selection)$. Our next question, therefore, is how these two likelihoods should be conceptualized.

2. The Two Hypotheses

Let's begin by temporarily setting to one side examples of complex adaptive features such as the vertebrate eye and consider instead an ostensibly simpler quantitative character—the fact, let us assume, that polar bears have fur that is, on average, 10 cm long. Which hypothesis—selection or drift—confers the higher probability on the trait value we observe polar bears to have?[6]

I will assume that evolution in the lineage leading to present day polar bears takes place in a finite population. This means that there is an element of drift in the evolutionary process, regardless of what else is going on. The question is whether selection also played a role.

---

[5] I am grateful to Branden Fitelson for discussion on this point.

[6] Since we are talking about a continuous variable, the proper concept is *probability density*, not *probability*, and even so, the probability (density) of the bears' having an average fur length of *exactly* 10 cm. is zero, on each hypothesis. Thus we need to talk about some tiny region surrounding a value of 10 cm. as the observation that each theory probabilifies. The subsequent discussion should be understood in this way.

Elliott Sober

Thus, our two hypotheses are *pure drift* (PD) and *selection plus drift* (SPD). Were the alternative traits identical in fitness or were there fitness differences among them (and hence natural selection)? I will understand the idea of drift in a way that is somewhat nonstandard. The usual formulation is in terms of random *genetic* drift; however, the problem I want to address concerns fur length, which is a *phenotype*. To decide how random genetic drift would influence the evolution of this phenotype, we'd have to know the developmental rules that describe how genes influence phenotypes. I am going to bypass these genetic details by using a purely phenotypic notion of drift. Under the PD hypothesis, a population's probability of increasing its average fur length by a small amount is the same as its probability of reducing fur length by that amount.[7] Average fur length evolves by random walk. I'll also bypass the genetic details in formulating the SPD hypothesis; I'll assume that the SPD hypothesis identifies some phenotype (O) as the optimal phenotype and says that an organism's fitness decreases monotonically as it deviates from that optimum. Thus, if 12 centimetres is the optimal fur length, then 11 is fitter than 10, 13 is fitter than 14, etc. Given this singly-peaked fitness function, the SPD hypothesis says that a population's probability of moving a little closer to O exceeds its probability of moving a little farther away. The SPD hypothesis says that O is a *probabilistic attractor* in the lineage's evolution. For evolution to occur, either by pure drift or by selection plus drift, there must be variation. I'll assume that mutation always provides a cloud of variation around the population's average trait value.

The dynamics of selection plus drift (SPD) are illustrated in Figure 1, which comes from Lande (1976), whose phenotypic model is the one I am using here. At the beginning of the process, at t_0, the average phenotype in the population has a sharp value. The state of the population at various later times is represented by different probability distributions. Notice that as the process unfolds, the mean value of the distribution moves in the direction of the optimum specified by the hypothesis. The distribution also grows wider, reflecting the fact that the population's average phenotype becomes more uncertain as more time elapses. After infinite time (at t_∞), the population is centred on the putative optimum. The speed at which the population moves towards this final distribution depends on the trait's heritability and on the strength of selection,

[7] Except, of course, when the population has its minimum or maximum value. There is no way to have fur that is less than 0 centimetres long; I'll also assume that there is an upper bound on how long the fur can be (e.g., 100 centimetres).

130

Is Drift a Serious Alternative to Natural Selection?

Figure 1

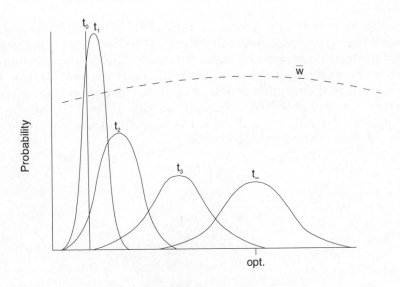

Average phenotype in the population

which is represented in Figure 1 by the peakedness of the $\bar{w}$ curve; this curve describes how average fitness depends on average fur length. The width of the different distributions depends on the effective population size N; the larger N is, the narrower the bell curve. In summary, the SPD hypothesis models the process of selection plus drift as the *shifting and squashing of a bell curve*.

Understood in this way, the SPD hypothesis constitutes a relatively simple conceptualization of natural selection in a finite population. The SPD hypothesis assumes that the fitness function is singly peaked and that fitnesses are *frequency independent*—e.g., whether it is better for a bear to have fur that is 9 centimetres long or 8 does not depend on how common or rare these traits are in the population. I also have conceptualized the SPD hypothesis as specifying an optimum that remains unchanged during the lineage's evolution; the optimum is not a moving target. Indeed, the hypothesis assumes that there is a fur length that is optimal for all bears, regardless of how they differ in other respects. I have constructed the SPD hypothesis with these features, not because I think they are realistic, but because they make the problem I wish to address more tractable. My goal, recall, is to identify the information one must have on hand if one wishes to say whether

SPD or PD has the higher likelihood. Informational requirements do not decline when models are made more complex; in fact, they increase.

Figure 2 depicts the process of pure drift (PD); it involves just *the squashing of a bell curve.* Although uncertainty about the trait's future state increases with time, the mean value of the distribution remains unchanged. In the limit of infinite time (at t_∞), the probability distribution is flat, indicating that all average phenotypes are equiprobable. The rate at which the bell curve gets squashed depends on N, the effective population size; the smaller N is, the faster the squashing occurs.[8]

Figure 2

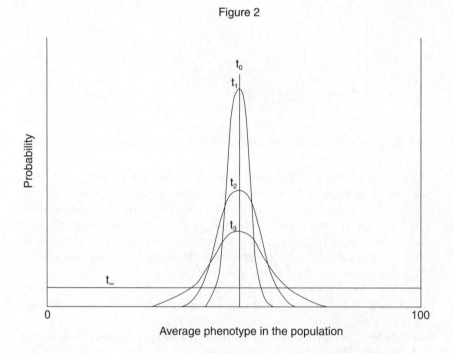

Average phenotype in the population

[8] The case of infinite time makes it easy to see why an explicitly genetic model can generate predictions that substantially differ from the purely phenotypic models considered here. For example, under the process of pure random *genetic* drift, each locus is homozygotic at equilibrium. In a one-locus two-allele model in which the population begins with each allele at 50%, there is a 0.5 probability that the population will be *AA* and a 0.5 probability that it will be *aa*. In a two-locus two-allele model, again with each allele at equal frequency at the start, each of the four configurations *AABB, AAbb, aaBB,* and *aabb* has a 0.25 probability. Imagine that genotype determines phenotype (or that each genotype has associated with it a

Is Drift a Serious Alternative to Natural Selection?

Figure 3

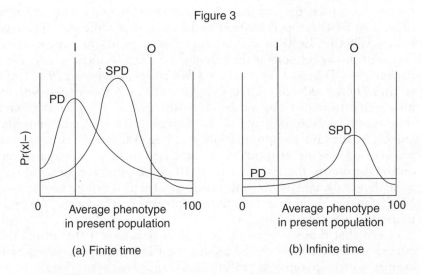

(a) Finite time (b) Infinite time

For both the PD and the SPD curves, it is important to understand that the curves do not describe how an individual's fur length must change, but rather describe possible changes in the population's average fur length. It is perhaps easiest to visualize what is involved by thinking of each curve as describing what will happen if 1000 replicate populations are each subjected to the SPD or the PD process, where each begins with the same initial average fur length. After a given amount of time elapses, we expect these different populations to have different average fur lengths; these different averages should form a distribution that approximates the theoretical distributions depicted in the figures. What these curves say about a single population is that there are many different average fur lengths it might have, and that these different possibilities have the different probabilities represented by the relevant curve.

We now are in a position to analyse when SPD will be more likely than PD. Figure 3a depicts the relevant distributions when there has been finite time since the lineage started evolving from its initial state (I). Notice that the PD distribution stays centred at I, whereas the SPD curve has moved in the direction of the putative optimum (O). Notice further that the PD curve has become more flattened than the SPD curve has; selection impedes spreading out.

different average phenotypic value) and it becomes obvious that a genetic model can predict nonuniform phenotypic distributions at equilibrium. The case of selection-plus-drift is the same in this regard; there are genetic models that will alter the picture of how the average phenotype evolves. See Turelli (1988) for further discussion.

Figure 3b depicts the two distributions when there has been infinite time. The SPD curve is centred at the optimum while the PD curve is flat. Whether finite or infinite time has elapsed, the fundamental fact abut the likelihoods is the same: *the SPD hypothesis is more likely than the PD hypothesis precisely when the population's actual value is 'close' to the optimum.* Of course, what 'close' means depends on how much time has elapsed between the lineage's initial state and the present, on the intensity of selection, on the trait's heritability, and on N, the effective population size. For example, if infinite time has elapsed (Figure 3b), the SPD curve will be more tightly centred on the optimum, the larger N is. If 10 is the observed value of our polar bears, but 11 is the optimum, SPD will be more likely than PD if the population is small, but the reverse will be true if the population is sufficiently large.

Given that there are several biological parameters that affect the curves associated with the SPD and the PD hypotheses, it is worth asking which parameter values make it easier to discriminate between the two hypotheses and which values make this more difficult. One crucial factor is the amount of time that has elapsed between the ancestor and the present day species whose trait value we are trying to explain. With only a little time, the predictions of the two hypotheses are mainly determined by I, the population's initial condition, and so the two hypotheses will be pretty much indistinguishable. Only with the passage of more time do the processes postulated by the two hypotheses significantly influence what they predict; with infinite time, the predictions are determined entirely by the postulated processes and the initial condition has been completely 'forgotten.' This means that more time is 'better,' in terms of getting the two hypotheses to make different predictions. The same point holds for the intensity of selection and the heritability; for a fixed amount of time since the initial state I, the higher the values of these parameters the better, in terms of getting the SPD curve to shift significantly away from the PD curve. It is more difficult to gauge the net epistemological significance of N, the effective population size; as noted before, small N makes the PD curve flatten faster, whereas large N makes the SPD curve narrower.

Although the criterion of 'closeness to the putative optimum' suggests that there are just two possibilities that need to be considered in deciding whether SPD is more likely than PD, it is more fruitful to distinguish the four possibilities that are summarized in the accompanying table. In each, an arrow points from the population's initial state (I) to its present state (P); O is the optimum postulated by the SPD hypothesis. The first case (a) is the most obvious; if the optimum (O) turns out to be identical with the population's actual trait value (in our example, fur that is 10 cm. long), we're done—SPD has the higher likelihood. However, if the present trait value is different from the optimum value, even a little, we need more information. If we can discover what the lineage's initial state (I) was, and if this implies that (b) the population evolved *away* from the putative optimum, we're done—PD has the higher likelihood. But if our estimates of the values of I and O entail that there has been (c) overshooting or (d) undershooting, we need more information if we wish to say which hypothesis is more likely.

		Which hypothesis is more likely?
(a) present state coincides with the putative optimum	---|----------|---------------- I → P=O	selection-plus-drift
(b) population evolves away from the putative optimum	---|----------*------------|--- P ← I O	pure drift
(c) population overshoots the putative optimum	---|----------|------------|--- I → O → P	?
(d) population undershoots the putative optimum	---|----------|------------|--- I → P O	?

3. Estimating Biological Parameters

If answering the question of whether SPD is more likely than PD depends on further details, how should those details be obtained? One possibility is that we simply *invent* assumptions that allow each hypothesis to have the highest likelihood possible, and then compare these two 'best cases.' With respect to the SPD hypothesis, this would involve assuming that the actual fur length of 10 centimetres also happens to be the optimal value, that the population has been evolving a very short time, that its initial state was the same as its present state, and that the population is extremely large. The net effect of these assumptions is to push the likelihood assigned to SPD very close to the maximum possible value of unity. The problem is that this is a game that two can play. By assuming that the population was large, that there has been little time since the population started evolving, and that the population began with a trait value of 10, the PD hypothesis will have that same high likelihood.

Simply inventing favourable assumptions has a second defect, in addition to the fact that it leads to a stand-off between the two hypotheses. The problem is that the assumptions are merely that— they are *invented*, not *independently supported*. When we want to know whether SPD is more likely than PD, we are not asking whether we can invent a detailed description of selection that has a higher likelihood than any hypothesis about drift that we are able to invent. Rather, what we want to know is how SPD and PD compare when each is fleshed out in ways that are independently plausible.[9]

This means that we can use the four possible relationships depicted in the table to construct the protocol for asking questions presented in Figure 4. We first must figure out what the optimal fur length would be for polar bears, if fur length were subject to natural selection. If it turns out that the optimal value (O) is identical with the observed present value (P), we need go no farther—we can conclude that SPD is more likely than PD. However, if the optimum and the actual value differ,[10] we must estimate what the ancestral condition (I) was at some earlier point in the lineage. If the estimated values for O and I, and the observed value for P, are such that I is between O and P, we are finished—we can conclude that PD is more likely than SPD. However, if I is not between O and P, we must estimate additional biological parameters if we want to say which hypothesis has the higher likelihood.

Figure 4

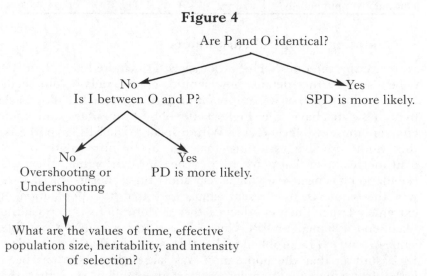

Are P and O identical?

No — Is I between O and P?

Yes — SPD is more likely.

No — Overshooting or Undershooting

Yes — PD is more likely.

What are the values of time, effective population size, heritability, and intensity of selection?

[9] I criticize 'intelligent design theory' for being unable to provide independently supported information about the putative designer's goals and abilities in Sober (2002a, 2004a, 2004b).

[10] The question of whether O and P are identical must be approached statistically. If O = 10.01 and the 100 sampled polar bears have a mean fur length of 10.0, the conclusion may be that O and P are not statistically distinguishable.

Is Drift a Serious Alternative to Natural Selection?

Let us begin with the first question in the protocol. If present day polar bears have an average fur length of 10 cm, how are we to discover what the optimal fur length is? If there is, as I'm assuming, variation in the present population around its mean value, we can observe the survival and reproductive success of individuals that have different trait values. We also might wish to conduct an experiment in which we attach parkas to some polar bears, shave others, and leave others with their fur lengths unchanged. We then can monitor what happens to these experimental subjects, and these observations will allow us to estimate the fitness values that attach to different fur lengths. This experiment will allow us to construct an empirically well-grounded estimate of what the optimal fur length is.

There is a second approach to the problem of identifying the optimal fur length, one that is less direct and more theoretical. Suppose there is an energetic cost associated with growing fur. We know that the heat loss an organism experiences depends on the ratio of its surface area to its volume. We also know that there is seasonal variation in temperature. Although it is bad to be too cold in winter, it also is bad to be too warm in summer. We also know something about the abundance of food. These and other considerations might allow us to construct a model that identifies what the optimal fur length is for organisms that have various other characteristics. Successful modelling of this type does not require the question-begging assumption that the bear's actual trait value is optimal or close to optimal. This methodology has been applied to other traits in other taxa (Alexander 1996; Hamilton 1967; Parker 1978); there is no reason why it should not be applicable in the present context.

As noted earlier, the simple model of selection we are considering assumes a stationary target—the optimal fur length for bears *now* is the same as the optimum that existed while the lineage was evolving. This is almost certainly a highly unrealistic assumption. If we dropped it, we'd have to worry about how an estimate of present optimal values would allow one to infer what trait value was optimal during the time the trait was evolving. As Tinbergen (1964, p. 428) observed '[w]hen one finds that a certain characteristic has survival value ... one has demonstrated beyond doubt a selection pressure which prevents the species in its present state from deviating ... However, the conclusion that this same selection pressure must have been responsible in the past for the *moulding* of the character studied is speculative, however probable it often is.'

Although the SPD hypothesis' assumption of a stationary target allows us to bypass this question, the question of how to infer past from present cannot be evaded in connection with the second question in the protocol described in Figure 4. We need to decide whether I, the state the population occupied at some earlier time, falls between O and P. The natural way to address this question is to estimate I. Biologists attempt to solve this estimation problem by exploiting the fact that polar bears and other bears alive today share common ancestors. By using other traits that these bears possess, they infer a phylogenetic tree of the sort depicted in Figure 5 in which polar bears and their relatives are tip species. The fur lengths of polar bears and their relatives can then be written onto the tips of that tree. The observed character states of these tip species provide evidence about the character states of ancestors, which are represented by interior nodes. What inference procedure should we use to infer these ancestral trait values?

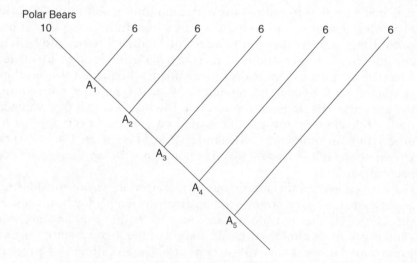

Figure 5

Before addressing that question, I want to explain why Figure 5 shows that our question about SPD versus PD is ambiguous—there are many SPD versus PD questions about polar bear fur length, not just one. It is obvious that present day polar bears have multiple ancestors, and equally obvious that different ancestors may well have had different fur lengths. If these were all known, the problem of explaining why polar bears now have fur that is 10 centimetres long would decompose into a number of subproblems—why the fur length present at A_5 evolved to the length present at A_4, why A_4's fur length evolved to the value found at A_3, etc. SPD may be a better answer than PD for some of these transitions, but the reverse might be true for others. Similarly, suppose we infer the fur length of just one of these ancestors and ask whether the evolution of fur length from that ancestral value to the 10 cm we observe in present day polar bears favours SPD or PD. The answer may depend on which ancestor we consider. If the inferred optimum is 12 and we infer that $A_2 = 11$, then the lineage leading from A_2 to the present has evolved away from the putative optimum, and we conclude that PD is more likely than SPD. If, however, we focus on A_3, and infer that $A_3=8$, then the lineage leading from A_3 to the present under-shot the optimum, and we are in case (c) described in the Table; with further biological information, it may turn out that SPD is more likely than PD. The question of whether SPD or PD is the more likely explanation of an observed trait value thus needs to be relativized to a choice of ancestor.

Now back to the problem of inferring the character states of ancestors. A standard method that biologists use is *parsimony*—we are to prefer the assignment of states to ancestors that minimizes the total amount of evolution that must have occurred to produce the trait values we observe in tip species. This is why assigning ancestor A_1 in Figure 5 a value of 8 and the other ancestors a value of 6 is said to have greater credibility than assigning them all a value of 10. But why should we use parsimony to draw this inference? This is a large question, which I won't attempt to answer here. However, a few points may be useful. First, it turns out that if drift is the process at work in a phylogenetic tree, then the most parsimonious assignment of trait values to ancestors (where parsimony means minimizing the *squared* amount of change) is also the assignment of maximum likelihood (Maddison 1991). On the other hand, if there is a directional selection process at work, parsimony and likelihood can fail to coincide (Sober 2002b). This point can be grasped by considering a very simple example—the lineage leading from a single ancestor to present day polar bears. If bears now have a trait value of 10, the most parsimonious assignment of character state to the ancestor is, of course, 10. But suppose the lineage has been undergoing strong selection that is pushing the lineage towards an optimal fur length of (say) 13; if so, the most likely assignment of trait value to the ancestor is some number less than 10; the exact value of that best estimate depends on the amount of time separating ancestor and descendant, the intensity of selection, and the heritability.[11] It follows that parsimony does not provide evidence about ancestral character states that is *independent* of the PD and SPD hypotheses we wish to test.[12]

Given that it is question-begging in the context of testing drift against selection to use parsimony to infer the initial state (I) of the lineage leading to present day polar bears, one remedy may be to consider a range of possible values for I. If the drift hypothesis says that the maximum likelihood estimate of the fur length of an ancestor is 8 and the selection hypothesis says that the maximum likelihood estimate is 6, then perhaps one should see how setting I to different values between 6 and 8 affects the likelihood comparison of PD and SPD. If the greater likelihood of one hypothesis over the other is robust, then the problem of inferring I can be set to one side. However, I see no reason to expect that the problem will usually disappear in this way.[13]

Similar issues arise in connection with the last question in the protocol. If O≠P and if I is not between O and P, then we need estimates of effective population size, heritability, intensity of selection, and so on. If we can't answer the questions in this protocol, we are in no position to say which hypothesis is more likely.

[11] Here's an analogy: imagine you want to swim across a river that has a strong current. The way to maximize your probability of reaching a target on the other side is *not* to start directly across from it; rather, you should start a bit upstream. How far upstream you should go depends on the width of the river, the strength of the current, and on how strong a swimmer you are.

[12] This is the central problem with the procedure for testing adaptive hypotheses proposed by Ridley (1983); see Sober (2002b) for further discussion.

[13] The discovery of fossils helps solve this problem, but does not solve it completely. Even if fur length could be inferred from a fossil find, it is important to remember that we can't assume that the fossils we observe are *ancestors* of present day polar bears. They may simply be *relatives*. If so, the question persists—how is one to use these data to infer the character states of the most recent common ancestor that present day polar bears and this fossil share? The fact that the fossil is closer in time to this ancestor than is an organism that is alive today means that the fossil will provide stronger evidence. If present day polar bears have a fur length of 10 and the fossil has a fur length of 6, and it is known that the fossil is temporally much closer to the most recent common ancestor than present day polar bears are, then the maximum likely estimate of the ancestor's character will not be 8, but will be closer to 6 (assuming a pure drift process). Likelihood and parsimony do not agree in this case.

Is Drift a Serious Alternative to Natural Selection?

My analysis of how the PD and SPD hypotheses ought to be compared rests on the demand for 'independent evidence' concerning the values of various biological parameters. Some of these parameters are shared between the two models. For example, the likelihood of each depends on what the initial state (I) of the lineage was, on how much time elapsed between I and the present state P, and on the effective population size. The demand for independent evidence in these cases is the demand that the estimate not depend on assuming that the PD hypothesis is true or on assuming that the SPD hypothesis is true. However, there are parameters in the SPD hypothesis that do not occur in the PD hypothesis—most obviously the putative optimum O. What would it mean to have 'independent evidence' concerning the value of O? After all, if an optimal phenotype exists, the SPD hypothesis must be true and the PD hypothesis false. Here the demand for independent evidence is the demand that one's estimate of O not rest on the assumption that the present state P of the population is optimal or close to optimal. The point is to find the most reasonable estimate of O, on the assumption that the SPD hypothesis is true.

4. A Digression on Dichotomous Characters

Perhaps the epistemological difficulties just described would disappear if we redefined the problem. Instead of asking why polar bears now have fur that is 10 centimetres long, perhaps we should ask why they have 'long' fur rather than 'short.' Isn't it clear that polar bears are better off with long fur than they would be with short? If so, long is the *optimal* fur length in this dichotomous character. Doesn't this allow us to conclude without further ado that SPD has higher likelihood than PD, according to the protocol described in Figure 4? Apparently, you don't need to know the ancestral fur length or other biological details to make this argument.

It is interesting how often informal reasoning about natural selection focuses on dichotomous qualitative characters. For example, sociobiologists ask why human beings 'avoid incest,' not why they avoid it to the degree they do. The adaptive hypothesis is that selection favours outbreeding over inbreeding. This hypothesis renders the observed 'avoidance of incest' more probable than does the hypothesis that says that a pure drift process occurred. Of course, the problem gets more difficult if we estimate how much inbreeding there is in human populations and then ask whether that quantitative value is more probable under the SPD hypothesis or the PD hypothesis. However, why can't an adaptationist admit that this quantitative problem *is* more difficult and still insist on the correctness of the simple likelihood argument just described to solve the qualitative problem?

There is a fly in the ointment. What does it mean to say that fur is 'long' rather than 'short?' No matter where the cut-off is drawn to separate 'short' fur from 'long,' it will do violence to the trichotomy implicit in our fundamental finding about Figure 3— that SPD is more likely than PD when the observed fur length is 'close' to the optimum, whereas fur lengths that are too long or too short render PD more likely than SPD. Long fur is not, contrary to appearances, unambiguous evidence favouring the hypothesis of natural selection.

The problem with imposing dichotomous descriptors ('long' versus 'short') on a quantitative character in the case of fur length seems to arise from the fact that fur length has an intermediate optimum. But why should this be a problem in connection with a feature like incest avoidance, where the less of it the better (or so I will assume for the sake of posing this problem)? In this case, there will be two regions of parameter space, not three. If human beings have a rate of incest that is 'close' to zero, then SPD is likelier than PD; otherwise, the reverse is true. The problem is to say how close is close enough (Sober 1993). How much incest is consistent with saying that SPD is more likely than PD? Of course, if human beings had a zero rate of incest, we'd be done—SPD would be more likely than PD. But if the rate is nonzero, it is unclear how to classify the observation, and so it is unclear whether SPD is more likely. We need further biological information to answer this question. Moving to a dichotomous description of the data doesn't change that fact.

5. The Significance of Adaptive Complexity—from Fur Length to the Camera Eye

It may strike the reader that the example I have been considering— fur length in polar bears—is rather simple and therefore differs in important respects from the problem of testing adaptive hypotheses about a complex structure like the vertebrate eye. In fact, I'm not so sure that bear fur length really *is* so simple. But even if it is, the problems just adumbrated apply with equal force to the task of explaining complex adaptive features. There are additional wrinkles, as we shall see, but questions concerning the relationship of the initial state (I), the present state (P), and the optimal state (O) remain relevant to identifying the predictions of the SPD hypothesis.

Fur length has an obvious 'transformation series.' If a population is going to evolve from an average fur length of 3 cm to an average of 5 (let us assume by a series of small changes), then it must pass through an average that is around 4. But consider the evolution of the camera eye in the vertebrate line. If we trace this lineage back far enough, we will find an ancestor that does not have any eye at all. Again assuming that changes must be small, we can ask what the intermediate stages were through which the lineage must have passed as it evolved from no eye to a camera eye. A more general approach would be to conceive of this problem probabilistically; there may be more than one possible transformation series, with different probabilities attaching to different possible changes in character state. The reconstruction of this transformation series is a nontrivial evolutionary problem.

There are nine or ten basic eye designs found in animals, with many variations on those themes. In broad strokes, this variation can be described as follows: vertebrates, squid, and spiders have camera eyes, most insects have compound eyes (but so do many shallow water crustacea), the *Nautilus* has a pinhole eye, the clam *Pectem* and the crustacean *Gigantocypris* have mirror eyes, and flatworms, limpets, and bivalve molluscs have cup eyes. When biologists place these features at the tips of an independently inferred phylogenetic tree (and use parsimony to infer the character states of ancestors), they conclude that these and other basic designs evolved somewhere between 40 and 65 times in different lineages (Salvini-Plawen and Mayr 1977; Nilsson 1989). For each monophyletic group of tip species that share a given eye design (e.g., vertebrates with their camera eyes), we can ask whether the trait value exhibited favours SPD over PD.

The first question in the protocol described in Figure 4 is to determine which design is optimal for each species or taxonomic group. In the case of polar bear fur length, we considered a simple experiment that could provide information about this. Is there a similar experiment for the case of eye design? Present technology makes this unfeasible. Although it is easy enough to remove or diminish the efficiency of whatever light-sensitive apparatus an organism possesses, it is harder to augment those devices or to substitute one complex structure for another. On the other hand, considerable information is now available concerning the optical properties of different eye designs, though a great deal remains to be learned. Nilsson (1989, p. 302) agrees with Land's (1984) contention that 'if the *Nautilus* had a camera-type eye of the same size, it would be 400 times more sensitive and have 100 times better resolution than its current pinhole eye.' He has similar praise for camera eyes as compared to compound eyes: 'if the human eye was scaled down 20 times to the size of a locust eye, image resolution would still be an order of magnitude better than that of the locust eye. Diffraction thus makes the compound eye with its many small lenses inherently inferior to a single-lens eye (Nilsson 1989, p. 306).'

If the camera eye is *globally* optimal, the protocol described in Figure 4 may appear to entail that SPD is more likely than PD with respect to the organisms that have camera eyes. However, this protocol was predicated on the assumption of a monotonic fitness function. As it turns out, current thinking about eye evolution rejects monotonicity. This means that we have to rethink the protocol in the context of the idea of multiple adaptive peaks. Biologists have been led to reject monotonicity by considering why the camera eye isn't more widely distributed, given that the camera eye seems to be fitter than both the pin hole and the compound eye. Spiders and squid are as lucky as we are, but bees and the *Nautilus* are not. Why not? Nilsson (1989, p. 306) suggests that compound eyes are trapped on a local adaptive peak. He agrees with Salvini-Plaven and Mayr (1977) that

> ... at an early stage of evolution, the simple eye would be just a single pigment cup with many receptors inside ..., whereas the compound eye would start as multiple pigment cups with only a few receptors in each ... At this low degree of sophistication, neither of the two designs stands out as better than the other. It is only later, when optimized optics have been added, that the differences will become significant. But then there is no return, and the differences remain conserved.

Expressed in terms of the idea of a transformation series, the thought is that evolving from a compound eye to a camera eye would have to retrace steps—there is no way to go directly from one complex design to the other—and the retracing would involve passing through arrangements of lower fitness.

How does this non-monotonic fitness function affect the protocol for testing SPD against PD? If the population's initial state (I) and its present state (P) are in the zone of attraction of the same adaptive peak, the analysis proceeds as before. However, if I is in the zone of attraction of local optimum O, but the lineage evolves to a point in the zone of attraction of O′ (where O ≠ O′), the analysis will be more complicated. The probability that a population beginning in the zone of attraction of O will 'jump across a valley' and end in the zone of attraction of O′ (where O ≠ O′) depends on the height of O, the effective population size, the amount of time there is between the initial state and the present, the heritability, and the width of the valley (Lande 1985). This means that a population that now sits on top of the *global* adaptive peak can still be such that SPD has lower likelihood than PD, if the population's initial state and its other parameters have the right values. The protocol described in Figure 4 therefore needs to be modified. With multiple peaks, the fact that P=O (where O is *any* of the optima, even the global optimum) does not suffice to settle which hypothesis has the higher likelihood. The protocol needs to begin, not with the question of whether P=O, but rather by asking whether P=O (for some optimum O) *and* whether I is in the zone of attraction of O. The lineage's initial state (I) must enter the protocol from the outset. The shift from a monotonic fitness function to one with multiple peaks thus requires that the test procedure be more historical.

Are there are other differences between polar bear fur length and the vertebrate eye that affect how SPD and PD should be tested? What of the alleged fact that the collection of traits that we call 'the vertebrate eye' is more complex than the simple trait of having fur that is 10 cm long? Complex traits are often said to have a larger number of components than simpler traits. To explore this idea, let's consider a complex trait T^* that can be understood as the conjunction of a number of simpler constituent traits T_1, T_2, ..., T_n. The vertebrate eye is 'complex' because it has this feature *and* that feature *and* this other feature besides. If the PD hypothesis says that these traits evolved independently of each other, then the likelihood of the PD hypothesis decomposes as follows:

$$Pr(T^*|PD) = Pr(T_1 \,\&\, T_2 \,\&\, ... \,\&\, T_n \,|PD) = Pr(T_1|PD) \cdot Pr(T_2|PD) \cdot ... \cdot Pr(T_n|PD).$$

It isn't inevitable that a hypothesis invoking drift without selection should take this form; for example, two genes that are closely linked may each experience random drift. However, for the sake of a simple example, let's consider this formulation of the PD hypothesis.

What does the SPD hypothesis say about the evolution of the complex trait T^*? Let's begin with the easiest case, in which selection is taken to act simultaneously and independently on each of the simple constituents. In this case, the likelihood of the SPD hypothesis is

$$\Pr(T^* | SPD) = \Pr(T_1 \ \& \ T_2 \ \& \ \dots \ \& \ T_n \ | SPD) = \Pr(T_1 | SPD) \cdot \Pr(T_2 | SPD) \cdot \dots \cdot \Pr(T_n | SPD).$$

If each component trait T_i favours SPD over PD—that is, if $\Pr(T_i | SPD) > \Pr(T_i | PD)$, for each i—then

$$\frac{\Pr(T^* | SPD)}{\Pr(T^* | PD)} > \frac{\Pr(T_i | SPD)}{\Pr(T_i | PD)}.$$

The complex trait provides stronger evidence for SPD over PD than does any of its simple constituents.[14]

Here's an analogy: Suppose an investment firm predicts that stock T_1 will rise in price tomorrow, and the prediction comes true. This successful prediction offers some evidence, if only a little, that the firm's prediction was based on knowledge of the stock market[15] rather than being the result of a coin toss the firm performed. The evidence favouring intelligent design over chance increases as the number of correct predictions increases. The 'simple' fact that stock T_1 increased in price counts as evidence, but far more weighty is the 'complex' fact that the company correctly predicted price increases for T_1, T_2, ..., and T_n. It isn't that complex facts are automatically evidence for design over chance, whereas simple facts are not; rather, the point is that when several simple facts are each evidence for design over chance, the complex constructed from those simples is stronger evidence still (assuming some degree of conditional independence amongst them). What holds for intelligent design versus chance holds also for SPD versus PD.

The above argument shows how a complex character is related to its simpler constituents *if* each of those constituents favours SPD over PD. But how does the complexity of a trait affect how fast the trait can be expected to evolve towards its optimum? Wagner (1988) and Orr (2000) show that the complexity of a trait, as measured by the number of independent dimensions that are needed to score different trait values for their relative fitness, is relevant to the rate

[14] Notice that I am here comparing a complex trait with each of its simpler constituents. I am not comparing complex and simple traits that are not related in this way. I see no reason to believe the stronger thesis that *all* complex adaptive features provide stronger evidence for SPD over PD than *any* simple adaptive feature provides.

[15] Here I assume for the sake of a simple example that the firm wants to make accurate predictions.

of evolution under SPD—for fixed mutation size, distance from the optimum, and population size, more complex traits evolve more slowly under SPD. This means that the complexity of a trait is relevant to the answers we will get when we ask the questions described in our protocol; however, notice that the questions we need to ask are the same for both simpler and more complex traits.

I just conceptualized the SPD hypothesis as saying that selection acts independently and simultaneously on each constituent of the complex trait T^*. However, selection processes are often not thought of in this way. Consider, for example, an SPD hypothesis concerning a complex trait that has two constituents, T_1 and T_2, where the hypothesis says that the process begins with T_1 undergoing selection, and that T_2 is favoured by selection only after T_1 has become pretty common; before that time, T_2 is subject to drift. Here selection for T_1 and selection for T_2 occur sequentially, not simultaneously. This is a more complicated formulation of the SPD hypothesis than the one just described, but the point of relevance is the same. If SPD is more likely than PD with respect to the evolution of trait T_1, and the same is true with respect to trait T_2, then the complex trait T^* will favour SPD over PD more strongly than either of the simple constituent traits does. The complexity of T^* is in this sense relevant to the problem of testing selection against drift, but not because this property of T^* allows one to ignore the protocol presented in Figure 4.

As a third and final formulation of SPD, it is interesting to consider traits that have the property that intelligent design theorists term 'irreducible complexity' (Behe 1996). The idea is not new; it is exemplified in what Paley thought was special about the vertebrate eye. The eye has a number of parts and these parts must be arranged *just so* if the eye is to perform its function. The fitness function implicit in this idea is that T^* is a conjunction of n quantitative traits T_1 & T_2 &...& T_n, where there is a fitness advantage to an organism only if it has a rather narrowly circumscribed value for each conjunct. This is easy to visualize if T^* has just two conjuncts, T_1 and T_2. Imagine a plane whose x- and y-axes represent values for T_1 and T_2 and where the elevation above the plane represents fitness. T^* will be irreducibly complex if the fitness surface is flat, except for a narrowly circumscribed bump, which represents the fitness advantage an organism receives if it has the right values for both T_1 and T_2.

Before discussing how irreducible complexity affects the comparison of the SPD and PD hypotheses, I want to comment on what intelligent design theorists say about such traits. They claim that no mindless natural process can produce adaptive traits of this sort. This assertion involves a double overstatement. First, intelligent design theorists do not have the power to foresee the mindless processes that science will someday learn to describe (neither does anyone else, of course). Second, evolutionary theory doesn't say that irreducibly complex traits *cannot* evolve; at most, the theory says that they have a *low probability* of evolving (Sober 2002a). But, as noted at the start of this paper, the fact that the probability of T* is low, given SPD, is not sufficient for any conclusion about SPD to be drawn. The relevant question must be comparative.

The competing hypotheses we have been considering—SPD and PD—each regard the lineage leading to the present trait value P as beginning in some initial character state I. Our present question is is whether SPD makes the attainment of P more probable than PD does, if the fitness function exhibits irreducible complexity. If P is optimal, the answer is *yes* (note that there is just one adaptive peak on the surface we are taking to characterize the idea of irreducible complexity). However, there is a difference that irreducible complexity introduces. Irreducible complexity involves a fitness function that is flat except that there is a narrowly delimited bump on it; the contrasting case is a fitness function that everywhere slopes upward towards a single peak. When a trait evolves from I to the optimal value of O, the idea of irreducible complexity entails that the trait must first move through a pure drift process before it reaches the small region in which selection can take it to the optimal value O; in contrast, if the fitness function is monotonic, evolving from I to O will be driven by selection from start to finish, This means that if the observed trait T* coincides with what the SPD hypothesis says is the optimal trait value, and if T* is also irreducibly complex, then T* favours SPD over PD *more weakly* than would be the case if T* were optimal but not irreducibly complex. The likelihoods of SPD and PD are more similar for traits that are irreducibly complex than they are for traits that are not.

I have described four ideas about how the complexity of a trait might be understood. In the first, we shifted from a monotonic fitness function to multiple adaptive peaks, and the result was that the protocol described in Figure 4 had to be modified, even though the relationship of I, O, and P remains critical. In the next three interpretations, a complex trait was understood as one that has a number of constituents; in (i) selection acts simultaneously and independently on each conjunct; in (ii), it acts sequentially on each conjunct; in (iii) selection occurs only when an organism has the right trait value for each of the constituent conjuncts. These differences can affect whether SPD or PD will have the higher likelihood, but they do not affect the questions about those hypotheses that need to be addressed.

6. Concluding Comments

I have focused in this paper on the task of deciding whether selection or drift, each conceptualized phenotypically, is the better explanation of a single trait value found in a single species or taxonomic group. The reason I formulated the problem in this way is that it is simple (and so it is a good place to begin) and also because many biologists invoke natural selection to explain observations of this kind and would be loathe to think of drift as an alternative that is worth considering. For example, sociobiologists and evolutionary psychologists often focus on traits they think are universal in our species and seek to explain them in terms of natural selection.[16] If the trait is adaptive, the drift hypothesis gets dismissed out of hand. And if the trait is both adaptive and complex, the suggestion that drift should be considered will strike many biologists as both pedantic and obscurantist. I have described the biological information that is needed if one wants to defend the claim that selection is more likely than drift. Appeal to intuition is not enough. I also have described some of the difficulties that must be overcome if such information is to be obtained. Although it may seem 'obvious' that adaptive features are better explained by appeal to selection than by appeal to drift, producing evidence for that 'obvious' claim is far from trivial. And the fact that the adaptive feature is 'complex' does not let one off the hook.

Although this paper addresses the problem of explaining a single trait value found in a single group of organisms, some biologists will be disinclined to consider this an appropriate datum for testing selection against drift. Rather, their preference will be to consider

[16] It is a familiar point in the debate about adaptationism that the genetic system can prevent the fittest of the available phenotypes from evolving to fixation; see Sober (1993), pp. 123–7 for a simple exposition of this point in connection with the idea of heterozygote superiority and footnote 8 of the present essay for the bearing of this point on the SPD and PD hypotheses. I have chosen to explore purely phenotypic models in order to show that it is far from inevitable that selection is more likely than drift as an explanation of complex adaptive features, even when we restrict our attention to such models.

facts about the distribution of character states across a group of taxa. Instead of asking why polar bears have fur that is 10 cm long, they will want to ask why bears living in colder climates tend to have longer fur than bears living in warmer climates. The choice between these *explananda*—a point value for a single taxon versus a correlation within a group of taxa—is significant. This is because the protocol for testing SPD against PD is different in the two cases. The protocol for explaining a point value is given in Figure 4. For discussion of the protocol relevant to explaining a correlation, see Sober and Orzack (2003). It turns out that less biological information is needed for one to decide between selection and drift in this case.

Regardless of how shifting the *explanandum*—from the point value of a single taxon to a correlation within a set of taxa—changes the epistemological landscape, the argument of this paper constitutes a challenge to those who wish to address *explananda* of the first kind. Although biologists sometimes assert that the traits they study are 'optimal,' they often are happy to grant that their confidence in the role played by natural selection does not require strict optimality. The vertebrate eye has a blind spot, but this imperfection has not made many friends for the hypothesis of random genetic drift. After all, even if a complex adaptive feature is imperfect, it still is complex and adaptive, and that is the end of the matter, or so one might be inclined to think. However, according to the protocol described in Figure 4, imperfection (in the sense that the observed trait value differs from what one thinks is the optimal trait value) requires that other questions be asked and answered. Paley (1802) thought it was intuitively obvious that the watch found on the heath favours intelligent design over chance, and that this conclusion does not depend on whether the watch keeps perfect time.[17] Latter day adaptationists have followed Paley's lead. According to the models of selection and drift explored here, the problem is in fact more subtle.

In the Spandrels article, Gould and Lewontin complain that if one adaptive hypothesis is refuted, it is *easy*—indeed, *too easy*—to invent another. They do not say so, but the same point applies to a pluralistic hypothesis that accords an important role to selective and to nonselective processes as well; if one hypothesis of this type is

---

[17] In defiance of Gould's (1980) argument concerning the panda's thumb, Paley (1802) thought that intelligent design hypotheses are not refuted by adaptive imperfection. In Sober (2004a), I agree with Paley against Gould on this point.

refuted, another hypothesis of the same kind can be invented (Sober 1993). This *tu quoque* does not mean that Gould and Lewontin's criticism is wrong; rather, the lesson is that every theoretical approach must come to terms with this problem. In the present context, the solution I have suggested is to require that biological parameters be estimated on the basis of independent evidence. It is easy enough to *stipulate* that the optimal fur length for polar bears is 10 cms; what is more difficult is to justify this estimate in terms of independently plausible observational and theoretical considerations. If one adaptive hypothesis fails, by all means let another be invented! But inventing parameter values is not the same thing as justifying them; and justifying the estimates used in a hypothesis is not the same thing as testing that hypothesis against alternatives.

Acknowledgments

My thanks to James Crow, Branden Fitelson, Patrick Forber, Richard Lewontin, Will Provine, and Larry Shapiro for useful discussion, and to Johan Van Bentham for his serendipitous reference to Rumsfeld.

References

Alexander, R. M. 1996. *Optima for Animals*. Princeton: Princeton University Press.
Behe, M. 1996. *Darwin's Black Box*. New York: Free Press.
Crow, J. 2000. 'The Future of Forensic DNA Testing—Predictions of the Research and Development Working Group.' *National Institute of Justice*: NCJ 183697.
Edwards, A. 1972. *Likelihood*. Cambridge: Cambridge University Press.
Fisher, R. 1925. *Statistical Methods for Research Workers*. Edinburgh: Oliver and Boyd.
Forster, M. and Sober, E. 2004. 'Why Likelihood?' In M.Taper and S. Lee (eds.), *The Nature of Scientific Evidence*, Chicago: University of Chicago Press.
Gould, S.(1980. *The Panda's Thumb*. New York: Norton.
Gould, S. and Lewontin, R. (1978): 'The Spandrels of San Marco and the Panglossian Paradigm—A Critique of the Adaptationist Paradigm.' *Proceedings of the Royal Society B*, **205**, 581–98.
Hacking, I. 1965. *The Logic of Statistical Inference*. Cambridge: Cambridge University Press.

Elliott Sober

Hamilton, W. D. 1967.: 'Extraordinary Sex Ratios.' *Science*, **156**, 477-488.

Kingsolver, J. and Koehl, M. 1985. 'Aerodynamics, Thermoregulation, and the Evolution of Insect Wings—Differential Scaling and Evolutionary Change.' *Evolution*, **39**, 488–504.

Kirkpatrick, M. 1996. 'Genes and Adaptation—a Pocket Guide to the Theory.' In M. Rose and G. Lauder (eds.), *Adaptation*. New York: Academic Press, pp. 125–46.

Land, M. 1984. 'Molluscs.' In M. Ali (ed.), *Photoreception and Vision in Invertebrates*. New York: Plenum, pp. 699–725.

Lande, R. 1976. 'Natural Selection and Random Genetic Drift in Phenotypic Evolution.' *Evolution*, **30**, 314–34.

Lande, R. 1985. 'Expected Time for Random Genetic Drift of a Population between Stable Phenotypic States.' *Proc. Nat. Acad. Sci. USA*, **82**, 7641–5.

Leeds, S. 2000. 'Other Minds, Support, and Likelihoods.' unpublished manuscript.

Maddison, W. 1991. 'Squared-Change Parsimony Reconstructions of Ancestral States for Continuous-Valued Characters on a Phylogenetic Tree.' *Systematic Zoology*, **40**, 304–14.

Nilsson, D. 1989. 'Vision Optics and Evolution.' *Bioscience* 39: 298–307.

Orr, A. (2000): 'Adaptation and the Cost of Complexity.' *Evolution*, **54**, 13–20.

Orzack, S. and Sober, E. 2001. 'Adaptation, Phylogenetic Inertia, and the Method of Controlled Comparisons.' In S. Orzack and E. Sober (eds.), *Adaptationism and Optimality*, Cambridge University Press, pp. 45–63.

Paley, W. 1802. Natural Theology, or, Evidences of the Existence and Attributes of the Deity, *Collected from the Appearances of Nature*. London: Rivington.

Parker, G. 1978. 'Search for Mates.' In J. Krebs and N. Davies (eds.), *Behavioral Ecology—An Evolutionary Approach*. Oxford: Blackwell.

Ridley, M. 1983. *The Explanation of Organic Diversity*. Oxford: Oxford University Press.

Royall, R. 1997. *Statistical Evidence—a Likelihood Paradigm*. London: Chapman and Hall.

Salvini-Plaven, L. and Mayr, E. 1977. 'On the Evolution of Photoreceptors and Eyes.' In M. Hecht, W. Sterre, and B. Wallace (eds.), *Evolutionary Biology*, vol. 10, New York: Plenum, pp. 207–63.

Sober, E. 1993. *Philosophy of Biology*. Boulder: Westview Press.

Sober, E. 2002a. 'Intelligent Design and Probability Reasoning.' *International Journal for the Philosophy of Religion*, **52**, 65–80.

Sober, E. 2002b. 'Reconstructing Ancestral Character States—A Likelihood Perspective on Cladistic Parsimony.' *The Monist*, **85**, 156–76.

Sober, E. 2004a. 'The Design Argument.' In W. Mann (ed.), *The Blackwell Guide to Philosophy of Religion*. Oxford: Blackwell Publishers.

Sober. E. 2004b. 'Intelligent Design is Untestable. What about Natural Selection?' In P. Hajek, L. Valdes-Villanueva, and D. Westerstahl (eds.),

Proceedings of the 11th Congress of the International Union for History and Philosophy of Science, Division of Logic, Methodology, and Philosophy of Science. Elsevier.

Sober, E. and Orzack, S. 2003. 'Common Ancestry and Natural Selection.' *British Journal for the Philosophy of Science,* **54**, 423–37.

Tinbergen, N. 1964. 'On Aims and Methods of Ethology.' *Zeitschrift für Tierpsycologie,* **20**, 410–33.

Turelli, M. 1988. 'Population Genetic Models for Polygenic Variation and Evolution.' In B. Weir, E. Eisen, M. Goodman, and G. Namkoong (eds.), *Proceedings of the Second International Conference on Quantitative Genetics.* Sunderland, MA: Sinauer, pp. 601–18.

Wagner, G. 1988. 'The Influence of Variation and of Developmental Constraints on the Rate of Multivariate Phenotypic Evolution.' *Journal of Evolutionary Biology,* **1**, 45–66.

Evolution and Aesthetics

ANTHONY O'HEAR

I want to begin with four quotations, fairly typical of their type, and germane to our topic because they encapsulate what many artists and art lovers feel about art and music. These feelings are often inchoate, to be sure, and in the cold light of analytical day they may look extravagant and exaggerated. But they do capture something of the experience people often have of art and beauty, and for that reason alone must be given some phenomenological plausibility at least.

First quotation: 'It is reserved to art to salvage the kernel of religion, inasmuch as the mythical images which religion would wish to be believed as true are apprehended in art for their symbolic value, and through ideal representation of those symbols art reveals the concealed deep truth within them.'

Second quotation: '(In art) for a brief moment we really become the primal essence itself, and feel its unbounded lust for existence, and delight in existence. Now we see the struggles, the torment, the destruction of phenomena as necessary. For all our pity and terror we are happy to be alive, not as individuals but as *the* single living thing, merged with its creative delight...'

Something of what we experience in, say, *Tristan und Isolde* may be alluded to be these two extracts. In this context, we might also think of the experience of some of Titian's late paintings, *The Flaying of Marsyas*, (Archiepiscopal Palace, Kromeriz), for example, or of the exuberance of some of Rubens, his hunting scenes, say, or of the implacability of Homer and of Aeschylus, of the mystical vision in John Cowper Powys's *A Glastonbury Romance*, or of some of D. H. Lawrence, and of the serious vein underlying the silvery brilliance of Ovid's *Metamorphoses*. And we could think of the evocation of the sublime in so many of Turner's canvasses. Mention of Turner might remind us that many people have analogous experiences in observing aspects of the natural world and feeling themselves a part of nature.

But leaving nature aside for the moment, our third quotation, taking up some of the theme of the first, says 'Good art, thought of as symbolic force, rather than statement provides a stirring image of a pure, transcendent value, a steadily visible enduring human good... in an unreligious age... the clearest expression of something grasped as separate and precious and beneficial.'

And finally, 'our highest dignity lies in the meaning given to us by works of art; it is only as an aesthetic phenomenon that existence and the world are eternally justified.'

Notice that Nietzsche (for it is, of course, Nietzsche's notorious claim on art's behalf in *The Birth of Tragedy*) does not say that the world is justified (or not) as an evolutionary process, or as chains of survival and reproduction, or as blind drive to procreate, or as random variation and selective retention. It is justified as an aesthetic phenomenon, and at least in *The Birth of Tragedy*, it actually is justified. Notice, too, in our third quotation Iris Murdoch—for it is she—speaks of an enduring human good, but also of a transcendent value. And analogous, non-naturalistic remarks could be made of quotation 1 (Wagner) and of quotation 2 (Nietzsche again).[1]

I am not going to discuss these quotations directly, beyond insisting that they do represent aspects of a vision of art and beauty, with a long history and still resonating—if beneath the surface—with many to-day. Nevertheless, examining what might be called the evolutionary account of art and beauty, as given by Darwin and his followers, may throw some indirect light on them, as I will suggest at the end of this paper. However, even at this stage, it will be obvious that the sentiments underlying my quotations will be in no little tension with what many take to be the message of orthodox Darwinism.

In so far as Darwinism is a doctrine of causal meaninglessness—indeed, in the hands of authors such as Jacques Monod and Richard Dawkins, perhaps *the* doctrine of causal meaninglessness—anyone in the least degree affected by any of the four quotations will have to treat a wholly Darwinian account of art and of our sense of the beautiful with extreme suspicion. At the very best, it will be radically incomplete. For, without any supplementation, Darwinism explains phenomena, to the extent that it does explain them, in terms of a blind, unconscious and unintelligent nature populated with creatures driven for no purpose to survive for a

---

[1] The first quotation is from Richard Wagner, 'Religion und Kunst' in his *Gesammelte Schriften und Dichtungen*, 2nd edition, Leipzig, 1888, vol. x., p. 211; the second is from Friedrich Nietzsche, *The Birth of Tragedy*, 1871, section 17; the third from Iris Murdoch, *The Fire and the Sun*, Oxford University Press, 1977, pp. 76–7; and the fourth from Nietzsche's *The Birth of Tragedy*, section 5.

time, if they are lucky, to reproduce themselves, again given good fortune, and then to die; and all this for no other reason than the fact that they have these drives and enough physiological and behavioural adaptations to survive and reproduce, and with no result other than that with luck and the cunning of the randomly produced adaptiveness some of them do actually succeed in reproducing themselves, and in some cases producing offspring actually better fitted to their environments than their parents.

We should not be so impressed by the rhetoric of creationists or of their polar opposites, evolutionary atheologians like Monod and Dawkins into thinking that Darwinism is formally incompatible with religious belief or meaning. Nevertheless it cannot be denied that Darwinism has been a major weapon in the hands of those concerned to deny any meaning to our existence or that of the universe as a whole. It has been such a weapon precisely because, on its surface at least, Darwinism analyses life, including human life, in terms of five billion years of processes of random variation and selective retention. We, as every other living thing, are products of chance mutations in the genetic structure of earlier creatures, as are all our traits and dispositions, which, directly or indirectly, have been selected because of their contribution to survival and reproduction. According to Darwin, all living things strive to reproduce themselves at a geometrical ratio, and according to what he called the 'law of natural selection', according to which any variations in the 'least degree injurious' will be 'rigidly destroyed'.[2] This picture is not, as has just been noted, formally incompatible with meaning, religious or otherwise, but any such meaning will have to be added to it.

So, maybe there are aspects to our existence which do point beyond the blind drive to survive and reproduce. And maybe, if there is anything in our initial quotations, our intimations of beauty and other aesthetic properties are such aspects. In any case we do seem to spend an awful lot of time and effort in pursuing aesthetic ends. We beautify and decorate our environments, public and private, we create and appreciate works of art, and we seek and appreciate the aesthetic aspects of nature. And we do all these things in a way which seems to have little to with survival and reproduction, and which may at times interfere with survival and reproduction, as when artists starve in garrets or when opera fanatics spend their fortunes and ruin their marriages in pursuing

[2] Charles Darwin, *The Origin of Species*, 1859, First para. of Chapter 4, Penguin Edition, Harmondsworth, 1882, p. 131.

their passion or when young girls devote all their time and energy to ballet training, all in apparent violation of Darwin's law of natural selection and without any indication of the types in question dying out. So even at the crudest level, does not aesthetic interest provide a counter-example to the theory of evolution?

Darwin was himself worried by the threat aesthetics posed for his theory for at least two reasons. In the first place, if aesthetic sensibility were confined to human beings, it would—against his theory—suggest a radical discontinuity between humans and other animals. Then, secondly, even in the animal kingdom there are aesthetic contrivances, such as the tails of peacocks and the plumage of humming birds. These contrivances seem to contribute nothing to survival and reproduction, but they are costly to produce, and in the case of peacocks' tails they may actually be injurious to their possessors in preventing or impeding flight.

In *The Descent of Man* Darwin tackled both these questions. His strategy was to show that both the appearance of beauty, as in the peacocks' tails, and the taste for it, as in the case of peahens' choices, go hand in hand as mutually supporting and demanding players in the struggle for existence. And, insofar as peahens and the like have an aesthetic sensibility, there is no discontinuity between us and the rest of the animal kingdom, even if our aesthetic tastes are more developed than those of most other animals.

What Darwin argued was that the elaborate displays found among animals and birds, particularly during mating, could be explained only on the assumption that birds and animals were capable of appreciating beauty. That is the only way in which we could explain why so much effort, metabolic and behavioural, went into producing these things, as beyond certain in-built preferences for regularity and symmetry, 'why certain bright colours should excite pleasure cannot be explained'.[3]

Darwin was concerned to demonstrate continuity between humans and other animals, so if he could show that there was in animals a genuine aesthetic sense, one large ostensible discontinuity would have been eliminated. The tails of male peacocks and the songs and plumage of many other birds are, in Darwin's own terms, elaborate, graceful, splendid, beautiful and highly ornamented. That the females of the species in question appreciate these things cannot be denied, says Darwin, and in just the same way that human females do, who deck themselves out with the same plumes

[3] Charles Darwin, *The Descent of Man*, 1871, quoted from the second edition, 1874, vol. I, p. 141.

of the same birds. And in the animal kingdom, it is the most splendid and beautiful males who succeed in getting the most and best females—as, in the case of peahens selecting the peacocks with the most luxuriant tails, has more recently been confirmed systematically by experiment and observation.

But do the peahens who chose the peacocks with the best tails do so because they admire their beauty? That they might not be chosing on aesthetic grounds was actually the subject of an early dispute between Darwin and Alfred Russel Wallace. Wallace was in general somewhat un-Darwinian in emphasizing differences between humans and other animals, a point to which we will return. But in the matter of female choice of mates, Wallace was more Darwinian than Darwin himself in denying that there was anything functionless or purely aesthetic in behaviour which played so significant a role in the development of a species.

Darwin himself argued that selection pressures alone, building on some initially inexplicable caprice or aesthetic preference could have been enough to explain the apparent admiration female birds had for the extravagance of their mates, and for the development within a species of males with ever more elaborate tails, songs and plumage. In the development of the species in question, females initially had preferences for males with the attributes in question. The resultant pairings produced off-spring with similar tastes and attributes. The most splendid of the new males are then, in their turn chosen by the ever more choosy females descended from the original choosers, and one more twist is given to the evolutionary spiral, which will go on developing until checked by some countervailing pressure.

The evolutionary potential of this sort of selection pressure and its trajectory moving far from its original starting point was well demonstrated by R. A. Fisher in 1930.[4] Fisher showed that once a preference gets embedded in a population, it will tend to move forward with ever increasing rapidity under its own momentum. It may even, as is the case with peacock's tails, produce unwieldy and, from the point of view of simple survival, potentially injurious adaptations. After all, peacocks with splendid tails are pretty poor flyers, and so more vulnerable to predators than they would be were their tails more modest. Does this example refute Darwin's principle about the the inevitable eradication of variations in the least degree injurious? Darwin thought not, because what the

[4] see R. A. Fisher, *The Genetical Theory of Natural Selection*, Clarendon Press, Oxford, 1930.

Anthony O'Hear

luxuriantly tailed peacocks may have lost in terms of sheer survival, they more than made up for in reproductive advantage over their less well endowed competitors. Injury and advantage in evolutionary terms are many faceted, and cannot be read off from a creature's performance on just one dimension.

Darwin, supplemented by Fisher, provide a convincing enough account of how in a particular species, the development of what is for us aesthetically pleasing characteristics can occur as a result of female choice (and specifically as a result of what Darwin somewhat ungallantly refers to as the initially inexplicable operation of female caprice). But what he does not show is that either in the beginning of the evolutionary trajectory or at its end the females are choosing for aesthetic reasons. And it was on precisely this point that Wallace parted company with Darwin. Wallace insisted that in the human realm aesthetic response is part of our 'spiritual nature'—which we did not share with animals—whereas what looks to us like an aesthetic response in the animal realm is actually no such thing. For big tails, fine plumage and vibrant songs presuppose in their owners health, strength and vitality; ornamental display can also be a sign of territorial dominance, which also indicates general strength and superiority.

How does Darwin know that the females are not choosing their beautiful males because what we see as their beauty is symptomatic of other more utilitarian qualities? Could nature ever endow its creatures with properties and tastes which were not, in Wallace's terms, 'sensible'?[5] Evolution is a process powered by the drives individuals have to survive and reproduce and shaped by the environmental response to the means by which different creatures seek to satisfy those drives. Could evolution ever allow its creatures to waste time and effort on drives and properties which are literally useless? Wallace, more selectionist here than Darwin, thought not. Every trait of any significance had to endow its possessor with direct adaptive advantage in survival and reproduction. Caprice alone and aesthetic sense could play no significant role in a domain governed by the iron logic of natural selection, and certainly not to the extent envisaged by Darwin and Fisher.

How, then, might it be possible to decide between the view that aesthetic preference in animals is really aesthetic and the view that what looks to us to be aesthetic preference, on the part of peahens say, is really a preference for other qualities which go along with the

[5] On Wallace and aesthetics, see Helena Cronin, *The Ant and the Peacock*, Cambridge University Press, 1993, pp. 186–91.

160

aesthetic, and which are not chosen via aesthetic appreciation? The problem is that there is no direct way of deciding. All we have is broad brush behaviour, which is susceptible of several interpretations. What we cannot do is ask a peahen why she makes the choices she does, or what precisely it is she admires in her mates. Nevertheless, if we compare what we see of peahens and other animals in this area with what seems to be crucial in human aesthetic judgments, that animals have a genuine aesthetic sense can come to seem highly doubtful.

We can usefully begin this enquiry by considering some of the things Kant says about aesthetic judgments.[6] In the first place, they are seen by Kant, correctly in my view, as both disinterested and universal, and right at the start we have a difference. For, whatever else the peahen is doing when she chooses the peacock with the best tail, she is judging neither disinterestedly nor universally.

In speaking of aesthetic appreciation as disinterested, what Kant means is that we are not interested in consuming or possessing the object we are reacting to. We are interested in its 'real existence' and contemplate it for its own sake, rather than as something which we could consume or sell or use. Of course, one might have both an aesthetic interest in something and some other interest. An art dealer might admire a painting for aesthetic reasons and for its monetary value to him; a landowner might appreciate his estate both for its beauty and for the lustre it added to his reputation. But in each case, it is possible, theoretically at least, to distinguish the aesthetic from the other interest.

The disinterestedness of the aesthetic judgment can be characterized in terms of the object in question being contemplated rather than used, and this goes even for cases where one admires something aesthetically for its fittedness to function. That is to say, we can speak of a beautiful car or aeroplane, and part of what we are admiring here may be the way the design refers to what it is intended to do, and, by its sleek lines or whatever, symbolizes that. But in saying that, say, the racing cars of the 1950s were beautiful in comparison to today's F1 monstrosities, we will be standing back from actually using the cars, even if the contemplation does eventually issue is use (though in this case, today's Ferrari would undoubtedly outperform its 1950s predecessor). Aesthetic enjoyment is, in Kant's terms, a 'reflective' rather than an 'organic' or 'appetitive' pleasure.

Matters may seem more complicated when we turn to sexual

[6] in Immanuel Kant, *The Critique of Judgement*, 1780, sections 1–60.

beauty. In admiring a beautiful woman is the man disinterested? Or is he looking at her as a potential or even an actual lover? This is a question which takes us back to Plato. In *Phaedrus* (250ff) Plato had argued that our first perception of beauty comes when we fall in love with a beautiful youth. The lover shudders with awe and reverence, as at the sight of a god. He is seized by a strange sweating and by fever. Warmth enters the soul through the beauty coming in through the eyes. The soul grows wing and aches, as when a child is teething. When he is parted from the loved one, he is maddened, and will suffer any shame to get back in the presence of the beloved.

In his discussion of the power of sexual attraction, Plato undoubtedly touches on aspects of our emotive life which Kant would rather we forgot. In Plato's descriptions any reflective enjoyment is intermingled with the appetitive and the organic. In this Plato may be telling us something about the genesis of our aesthetic sense which Kant overlooks, and which points more in the direction of Darwinian accounts of beauty. For many people a strong and particular feeling for beauty and for the aesthetic does seem to accompany adolescence and sexual awakening. But not the only or necessarily the earliest intimation of the aesthetic. Even quite young children are often moved by the beauties of nature, in a purely contemplative way.

In any case, even if there are experiences of sexual beauty which are, in a sense, mixed, and which might point to some of our experience of beauty as being rooted in our physical nature, as Plato points out the madness and the would be consumption of the lover is only the first stage in the soul's ascent to the beautiful. When sanity returns, the lover will experience beauty in a calm way; his sense of the beautiful diffuses itself over all parts of material creation, where it is to be found, and not just the sexual. He turn from the 'slavish and illiberal' devotion to 'individual loveliness' to set sail on the 'open sea of beauty', before eventually finding rest in Beauty itself, something wholly abstract and non-material. (See *Symposium*, 210–2)

As we shall see, in terms of Kantian aesthetics abstract, non-material beauty is a step too far. But what Plato says about the second stage is suggestive, even in the case of the beauty of beautiful bodies. A calm, disinterested appreciation here is not out of the question. There can be a chaste, non-possessive appreciation of female beauty, either in the flesh or in the painted image. Despite the claims of John Berger, not every painted nude is an incitement to male possession or fantasy, even if many are. Titian's *Education of Love* (Borghese Gallery, Rome) is certainly a celebration of female flesh, but it is at the same time a reminder of the poignancy and uncertainty of love and of the pain of the experience (in the painting the achingly beautiful Venus is binding the love-inducing gaze of Cupid). In his later work Rubens continually and, in my view successfully, used female nudity, including exuberant depictions of his own wife's abundant and fleshy beauty, to evoke the blessings of peace and of fertility. Even Titian's *Venus of Urbino* (Uffizi Gallery, Florence) and Velasquez's *Rokeby Venus* (National Gallery, London), though certainly reminders of the most organic pleasures possible and of the processes of reproduction, are reflective reminders, which can and should be viewed aesthetically, that is disinterestedly, reflectively and without engaging desire.

What is striking about the reflectiveness which Kant sees in the aesthetic judgment is that there is no obvious analogue in the animal realm. We say that the peahen admires the peacock's tail only because she chooses the cock. The judgment, if such it is, is interested, organic, the manifestation of a very basic desire, which is indeed the only criterion for the existence of any judgment on the hen's part. She is only at the stage of Plato's maddened lover, if indeed she is even that far. We hear no stories of animals admiring some aesthetic feature of their environment reflectively and disinterestedly. And even if we are able to discern rhythm and melody in the song of a bird, it is far from clear that the birds do. Even less do they treat their songs aesthetically, using them as material to be developed musically, as, by contrast, the composer Messaien tried to do (with, in my opinion, rather mixed success).

If disinterested aesthetic judgments are not found in the animal kingdom, nor are universal ones. When the peacock with the most beautiful tail is chosen by a peahen, she is not implying that all observers, or even all peahens, should concur in finding it beautiful. Nor, when I declare a preference for dark over milk chocolate am I saying that every right-minded person should agree. But when I say that Beethoven's late quartets are great works of art, spiritually deep, full of exquisite lyricism, earthy humour and fascinating counterpoint, I am intending that what I say should command general assent. The fact that some of Beethoven's contemporaries failed to appreciate the late quartets means that I am committed to saying that they were in error over them, that for whatever reason (unfamiliarity or surface strangeness, perhaps) there was some failure in their appreciation. I am not simply saying that these contemporaries of Beethoven were unable to see that future generations of listeners would find the quartets deep, humorous, lyrical, and so on.

Anthony O'Hear

In my view, the most natural way of explaining the Kantian universality of the aesthetic judgment, to which, it should be stressed, no equivalent can be found in the kingdom of non-linguistic animals, is to say that those who fail to agree with some generally acceptable aesthetic judgment are mis-perceiving something in the work in question. In my view, but not in Kant's. As is well-known, Kant emphasized the universality of the aesthetic judgment, while denying its objectivity. He thought that when I judge something beautiful or ugly or elegant, and so on, I am speaking not about real features of the object in question, objectively present in it. What I am indirectly, but really referring to, are feelings the object conjures up in me, in my breast. Aesthetic judgments are, in Kant's terms, subjective.

Part of the reason for this was that Kant thought that aesthetic judgments were singular. That is to say, an aesthetic judgment is one which is always, on the surface at least, about particular unique properties of the particular object it is (ostensibly) about. Many will agree with Kant here, up to a point. An aesthetic judgment by me about a work of art, say, requires experience by me of that specific object, and its unique combination of properties. A mere description will not suffice if I am interested in making a judgment about its aesthetic value. Nor will it be possible to sum up my grounds for my judgment in any general formula, which does not refer to specific features of the object in question. Thus, you can say that in a good painting a balance of form and detail is needed, but that general principle will not tell us why, let us say Veronese's *Marriage Feast at Cana* (Louvre, Paris) is an aesthetic triumph, while Frith's *Derby Day* (Tate Gallery, London), with much the same amount of form and detail, is hardly a painting at all. To make a judgment of that sort with any degree of confidence, you will have actually to look at the works in question and analyse the experience they conjure up.

But even if, as Kant rightly implies, aesthetic judgments cannot be usefully captured in terms of general formulae, it is simply prejudice to say—as Kant appears to do—that a non-formalisable judgment cannot be objective, or about real properties of objects. Judgments about the guilt or innocence of an accused person in court are also singular and non-formalisable, in much the same sort of way as aesthetic judgments, but they are certainly about something objective. Nor is their singularity and non-formalisability the main reason for Kant denying objectivity to aesthetic judgments. The deeper reason seems to be due to his realisation of what we might call the 'magnetism' of value. Beauty is something that attracts us, and ugliness repels, and so on with other aesthetic (and ethical) properties. But how can they do this if they are straightforward properties like squareness or redness, which have no necessary affective charge? If the recognition of beauty or of ugliness were due to something happening in us rather than to something outside us, that problem would be quickly solved. But, I think, far too quickly.

For it is not the case that every time I recognize something as beautiful I am then and thereby attracted to it, any more than I am always drawn to do the right thing and never the wrong thing. One could well—in one's youth, perhaps—admit the beauty of the painting of Raphael or the fineness of the poetry of Horace without being particularly attracted to either. The point is that while aesthetic and moral properties characteristically do engage us and are rooted in our genetically given constitution and our psychology, they can and do transcend their origins in such a way as to open a theoretical gap between recognition of a given property and actual responses in particular cases. No such normative gap—a gap which allows us to say that someone *ought* to like or admire some aesthetic feature of an object, even though they don't—exists in the animal case. They just respond or fail to respond. There would just be no sense in arguing that a peahen who failed to respond to the most luxuriant tail in her vicinity was making a mistake in judgment, as opposed to simply lacking a particular behavioural response.

In analysing aesthetic judgments as obliquely referring to the emotions which objects of aesthetic value stir up in us, Kant was, as in so much else, following Hume. For Hume, seeing an object as beautiful or ugly is a matter of 'gilding or staining it with the colours borrowed from internal sentiment'. Nevertheless, like Kant, Hume is also insistent on the universality of the aesthetic:

> the same Homer, who pleased at Athens and Rome two thousand years ago, is still admired at Paris and at London. All the changes of climate, government, religion, and language have not been able to obscure his glory. Authority or prejudice may be able to give a temporary vogue to a bad poet or orator; but his reputation will never be durable or general. When his compositions are examined by posterity or foreigners, the enchantment is dissipated and his faults appear in their true colours. On the contrary, a real genius, the longer his works endure, and the more wide they are spread, the more sincere is the admiration which they meet with.[7]

Hume, like Kant, wants to hold both that aesthetic judgments are potentially universal and that their source and ultimate reference is

[7] David Hume, 'Of the Standard of Taste', 1757, para 11.

human taste; both, that there is such a thing as good taste, vindicated and manifested through universal assent and the test of time, and that this good taste is not objectively warranted by the objects themselves, but is a matter of those objects attracting our feelings or (in Hume's case) of their being gilded and stained by them. For Hume, as for Kant, the cross-cultural and trans-temporal critical-creative dialogue which elicits the cool, reflective and disinterested judgment that Homer is a poet of great stature, is ultimately a dialogue about what exists (or ought to exist) only in our minds. It is not about anything which is really or objectively there.

But why 'ought to exist' and how universal, if these judgments are not based on something which is actually there, and actually there apart from any feelings I or anyone else happen to have at any time? And what is the dialogue about, if it is not a dialogue about the *Iliad* itself? The attempt of Hume and Kant to subjectivise the aesthetic judgment is hard enough to accept in itself, but is particularly hard in the context of its supposed normativity and universality. It is time to suggest an approach to beauty which maintains its objectivity, but which does not deny its roots in human, and ultimately instinctual responses, nor its valuational— that is magnetizing—nature.

To find the Rokeby Venus beautiful is to make an objective judg-ment (and one which most people acquainted with the painting would agree with), but it is not to make a judgment which is factu-al in the scientific sense. It is a judgment which needs a specifically human sensibility to discern, and which will not be captured by the more universally intelligible concepts and theories of natural science. But to deny it objectivity on those grounds alone would simply be to indulge in a piece of philosophical dogmatism, according to which only the scientifically accessible is granted the title of real. So, on the view being advanced here, aesthetic judgments are indeed *our* judgments, that is judgments made possible only by our biological and cultural traditions, but they nonetheless reveal genuine properties of the objects in question.

When Hume and Kant and their followers deny this, they are in fact saying little more than that beauty is not a formalisable property, nor one which could feature in those types of scientific theory which deliberately prescind from properties which would be intelligible only to creatures with a very specific—in this case human—sensibility. To be sure, as already hinted at by the difficulty of finding rules for beauty, and by its extreme context dependence, there will be no set of physically determinable properties shared by and only by beautiful objects, such as sunsets, sunflowers, pictures of sunflowers and musical evocations of sunsets. But that a Mediterranean sunset, a field of sunflowers, Van Gogh's *Sunflowers* and Strauss's *Im Abendrot* are all beautiful is certainly something experienced by most of us as true, as demanded by the objects just mentioned, and as authoritative and compelling as anything in science. They are also judgments on which there is perhaps surprising convergence among different people and at different times, in the making of which people certainly believe themselves to be speaking about qualities of the things they are seeing or hearing, and not about feelings in their own breasts.

Indeed, that beauty is not just a projection or a matter of internal sentiment merely is strongly suggested by the experience most of us have had of learning that something is generally regarded as beautiful, of not initially appreciating it as such, and then, with further acquaintance, care and attention coming to find it beautiful (a phenomenon memorably described by Proust in a number of passages). In other words, what *is* beautiful actually directs, shapes and explains our experience of its being beautiful. It is not as if the feelings in us towards that thing existed prior to our assimilation of standards of true beauty, standards which we take to have an existence and a logic independent of empirically given feelings people have. In other words, whatever its origin may have been in ancestral sensibility, taste and instinct, in the human world as we know it, beauty is something objective and outside of us, commanding our attention and allegiance individually and collectively.

As far as the logic of beauty goes, it is perfectly possible that some aesthetic prophet could demonstrate to a whole people that there was something amiss about its taste—as, with some success and justification, Ruskin and Pugin did in nineteenth century England. And some might feel there is an even more pressing need for a Ruskin of the present day to reveal the aesthetic of the Disney empire as not so much popular as vulgar, garish and mawkish. (And maybe also we need some person with the authority of a Ruskin or a Carlyle to pull us all up over our connivance in rap and pop music and in the sheer lowness of popular television—though it is arguable that if there were such a person, these appalling phenomena would never have come to play so large a part in national and publicly funded life.) All this aside, though, when we read great criticism—Ruskin on Turner, say, or Nietzsche on Wagner, or Leavis on Eliot—what we have does not have the logical form of mere expression of emotion. These critics are pointing to features of the

Anthony O'Hear

works they are discussing, and drawing judgments about those works, which we are urged to accept, based on the features they have pointed to. The criticisms demand us to respond to the works in a particular way, in a way we may not previously have realized, because of what they show us about the works; if we disagree—as in at least two of the cases we probably should—we will have to point to countervailing features which override the original judgment.

Note, incidentally, how discourse of this sort reinforces Kant's views on the universality of the aesthetic judgment, and also on its singularity: that, to stay with our examples, religiosity like Eliot's, but in hands other than his, or a neurasthenic sensibility like Wagner's, but without his colossal grasp of structure, might well have had the dire effects Leavis and Nietzsche purported to find in the works as a whole. While there are reason which support and must support aesthetic judgments, an aesthetic judgment will always depend on the precise and unique way a particular set of reasons bears on the specific case.

Reflection on the way discussions about beauty actually proceed shows clearly that neurological and evolutionary accounts of the perception of beauty are necessarily incomplete (at best). To take an example of the former, P. W. Atkins has written of the near universal and favourable recognition of the golden section as being 'like the resonance of an electronic circuit to a distant transmitter, when a certain frequency can induce an enhanced power'. Particular circuits in the brain respond to the scanning of golden sections, the brain itself then responds in 'an enhanced manner' and our response is 'the one that normally correlates with perceived "beauty"'.[8] What is perceived as beauty, on this neurological account, is what meshes with our brain circuitry, which is itself a product of our DNA. As our DNA, and the behaviour it provokes, is itself part of our evolutionary history, an account like Atkins' will both fit into and fill out an evolutionary perspective.

The connexion is made explicitly by E. O. Wilson. In *Biophilia* he writes that aesthetic contrivances 'play upon the circuitry of the brain's limbic system in a way that ultimately promotes survival and reproduction'.[9] Wilson's idea is that aesthetic interest has been embedded in us because of the general usefulness of curiosity and the search for connexions and similarities. More specifically, because of our ancestral past, we are disposed to find beautiful

[8] P. W. Atkins, 'The Lion, the Rose and the Ultimate Oyster', *Modern Painters*, 2/4, Winter 1989, pp. 50–5.

[9] E. O. Wilson, *Biophilia*, Harvard University Press, 1984, p. 61.

scenes and bodies which contribute in various ways to survival and reproduction. Thus it has recently been shown that, various allegedly superficial differences in taste aside (as between the large women of Renoir and Rubens, say, and the more gamine figures fashionable in the 1960s), men universally prefer women with figures with the same (low) waist-hip ratio, of about 0·70%, which is constant as between both Renoir's beauties and those of today.[10] Perception of this ratio in a woman is supposed to indicate to the males the woman's potential fertility and absence of actual pregnancy, which in turn is supposed to explain why men find women of this type beautiful. Men also prefer women with other characteristics, such as bright eyes and good complexions, which indicate youth (and hence ability to have healthy children). Wilson himself would explain the near-universal predilection for pictures for what are in effect Claude-type classical landscapes in terms of our ancestors having been disposed to favour landscapes which were conducive to survival on the savannah—that is to say, places where there was good vegetation, a source of water, such as a river or a lake, and also some higher ground to facilitate the perception of prey and predators.[11]

In fact this idea of the universality of what has been called by Denis Dutton a 'pervasive Pleistocene taste in landscape' has in a sense been confirmed by the researches of two emigré Russian artists, Vitaly Komar and Alexander Melamid, in 1993. Kómar and Melamid surveyed people around the world, and found that their taste in landscape was pretty constant, and much as Wilson had suggested, with the addition that there was a marked preference for some famous human figure in the picture. On this basis, and clearly ironically, they then concocted an impossible mélange of these elements, which they called *America's Most Wanted*, a Hudson River School scene, with George Washington standing beside a lake in which a hippo is disporting itself.[12]

I do not want to deny that at some level perception of aesthetic properties, and aesthetic interest more generally, is based in our physical constitution, our brain structure, and hence indirectly in our evolution. It is indeed this grounding in the physical which

[10] c.f. Steven Pinker, *How the Mind Works*, Penguin, London, 1998, pp. 485–7.

[11] c.f. *Biophilia*, pp. 109–11.

[12] c.f. Denis Dutton, 'Art and Evolutionary Psychology' in Jerrold Levinson (ed), *The Oxford Handbook of Aesthetics*, Oxford University Press, 2002, in which there is a full discussion of Komar and Melamid, and of much else relevant to our present theme.

leads me to reject the Platonic notion of a non-physical aesthetic. Our common biology also provides the start of an explanation as to why there are aesthetic universals, aesthetic preferences common to us all, to the extent that there are such things; though I do not believe that this is a purely physical matter. Aesthetic interest is connected to a wider sense of human flourishing and human poten-tiality, which though at some level is also common to us all, takes us beyond purely biological imperatives.

But what I do want to question is the view implicit in Atkins, at least, that the perception of beauty is an automatic response to a generalisable stimulus. The same golden section can be made out in many different objects: a prehistoric palace in Mexico, a temple in Greece, a sketch by Le Corbusier, numerous renaissance paintings, the Palazzo della Cancelleria in Rome, and, of course, in a Euclidean textbook. Even if the perceiver saw all of these things as balanced, this is not the same thing as harmonious, let alone as beautiful. It is only the right sort of balance which is harmonious or beautiful, or balance in a particular context. Even if modernist architects and their propogandists have forgotten it, Alberti's adage that the beauty of ornament must be added to the harmony of proportion remains true. But what is the right combination of proportion and ornament? And it would be simply absurd to say that the aesthetic interest in Raphael's *The Crucified Christ with the Virgin Mary, Saints and Angels* (National Gallery, London) is some-how explicable in terms of the geometry underlying the painting. Even if geometry is a necessary condition to an aesthetic like Raphael's it is not a sufficient condition. All the humanity and all the religion in the painting would be overlooked on an account framed in terms like those used by Atkins. (And it is surely significant in this context that Clement Greenberg who attempted a similarly reductive aesthetic was also the great spokesman for abstract painting, arguing heroically—or quixotically, as the case may be—that the history of painting should be seen as a history of a drive to the painterly purity of abstraction. But, for all the persuasive power of critics and others committed to abstraction, it is hard to see anyone finding the golden section on its own of even fleeting aesthetic interest.)

What goes for the golden section also goes for waist-hip ratios of 0·70% and for Claudian landscapes. These features would provide at most a substratum of what is required for true beauty and for real aesthetic interest. In fact it is doubtful that they do even that. For many people, including possibly for the painter himself, Rubens' most touching depiction of female beauty is the painting called *The*

Little Fur (Kunsthistorisches Museum, Vienna), in which Hélène Fourment is precisely not painted as an ideal subject for evolutionarily determined male admiration, but rather as a real woman, beautiful and beloved, to be sure, but also with the imperfections of reality, and, as far as one can see, with a waist-hip ratio which is certainly not 0.70%. In other words, to reduce beauty, even female beauty to some standard format is just crass, as it simply ignores the full human context in which the beauty of a person is actually recognized.

This point becomes even clearer when we turn to landscape. Whatever Wilson and those polled in public opinion surveys might say about their preferred scenes, it is noteworthy that Ruskin found Claude's approach to the subject insipid. Although Claude had a 'fine feeling for beauty of form' and 'considerable tenderness of perception', the overall effect is of a kind of 'feminine charm' and of an artist 'incapable of enjoying or painting anything energetic or terrible.'[13] Ruskin had a point. To maintain aesthetic interest, an artist has to do more than give us a formulaic chocolate-box landscape. But once the task of the landscape painter is seen as, at least in part, showing us things we might not otherwise have noticed or appreciated, it becomes far from clear that he or she has to stick with scenes our savannah roaming ancestors might have found conducive to their survival. And in fact they don't, even on chocolate boxes. Since Turner and Ruskin, at least, mountains and stormy seas have featured hugely in landscape taste, and since Sidney Nolan and Fred Williams deserts too, all terrains one imagines early man would have done his level best to avoid, and which evolution should therefore have given us a predisposition to find ugly. Post romanticism we do not, of course, have any such predisposition or not in all cases, though we do in some, those too dreary and desolate, perhaps. But how dreary is too dreary? Couldn't a Turner or a Graham Sutherland even change our earlier assumptions about that? We are back with the Kantian insistence on the non-generalisable nature of aesthetic judgments, just as we are when we enquire as to just what degree of roughness might prevent our Claudian sylvan glade (complete with picturesque rocks) from being insipid.

Aesthetic judgments focus on the precise detail of a given work or object, and they are also normative. They are about how this particular thing ought to be, with its full human resonance. They are judgments which are elucidated by giving reasons and how they

---

[13] John Ruskin, *Modern Painters*, vol. v, part ix, ch. 5, 1860, as in the Cook and Wedderburn edition, London, 1903–12, Vol. vii, p. 319.

apply in the particular case, and how the particular thing relates to other aspects of our lives and the human world generally. In this sort of discussion, appeals to brain circuitry or to evolutionary history will be strikingly irrelevant. They may tell us something about the origins of some of our preferences in an entirely general way, but they will tell us nothing about how or why this bit of ornament in a building enhances or destroys its overall harmony, or why *The Little Fur* is so humanly resonant, or why D. H. Lawrence's novels are so much fuller and more convincing than his essays, even when both seem, on the surface, to be conveying the same general messages.

To put this point another way, our experiences of beauty and other aesthetic properties (including negative ones) are not like certain nerves or neurones being stimulated. They are not just a matter of the senses or the brain being appeased. They are not like hunger or thirst or our drives to reproduce being assuaged or aroused. Aesthetic experience always involves reflection and judgment. At the very lowest level it always involves a perception of the beautiful object as an object of such and such a sort, and beautiful in such and such respects. As a result of this intentionality of the aesthetic judgment, critics of a judgment of ours can then point to features of the object we have missed or comparisons we should have made or connexions we should have drawn. We might then be led to revise or refine or reject our original judgment, and so to modify the experience.

There is nothing analogous in sensory stimulation, whether this is pleasurable or painful. Even though selective attention can modify an experience of pure pleasure or pure pain, what is at issue in these cases is an experience unmediated by thought or judgment, and not responsive to reasoning in the way judgments, including aesthetic judgments are. We can have aesthetic or quasi-aesthetic judgments closely tied to or based on sensations, as in the case of wine-tasting perhaps, but even here, in the element of judgment involved, the experience takes on rational and cognitive dimensions transcending the purely sensory. In a positive aesthetic experience, the pleasure in question is not just experienced; it is perceived as having a value, and if Kant is right, as having a universal value, and also as being bound in with all sorts of other attitudes and values we have or ought to have. Art may be for art's sake, but it is never just for art's sake. It is because of the valuational dimension of the aesthetic that aesthetic judgments are open to criticism and refinement, and, for the subject of an aesthetic experience, life is improved cognitively, emotionally and even morally.

The neural circuitry and evolutionary accounts of the experience of beauty overlook the intentionality of aesthetic experience and the role that reason-giving and justification play in refining our sense of the beautiful. They are thus unable to account for the way that far more than the formal properties of things contributes to our sense of what is beautiful and why, in our aesthetic endeavours the clichés of chocolate box and pin-up will not do. Related criticisms can be made of the recent attempts by writers like Steven Pinker and Geoffrey Miller to account for artistic endeavour in terms of the status and sexual advantage successful artists and owners of art secure as a result of their work and possessions.

Some artists certainly do succeed in this way. Due to the acclaim their work brings them, and seeing artistic motivation in terms of sexual success or status more generally would certainly bring it within the general orbit of evolutionary explanation, where what is done is done for advantage in survival and or reproduction. To this fairly crude notion Miller adds a refinement in his book *The Mating Mind*.[14] What attracts potential mates to successful artists is their skill in performance, the rarity of great performance, and its consequent expense and difficulty. So, on this view, art is explained in terms of sexual selection, artistic virtuosity being valued by potential mates both for its rarity and as a symbol of other skills in the performer. Again, at one level, this theory is not entirely baseless; one has to think only of the careers of the likes of Paganini and Liszt, Picasso and Augustus John.

However, in either simplistic or sophisticated versions, the sexual selection view explains at most one side of artistic activity. It explains at some level why the artists might want to be artists, and why some of them might drive themselves beyond the norm. It does not explain why women mob them, if mob them they do, and why the rest of us shower them with wealth and adulation. Leaving aside the obvious point that in mature artistic traditions virtuosity in itself is not the only or indeed the most admired quality in an artist, the sexual selection account fails to explain why it is precisely artistic virtuosity which is so admired, as opposed to virtuosity in, say, arithmetic or coal mining or sheep-shearing. Nor, at a more profound level, does it explain what the artist himself finds worthwhile in his performance, and leads him on to master it in the way he does. Picasso was promiscuous and highly sexed, and artistic success undoubtedly enabled him to satisfy himself in these ways

[14] Pinker, in *How the Mind Works*, pp. 522–4, Miller in *The Mating Mind: How Sexual Choice Shaped the Evolution of Human Nature*, Doubleday, New York, 2000.

beyond most men's wildest dreams, but this was a by-product of his artistic genius. He had first to succeed artistically, and to do this he had to understand and feel what art was about, and having grasped this, he had both to be able to innovate artistically, and to want to innovate artistically. He, like his admirers, had to be gripped by a sense that art was worth doing for itself and on its own terms—for it is because he and they have this sense that he is admired for his supreme ability at that. He is not admired because of the wealth and riches he gets through art; unlike a business man who is admired because of the riches his work brings, an artist is admired for his work, and logically admiration for his riches come afterwards. The sexual selection accounts of artistic activity are, in other words, externalist accounts, touching on some of the dynamics of artistic communities and esteem, but they tell us nothing about the meaning or justification of judgments of beauty, about their internal logic or value.

An evolutionary theorist like Miller could grant some of this. He could admit that to see a given behavioural trait as having had a certain function in its evolutionary history is not equivalent to its having that function now. On this view, in prehistory virtuosic artistic performances, by their rarity and skill, demonstrated rarity and skill in their possessors, who were thereby, like peacocks with luxuriant tails, preferred by potential mates; and because of this the taste for art and ability in it got into our genes. But then, this taste having got into our genes, so to speak, we can now value art and artists for other reasons than those to do with mate acquisition. But this concession is not enough. It is not just true (though it is) that artistic motivation nowadays floats free of its evolutionary origins, with a logic and system of values of its own, unconnected to whatever might have been true in the remote past. Even this modified evolutionary account fails to explain why it was *artistic* virtuosity which was admired in the first place. In sum, if there is anything to the 'performance' account of our aesthetic taste and sensibility, the direction of explanation must be exactly the opposite to that postulated by Pinker and Miller. That is, it is because artistic performance is admired for aesthetic reasons, that outstanding performers become attractive to potential mates and gain high status, rather than the other way round.

So, what then is aesthetic experience based in? It involves, at various levels, a delight in appearance, to be sure, a harmony for a time between us and how things appear. But does it take us any further than that? Does it, as our opening quotations suggested, suggest any deeper transcendence of the immediate? Does it intimate to us that we are 'at home' in the universe, as religion at one time preached, and as, in different ways, science and morality might contest (science by telling us that the world is really very different from how it seems, morality—at least on some accounts—by imposing on us duties which we either cannot fulfil or which have to be fulfilled at supreme personal cost)?

This is not the place to attempt an answer to these questions, or even any adequate analysis of their meaning. But our reflections on evolution prompt the following dilemma. Either, as our opening quotations implied, art and aesthetic experience really do point to some transcendence of the material world; in which case, evolution cannot give us a full account of human life and experience. Or, alternatively, art is a purely human creation and aesthetic experience has no transcendent dimension. In which case, something like an evolutionary explanation of these phenomena would in all likelihood be called for, even if we are at the moment far from any such account. At any event, any sense of transcendence aesthetic phenomena evoke would itself be illusory.

Maybe this sense of transcendence—which certainly does attach to many works of art of the past—has in some obscure way helped the species to survive and reproduce. It would be much the same way as, according to Michael Ruse, the (for him) equally illusory belief in an objective moral reality may in the past have helped human communities and individuals to flourish evolutionarily.[15] In both cases, the picture would be of survival devices tricking us into feelings of transcendence and illusions of objectivity for their own devious ends. But then, if this is true and it is generally realized to be true, we will look back on those forms of art which do intimate transcendence of some sort as belonging to a certain primitive and backward stage of humanity, as do the religious traditions out of which so many of them grew. In such circumstances, and in the absence of any transcendent ambition or dimension, art itself is likely to degenerate, as Ruskin predicted as early as 1846, into what he called mere aesthesis, 'mere amusement, ministers to morbid sensibilities, ticklers and fanners of the soul's sleep'—much like what you can see in to-day's most admired galleries of contemporary art, in fact.[16] Perhaps, too, surveying the cultural scene of the West to-day, both high and low, we might recall Darwin's own strictures about the 'babarous races of men', with

[15] c.f. Michael Ruse, in 'Evolution and Religion', paper presented at The Royal Institute of Philosophy's schools' conference, Warwick, 1995.

[16] Ruskin, *Modern Painters*, vol. ii, part iii, ch. 1, 1846, as in Cook and Wedderburn, vol. iv, p. 36.

their 'hideous ornaments and equally hideous music'.[17] Post Darwin, and perhaps in part because of Darwin, the aesthetic wheel would seem to have turned full circle.

---

[17] Charles Darwin, *The Descent of Man*, vol. 1, p. 142.

The Problems of Biological Design

TIM LEWENS

I. Selection and Design

Here is one way that philosophers and biologists sometimes speak of Darwin's explanatory innovation: 'Eyes, organs of echolocation, camouflage and the like are all wonderful instances of contrivance, of complex adaptation, of good design. Paley and the other natural theologians sought to explain this good design by appeal to an intelligent designer. Darwin, on the other hand, offers us a superior explanation for the appearance of this same property: Darwin shows us that we can explain good design through the action of selection. Indeed, selection is the only process that can explain good design in nature. And that is why evolutionary biologists can continue to use a version of the argument from design called the *argument from biological design*: when we see an instance of good design in nature, we should infer not the guiding hand of God, but the hand of selection at work.'

This way of talking about design and selection raises three inter-related problems. They are the problem of *continuity*, the problem of *monopoly*, and the problem of *inference*. The problem of continuity arises when we ask whether modern evolutionary biology and natural theology both seek to explain the same phenomena. What does this question mean? A very weak reading of continuity is easy to come by, and this reading will yield an affirmative answer to our question. It is true that some of the specific traits that are the objects of natural selection explanations—most obviously traits like eyes and wings—are the same as those that Paley was interested in. But can we go any further than this in uniting the two schools of thought? Is there some sense in which both aim at an understanding of 'good design'? One might think the answer must be no, on the grounds that Darwin shows that there is no design in nature to be explained. Yet biologists sometimes link the explananda of their theory quite explicitly to those of Paley. John Maynard Smith writes that 'the main task of any theory of evolution is to explain adaptive complexity, that is, to explain the same set of facts that Paley used as evidence of a creator'.[1] In claims

[1] J. Maynard Smith, 'The Status of Neo-Darwinism', *Theoretical Biology*, C. H. Waddington (ed.) (Edinburgh: University Press, 1969).

177

such as this it seems that 'adaptive complexity' is supposed to mean roughly the same thing as 'good design'; the different terms are chosen only to avoid the connotation of 'good design' that the property is a product of an intelligent designer. Richard Dawkins is even more explicit than Maynard Smith in his alliance with natural theology. Natural selection is the 'Blind Watchmaker': it has no foresight, but it still makes watches—i.e. well-designed entities.[2] Dawkins is quite open about his regard for Paley:

> I suppose people like me might be labelled neo-Paleyists, or perhaps 'transformed Paleyists'. We concur with Paley that adaptive complexity demands a very special kind of explanation: either a Designer, as Paley taught, or something such as natural selection that does the job of a designer.[3]

This brings us to the problem of monopoly. Dawkins does not merely note the phenomena of good design in nature, he also argues that selection is the only process that could explain their appearance.[4] There are apparent counter-examples to this claim. One might think that 'self-organization' can explain some instances of good design, or one might prefer less exotic examples such as the simple physical processes that produce the regular structures of crystals.[5] The obvious counter-argument for Dawkins to fall back on (also tentatively suggested by Sober[6]) is to say that such things as self-organization or crystal formation produce instances of regularity, order, or pattern, but not good design. The problem of monopoly is to give an account of what good design is, and how it differs from order, without thereby making the claim of monopoly vacuous. If 'well-designed' ends up being defined as 'produced by natural selection', then of course selection is the only property that can explain good design, but this will hardly be an important claim.

The problem of inference is to clarify and evaluate the argument from biological design; that is, the argument that takes as a premise the fact that some trait is well designed, and uses this as a basis for concluding that the trait was shaped by natural selection. The

[2] R. Dawkins, *The Blind Watchmaker* (London: Penguin, 1986).

[3] R. Dawkins, 'Universal Darwinism', *The Philosophy of Biology*, D. Hull and M. Ruse (eds.) (Oxford: Oxford University Press, 1998), p. 16.

[4] Ibid., 15–16.

[5] Self-organization is much discussed in S. Kauffman, *At Home in the Universe* (London: Penguin, 1996).

[6] E. Sober, 'Six Sayings About Adaptationism', *The Philosophy of Biology*, D. Hull and M. Ruse (eds.) (Oxford: Oxford University Press, 1998), p. 74.

natural theologians would argue from the proposition that a trait T is well designed for an effect E to the proposition that T was designed for E by God. Contemporary evolutionists appear to keep this inference almost entirely intact. They argue from the proposition that T is well designed for E to the proposition that T was designed for E by natural selection. A very clear statement of this view appears in work by Pinker and Bloom, who say that 'evolutionary theory offers clear criteria for when a trait should be attributed to natural selection: complex design for some function, and the absence of alternative processes capable of explaining such complexity'.[7] The problem of inference is once again to explain what 'complex design' means here, and to see how the biological argument from design holds up in the light of the account of good design we arrive at.[8]

II. Defining Design

It is easiest if we begin with the problem of inference; I will make some comments about the problems of continuity and monopoly in the final section of the paper. Proponents of the argument from biological design think that there is a property of good design, which indicates the action of selection when it is present in organic nature. They agree that sometimes good design really is explained by intelligence—namely when it is manifested by things like watches and computers. In order to get to an understanding of the nature of design and design arguments I want to look first at the ways in which we infer the presence of intelligent designers from the makeup of objects. Is there a property of 'good design' that tells us when an intelligent agent has been at work? Let us consider this definition of good design:

DI: T is well designed for some effect E iff in the right context T would produce E better than a range of alternatives $T_1...T_N$.

DI makes good design an intrinsic property because having this property does not depend logically on the context T is in, nor on T's history. I introduced a range of alternatives into this definition to

[7] S. Pinker and Paul Bloom, 'Natural Language and Natural Selection', *Behavioral and Brain Sciences* **13** (1990), 707.

[8] A very useful paper that discusses this inference in far more detail, and gives many more examples of its use and defence, is G. Lauder, 'The Argument from Design', *Adaptation*, M. Rose and G. Lauder (eds.) (San Diego: Academic Press, 1996).

give some sense to the idea that T is good at E-ing. This just means that T is better at E-ing than these alternatives. One might rightly worry which alternatives we are allowed to consider. I want to set this question aside, because as it stands DI isn't much use to us however we might spell this out.

If an object is well designed for some effect E in the sense of DI, then should we conclude that some intelligent agent probably designed it for E? No. If we follow this pattern of argument we need only find an effect of an object that is unique to it, and we will conclude that it is well designed for that effect. So pick any large rubbish tip you like. That tip has a very specific effect; it looks and smells a certain way. It is much better configured to look and smell that way than any other rubbish tip—had its organization been a little different then it would have looked different, its shape would have been different, it would have smelled a little different. The rubbish tip is well designed in the sense of DI for looking and smelling the way it does, but this is not evidence for the tip having been produced by intelligence. The problem here is not that intelligent design is a poor explanation in comparison to natural selection—that the tip is well-designed for appearing the way it does is evidence neither for the action of intelligence, nor for the action of selection.

Perhaps we can revise our version of the design argument a little, but keep a central place for DI's account of good design. We might think that some configurations of matter do not require an intelligent design process to explain them, because their presence is made very likely, and hence explained, by the action of some other, simpler, set of processes. A stone is good at weighing down papers, but the stone's capacity to do this can be explained quite simply without recourse to intelligent intervention. But, the intuition goes, some systems rely on such delicate arrangement for the performance of their effects, that we cannot assume that natural processes could have produced those effects without guidance.

Suppose, then, we revise the design argument like this. If an object is well designed for some effect in the sense of DI, and if the configuration required for that effect would be unlikely to arise in the absence of a process of intelligent design, then intelligent design is probably responsible for its configuration. As is probably obvious to most readers, this does not help with the problem at hand, for even this revised version tells us to infer that an intelligent design process produced the rubbish tip. There are many apparently equally likely ways the rubbish tip could have turned out. On the assumption that the tip is not the product of an intelligent agent adjusting it to have just the configuration it does, then its having just that configuration is a highly unlikely outcome. Its configuration is far better than alternatives at producing the effect of looking just that way to perceivers. So the tip was probably designed by an intelligent agent to look that just that way to perceivers.

The creationist Michael Behe slips up badly here in his characterization of the argument from design. He writes that:

> For discrete physical systems—if there is not a gradual route to their production—design is evident when a number of separate, interacting components are ordered in such a way as to accomplish a function beyond the individual components. The greater the specificity of the interacting components required to produce the function, the greater is our confidence in the conclusion of design.[9]

This makes the inference to intelligent design vacuous. Almost any system has some effect or another that depends on its internal components being organized just so, the rubbish tip's appearance to human observers included. We can even assume, in line with Behe's exclusion from this inference schema of systems for which gradual alteration can explain their effects, that the rubbish tip's look and smell are quite sensitive to changes in its internal configuration, so that slight differences to how it is organised make a big difference to how it looks and smells. We should not be at all confident that the rubbish tip was designed by an intelligent agent to look and smell just the way it does, but Behe's recipe tells us we should very confident of this. That is why Behe's version of the design inference should be rejected—not just when using it to make inferences about divine design and the natural world, but when we consider whether objects are designed by humans, too.

It is possible that Behe thinks we really do have decent evidence, in virtue of the rubbish tip's unlikely configuration, for the claim that someone designed it that way. Behe thinks the hypothesis that Italy was designed by someone who is a fan of boot-shaped countries should not be ruled out too quickly. He writes:

> Italy may have been intentionally designed to look like a boot, but maybe not. There is not enough data to reach a confident conclusion.[10]

This extraordinary claim could only come from someone who rules out sources of data external to the object itself in evaluating

---

[9] M. Behe, *Darwin's Black Box: The Biochemical Challenge to Evolution* (New York: Simon and Schuster, 1996), 194.

[10] Ibid., 198.

whether the object has been intelligently designed for one of its effects. Yet these data are crucial. Here lies the defect of trying to use a property like good design in the sense of DI as the sole basis for inferring intelligent agency. Establishing that something is well designed in this sense does not show that we should invoke either intelligence or selection to explain its makeup. Of course it is true to say that someone very powerful *could* have designed Italy to look like a boot, and she may have been more modest than the character Slartibartfast from Douglas Adams' *Hitchhikers' Guide to the Galaxy*, whose name is left carved in the fjords of Norway. But it is also true that someone *could* have designed a rubbish tip to look just like that. That fact about a remote metaphysical possibility isn't enough to shake our confidence in the lack of intelligent agency overseeing the building of rubbish tips, and the mere possibility that Italy was intelligently designed shouldn't shake our confidence in the lack of intelligence overseeing Italy either. The moral of the failure of DI as a sole ground for inferences to intelligent design is that it shows the importance of extrinsic information—facts that relate to things other than an object's structure and capacities—for assessing whether an object has been intelligently designed. Such facts include, in the case of inferences to intelligent design, infor-mation about the goals and powers of potential designers. No actual individual, it seems, has any interest either in making a rubbish tip look and smell just like that, nor in shaping Italy to look like a boot. True enough, some modern art really is structurally indistinguishable from undesigned rubbish, but we can tell that this art was designed by an intelligent agent all the same by drawing on rich, extrinsic, contextual data about the places where the work is found, the conventions for displaying artworks, facts about recent trends in the art world and so forth. Design inferences require information about far more than the structure and capacities of an object if they are to be reliable.

III. Cosmic Design

These observations about design inferences in the case of rubbish tips and artworks undermine cosmic intelligent design arguments that seek to attribute the means/ends organization of the universe to an intelligent designer. When we recognize structures as intelligently designed, it is (in part) in virtue of our knowledge of the goals and powers of intelligent agents. It is in part because we know that people like to eat food and are able to make medium sized tools that we can infer that objects that would be very helpful in catching and killing edible animals were probably intelligently designed for that effect. That means that if we want to infer the existence of a cosmic designer from the structure of the universe, we would need evidence of the cosmic designer's goals and powers.[11] Yet those who think they can infer the existence of an intelligent designer from, say, the 'fine-tuning' of certain universal constants, rarely think they have evidence of the designer's goals and powers, except for the evidence provided by the fine-tuning of those constants themselves. In other words, the fact that the universe is good at producing life is taken by itself to be evidence of a designer who is keen on a life-bearing universe, who has the power to make such a thing, and who has built something to meet her goal. But inferring goals, powers and a design process as an explanatory package-deal is analogous to inferring merely from the existence of a rubbish tip the existence of a designer with the goal of making a tip with just that makeup, a designer with the power to produce such a tip, and the process of design that explains how the tip gets to have just that makeup. Since this is not how we make inferences about the design history of artefacts, analogy cannot be used to show that our practice of inferring that a watch is intelligently designed commits us to inferring also that the universe is intelligently designed on the basis of the suitability of its universal constants to the existence of stars, organic life, or whatever.[12]

In general, we are exceptionally cautious about making package-deal design inferences, even when we have evidence that an agent will benefit from an apparently unlikely outcome. National Lottery winners have a clear interest in what appears to be an unlikely result. The hypothesis that Fred won the National Lottery fair and square makes Fred's winning exceptionally unlikely, and the same goes for every lottery winner. So should we infer to an apparently better explanation—namely that every lottery is fixed, and therefore each winner was always very likely to win after all? No: sometimes very unlikely things happen, even unlikely things that are in the interests of some agent. Yet we are far more confident of claims about lottery fixing if we have information that Fred has a brother who works the lottery machine. Once again, we insist on rich

[11] I owe this point to E. Sober, 'The Design Argument', *The Blackwell Guide to the Philosophy of Religion*, W. Mann (ed.) (Oxford: Blackwell, forthcoming).

[12] Some useful papers on cosmic design arguments are collected in *God and Design: The Teleological Argument and Modern Science*, N. A. Manson (ed.) (London: Routledge, 2003).

background information to bolster our inferences; we do not trust package-deal operators.

IV. The Biological Argument from Design

It is now time to assess the biological argument from design directly. Pinker and Bloom's criterion of 'complex design for some function and the absence of alternative processes capable of explaining such complexity' as a mark of the hand of natural selection threatens to make the biological argument from design vacuous. For it seems at first glance that they must mean one of two things when they write of 'complex design for some function'. If they wish to allude to the dominant account of functions, then the argument from function to selection appears to become trivial. Many philosophers these days defend what is called the 'Selected Effects' account of functions, which tells us that claims about functions are claims about selection histories.[13] If this account is the right one, then it is a conceptual truth that traits that have E as a function were selected for E—the function claim is not evidence for the selection history, rather, they are logically equivalent propositions.[14]

Perhaps we should try a second reading of Pinker and Bloom's claim. Suppose that when they write of 'complex design for some function' they mean only that the trait is good at producing some effect. This reading makes their criterion for the hand of selection stumble in just the same way that Behe's criterion for intelligent design stumbles. For this version of the argument from biological design implies that once we find some effect that (i) a trait would be particularly good at, and which (ii) relies on the trait being in a state that would be very unlikely to arise in the absence of selection for that effect, then we should conclude that the trait has probably been shaped by selection for that effect. But then we need only find some unlikely configuration of matter (organic matter this time), find some effect it has that relies on it being organised just that way, and we will conclude that it was probably shaped by selection to be like

[13] This is not the place for comprehensive references to the Selected Effects account. Many of the most important papers are collected in *Nature's Purposes: Analyses of Function and Design in Biology*, C. Allen, M. Bekoff and G. Lauder (eds.) (Cambridge, MA: MIT Press, 1998).

[14] For an evaluation of the Selected Effects account see chapter five of T. Lewens, *Organisms and Artifacts: Design in Nature and Elsewhere* (Cambridge, MA: MIT Press, 2004).

that. So because the pigmentation of the Friesian cow is well designed for the effect of camouflaging these cows in a Gateway computer factory, we should conclude that the Friesian's pigmentation was probably shaped by selection for this camouflaging effect. After all, it is surely unlikely that pigmentation would appear with just those colours in just that orientation in the absence of selection for that pattern, and the excellence of the pigmentation in producing this effect therefore seems to demand a selective explanation.

Thankfully we needn't abandon design arguments in biology, because they do not work in quite the way one might take Pinker and Bloom to imply. Just like arguments for intelligent design, they are also heavily constrained by contextual evidence, and rightly so. The first thing we need to note here is that the argument from biological design is typically used to determine whether a trait has been 'shaped' by selection, not merely whether the trait has increased its frequency in virtue of some effect.[15] That is, the argument is used to determine whether the trait is a product of a process that acts over time to build structures that become progressively better at meeting demands of the local environment. It is not a trivial truth, even on the dominant account of functions, that if something has a function it achieves through some complex arrangement of parts, then it has probably been shaped by selection for that function.

One important set of information that helps determine whether a trait is indeed the product of selective shaping for some effect E is information that tells us not just whether the trait in question would have been good at producing E, but whether E-ing would have contributed to fitness in the organism's past. After all, the trait might be excellent at E-ing, but E-ing may be completely irrelevant to the organism's prospects for survival. That is why the excellence of Friesian cow pigmentation in providing camouflage in a computer factory is not evidence of selection for this effect, for this effect was of no relevance to the cows' survival. To determine whether some effect of a trait was fitness enhancing in the organism's past, we need to know facts extrinsic to the trait itself, such as whether other traits could have interacted with the trait in question in the appropriate way, and whether the organism's environment was such that E-ing would have been valuable.

Richard Dawkins finds an interesting way of saying something right about these kinds of design arguments when he gives this informal definition of good design:

[15] I discuss this notion of 'shaping' in more in op. cit., note 14, chapter 2.

We may say that a living body or organ is well designed if it has attributes that an intelligent and knowledgeable engineer might have built in order to achieve *some sensible purpose*, such as flying, swimming, seeing, eating, reproducing, or more generally promoting the survival and reproduction of the organism's genes [my italics].[16]

Dawkins will go on to say that good design in this sense can only be explained by natural selection, with the result that good design is diagnostic of the action of selection. The specification of a 'sensible' purpose sounds strange here. Why on earth would an intelligent and knowledgeable engineer think that building a machine for eating, or for reproducing is a sensible endeavour? She probably wouldn't, but the demand that the effects of a trait must be sensible is really just a roundabout way of saying that they must make some contribution to survival and reproduction. Almost anything could make such a contribution, given the right environment. So Dawkins had better not be licensing an inference of the form 'it is possible that T augmented fitness by E-ing, and T is very well suited to E-ing, so T was probably shaped by selection for E-ing'. That pattern of inference would enable us to conclude that cowhides probably have the pigmentation they do because they have afforded camouflage in computer factories. Let us read Dawkins charitably as drawing attention to our need for information about what the past environments of traits have been like if we are to say what effects are sensible, hence what a trait has been shaped for. This reminds us that we must also handle with care Dennett's perfectly legitimate appeal to the good design of *Archaeopteryx*: 'An analysis of the claw curvature, supplemented by aerodynamic analysis of wing-structure, makes it quite plain that the creature was well-designed for flight'.[17] We must not suppose that this claim instantiates a generally reliable inference schema from 'T would have been excellent at E-ing' to 'T was probably shaped by selection for E-ing'. There is nothing wrong with Dennett's claim about *Archaeopteryx*, but there is no such reliable design argument, either.

V. Design Problems

My reconstruction of the argument from biological design allows us to see some of its limits quite clearly. When a trait augments the

[16] Op. cit., note 2, 21.

[17] D. C. Dennett, *Darwin's Dangerous Idea* (New York: Norton, 1995), 233.

fitness of its bearer, and when this relies on a very specific set of relations between its parts, it is often the case that the best explanation for this state of affairs is that the trait has been shaped gradually by selection to acquire that structure. There are, however, alternative explanations. Perhaps the organism/environment relation that results in the trait in question augmenting fitness is produced not by gradual alteration of the trait to match its environment, but instead by gradual migration of the species into an environment in which the pre-existing trait enhances fitness. This is a selective explanation of sorts, because one can suppose that the relational trait of *being in a better habitat* is one that increases its frequency in a population of organisms in different habitats. But clearly the metaphor of selection as craftsman—the metaphor encouraged by thinking of selection as a stand-in for the natural theologians' divine artificer—is inappropriate here. Selection does not shape these organisms to match their environments; rather, the environment changes to match the organisms.

This means that talk of 'good design' in contemporary biology may not be entirely innocent. In the realm of artefacts, good design is typically explained by good designers. Transferring this principle to the organic world, Dawkins implies that good design is also explained by a good designer, albeit a blind one. When selection is characterised in this way as a craftsman—as the 'Blind Watchmaker'—we are liable to overlook explanations for adaptation that turn to migration, rather than mutation. Migration explanations are selection explanations, but not explanations that have obvious analogues in intelligent design processes. Craftsmen shape artefacts to fit design problems; they rarely seek design problems to fit to artefacts. But selection is not constrained in this way, in spite of the watchmaker label that talk of biological design, and the consequent projection of a biological designer, invite.

VI. Continuity, Inference and Monopoly

It is time to bring together some answers to the three problems of biological design. Here I will tackle continuity first, then inference, then monopoly. In sections two, three and four we saw that there is no intrinsic property of 'good design' that is reliably diagnostic of either intelligent agency or of natural selection as the shaper of material form. This means that if any property of 'good design' is diagnostic of such historical processes, the property in question would have to be characterized extrinsically. This observation makes things difficult for the claim of continuity. That claim seems to demand that one single property of 'good design' shows us reliably that either intelligence, or selection, is historically responsible for some aspect of form. Only if that is true can we say that evolutionary theory focuses on the same class of phenomena as natural theology—namely, the well designed traits. Yet it is hard to see how one single property of good design can be possessed by both organisms and artefacts, if that property must be characterized extrinsically.

For artefacts, the property of being well designed that indicates an intelligent design history must be something like the property of being well suited to the needs or desires of users. On the face of it, this cannot be what biologists are talking about when they speak of well designed traits, for biological traits, one might think, rarely have genuine users, and certainly not users with desires. Users, it seems, are agents, and the well-designed sexual organs of plants (for example) do not derive their good design from the satisfaction of any agent's needs. For organisms, when we talk of a trait being 'well designed' we can only mean something like 'augmenting fitness in actual environments'. Such a reading of 'well designed' meshes with what Dawkins and Pinker say about the argument from biological design itself. So it is hard to see how intelligent design and natural selection can be said to explain the same property, even though the properties each process is believed to explain are given the same name.

It is nonetheless possible to explain the appeal of the continuity claim, for in a variety of metaphorical senses we can assert that fitness-augmenting traits answer needs or desires. On the one hand, there is a metaphorical sense in which one might say that an organism's environment lays down desiderata for how the organism should be constructed. Biologists of various kinds regularly refer to environmental problems in this sense. Alternatively, one might think loosely of an individual organism, or even of some type of gene, as the user or manipulator of organic traits, while thinking metaphorically of the maximization of fitness as the primary goal or desire of organisms or genes. In these ways, both the natural theological and the evolutionary conceptions of being 'well designed' are united under the general concept of a structure in virtue of which needs or desires are efficiently satisfied.

Second, the problem of inference. Is there a good inference from 'X is well designed for E' to 'X is shaped by selection for E'? As we saw, the answer is 'yes', but with qualifications. Sometimes having some fitness-augmenting effect indicates selective shaping, but not always, and it is a fault of phrasing this biological inference in the language of design that we are liable to overlook explanations for the existence of fitness-augmenting traits that look to migration, rather than the gradual modification of a trait in the face of a largely stable environment.

Third, the problem of monopoly. Does selection provide the only legitimate explanation of good design? It turns out that there is no pressing need for biology to answer this question in the affirmative. When we defended the argument from biological design we did so by restricting our understanding of 'well designed trait' to 'trait that augments fitness in actual environments'. The justified use of specific instances of the biological argument from design does not require that selection has a monopoly on the explanation of 'good design', where 'good design' is understood in an overarching sense; it requires only that selective shaping is typically the best explanation for the existence of fitness-enhancing traits. The battle against creationism also requires no defence of the overarching monopoly claim: that battle requires at the most that we show that there are no actual phenomena whose existence is better explained by the action of a divine creator than it is by non-intelligent processes.[18]

Not only does biology require no defence of the claim that selection is the only process that can explain good design understood in a general sense, it may be a mistake to try to formulate such a defence. At the beginning of the paper we considered bolstering the claim of monopoly by distinguishing between design and order. We briefly mentioned the argument that although processes other than selection might explain order, they cannot explain design. The attempt to distinguish design in general from order in general is made more difficult by the extrinsic nature of the property of being well designed. When discussing 'good design' in the context of artefacts we saw that any configuration of matter could be indicative of an intelligent design process, just so long as we suspect there might be agents who have interests in bringing such configurations about, and who have the ability to do so. Intelligent agents sometimes design chaotic configurations of rubbish; sometimes ordered patterns are designed by intelligent agents, too. Conversely, unless we think that agents exist with the right goals and powers, we need not recognize any state of affairs as 'well designed'. So, in the domain of artefacts, the

[18] Here I am expanding on what I take to be Sober's view, op. cit., note 6, 75.

contrast between ordered patterns and designed patterns also demands that we specify some set of needs or desires of users by which to reckon design good or bad. For organisms, the distinction will be drawn instead in terms of whether the trait in question is merely regular, or whether it also augments fitness. The lesson here is that one cannot draw a generic distinction between order and design; we can only draw local distinctions between order and design within whichever domain (organic, technical) we are considering.

The extrinsic nature of the property of being 'well-designed' thus makes it difficult to spell out what that property is in general terms, such that we might plausibly claim that in all domains good design is explicable only by selection. Within the domain of biology we can assert a restricted monopoly claim, namely that whenever some trait contributes to fitness in an actual environment, shaping by selection is the explanation. If we want to generalize this assertion, and use it as a basis for the claim that selection explains good design in all domains, then we would need to understand fitness as the kind of property that need not be restricted in its instantiation to the biological realm. Indeed, one might try to unify the concepts of good organic design and good technical design through an appeal to some kind of evolutionary model of creativity.[19] That project is beyond the scope of this essay.[20] But what are the prospects for this kind of monopoly claim when we consider the domain of biology alone? Fitness-enhancing traits need not always be explained by selection acting on gradual variation. To take one contentious example, macromutation may sometimes produce fitness-enhancing traits, too. So selective 'shaping' is not the sole explanation for how such traits come to be. One could reply to this by saying that fitness-enhancing traits produced by macromutation are not 'well-designed', for on those rare occasions when macromutation does produce a novel, beneficial trait, that trait will almost certainly be very simple. 'Complex' traits cannot be produced by anything other than selection, and well-designed traits should be defined as complex. But what does 'complex' mean here, and how does the addition of this condition of complexity change our definition of good design? Maybe we will say that traits of complex design are those whose contribution to fitness relies on

---

[19] Dennett has long been a defender of such evolutionary models of creativity. See op. cit., note 17, and also P. Griffiths, 'Functional analysis and proper function', *British Journal for Philosophy of Science* **44** (1993), 409–22.

[20] For more thoughts on this see op. cit., note 14, chapter seven.

interrelations between heterogeneous parts that would be exceptionally unlikely to arise together through macromutation. We could say this, but to do so threatens a form of creeping vacuity in the claim of monopoly. It threatens vacuity because it is a step on the path to defining 'well designed' as 'of a form most likely to be produced by selection acting on gradual variation'. If this is the definition of good design, then of course selection is the best explanation of the occurrence of good design. Arriving at this claim does not, however, signal a victory of good sense over creationism. We have seen that the monopoly claim is not needed in arguments against creationists. Better, perhaps, to avoid playing monopoly all together.[21]

[21] I am grateful to the audience at the Royal Institute of Philosophy where this talk was first given in February 2004, and to the audience at Shanxi University, China, where a revised version was given in April 2004. I also owe thanks for comments to André Ariew, Emma Gilby, Griff Gilby, Peter Lipton, Matteo Mameli, Hugh Mellor, Anthony O'Hear, Samir Okasha and David Papineau.

Are There Genes?[1]

JOHN DUPRÉ

Introduction

Contrary to one possible interpretation of my title, this paper will not advocate any scepticism or ontological deflation. My concern will rather be with how we should best think about a realm of phenomena the existence of which is in no doubt, what has traditionally been referred to as the genetic. I have no intention of questioning a very well established scientific consensus on this domain. It involves the chemical DNA, which resides in almost all our cells, which is capable of producing copies of itself that accurately reproduce a very long sequence of components, and which plays a role in the physiology of the cell which in certain basic respects is quite well understood. This substance has also achieved a remarkable iconic status in contemporary culture. It is seen as fundamental to personal identity both in the practical sense of providing a criterion of identity through DNA testing, and in the much deeper sense of being seen as, somehow, defining who we are. The latter role is illustrated, for example, by the recent debate about the right of children conceived by sperm donation to know who are their fathers. Such people, it is passionately argued, must be able to find out where they came from, who they really are. On a daily basis we are confronted with claims about the discovery of the genetic basis of—or in fact very often the 'gene for'—all manner of psychological and physical characteristics, and all kinds of disorders. This holds out apparent possibilities for curing or preventing diseases or for eugenic control over future generations. But more subtly it contributes to an increasingly general assumption that what we are depends more than anything else on our genetic endowment.

In this paper I want to address the question how we should best understand the phenomena that underlie all these ways of thinking.

[1] The support of the Economic and Social Research Council (ESRC) is gratefully acknowledged. The work was part of the programme of the ESRC Research Centre for Genomics in Society (Egenis). I am also grateful to several colleagues in Egenis for advice and comments on earlier drafts.

John Dupré

A general thesis about which I shall say something, is that what scientific experts say doesn't in fact provide much support for these wider general cultural understandings of genetics and of DNA. But my main focus will, as my title suggests, be largely ontological. I want to start not with genes, but with the genome, the totality of our genetic material. What kind of a thing is this, and in what sense may it usefully be considered as composed, at least in part, of genes? As I have already indicated, one thing the genome is is a quantity of a particular chemical, DNA. But presumably there is more to the genome than just what it is made of.

In the end, of course, our account of what such a thing as a genome is can only be derived from the science through which such an object is presented to us. However rather than approach the science directly, in order to bring into contact this scientific picture and more popular understandings of the genome, I shall consider some of the very familiar metaphors through which genomes (and genes, and DNA) are often described by scientific experts and assimilated by a wider public. The genome is often said to embody a code; to be a repository of information; to provide a blueprint for the developed organism; or perhaps a recipe; and so on. All of these are clearly metaphorical, and my proposal is to assess the aptness of these metaphors in relation to our contemporary scientific understanding of what genomes are and what they do. With a better understanding of this question it should be easier to see what turns on the idea that the genome contains or consists of genes, what kinds of things genes are or might be, and whether they provide a useful way of distinguishing components of the genome.

Let me repeat that although I shall be critical of some of the metaphors used to describe genes and genomes, this is not intended as criticism of the science which these metaphors are used to describe—indeed the criticism is largely dependent on taking the science on trust. I certainly do think philosophers can sometimes usefully criticise parts of science, and I have occasionally attempted this myself. But this is not my present aim and in fact the area of science I am talking about is one which, on the whole, I find impressive and admirable. Although the metaphors I'm considering no doubt play a role in the thinking of scientific practitioners, in the present case I suspect the role is often minimal or, at any rate, harmless. Contemporary genomics and molecular genetics is thoroughly, and in this case admirably, mechanistic. It is about molecules fitting together (like locks and keys), molecules being spliced together or cut in pieces, and channels in cell walls through which molecules are pumped. Now of course mechanism is itself a

194

metaphor—the cell is not a machine—but it is a very different metaphor from the ones I am considering. I don't want to talk about these little, local metaphors—locks and pumps—but about the much larger metaphors in terms of which the whole project of genetics has been presented—codes, blueprints, secrets of life, and so on.

These big metaphors matter not so much to the scientists on the coal face working on the mechanical details of the cells but rather to the people away from the frontiers of molecular biology who assimilate them. I mentioned the recent proposal that people conceived through sperm donation in the UK should in the future have a right to know the identity of their biological father. In defending this measure, scientists, experts of various kinds, and members of the public, speak of the importance to people of knowing their genetic origin. Since most of these people are not familiar with the technical details of the science—would probably not know a cytosolic channel partner from a translocation substrate—they are appealing to some image of the science which, I suggest, is very substantially formed by the metaphors promulgated by experts.

And something similar happens within science, now broadly conceived. One of the most effective disseminators of genetic metaphors has been Richard Dawkins[2], not a geneticist but an evolutionist. On the murkier fringes of evolutionary theory, new wave sociobiologists, or evolutionary psychologists as they are now known, often appeal to Dawkins's image of genetics to justify stories they tell about the evolution of the human mind. And these stories, unlike the work on the genomic coal face are often the subjects of international best sellers, presumably effecting images of the genetic among the general public. My claim is that these metaphors often misrepresent the science not usually, to repeat, to the scientists themselves, but rather to a range of scientific and non-scientific consumers of these metaphors.

Genetics and Genomics

As the director of a research centre with the word 'genomics' in the title, I am often made aware that many people do not know what this is. Most people have heard of the human genome project, but it is not my impression that a high proportion know what it was. And it

[2] See especially *The Selfish Gene* (Oxford: Oxford University Press, 1976).

is not trivial to say what the genome is. The first definition I found on Google defines the genome as the complete set of genes, which would cover about 3% of the genome on a typical estimate. Much better would be the complete set of chromosomes, which at least includes those parts that nobody thinks constitute genes. It is, however, more than a quibble to point out that a set is, on the face of it, an abstract object. It is more than a quibble because there is a real issue whether a genome should be considered as something abstract or something concrete. The common idea that the genome just is a sequence of base pairs (or even letters representing base pairs) suggests an abstract object—perhaps a canonical or standard genotype. But it is much better, I suggest, to think of the genome as something concrete—an object that occupies part of the nucleus in the centre of most organic cells. To mention just one reason for this preference, it seems quite likely that chromosomes themselves are not fully independent free-floating objects, but are structurally related to one another in functionally significant ways. Whether the genome is a distributed object or a single connected object is an empirical issue that will not be crucial for this paper; but I shall mention some reasons why it should be thought of as an object.

By contrast to this solidly material picture of the genome, genes turn out to be a much trickier matter. As already mentioned, only a small proportion of the genome is thought by anyone to be composed of genes. And whereas there are some potential pitfalls in attempts to define the genome, when we come to definitions of the gene we encounter fundamental disagreement. Anyone who doubts this should look at the Representing Genes project at the University of Pittsburgh[3], which has involved empirical investigation of the reaction of biologists' to various definitions of genes. The study confirmed the expectation that biologists with different interests tended to understand quite different things by this term. At any rate, for now I shall mean by 'gene' some—to be determined—principled subdivision of parts of the genome. Whether there are any principles adequate to motivate such a subdivision is a question this paper will address.

My own predominant opinion is that the concept of a gene is a misleading one. I do not think it misleads scientists who work on these things so much as the various other specialists and members of the general public who hear about them and derive more or less accurate pictures of the workings of our cells and our bodies. But these misunderstandings are deep and important. So even if it is

---

[3] See http://www.pitt.edu/~kstotz/genes/genes.html

unlikely that talk of genes will be abandoned altogether, we can hope that it may be treated with a healthy pinch of salt.

So what is a gene, or, if there are none, what would one be if there were any? The concept is often associated with the name of Mendel, though as is well known Mendel's work was discovered only posthumously in 1900, some years after his death, and the word 'gene' was not introduced until 1909 by Johannsen[4]. The crucial idea, associated rightly or wrongly with Mendel, was of discrete units of inheritance, discrete all or nothing causes of phenotypic traits. The familiar so-called Mendelian ratios between traits such as smooth or wrinkled and green or yellow seeds in peas were widely taken as evidence that these traits were caused by specific heritable factors. The hypothesis was developed that these factors came in pairs and that alternative variants (alleles) could make up these pairs. Particular variants could be preferentially expressed— or dominant—over others, so that just one copy of the dominant allele for green seeds would suffice to produce green seeds, whereas two yellow seed alleles would be required for yellow seeds. The additional assumption that these alleles were randomly assorted during sexual mating generated the simplest classical Mendelian ratios, those for two factors with complete dominance.

Essentially this picture underlay the classic studies on inheritance in fruit-flies (*Drosophila melanogaster*) undertaken by Thomas Hunt Morgan, his students Alfred Sturtevant and Herman Muller, and others. One of the most salient outcomes of this research was the observation of departures from Mendelian ratios that could be attributed to the association, or perhaps physical proximity, of genetic factors. This phenomenon, genetic linkage, was used by Sturtevant in 1911 to construct the first genetic linkage maps, proposing an ordering of the genes identified by a phenotypic difference[5]. Inevitably interest developed in the search for a physical realisation of the gene, and this early mapping work was important in developing support for the view that chromosomes, identifiable as fibrous structures in the cell, were the physical basis of genes. This theory was eventually accepted universally in the aftermath of the disclosure of the structure of DNA in 1953.

The crucial point in this story is the progression from purely theoretical entity—the hypothetical cause of inherited differences in

[4] Willhelm Johannsen, *Elemente der exakten Erblichkeitslehre.* (Jena: Gustav Fischer, 1909).

[5] A. H. Sturtevant, 'The Linear Arrangement of Six Sex-Linked Factors in *Drosophila*, as Shown by their Mode of Association', *Journal of Experimental Zoology* 1 (1913), 43–59.

phenotype—to a well-described structure, the DNA molecule. What I want to argue is that this transition actually involved the discovery that nothing fitted well with the concept underlying the original theoretical entity, 'gene'. Thus the famous results of Watson, Crick (and others) as well as being a natural culmination of the project of classical genetics, proved also to be the beginning of its end.

To avoid excessive circumlocution, I shall use the term 'gene' for the time being to mean any region of the genome containing coding sequence. Something like this is assumed when, for example, we are told how many genes there are in the human genome, though estimates vary from a now popular figure of about 30,000 to as many as 100,000. One of many difficulties is that genes are assumed to contain non-coding regions (introns), but clearly there must be a question whether a non-coding sequence is an intron or the gap between two genes. At any rate, it will become clear that this very rough definition fits poorly with many other assumptions that are made about the gene.

Another conception of the gene, not entirely a straw man, is as the material cause of a phenotypic feature. I suppose nobody quite believes that there are strings of bases that can be properly understood as the full and sufficient cause of a Roman nose or an artistic temperament. However there is considerable pressure towards beliefs of this sort apparent in, and perhaps in part stemming from, some of the most widely familiar metaphors in terms of which the genome is described. It is still common to hear the genome described, for instance, even by eminent experts, as a blueprint for the organism. And one point about blueprints is that there is a systematic mapping from parts or features of the blueprint to parts or features of the thing for which it is a blueprint. And talk of genes for this or that phenotypic trait might naturally be taken to give us the mapping from genome to phenotype. Perhaps not many people will defend the blueprint metaphor very far these days if pushed, however. A common retreat is to the metaphor of a recipe. Certainly this overcomes the immediate objection: one doesn't expect distinct parts of the cake that correspond to the flour or the sugar, for instance. But this metaphor is still quite inadequate. With due allowance for an element of assumed common knowledge, the recipe is a complete set of instruction for how to make the cake. The massive insufficiency of the genome, let alone merely the genome sequence, to determine the development of the phenotype points to deeper ways in which standard metaphors for describing the relation of the genome to the phenotype are inadequate. To explain why this is so, it will be useful to return to my highly schematic and simplistic historical narrative.

Investigations following the discovery of the structure of DNA led eventually to the unravelling of the so-called genetic code, the mapping of triplets of the bases composing the DNA molecule on to specific amino acids, and hence the ability to correlate stretches of DNA with complex amino acid sequences, or proteins. An immediate worry—if hardly a surprising one—arising from the identification of the mode of action of DNA is that this action, the production of specific proteins within cells, is at a considerable causal distance from the phenotypic traits with which the story began. This causal distance immediately explains the classic philosophical objection to the attempt to identify classical Mendelian genes with parts of the chromosome: the relations between bits of chromosomes and Mendelian, or just phenotypic, traits are many/many.[6] Even the sketchiest conception of the processes connecting the production of a protein to the shape of a nose, let alone to, say, a sensitivity to violation of social contracts, makes it obvious that such a process will interact with many other proteins on the way. And it is at least likely that the ramifications of the production of a protein will be felt at many different points on the phenotype. These phenomena are referred to as pleiotropy—the multiple effects of a single gene—and polygeny—the multiple genes involved in producing a phenotypic effect.

The consequence of this on which I want to focus here is that polygeny and pleiotropy make phenotypic features generally poorly suited to distinguishing particular genes. An expression such as 'gene for measuring waist-to hip ratio', in the unlikely event that it has any referent at all, must trace back to many segments of the genome[7]. Conversely, many segments of genome will trace forward to a phenotypic feature of interest. What we so far lack, therefore, is a principle for identifying bits of the genome as individual genes. An obvious solution, and one that still appeals to many thinkers, is merely to move the effect much closer to the gene, and identify genes as the templates for particular proteins.[8] The problem with

[6] This point was clearly established thirty years ago by David Hull, *The Philosophy of Biological Science* (Englewood-Cliffs, NJ: Prentice-Hall, 1974).

[7] This improbable but widely cited candidate for an evolved product of genetic processes is due to Devendra Singh, 'Adaptive Significance of Waist-to-Hip Ratio and Female Physical Attractiveness', *Journal of Personality and Social Psychology* 69 (1993), 293–307.

[8] A sophisticated attempt of this sort is Kenneth Waters, 'Genes made molecular', *Philosophy of Science* 61 (1994), 163–85.

this, however, is that it has become increasingly clear that even the relationship between bits of DNA sequence and proteins is many/many. A typical stretch of DNA that appears to correspond more or less to what used to be thought of as a gene contains a series of coding sequences, called exons, separated by non-coding sequences, called introns. When the gene is transcribed into messenger RNA, this can be done in a variety of ways selecting from the available exons to produce various different RNAs. These RNA sequences in turn may subsequently be spliced on to other sequences, perhaps deriving from DNA from other parts of the genome. The RNA is then translated into polypeptide sequences which may themselves be spliced to further polypeptides after translation. The upshot of all this mess is then that the final protein product may contain sequences derived from DNA from diverse parts of the genome; and coding sequences of DNA may contribute to the production of a range of final protein products. So the genome cannot be classified into parts based on the proteins that it generates any more than it can in terms of phenotypic traits, and for just the same reason: in both cases the processes intervening are too complex and diverse.[9]

Both the many/many relations and the diversity of process can be elegantly illustrated by comparing the genetic basis of sensory mechanisms in the ear and in the nose. A gene that is involved in the production of the hairs in the cochlear cells in the ear produces several hundred distinct protein products that provide the variable-lengthed hairs sensitive to different sound frequencies.[10] By contrast, the many different cells in the nose sensitive to distinct molecules each employ a protein product from a distinct gene in tuning their sensitivity to a different molecule.[11] Interestingly, both these systems have undergone substantial recent evolution, suggesting that these are two different mechanisms for providing a certain kind of (relatively) rapid evolutionary response. I must confess,

[9] For details of these difficulties, see Thomas Fogle, 'The Dissolution of Protein Coding Genes in Molecular Biology', in *The Concept of the Gene in Development and Evolution*, Peter Beurton, Raphael Falk, and Hans-Jorg Rheinberger (eds.) (Cambridge: Cambridge University Press, 2000), 3–25 ; Lenny Moss *What Genes Can't Do* (Cambridge, Mass.: MIT Press, 2003).

[10] See Douglas L. Black, 'Splicing in the Inner Ear: a Familiar Tune, but what are the Instruments? *Neuron,* 20 (February, 1998), 165–8.

[11] See Shou Serizawa et al., 'Negative Feedback Regulation Ensures the One Receptor—One Olfactory Neuron Rule in Mouse', Science 302 (19 December, 2003), 2088–94.

however, that whereas there is no doubt that scientists describe these systems in these quite different ways, in the absence of greater clarity about the interpretation of the word 'gene' it is difficult to be sure how fundamental this difference is. What is clear, though, is that these findings illustrate the great diversity and complexity in the relations between genotype and phenotype.

A more familiar problem is that most of the genome is not even a candidate for analysis into genes in the way currently being considered, simply because it does not consist of sequences that provide information for protein production. As is now widely known, many active parts of the genome function by promoting or inhibiting the transcription of other sequences. Other parts are transcribed into RNA that has various cellular functions, but is not translated into polypeptides. And most of the genome appears to have functions of neither kind, and has been widely assumed to have no function at all. It has sometimes been referred to as 'junk DNA', and is thought to constitute the very large majority of most genomes, though in a moment I shall suggest that this junk maybe less junky than often supposed.

Before pursuing the question of genes any further, it will be better to return to the genome—the entire collection of nuclear DNA in an organism. I shall approach the genome this time through another metaphor, equally familiar in presentations of genetics, that of information.[12] The first thing to explain here is the sense in which this term is a metaphor. There is a technical sense of 'information' in which information is the inverse of uncertainty. A source is said to carry information about a target if knowledge of the source reduces uncertainty about the state of the target. In this sense, the genome is, undoubtedly rich in information. The outcome of human development is, in general outline, stunningly predictable. And if we scramble the genome a bit the outcome will very rapidly become less predictable. The only problem is that in this thin sense of information there is no special sense in which the genome is more a bearer of information than is any other essential developmental resource. As is often remarked, DNA can do nothing without a cell replete with the mass of chemical machinery need for its transcription and translation, and this machinery is as rich in information (in the present sense) as is the DNA.

[12] The critique here has been developed extensively in the context of developmental systems theory. See Susan Oyama, *The Ontogeny of Information* (New York: Cambridge University Press, 1985); Paul Griffiths and Russell Gray, 'Developmental Systems and Evolutionary Explanation', Journal of Philosophy 91 (1994), 277–304.

Of course this also implies that there is this thin sense in which bits of the genome carry information about features of the phenotype, and this will be appealed to when I discuss a very minimal sense in which the concept 'gene' still does useful work. A certain repetitive DNA sequence on human chromosome 4 carries the information that a person is almost certain to suffer the devastating neurological deterioration characteristic of Huntington's disease in middle age, for instance. Similarly, of course, the deposits of fatty material in a person's arteries carries information about the probability of sudden death. It is not obvious what is uniquely information-bearing about genes.

Part of the attraction of the informational view of the genome is that it appeals to a much richer idea of information and suggests a view of the sequence as something quasi-linguistic—linguistic not so much by analogy to the informal everyday languages of human chatter, but to the much more formal instances of the machine languages and programming languages of information technology. This parallel carries with it a certain temptation to abstraction. Though a sequence of machine code requires a machine to implement the programme it contains, it is often suggested that there are indefinitely many possible such machines. All the information is in the sequence and the programme it contains. When distinguished scientists display the rightly celebrated achievement of having determined, more or less, the sequence of nucleotides in the human genome; and when they go on to claim that this contains the blueprint for a human, or all the information necessary to build a human, we naturally think of such parallels from computer science. And naturally, too, we think of the rest of the cell as relatively undistinguished hardware implementing the programme in the genome.

One important move away from this picture is to recall the suggestion that the genome, rather than an abstract string of information, is a concrete material object occupying space.[13] An initial observation that might encourage this perspective is that there is about a 2m length of DNA in the human genome, whereas the cell is about 20 micrometres. This difference of about 8 orders of magnitude requires some fairly serious crunching up (or, technically, condensation) of the DNA. This is increasingly proving relevant to one of the most fundamental issues in molecular

[13] See, for instance, Timothy O'Brien et al., 'Genome Function and Nuclear Architecture: From Gene Expression to Nanoscience', Genome Research (2003), (http://www.genome.org/cgi/doi/10.1101/gr.946403) 1029–41.

biology, what determines which parts of the genome are being transcribed in any particular cell. The common computer analogy may make us think of this in terms of a sequential programme, one piece of transcription following another in a (somehow) predetermined sequence. But this, apart from bringing in an assumption of predetermination that sounds improbable in view of the general ability of organisms to respond to conditions of their environment, seems largely to beg the question of what determines changes in the sequence of activities. A sensible development of the computer metaphor will have changes determined by concentrations of products from previous stages, and this is no doubt an important part of the story. But it is also increasingly clear that part of the relevant mechanism is structural. As the chromosome condenses into more concentrated forms, the accessibility for transcription decreases, and particular parts of the structure become more or less available. More subtly, it is clear that chemicals, for example chemicals that degrade RNA or DNA, cannot be allowed to go just anywhere within the cell, or even the nucleus, and must be restricted to particular locations. Complex structures, membranes, barriers, and mechanisms are gradually being revealed within the cell. The cell is, in short, a highly structured space. It sometimes appears as if the cell is imagined as consisting of a nugget of information floating in a homogeneous chemical soup. In reality, this is as promising as throwing the components of a car into a vat of oil and expecting to drive the resultant mess down the motorway. A speculative thought about the structure of the genome that I won't explore here, is that it disposes of the notion that most of the DNA in most genomes is junk. Clearly large stretches of repetitive sequence, even if they have no coding function, will make a difference to the shape of the molecule and hence, very probably, have some effect on the functioning of the mechanism. Moreover stretches of junk will alter the distance between coding sequences and it is quite possible that this will also have functional consequences. My point here is not, of course, to advocate any such empirical thesis. It is rather to emphasise that the notion of DNA as junk is very much dependent on the picture of DNA as information bearer. From the perspective of DNA as part of a spatially integrated mechanism the metaphor of 'junk' actually makes little sense. And this is, apart from anything else, an excellent illustration of the sometimes unexpected implications of metaphors in this area.

Emphasis on the structural complexity of the genome motivates metaphorical appeals to mechanism rather than information technology. And when one starts to think of the cell as a piece of exceedingly complex and intricate machinery, the question what is so special about the genome arises with new force. A mechanism depends on the interactions between parts, and however ingenious a particular component may seem to be, it is difficult to see how it can have any ontologically special status. It is tempting to argue that it is merely a historical accident, consequent on the fact that it was possible to learn something about genomes long before the techniques were developed for detailed investigation of cellular mechanisms, that leads us to attribute a special significance to the genome.

I do, as a matter of fact, think it is therapeutic to take very seriously the downgrading of the genome that has been proposed by some thinkers (including, on occasion, myself). The genome is part of the cellular mechanism and is entirely devoid of function apart from its meshing with the rest of the cellular machinery. In addition, contrary to what was for a long time known as the 'central dogma' of molecular biology, that information flowed only from DNA to RNA to proteins, it is becoming increasingly clear that the interaction between DNA and the rest of the cell is thoroughly interactive. A successor to the human genome project, the epigenome project, is devoted to the mapping of the sites at which the best understood of the mechanisms of action on the genome, methylation, can act.[14] It is, at any rate, no longer possible to think of DNA as an executive molecule, handing down instructions to its cytological minions. However, it is still worth exploring the intuition that sees something unique about the DNA molecule.

It is sometimes argued that there must be something like DNA for organisms to be possible at all (DNA as the conclusion of a transcendental argument). There are, in fact, two versions of such an argument, the phylogenetic and the ontogenetic. The supposedly necessary features in question are richness of information content, stability, and perhaps a capacity for self-replication. Nothing I have said critical of the unique informational status of DNA should be taken to deny the obvious fact that the DNA molecule is capable of storing enormous quantities of information—and here 'information' can be under-stood in the technical sense of reduction of uncertainty. Each of the three billion bases in the human genome has the potential to make a difference to some developmental process by virtue of its selection from the four possible bases, and hence each base at least in a coding part of the sequence potentially carries information about

[14] For details, see http://www.epigenome.org/index.php

the development of the organism. It is also indisputable that a great deal of information must be deployed in ontogeny. It may well be said that the central problem of biology is the reproduction of form—the ability of organisms to produce descendant organisms of the right kind, and one approach to that problem is to look for the information that guides ontogeny. On the other hand, and this is the point that drives much criticism of overly gene-centred views of development, in principle the necessary information can be dispersed across a variety of locations. In species deploying parental care, most notably our own, a good deal of development may be dependent on this. But more generally, the transmission of an entire cell—the minimum that is physically passed from parent to off-spring—will involve the passing on of a great deal of structure and material in addition to the DNA sequence.

What about stability? It is often noted that DNA is a very stable molecule, especially for one of such high molecular weight, and certainly it is important that a good deal of developmental information is transmitted reliably. Stability of individual molecules may be important, but an even more interesting feature of DNA is its ability to replicate—to produce molecules that are accurate copies of itself. Richard Dawkins has notoriously elided these two properties, describing DNA molecules as achieving, through stability and copying fidelity, immortality. Without worrying too much about immortality, it seems to me implausible that self-replicating parts are a priori required for a replicating whole. One might perhaps imagine a lineage of pieces of paper, which achieve reproduction through photocopiers that copy instructions for the construction, use and maintenance of photocopiers, and distribute these instructions to symbiotic humans. Moreover, complex structures in the cell replicate in cell-division without apparently being composed of self-replicating parts. Nonetheless, there is a very strong intuition that such a molecule is an extremely good idea, an intuition worth some further exploration.

An analogy that seems to me potentially useful here is one that subtly but importantly modifies the standard information metaphor, and that is the idea of data storage. Storage is immediately suggested as a function by the reference to stability: when one stores things one generally hopes that they can be retrieved in a condition very similar to that in which they were put away. (An interesting, but not presently relevant, exception is provided by such things as wine or cheese, that may even come out better than when they went in.) One also stores things while one is not using them. Since most coding sequences are not being actively

John Dupré

transcribed at any time, they may reasonably be seen as in storage, and as just noted, it is to be hoped that they will exhibit a high degree of stability in this condition.

The conception of the genome as the cell's main device for data storage is rather different from most of the contemporary metaphors used for thinking of the function of the genome. First, it should be stressed that what is in question is long-term storage. If we spell out the inevitable parallel with computer technology, we are thinking of the genome as something like a hard disk. The parallel with active memory in a computer (RAM) is rather with RNA or protein molecules. But it will also occur immediately to the listener that programmes as well as data reside on the hard disk. So does the genome contain the developmental programme after all?

Of course the genome doesn't run any such programme, but in this respect there is no disanalogy with the computer. The hard disk stores the programme but doesn't run it. And this points to the important, if trivial, general observation about any programme, that it is always required in addition to a programme that there be a system capable of implementing it. A much more significant disanalogy stems from the phenomena of epigenesis. As noted above, the central dogma, of a one way flow of information from DNA to RNA to protein is increasingly untenable. It is now well-established that other elements in the cell can make permanent or transitory changes to the DNA that affect the likelihood of transcription. Of course it could be that these are instructions originating in programme parts of the DNA and implemented on data storage. But there are more basic reasons for thinking the programme metaphor, if not entirely misguided, is liable to mislead.

For one thing, the metaphor is deeply deterministic. There is little reason to think that development is a deterministic process. Note that this is not to say that development is an unreliable process. Quite the contrary: the process is too reliable in outcome to be plausibly modelled as a predetermined series of steps. This is perfectly familiar and unproblematic in our experience of human action. If I ask someone to go to the shop and buy me a loaf of bread, and they agree, I am fairly confident that the outcome will be as I intend. If I provide a deterministic programme—take 12 paces north-west, raise hand, turn knob, push, etc., there are too many unanticipated interventions that can derail the process for me to have much hope of success. Teleology is much better than deterministic causation at getting things done, and development is much too reliable to be seen as anything but teleological. I don't mean to monger mysteries here, or deny that the 'teleological' process is analysable in terms of a sequence of efficient causes. I am only claiming that the kind of algorithmic sequence of deterministic causes employed by (most) computers is not a plausible model. (No doubt the same can be said for similar models of the brain.)

This point is perhaps more obvious when we reflect that development is a very long process. Indeed human development has no obvious terminus short of death. While it is important that a normal human life-course takes place against a backdrop of species-typical developmental stages—infancy, childhood, puberty, adult-hood, middle age, senescence, etc.—the diversity of the lives that take place within this broad framework is such as to make the notion of a programme strikingly inappropriate. It will no doubt be suggested that if one abstracts the biological dimension of the life course one will find a programme at the common ontogenetic core. Though there is surely something in this, I still consider it more misleading than helpful. First, the length of time over which this programme is alleged to run makes the point that it must be thought of teleologically that much more compelling. But second, I doubt whether it makes sense, certainly for a human life, to abstract the biological from the social, cultural, and merely environmental. (And many non-humans have a social dimension to their lives, all have an environmental dimension.)

Let me summarise what I have suggested about the genome. It is a concrete structure rather than an abstract pattern, and as such it may be seen as part of the mechanism that constitutes the cell. No familiar mechanical metaphor very well characterises the genome, though perhaps that of a data storage device is the most useful. (There is also something important to be said along these lines about the relation between the genome and evolution.) The most accurate general description is perhaps a semi-technical one from theoretical biology, a developmental resource, one of a number of such that is required to solve the problem of organic reproduction. Let me turn, in conclusion, to the question whether this leaves us anything useful to say about genes?

Back to genes

Suppose we think of the genome as a material part of the cell, and as something like a data storage device. Might its parts be genes? The analogy suggests not. The parts of a hard disk are not chunks of data but mechanical components. Similarly the genome

John Dupré

certainly has structural parts—chromosomes, and within those, such things as centromeres and telomeres. Anyone tempted to believe that, say, my latest Kylie Minogue album was part of my hard disk need only be reminded that the relevant electronic data are likely to be scattered around different parts of the disk, an observation interestingly parallel with the distribution of the code required to make proteins around the genome. If someone claimed that they might just be spatially distributed parts, I would then point out that the same chunks of data on the same bit of disk might be parts of many different files, here reminding us both of the IT equivalent of pleiotropy and the lamentable ease of contemporary plagiarism.

Might the gene concept nevertheless prove to be useful in characterising information, in the sense simply of significant sequence, in the genome? The first thing to say is that this is in the end a question for genomic scientists rather than philosophers. Having said that, my impression is that the useful concepts for this task are likely to be at a lower level and more specific. The project of counting genes seems doomed to incoherence and this speaks unpromisingly for the future of the concept. The second thing to say, or to repeat, is that if such a concept does prove useful, it will prove incommensurable with the entire tradition of thinking of genes in relation to their phenotypic consequences. This does, at the least, present severe dangers of misunderstanding.

What residuum is there of the traditional concept? The first point here is that, in keeping with its Mendelian roots, it is a concept that applies only to the explanation of difference. It was a natural hope, perhaps, that the explanation of differences would have provided a path towards the general explanation of developmental outcomes, but this has not been the case. In the sense in which there is a gene for brown eyes there are no genes for eyes, tout court, because everyone has them. Those parts of the genomes in which variation is not permitted, that is, those in which it causes inviability, contain no genes. Clearly this is something that can be made no sense of within anything remotely related to the blueprint conception of the genome, and again there are obvious dangers of misunderstanding as this usage of the word 'gene' disseminates to the general public.

The irreconcilable tension between the molecular and the Mendelian rumps of the gene concept suggest that we would do well to canvass for the abolition of the word altogether. However there are contexts in which the Mendelian concept still lives a more active life, which we may have to respect. The first of these is in evolutionary theory. Since most evolutionary theory is focused on natural selection, and selection, by definition, is concerned only with differences, it is not surprising that evolutionists have generally found the Mendelian concept admirably suited to their needs. I think, as a matter of fact, that this has led to very serious problems as evolutionists have at the same time failed to take adequate account of the limitations of developmental interpretations of genetics. But this is something I have discussed at length in other places and will not go into here.

More relevant to present concerns is the case of medical genetics. Without wishing to speculate on the likely future achievements of this growing branch of medicine, it would be careless, at least, to legislate it out of a subject matter. And indeed it surely has a perfectly good subject matter: familiar and often devastating diseases such as cystic fibrosis and Huntington's are maladies directly caused by genes, and genes about which we often have detailed knowledge. We should at least be able to make sense of this kind of knowledge.

This is not, in fact, particularly difficult. Classic monogenetic diseases are diseases caused by errors in the genome. Typically this is the failure to make a functional protein due to an error in the DNA sequence. Unlike text, small errors can be fatal in DNA transcription and translation—one deleted base, for instance, will shift the whole reading frame to nonsense. 'Genes' for such diseases are, therefore, a set of possible errors in a particular area of the genome that produces a particular developmental or metabolic failure and a characteristic syndrome of symptoms. This is all quite unmysterious if tragic. Just two simple points should be stressed. First there is no specific physical structure that is, say, the gene for cystic fibrosis. Almost any disease gene will be a set of possible errors rather than a particular sequence. It is, perhaps, best seen as an abstract object. Second, a genetic disease implies no phenotypic characterisation of the normal, healthy state of that piece of the genome. It is part of the genome that contains information needed for building a protein, and the lack of the protein causes disease. One could, technically, I suppose, say that this was the gene for not having cystic fibrosis, but to do so would be, to say the least, misleading. If the subject matter of medical genetics turns out to be a set of abstract characterisations of some sites in the genome, it hardly looks likely to legitimate a general reinstatement of the phenotypic characterisation of genes. The dangers here, incidentally, are well illustrated by the widespread tendency to use genetic diseases such as phenylketonuria, which have serious effects on mental development, as evidence for the importance of behavioural genetics. I hope it is clear that this provides no such evidence.

Conclusion

The history of the term 'gene' has seen the increasing erosion of the assumptions with which its use has often been associated. This has led to a set of rather poorly defined and perhaps unnecessary uses in molecular genetics that reflect the contemporary understanding of the phenomena out of which the tradition of genetics arose, and a fringe of uses in such areas as evolutionary theory and medical genetics, essentially similar to traditional meanings but liable to carry strongly misleading implications to the unwary.

The concept is a wonderfully rich source of potential insight into the historical development of scientific concepts, and into the processes by which such concepts travel from one technical context to another and disseminate into public discourse. The present paper is intended to provide an introductory survey of some of the issues that arise within these projects.

Folk Psychology and the Biological Basis of Intersubjectivity

MATTHEW RATCLIFFE

1. The Usual Story

Recent philosophical discussions of intersubjectivity generally start by stating or assuming that our ability to understand and interact with others is enabled by a 'folk psychology' or 'theory of mind'. Folk psychology is characterized as the ability to attribute intentional states, such as beliefs and desires, to others, in order to predict and explain their behaviour. Many authors claim that this ability is not merely one amongst many constituents of interpersonal understanding but an underlying core that enables social life. For example, Churchland states that folk psychology 'embodies our baseline understanding' of others (1996, p. 3). Currie and Sterelny similarly assert that 'our basic grip on the social world depends on our being able to see our fellows as motivated by beliefs and desires we sometimes share and sometimes do not' (2000, p. 143). And, as Frith and Happé put it, 'this ability appears to be a prerequisite for normal social interaction: in everyday life we make sense of each other's behaviour by appeal to a belief-desire psychology' (1999, p. 2).

As there is general consensus concerning what folk psychology *is*, the focus of recent debates has been on *how* it is accomplished. 'Theory-theorists' claim that the term 'theory of mind' should be taken literally. Attribution of intentional states is enabled by a largely tacit, systematically organized body of knowledge concerning intentional states and their relations. 'Simulation-theorists', in contrast, maintain that our understanding of others depends upon a practical ability as opposed to an organized body of knowledge. Given the plausible assumption that most people have a similar psychological structure, the possibility arises of using one's own mental states and processes as a model for others, predicting what they would do by putting oneself in their situation or psychological predicament. Many different positions are encompassed by these two general approaches and others borrow elements from both[1].

[1] See Carruthers and Smith (eds.) (1996) and Davies and Stone (eds.) (1995a, 1995b) for various theory, simulation and hybrid approaches.

211

Matthew Ratcliffe

Questions also arise concerning the biological basis, development and evolutionary origin of folk psychology. Both theory and simulation accounts tend to maintain that folk psychology is 'modular', meaning that it is tailored to the solution of specific kinds of environmental problems and functions in a manner that is largely autonomous of other cognitive abilities. As Sperber and Wilson put it:

> Most theories of mind-reading [...] assume that it is performed not by a general purpose reasoning mechanism, which takes as premises a number of explicit hypotheses about the relationships between behaviour and mental states, but by a dedicated module. (2002, p. 10)

Modular accounts are closely associated with the view that folk psychology is an innate biological adaptation, which arose as a response to selection pressures favouring certain social abilities. As Carruthers puts it, 'there seems little doubt that our mind-reading (or "theory of mind") faculty has evolved and been selected for' (2000, p. 267). Others have suggested that folk psychology, despite having an innate, modular *basis*, also affords various developmental possibilities (Scholl and Leslie, 1999). But commitment to a substantial innate component is not universal. For example, Garfield, Peterson and Perry place more emphasis on developmental processes and claim that folk psychology is supported by an 'acquired module' (2000, p. 502), which forms through interaction between innate capacities and social environments. And Gopnik (e.g. 1996) plays down innate abilities even further, suggesting that folk psychology develops in a manner analogous to scientific theories. However, if, as in most accounts, a substantial innate component is postulated, there is the question of which selection pressures influenced its development. The 'core' of folk psychology is claimed to involve an ability to recognize that another's beliefs, desires and intentions differ from one's own. One context in which such an understanding could be put to use is in manipulating/deceiving others or being receptive to the possibility of their manipulating/deceiving you. Hence folk psychology is complemented by the 'Machiavellian intelligence' hypothesis (e.g. Byrne and Whiten, 1988), according to which a primary selection pressure driving human brain development was strategic interaction, with social competition leading to increasingly sophisticated mechanisms for mentalistic interpretation.

So, in summary, although there are many disagreements, almost all accounts accept (1), (2) and (3) below and many also accept (4) and (5):

Folk Psychology and the Biological Basis of Intersubjectivity

1. Social understanding and interaction are enabled by a 'folk psychology', whose 'core' is the ability to attribute intentional states to others in order to predict and explain behaviour.
2. Folk psychological abilities are facilitated by a largely tacit theory, an ability to simulate or a combination of the two.
3. Folk psychology has a modular basis.
4. Folk psychology is largely innate.
5. Folk psychology is an adaptation for strategic social interaction.

My focus here will be on (1). Accounts of how folk psychology is facilitated, how it developed and how it evolved all presuppose an understanding of what folk psychology *is*. Hence, if (1) turns out to be mistaken or substantially incomplete, it is likely (2), (3), (4) and (5) will also have to be abandoned or significantly revised.

Despite near universal acceptance of (1)[2], it is not at all clear how the claim that 'understanding others consists in the attribution of intentional states in order to predict and explain behaviour' (hereafter FP) is arrived at. FP is, by definition, 'commonsense' psychology. So, although much of its underlying structure may be tacit and only accessible through scientific study, some part of it must be evident in everyday commonsense. However, if one were to ask a variety of people on the street what their understanding of others consists of, it is doubtful that one would get FP or anything like it as a consistent response. Hence FP is something that philosophers and others claim to discover *in* commonsense, rather than something that is readily apparent *to* commonsense. The question thus arises as to whether it is indeed something internal to individuals, which is discovered, or whether it is an external systematisation, imposed by philosophers (Stich and Ravenscroft, 1996). In other words, is FP how we do think about others or is it just a way that some people think about how we think about others? If the latter is so, searching for underlying FP abilities or contemplating their origins and development would be misguided.

I will suggest that, although FP is generally regarded as an ability possessed by individuals, it is actually an abstraction from a much richer context of social understanding and interaction, which has no psychological reality as an autonomous ability. This abstraction has its source in an over-intellectualisation of social life. FP assumes that, in understanding others, we *observe* their behaviour and

---

[2] An exception is Gordon (e.g. 1996), who claims that an understanding of intentional states is generated by more fundamental intersubjective abilities.

employ some internal cognitive process in order to *postulate* intentional states as internal regulators of that behaviour. Hobson (1993a) and Gallagher (2001) both point out that the assumptions of detached observation and postulation emphasize the first- to third-person stance, where one looks upon another as a 'he', 'she' or 'it' and contemplates them from a distance. The 'first- to second-person' stance, through which another is encountered as 'you' is very different. In an 'I-you' scenario, one is engaged in complex interactions with others and the cognitive structure of interaction may be very different to that of non-participant observation.

Of course, one might claim that interaction involves exactly the same cognitive processes as observation, regardless of phenomenological differences. However, many practical activities are quite clearly not just a matter of applying internal cognitive abilities in an engaged, rather than observational, context. Clark gives the example of a jigsaw puzzle:

> Completing a jigsaw puzzle [...] involves an intricate and iterated dance in which 'pure thought' leads to actions which in turn change or simplify the problems confronting 'pure thought'. (1997, p. 36)

The ability to complete the puzzle is inextricable from one's ability to move and reposition the pieces, to perceive the results and further manipulate them. It is not that some internal capacity is *manifested* through interaction with an environment. The ability to complete the puzzle is indissociable from an ability to interact with and reconfigure the environment. One acts to reshape the environment and receives perceptual feedback, which changes the nature of the problem faced. Now compare completing a jigsaw to interacting with other people. Feedback from others in a social situation is far more complex than that gained from one's manipulation of an inert environment. There is intricate interaction of word, gesture, action, expression, gaze and tone. In what follows, I will argue that such interactions constitute a framework for interpersonal understanding. The ability to understand others is generated through one's interactions with them, rather than through internal capacities that are deployed upon others in contexts of interaction. I will start by focusing on the affective dimension of interaction and suggest that an affective, perceptual, practical grasp of others is central to interpersonal understanding. Furthermore, it does much of the work that postulation of internal states underlying behaviour is claimed to do. This might suggest that FP is an incomplete rather than mistaken account of human social ability. However, I will go on to argue that an understanding of intentional states is inextricable from contexts of interaction. Thus FP misinterprets the structure of intersubjectivity, construing an essentially practical, self-engaging process as detached and observational. I will conclude that intersubjectivity is consequently not founded on a domain-specific module in the brain but on a plethora of abilities.

2. Sartre on Intersubjectivity

In order to claim that FP inadequately describes commonsense interpersonal understanding, one cannot appeal to scientific studies of subpersonal processes, given that such things are not part of commonsense. However, one cannot simply ask people on the street either, given that much of commonsense is weakly tacit (by which I mean that it is ordinarily implicit but can, in principle, be made explicit). In my view, a good place to start is phenomenology, given that a goal of phenomenology is to make explicit the ordinarily taken for granted structure of experience. In this section, I will look at Sartre's phenomenological account of intersubjectivity or 'Being-for-others' in his *Being and Nothingness*. In so doing, my aim is not to provide a comprehensive summary or critique of Sartre's position but to draw from his phenomenological descriptions the view that our primary sense of others is perceptual, affective and interactive. Having done so, I will turn to sources other than phenomenology in order to support and elaborate this view.

Sartre employs the example of 'shame' to illustrate how others are encountered as *others*, as opposed to inanimate entities. For example, one can be peeping through a keyhole, spying on someone else's private pastimes (p. 259). One hears a step on the stair behind and is suddenly aware of being looked upon by another. This awareness of another's presence does not take the form of a detached inference but of a self-altering feeling. Sartre describes the phenomenology of shame as follows:

> I have just made an awkward or vulgar gesture. This gesture clings to me; I neither judge it nor blame it. I simply live it. [...] But now suddenly I raise my head. Somebody was there and has seen me. Suddenly I realize the vulgarity of my gesture, and I am ashamed. (p. 221)

It is clear that what Sartre calls 'shame' is a kind of affective response. It is 'an immediate shudder which runs through me from head to foot without any discursive preparation' (p. 222).

Matthew Ratcliffe

Registering the presence of another incorporates a change in one's own orientation towards the world, a *feeling* of being scrutinized that breaks up the coherence of one's prior concerns. The project of spying, in which one was previously absorbed, disintegrates. One is no longer a locus of practical projects but an entity that stands before somebody else, an object that is situated in the context of their projects. This affective re-orientation does not just accompany or facilitate the experience of another. It *is* itself one's sense of 'the Other'. Sartre does not construe affective transformation of oneself before the other as a one-off event but as a dynamic process of interaction, whereby self and other engage in a play of mutual objectification. A dance of changing affect first renders one an object before the other and then the other an object before oneself. So the experience of others involves mutual transformation. One is essentially *engaged* in this, rather than standing back as a detached onlooker. And this direct, perceptual, affective apprehension is more basic than any theoretical or detached understanding that one might also employ: 'The Other is present to me without any intermediary as a transcendence which is not mine' (p. 270).

Sartre claims that the feeling of shame has its source in 'the look' of the other, which directly elicits an affective response. By 'the look', he means something more abstract than a pair of eyes gazing at one:

> Of course, what *most often* manifests a look is the convergence of two ocular globes in my direction. But the look will be given just as well on occasion where there is a rustling in the branches, or the sound of a footstep followed by silence, or the slight opening of a shutter, or a light movement of a curtain. (p. 257)

Hence 'the look' is not something in the world with a physically identifiable structure. But surely if a 'rustling in the branches' can do it, some kind of cognitive process is required in order to infer the presence of another from an inanimate stimulus? Sartre claims that our most basic sense of the presence of others arises in a context of bodily interaction and it is clear that he thinks this, at least, requires no such inference. The other is directly apprehended, not just through her gaze, but in an affect-laden perception of her dynamic body: 'The Other is originally given to me as a *body in situation*' (p. 344). However, this is not to suggest that a 'mere body' is apprehended and mental states are then postulated as the causes of bodily movements. One perceives the other's body *as* a locus of experiences and projects. This perception is inextricable from an

216

affective transformation of one's own body, which one suddenly becomes aware of as a thing before the other. Hence 'the original bond with the Other', on which the objectifying interplay between self and other is based, 'first arises in connection with the relation between my body and the Other's body' (p. 361).

Sartre's depiction of Being-for-others emphasizes an irresolvable tension in interpersonal interaction. Both are locked in an objectifying dynamic; one objectifies the other or is objectified by the other. However, one might suggest that this is at best a description of certain pathological relationships and fails to capture the openness towards another that characterizes a loving relationship, for example. The claim that such relations take the form of one party objectifying the other is, at the very least, phenomenologically implausible. However, I do think that Sartre's discussion makes salient some important characteristics common to the phenomenology of all interpersonal interaction. We can reject the Sartrean emphasis on conflictual relations and build on the following insights into the structure of interpersonal experience and interaction:

1. Our sense of others as *others* is perceptual and phenomenologically direct.
2. We perceive others as animate beings, rather than as moving bodies with underlying mental states.
3. Perception of others incorporates changes in one's self-perception. It is not detached but self-engaging and dynamic.
4. Perception of others is essentially affective. One registers others through the way in which they induce affective changes in oneself.

If the above are indeed aspects of our everyday experience, then an appreciation of others is, in some respects at least, affective, practical, perceptual and direct, as opposed to detached, observational and indirect. Hence, if FP claims to comprehensively describe our everyday apprehension of others as *others*, it misinterprets a practical dynamic in terms of detached observation. However, our FP advocate could reply that FP *underlies* the affective transformations that Sartre describes. X is ashamed before Y because X believes that Y believes that spying is wrong; X also believes that spying is wrong; X believes that Y has seen X and so forth. Hence what looks like affect-laden perception is, upon reflection, supported by abilities to attribute various internal mental states. But the question arises as to why we *should* reinterpret the experience in these terms, even if we *can*. One reason to resist such a move is that complex affective engagement with others appears to be evident in very young infants, who do not have full-blown FP abilities. Indeed some descriptions of early infant-parent interactions incorporate insights I have drawn from Sartre's description of adult phenomenology, but without Sartre's narrow emphasis on conflict.

3. Affective Interaction

It is well established that very young infants respond to emotional expressions and gestures with attention, gaze, expression and sometimes imitation. Hobson (1993a, b; 2002) appeals to numerous studies of autistic and normal children of various ages to make the stronger claim that infant-parent interactions constitute a kind of proto-dialogue, which is enabled by mutual *perception* of affect in expression, during structured interaction. He suggests that, although young infants are unable to conceptualize intentional states, they display 'capacities to *perceive* a range of overt, bodily-expressed attitudes in other people' (1993a, p. 103). Interactions do not always take the form of simple 'perception-response' exchanges. They can be complex, structured patterns, which involve distinguishable stages such as initiation, mutual orientation, greeting, play dialogue and, finally, affective disengagement (2002, p. 35). Hobson claims that early interaction involves neither 'behaviour-reading' nor 'mind-reading' on the part of the infant. One need not *infer* meaning from behaviour. One apprehends it *in* the behaviour. Infants have 'direct perception of and natural engagement with person-related meanings that are apprehended in the expressions and behaviour of others' (1993a, p. 117). Others' expressions and gestures are *perceived* to be meaningful, through the affective responses they elicit. He argues that early interpersonal abilities do not depend on an infant's internal capacities, operating without the aid of interaction. They involve a mutual receptivity that is partly constituted by and grows through affective, bodily interaction: 'It is not the case that to begin with, behaviour is perceived in a cool, detached way' (1993b, p. 214). The structure of interpersonal understanding is instead a matter of 'relations'. Parent and child together configure a framework for their exchanges, through perception of gesture, expression and affect, and affective, expressive and gestural response. Interaction with others is thus inextricable from an infant's developing ability to understand them.

Folk Psychology and the Biological Basis of Intersubjectivity

Gallagher (2001) takes such developmental claims a step further, arguing that these early abilities are not only developmentally prior to FP but remain the primary means of interpersonal understanding in adults. A perceptual and affective appreciation of others, arising through our interaction with them, is all we require in many social scenarios. There is usually no additional need to posit underlying internal states. Gallagher suggests that most interpersonal understanding incorporates an 'I-you', rather than an 'I-she' structure. It is an 'embodied practice', rather than something that incorporates an objective, detached, intellectualized stance towards them:

> ... in most intersubjective situations we have a direct, pragmatic understanding of another person's intentions because their intentions are explicitly expressed in their embodied actions. (2001, p. 86)

I think Gallagher is right to emphasize the importance of perceptual-affective factors in adult interpersonal interactions. A good way in which to make something explicit is to look at those cases where it breaks down. And this is, I suggest, the case here. For example, Cole (1998; 2001) addresses the contribution made by facial expression and its perception to interpersonal interaction, by exploring cases where the ability to express oneself facially or to perceive facial expressions is impaired or absent. Personal interactions ordinarily involve an intricate interplay of perception of expression and expressive response. Breakdowns of this interaction are evident in those with various facial problems, such as Möbius syndrome, a form of facial paralysis. As Cole observes, 'those with facial differences describe a loss of social relatedness leading to profound social isolation and to an impoverished sense of self' (2001, p. 478). One's ability to interpret others is substantially diminished by a breakdown of normal interaction. And one's own sense of self is altered by the absence of those reciprocal gestures and expressions by which one is ordinarily affected. Cole describes one subject with facial paralysis as follows:

> ... without the feedback and reinforcement between people that facial gestures provide, there was little relatedness and engagement. Her loss of facial responsiveness made her feel somehow invalidated at her very core. (1998, p. 10)

Such cases make salient the way in which an interplay of affect and expression structures interpersonal understanding; one's perception of another's expression incorporates an affective

219

response, which is often manifested in one's own expressions. Others respond to this and so forth. Expressions are not best interpreted from a detached, observational standpoint but through the way in which they are modified in response to one's own expressions and gestures. This interplay constitutes an openness or receptivity to each other; a dynamic framework within which the task of mutual understanding is played out. We do not have to appeal to clinical cases in order to appreciate this. Most people have had the experience of a conversation where one feels detached from the other participant, as though one has somehow failed to make contact. The dance of expression, gesture and eye contact fails to flow, the conversation breaks down and one *feels* a failure to 'connect'. Breakdowns of mutual understanding need not take the form of an inability to infer the relevant intentional states. They more often involve a *feeling* of distance, an absence of the to-and-fro of expression and gesture that constitutes a harmonious back-drop for mutual understanding. Hobson notes that such feelings of detachment can be especially pronounced when interacting with autistic people:

> A person can *feel* that there is something missing when relating to someone who is autistic—it is as if one is in the presence of a changeling, someone from a different world—but this escapes the net of scientific methods. (2002, p. 49)

So why not admit that understanding others centrally incorporates perception of expression, gesture and feeling in contexts of interaction? One move would be to suggest that it is simply not possible to *perceive* the meaning of a gesture or expression; one can only perceive surface behaviour. However, this is certainly not an a priori truth and some recent findings in neurophysiology indicate that we may indeed have perceptual access to the meaning of certain expressions and gestures, and, more generally, to the teleological structure of action. I am referring to the discovery of mirror neurons in the mid 1990s. These are cells that discharge when one performs a certain kind of action and also discharge when one observes a conspecific performing a similar action. They were first found in the ventral premotor cortex of monkeys and have since been found in other cortical areas. There is also strong evidence of a more widespread mirror system in humans. In monkeys, mirror neurons are responsive to various kinds of hand actions, such as grasping, holding, tearing or manipulating. They do not discharge when the target object alone is presented or when an action is mimicked in the absence of a target object. Two different classes of mirror neuron have been identified. Strictly congruent neurons fire when one performs a specific action and also when a conspecific performs the same action in the same way. However, broadly congruent neurons are not sensitive to the precise manner in which the action is carried out but to the goal of the action. In other words, they are receptive to the teleological structure of action, rather than to similarity of movement. There are also broadly congruent neurons, which are sensitive to sequential actions, such as when an experimenter places food on a tray and when the monkey grabs it[3]. In humans, there is further evidence for gaze-sensitive mirror neurons (Fogassi and Gallese, 2002), in addition to cells sensitive to gesture and posture (Rotondo and Boker, 2002). Studdert-Kennedy (2002) hypothesizes that we also have a specialized mirror system for perceiving and imitating facial expressions. Hence the human mirror system may turn out to be more complex and differentiated than that of the monkey.

These findings have been taken by some to indicate that we are able to perceive much of the structure of action, rather than infer it from behaviour. In observing X perform action A, parts of one's own motor system are activated in the same way that they would be if one were to perform action A. Perception is structured by a proprioceptive mirroring that facilitates a perceptual awareness of agency:

> ... when 'reading the mind' of conspecifics whose actions we are observing, we rely *also*, if not mostly, on a series of explicit behavioral signals, that we can detect from their observed behavior. These signals may be *intrinsically meaningful* to the extent that they enable the activation of equivalent inner representations on the observer/mind-attributer's side. (Fogassi and Gallese, 2002, p. 30)

Gallese and Goldman suggest that the existence of a mirror system constitutes support for a simulation theory of FP, given that mirror neurons could be a precursor to and constituent of the ability to get oneself in the same 'mental shoes' as a target (1998, pp. 497–8). However, Gallagher points out that such an interpretation is not supported by the evidence. The motor system is activated *during* perception and 'there is no extra step involved that could count as a simulation routine' (2001, p. 102). One *perceives* the agency of others through a proprioceptive sense of one's own motor readiness,

---

[3] See Fogassi and Gallese (2002) and Rizzolatti, Craighero and Fadiga (2002) for discussion of all these findings.

rather than by perceiving behaviour and *then* employing an ability to simulate in order to interpret that behaviour as action.

Regardless of whether such interpretations of the nature and role of the mirror system receive further experimental support, they remain significant for current purposes, in showing how self-engaging perception of agency, gesture and expression is an empirical possibility and not something to be dismissed on the basis of a priori cognitive implausibility. So it is not at all clear why this phenomenologically pervasive aspect of interpersonal understanding and interaction should be re-interpreted in FP terms. Scrutiny of commonsense suggests otherwise and scientific findings show how what seems to be perceptual, direct and self-engaging might well be precisely that[4].

If we acknowledge that our understanding of others incorporates a kind of affective responsiveness, which is employed most effectively through contexts of interaction, emphasis on a circumscribed 'intersubjectivity' device or module starts to look misleading. A plethora of variably connected abilities play a role in affective interaction. These include expressing oneself facially and responding to facial expressions, responding to gaze, initiating and responding to gestures, and co-ordinating a variety of affective states. None of these is a peripheral accompaniment to some under-lying core and they do not together constitute a single device. We encounter others as whole organisms and with our whole organism. Intersubjectivity is not a single, discrete skill.

One could respond by conceding that FP is not all-encompassing; it is not a magic box from which *all* other interpersonal abilities spring but it does play a substantial role in interpersonal understanding, which cannot be wholly replaced by an account of perception of feeling in contexts of interaction. In the next section, I will argue that this too should be rejected. FP is not a separable component of intersubjectivity but something that has been abstracted from a broader framework of social interaction and misinterpreted.

---

[4] It is worth raising a note of caution here. That the mirror system facilitates perception of action does not imply that it also facilitates perception of feeling. For example, Hobson (2002, p. 56) discusses experiments which suggest that autistic people can understand the actions of others whilst failing to comprehend their emotions. However, if we have a proprioceptive awareness of others' action, gesture and expression, it is surely possible, and indeed likely, that this also applies to the perception of affect. After all, the 'mirror system' is unlikely to be a single, unified structure.

4. A Scaffold for Thought

In this section, I will suggest that linguistic exchanges between people are intricately connected with the kind of affective interaction sketched above. The nature and role/s of intentional talk can only be appreciated when considered as part of this rich context of verbal and non-verbal interaction. Thus FP is not a discrete ability but an abstraction from the realities of social life.

Brief reflection is enough to reveal that everyday face-to-face conversations are sculpted by a subtle, harmonious interplay of feeling, gesture, expression and action. For example, if one is met by a smile and or by an extension of one's previous comment, one may develop that comment further. One understands, through her smile, that another has understood and sympathized. The construction of conversational narratives is not simply a matter of having the capacity to infer intentional states and respond accordingly. It incorporates a background of affective and perceptual interaction, which serves to constrain and direct the mutually constructed narrative. The centrality of this kind of interactive narrative construction to interpersonal understanding is made salient by Bruner and Feldman (1993), who argue that the primary deficit involved in autism is not, as is often maintained, an impairment of FP, construed as a detached ability to attribute internal states. It is instead a failure to fully participate in the narratives that are ordinarily formed through interpersonal interaction. In linguistic interactions, autistic subjects fail to extend a previous speaker's comment or grasp 'where it is "going"' and their ability to tell coherent stories is impaired (p. 274). Bruner and Feldman also recognize that affect ordinarily plays a central role in narrative interaction. As they tellingly note:

> Although all but one of the subjects manifestly enjoyed having the conversations, the interviewer felt she had failed. In spite of the appearance of so much talk, she nevertheless *felt* that she had been unable to make contact[5]. (p. 277)

The interactive structure of face-to-face linguistic exchanges and their inextricability from an intricate dance of expression and gesture further diminishes the role of FP. In 'I-you' interaction, others are interpreted within a mutually created context, which massively constrains interpretation. Both parties' understanding of each other is progressively shaped and focused by an evolving

[5] My italics.

narrative, whose development is supported by interaction of gesture, movement, expression and tone. One does not need to predict what another will say, think or do from a neutral, detached perspective or assign internal states by *observing* behaviour. A shared context is constructed through *interaction* and it is within this context that one interprets. Interpretations are supported, shaped or rejected through interaction, through a frown, a laugh or a grimace. In order to understand another, one does not 'read' from afar; one acts, gestures, smiles, speaks and responds. Understanding others is a multi-faceted process, in which others' activities partly constitute the structures through which one understands them[6]. It is not a matter of detached observation of behaviour or deployment of a pre-given internal capacity. One actively investigates with word, gesture and expression. One creates the structures of interpersonal understanding through engagement.

It might be objected that such significant contextual constraints only apply to one-to-one interactions, whereas many other social encounters involve brief exchanges or prediction and explanation on the basis of observation. After all, I have focused throughout on 'I-you' interaction. But we often do understand others by observing them. Surely FP plays a significant role in such cases? Furthermore, what about exchanges of letters and e-mails, or telephone conversations, where much of the structure of face-to-face interaction is absent?

In order to placate such concerns, it should be acknowledged that interactions between two people A and B are not exclusively responsible for constraining their understanding of each other. Interpersonal exchanges do not take place in a desert but within a broader context of shared practices. This is the case from a very early age. For example, Hobson (2002, Chapter 2) notes that early adult-child interactions often involve structured play or games, where interaction is progressively constrained by established patterns of exchange and performance. These patterns are accepted by both as a background for more intricate and complex exchanges.

It is clear that not all such patterns are *created* through the interaction of parent and child. The parent already inhabits an intricate cultural framework of standardized practices and agreed patterns of interaction. Some of these are linguistically expressible and may indeed have been learned via linguistic communication. Others will involve forms of practical know-how that have never

[6] Morton (2003) discusses at length the extent to which interpersonal understanding involves responding to others in such a way as to make oneself intelligible to them.

been put into words. All may have originated through affective interaction between people. However, they now form a context within which interpersonal interpretation takes place, a background of institutions, prescriptive narratives, social roles, artefact roles and accepted ways of doing things. So the infant not only helps create standardized patterns of interaction but is also tuned into them through its interactions. This shared cultural context serves to constrain *all* personal interpretation. As Bruner puts it:

> ... human-beings, in interacting with one another, form a sense of the canonical and ordinary as a background against which to interpret and give narrative meaning to breaches in and deviations from 'normal' states of the human condition. (1990, p. 67)

In most circumstances, much of the interpretive work is done by shared context. It is ordinarily a presupposition of interpretation that we share many of the same practices and 'canonical narratives', which tell us 'what one does', 'what should be done'. 'what is to be done with artefacts of type X', or 'what those with social role Y are expected to do' in given situations. Hence first- to third-person interpretation does not require assigning internal mental states from some detached standpoint. A shared cultural context of established practices can do most of the work. Indeed, explanations are often take forms such as 'If X has social role M and is in Situation A, X will do what one does if one is an M in Situation A'. Such explanations do not involve the assignment of internal states but an understanding of normative practices and prescriptive narratives. Furthermore, one can still rely on perceptual/affective engagement in first- to third-person cases. One need not interact with someone in a complex fashion in order to be moved by her gesture and respond to her expressions.

What about those first- to second-person interactions, such as telephone and e-mail, where one is deprived, to various degrees, of gestural and expressive interaction? These need not be described in terms of an ability to infer internal mental states on the basis of observed evidence. They will still incorporate some degree of affective engagement and when such exchanges involve genuine personal understanding, rather than mere information exchange or pre-scripted professional performances, they tend to rely heavily on already established contexts of interaction. For example, when intricate narratives are constructed via telephone, conversations are ordinarily between friends or those who share a fairly specific set of interests and practices. In such cases, the 'rules of engagement' come largely pre-formed, so that both parties are already predictable to each other. The same goes for prolonged e-mail exchanges. The lengthy and elaborate first- to second-person exchanges between strangers, which (I'm told) take place in Internet chat rooms, are substantially constrained by shared practices, interests and codes of conduct. They may also involve the development of new practices and rules of engagement, suited to that particular medium of engagement. Furthermore, whether a 'chat room' facilitates fully enriched interpersonal understanding is debatable. Perhaps part of the appeal of such things is the mystery and unpredictability of the respondent.

But when are intentional states assigned? Bruner suggests that FP is employed in a way that is inextricable from participation in practices. Most of the time, people will do what is expected. It is only when things deviate from the norms of shared practices that an FP narrative is constructed:

> *The function of the story is to find an intentional state that mitigates or at least makes comprehensible a deviation from a canonical cultural pattern.* (1990, pp. 49–50).

Hence the assignment of intentional states is not something that we need do all the time in order to explain or predict the internal workings and behaviour of others. It is an occasional activity, whose purpose is to describe a person's unexpected actions in such a way that they make sense, given a shared background of practices and ways of doing things. It is part of a richer context of interpersonal understanding, a story told to make sense of apparently deviant activities by showing or trying to show how they accord with shared cultural frameworks through which we (or others) live[7].

Bruner's account of FP's role is of course debatable. Indeed, it is arguable that belief-talk plays a multiplicity of different roles in everyday social life. Morton (2003, Chapter 3) goes so far as to suggest that our commonsense psychology does not even incorporate a unitary conception of 'belief'. Different senses of the term may be at play in different contexts. But regardless of precisely how or when such talk is employed, it is clear that intentional state assignment is not an ever-present core underlying all interpersonal understanding and interaction. Even if some

---

[7] Goldie makes a complementary point with respect to emotion, observing that our understanding of emotions has a narrative structure; 'our thought and talk of emotions is embedded in an interpretive (and sometimes predictive) narrative which aims to make sense of an aspect of someone's life' (2000, p. 103).

belief-talk does involve postulating internal intentional states (for some purpose or other, whose nature will need to be clarified), it is clear that the ability to do so is inextricable from a much broader collage of abilities. Assignments are massively constrained by shared cultural context. They are also aided considerably by affective response, and perception of action and gesture, most often a context of interaction. Thus FP, construed as a *discrete* ability to attribute internal states from a detached observational standpoint, is a misleading abstraction from social life. It misrepresents one part of a multi-faceted process, where interaction with others and participation in a culture are constitutive of interpersonal understanding, as a detached, observational, internal ability to assign internal states to others. It then proceeds to claim that this distorted fragment underlies everything else.

5. The False Belief Task in Context

Much of the support for a domain-specific, discrete ability to assign intentional states to others is drawn from the many variations of Wimmer and Perner's (1983) False Belief Task (FBT). These tasks involve setting up a situation and asking a question about it, the answer to which requires a child to recognize that another person possesses a belief that differs from her own (true) belief. FBTs are often taken as evidence for a domain-specific ability, which arises at around four to five years of age and enables the attribution of internal mental states. However, I suggest that they indicate no such thing and cohere equally well, if not better, with the idea that an understanding of intentional states is embedded in broader contexts of interaction.

It is interesting to note that much younger children appear to display a grasp of epistemic differences between people, when in more familiar contexts of interaction. Papafragou (2002) notes that two-year-old infants will modify their requests for a hidden object, depending on whether or not an adult in the room has seen it or not. And Bloom and German observe that three-year-olds often pass more 'pragmatically natural' variants of the FBT, with simpler or more specific questions (2000, p. 27), adding that two-year-olds participate in pretend play, understand pretences, assign goals and imitate intended or completed actions.

If, as such findings suggest, an ability to understand others is bound up with interaction in a shared social context, the FBT is an inappropriate test of that ability. Most variants of the task involve decontextualized observation and hence strip away structures of interaction that are, I have suggested, constitutive of understanding. Indeed, it is arguable that the very design of the task and the importance ascribed to it simply presupposes that a detached ability to assign intentional states is central to interpersonal understanding. For example, Lord (1993) remarks that autism involves deficits in gaze, gesture, and verbal and nonverbal communication. Thus it does not appear to be a specific cognitive deficit. Despite this, an impaired ability to perform on FBTs is often taken not just to confirm the presence of autism but to exemplify the central underlying deficit (impaired FP). Lord indicates that this may amount to a self-fulfilling prophesy:

> It is not surprising that cognitive explanations have seemed so attractive, when what has been studied has for the most part been cognitive tasks that are set up in surroundings quite different from those of naturally occurring, affect-laden settings. (p. 310)

It is by no means clear that the skills measured by the FBT are a fundamental or discrete constituent of interpersonal understanding. For example, Garfield, Peterson and Perry (2001) note that children under four years of age are already 'able to perceive a wide variety of socially meaningful objects and properties in their social environments' (p. 532). They go on to cast more general doubt on the idea of a circumscribed FP by claiming that its acquisition is 'essentially social in character, and [...] the body of knowledge represented by [FP] is inextricably bound up with broader knowledge about persons and their lives' (p. 496). Commonplace interpretations of the FBT simply assume the fundamentality of a decontextualized ability to detect beliefs that differ from one's own. Even if they do succeed in measuring a discrete ability, they do not amount to a case for its primacy. It is for such reasons that Bruner and Feldman refer to passing the test as a 'False Belief Diploma', handed out at some arbitrary 'Graduation Day' during development (p. 269). FBTs may be good *indicators* that a certain developmental stage has been reached but an ability to pass them need not itself be the essence of intersubjectivity. Analogously, a smoke detector may indicate a house fire but a house fire is not itself comprehensively described as 'that which makes a smoke alarm go off'. It is not even clear that such tasks require the same *kind* of cognitive performance as everyday interpersonal understanding and interaction. Furthermore, although the developmental achievement required to pass these tests *can* be described in terms of a distinctive cognitive ability to 'attribute an internal mental state that differs from one's own', this by no means implies that it *should* be. As I have already suggested, such descriptions could well involve a misleading abstraction from what is really going on. Feelings and bodily reactions may well play a key role in the child's interpretation of the task, along with numerous other factors. Hence these tasks only constitute evidence for FP if they are interpreted through the lens of FP.

6. Evolution and Intersubjectivity

The account I have proposed suggests that intersubjectivity is enabled by myriad variably interconnected abilities, as opposed to an single 'underlying core'. We are evolved organisms, whose abilities are refined through interactions with our environments, rather than by observing the world from afar. It should come as no surprise that our ability to understand something as complex as each other is bodily, practical and multi-faceted. By implication, an account of the evolution of interpersonal understanding will need to incorporate a multiplicity of factors and stages. A speculative account of human cognitive evolution, proposed by Donald (1991), complements much of what I have said concerning perceptual and bodily interaction. Donald suggests that three major evolutionary accomplishments, which appeared in succession, distinguish us from our closest primate cousins:

1. Mimesis (an ability to re-enact events).
2. Speech (with an emphasis on the ability to construct narratives).
3. The ability to use the environment as an external storage system for symbolic representations.

The first two shifts, he claims, occurred at a biological level and involved genetic changes, whereas the third involved a reconfiguration of the organismic environment, which led to changes in brain development. For the sake of brevity, I will restrict my discussion here to Stage 1. Donald's description of mimesis is similar in many respects to the structure of affective interaction described in Sections 2 and 3. According to Donald, mimesis is an ability to re-enact events and actions. It is more sophisticated than mimicry or imitation, given that mimetic performances are structured by one's goals and intentions, but it can incorporate both. Donald emphasizes the role played by a range of bodily capacities and receptivities in facilitating mimesis: 'Tones of voice, facial expressions, eye movements, manual signs and gestures, postural attitudes, patterned whole-body movements of various sorts, and long sequences of these elements can express many aspects of the perceived world' (p. 169).

He goes on to argue that mimesis was not just an evolutionary precursor to modern human social abilities. It persists as a framework within which linguistic and other abilities are nested and structured:

> No matter how evolved our oral-linguistic culture, and no matter how sophisticated the rich varieties of symbolic material surrounding us, mimetic scenarios still form the expressive heart of human social interchange. (p. 189).

Mimesis, Donald claims, plays a key role in one-to-one social exchanges, in addition to activities such as games, customs and dance. It is an 'integral skill', utilising a number of different biological components and not something that could be subserved by a single, discrete, core biological capacity (p. 186). In suggesting that language is nested within mimetic abilities, Donald emphasizes that mimesis has a complex systematic structure, which includes many of the prerequisites for spoken language, such as 'intentionality, generativity, communicativity, reference, autocueing, and the ability to model an unlimited number of objects' (p. 171).

In endorsing Donald's account of intersubjectivity as a multi-faceted, multi-staged accomplishment, I do not want to dispute the popular claim that Machiavellian intelligence may have played some role in our evolution. However, given that intersubjectivity involves a range of abilities, it is unlikely that selection pressures favouring more refined abilities to interact strategically were the only major factors in play. What's more, an ability to detect deceit in others need not fall back on a detached ability to attribute intentional states. Anomalies in the interplay of expression, gesture and gaze could well contribute to the *feeling* that another is not to be trusted. I also suggest, tentatively, that acknowledgement of the multi-faceted nature of interpersonal understanding and the extent to which it is bodily, perceptual and affective, will serve to better clarify and maybe lessen perceived differences between ourselves and other species[8]. FP suggests that the differences between our social abilities and those of our closest primate relatives are largely

---

[8] See, for example, Dunbar (2000) and Whiten (2001) for survey and discussion of evolution of FP and comparisons between our own abilities and those of other primates.

due to our ability to attribute complex internal mental states, on the basis of behavioural observations. Given that intersubjectivity is practical, affective and perceptual, we should perhaps attend to other individually unremarkable differences, such as a more diverse range of facial expressions and a more refined affective receptivity to action, gesture, expression and tone.

7. Conclusion

In summary, FP is an abstraction from a complex of perceptual, affective, expressive, gestural and linguistic interactions, which are scaffolded by a shared cultural context. When talk of beliefs and desires is considered in context, it is clear that FP does not comprise a discrete ability. Even if and when intentional states are assigned, the ability to do so incorporates frameworks of shared culture and structures of interaction. Taking FP as the 'core' of interpersonal understanding involves extracting an aspect of social interaction from its context, reinterpreting it as an autonomous, decontextualized ability to observe and postulate, and then claiming that this abstraction is in fact the foundation of social life. I can see no rationale for popular descriptions of FP. It is possible that such abstractions serve some conceivable theoretical purpose but they do not reflect the structure of social life.

References

Baron-Cohen, S., H. Tager-Flusberg and D. J. Cohen (eds.) 1993. *Understanding Other Minds: Perspectives from Autism* (Oxford: Oxford University Press).

Bloom, P. and T. P. German. 2000. 'Two Reasons to Abandon the False Belief Task as a Test of the Theory of Mind', *Cognition*, 77, 25–31.

Bruner, J. 1990. *Acts of Meaning* (Cambridge Mass.: Harvard University Press).

Bruner, J, and C. Feldman. 1993. 'Theories of Mind and the Problem of Autism', in Baron-Cohen, Tager-Flusberg and Cohen (eds.), 267–91.

Byrne, R. and A. Whiten. (eds.) 1988. *Machiavellian Intelligence: Social Expertise and the Evolution of Intellect in Monkeys, Apes and Humans* (Oxford: Oxford University Press).

Carruthers, P. 2000. 'The Evolution of Consciousness', in Carruthers and Chamberlain (eds.), 254-275.

Carruthers, P. and P. K. Smith (eds.) 1996. *Theories of Theories of Mind* (Cambridge: Cambridge University Press).

Matthew Ratcliffe

Carruthers, P. and A. Chamberlain (eds.) 2000. *Evolution and the Human Mind: Modularity, Language and Meta-Cognition* (Cambridge: Cambridge University Press).

Churchland, P. M. 1996. 'Folk Psychology', in P. M. Churchland and P.S. Churchland. *On the Contrary: Critical Essays 1987–1997* (Cambridge Mass., London: MIT Press).

Clark, A. 1997. *Being There: Putting Brain, Body and World Together Again* (Cambridge Mass., London: MIT Press).

Cole, J. 1998. *About Face* (Cambridge Mass., London: MIT Press).

Cole, J. 2001. 'The Contribution of the Face in the Development of Emotion and Self', in Kaszniak (ed.), 478–82.

Currie, G. and K. Sterelny. 2000. 'How to think about the Modularity of Mind-Reading. *Philosophical Quarterly*, 50, 143–60.

Davies, M. and T. Stone (eds.) 1995a. *Mental Simulation: Evaluations and Applications* (Oxford: Blackwell).

Davies, M. and T. Stone (eds.) 1995b. *Folk Psychology: The Theory of Mind Debate* (Oxford: Blackwell).

Donald, M. 1991. *Origins of the Modern Mind: Three Stages in the Evolution of Culture and Cognition* (Cambridge Mass.: Harvard University Press).

Dunbar, R. 2000. 'On the Origin of the Human Mind', in Carruthers and Chamberlain (eds.), 238–53.

Frith, U. and F. Happé. 1999. 'Theory of Mind and Self-Consciousness: What is it Like to be Autistic?' *Mind and Language*, 14, 1–22.

Fogassi, L. and V. Gallese. 2002. 'The Neural Correlates of Action Understanding in Non-Human Primates', in Stamenov and Gallese (eds), 13–35.

Gallagher, S. 2001. 'The Practice of Mind: Theory, Simulation, or Primary Interaction?', in Thompson (ed.), 83–108.

Gallese, V. and A. Goldman. 1998. 'Mirror Neurons and the Simulation Theory of Mind-Reading', *Trends in Cognitive Sciences*, 2, 493-501.

Garfield, J. L., C. C. Peterson and T. Perry. 2001. 'Social Cognition, Language Acquisition and the Development of the Theory of Mind', *Mind and Language*, 16, 494–541.

Goldie, P. 2000. *The Emotions: A Philosophical Exploration* (Oxford: Clarendon Press).

Gopnik, A. 1996. 'Theories and Modules: Creation Myths, Developmental Realities, and Neurath's Boat', in Carruthers and Smith (eds.), 169–83.

Gordon, R. 1996. '"Radical" Simulation', in Carruthers and Smith (eds.), 11–21.

Hobson, P. 1993(a) *Autism and the Development of Mind* (Hove (UK): Lawrence Erlbaum Associates).

Hobson, P. 1993(b). 'Understanding Persons: The Role of Affect', in Baron-Cohen, Tager-Flusberg and Cohen (eds.), 204–27.

Hobson, P. 2002. *The Cradle of Thought* (London: Macmillan).

Kaszniak, A. (ed.) 2001. *Emotions, Qualia and Consciousness* (London: World Scientific).

Lord, C. 1993. 'The Complexity of Social Behaviour in Autism', in Baron-Cohen, Tager-Flusberg and Cohen (eds.), 292–316.

Morton, M. 2003. *The Importance of being Understood: Folk Psychology as Ethics* (London: Routledge).

Papafragou, A. 2002. 'Mindreading and Verbal Communication', *Mind and Language*, 17, 55–67.

Rizzolatti, G., L. Craighero and L. Fadiga. 2002. 'The Mirror System in Humans', in Stamenov and Gallese (eds.), 37–9.

Rotondo, J. L. and S. M. Boker. 2002. 'Behavioral Synchronization in Human Conversational Interaction', in Stamenov and Gallese (eds.), 151–62.

Sartre, J. P. 1989. *Being and Nothingness* (trans. H. E. Barnes) (London: Routledge).

Scholl, B. J. and A. M. Leslie. 1999. 'Modularity, Development and "Theory of Mind"', *Mind and Language*,14, 131–53.

Sperber, D. and D. Wilson. 2002. 'Pragmatics, Modularity and Mind-reading', *Mind and Language*, 17, 3–23.

Stamenov, M. I. and V. Gallese eds. 2002. *Mirror Neurons and the Evolution of Brain and Language* (Amsterdam, Philadelphia: John Benjamins).

Stich, S. and I. Ravenscroft. 1996. 'What Is Folk Psychology?', in Stich. *Deconstructing the Mind* (Oxford: Oxford University Press).

Studdert-Kennedy, M. 2002. 'Mirror Neurons, Vocal Imitation, and the Evolution of Particulate Speech', in Stamenov and Gallese (eds.), 207–27.

Thompson, E. ed. 2001. *Between Ourselves: Second-Person Issues in the Study of Consciousness* (Thornton, UK: Imprint Academic).

Walsh, D. (ed.) 2001. *Naturalism, Evolution and Mind* (Cambridge: Cambridge University Press).

Wimmer, H. and J. Perner. 1983. 'Beliefs about Beliefs: Representation and Constraining Function of Wrong Beliefs in Young Children's Understanding of Deception', *Cognition*, 13, 103–28.

Whiten, A. 2001. 'Theory of Mind in Non-Verbal Apes: Conceptual Issues and the Critical Experiments', in Walsh (ed.), 199–223.

The Loss of Rational Design

FRIEDEL WEINERT

I. *Introduction*

Charles Darwin published his *Origin of Species* on November 24, 1859. Whatever hurdle the theory of natural selection faced in its struggle for acceptance, its impact on human self-images was almost immediate. Well before Darwin had the chance of applying the principle of natural selection to human origins—in his *Descent of Man* (1871)—his contemporaries quickly and rashly drew the inference to man's descent from the ape. Satirical magazines like *Punch* delighted in depicting Darwin with his imposing head on an apish body. At the Oxford meeting of the British Association for the Advancement of Science (June 1860), Bishop Wilberforce asked T. H. Huxley triumphantly whether he traced his ancestry to the ape on his grandfather's or grandmother's side. A wave of evolutionary texts swept over Europe (L. Büchner, E. Haeckel, T. H. Huxley, J. B. Lamarck, C. Lyell, F. Rolle, E. Tyler and K. Vogt). Written in English, French and German, they all had a common focus: the place of humans in a Darwinian world, including religion and morality. Although Darwin contributed the new concept of sexual selection, his *Descent of Man* is more derivative, less original than his *Origin of Species*. By Darwin's own admission,

> the conclusion that man is the co-descendent with other species of some ancient lower and extinct form is not in any degree new.[1]

However, the contributions of Darwin's contemporaries are largely forgotten. Charles Darwin takes all the credit. A. R. Wallace, co-discoverer of the principle of natural selection, recognized the revolutionary potential of Darwin's theory:

> Never, perhaps, in the whole history of science or philosophy has so great a revolution in thought and opinion been effected as in the twelve years from 1859 to 1871, the respective dates of publication of Mr. Darwin's *Origin of Species* and *Descent of Man*.[2]

[1] C. Darwin, *The Descent of Descent* (1871), with an introduction by John Tyler Bonner and Robert M. May (Princeton: Princeton University Press, 1992), 5.

[2] A. R. Wallace, *Natural Selection and Tropical Nature* (London: Macmillan and Co., 1891), 419.

Friedel Weinert

Almost 150 years after Darwin's publications, researchers in biology still agree on the upheaval in human thinking, which Darwinism unleashed. Writing in 1974, Jacques Monod was quite confident

> that no other scientific theory has had such tremendous philosophical, ideological and political implications as has the theory of evolution.[3]

The distinguished evolutionary biologist Ernst Mayr is no less certain that the publication of the *Origin* 'represents perhaps the greatest intellectual revolution experienced by mankind.'[4] Reflecting the growing importance of the science of biology for the 21st century, Stephen Jay Gould accords Darwin a bigger impact effect than Copernicus.

> Of the two greatest revolutions in scientific thought, Darwin's surely trumps Copernicus in raw emotional impact... [5]

Copernicanism and Darwinism represent two prime examples of an important, yet often neglected aspect of science: that science comprises much more than erudite technicalities. Science is still too often seen as a highly complex, recondite activity, with no immediate philosophical consequences for human thought. And yet Copernicanism, Newtonianism and Darwinism are obvious counterexamples. In each case a scientific theory forced a re-evaluation of unquestioned presuppositions and accepted world-views. What is it in Darwin's theory of evolution that could yield such an impact on human thought? Why are his illustrious predecessors consigned to oblivion, when they shared many of Darwin's presuppositions? Why are they forgotten, when they anticipated some of his ideas on man? Jean-Baptiste Lamarck, for instance, who sadly figures today as one of the fools of science for his theory of use-inheritance, drew similar conclusions from his own views as did Darwin and his followers. In this paper I want to explore what is special about Darwinism. My *thesis* is that its profound impact is due to a remix of concept and fact. It is the com-

---

[3] J. Monod, 'On the Molecular Theory of Evolution', in M. Ridley (ed.), *Evolution* (Oxford: Oxford University Press, 1997), 389.

[4] E. Mayr, *What Evolution Is* (Basic Books, 2001), 9; E. Mayr, 'Darwin's Influence on Modern Thought', *Scientific American* (July 2000), 67–71.

[5] S. J. Gould, *The Structure of Evolutionary Theory* (Cambridge, Mass./London: The Belknap Press of Harvard University Press, 2002), 46; L. Büchner, *Sechs Vorlesungen über die Darwin'sche Theorie von der Verwandlung der Arten* (Leipzig: Theodor Thomas, 1868), 267.

bination of philosophical presuppositions with concrete scientific discoveries, which makes it a true revolution in thought. For the sake of a convenient label, I will call its effect the *loss of rational design*. Philosophical reflections and factual discoveries about man's lowly origin in the universe existed before Darwin. What makes Darwinism a revolution in thought is its unique meshing of philosophical ideas and empirical facts. From a revolution in thought we expect some conceptual upheaval, some new perspective. Let us take the year 1859 as a turning point in the history of human thought about humanity. We must consider what was said before in order to appreciate what was said after. We must look at the facts that were waiting for a theory to invest them with significance.

II. *Before Darwin*

What made Darwin a revolutionary thinker was his ability to switch *perspectives*, just like Copernicus. To describe planetary motions, Copernicus exchanged the viewpoint of a central, stationary earth with that of a planetary, moving earth. He claimed that this switch accounted better for the observable phenomena. Darwin performed a similar volte-face. He exchanged teleology for functionalism. Where nature seemed to display rational design he detected the operation of natural forces rather than the hand of a divine creator. This change of perspective has left traces in the interpretation of the famous watch analogy before and after Darwin. In his defence of Natural Theology (1802) the 18th century theologian William Paley proposed the celebrated watch analogy as an argument for the existence of God.

> In crossing a heath, suppose I pitched my foot against a *stone*, and were asked how the stone came to be there; I might possibly answer, that, for anything I knew to the contrary, it had lain there for ever: nor would it perhaps be very easy to show the absurdity of this answer. But suppose I had found a *watch* upon the ground, and it should be inquired how the watch happened to be in that place; I should hardly think of the answer which I had before given, that for anything I knew, the watch might have always been there.

Paley contrasts the simplicity of a physical object like a stone with the intricacy of an artificial object like a watch and concludes that the watch must have had a maker: that there must have existed, at some time, and at some place or other, an artificer or artificers, who formed it for the purpose which we find it actually to answer; who comprehended its construction, and designed its use.

Yet what is a human artefact, like a watch, compared with the complexity of the human eye? It seems unimaginable that the eyes of natural organisms could have been the product of blind forces. Paley therefore extends his analogy from the watch to the works of nature:

> every indication of contrivance, every manifestation of design, which existed in the watch, exists in the works of nature, with the difference, on the side of nature, of being greater or more, and that in a degree which exceeds all computation.[6]

Then, in 1859, Darwin proposed a change of perspectives. He provided biologists with a physical mechanism—natural selection— by which the process of evolution could be propelled in the absence of a pre-given goal. For the creationists, function comes first; the organ is tailored to it. For the evolutionists the organ rises first; it shapes its function. T. H. Huxley, one of Darwin's staunchest defenders, used the model of evolution to propose the gradual emergence of a watch—a process, which Paley had found impossible.

> Suppose, however, that any one had been able to show that the watch had not been made directly by any person, but it was the result of the modification of another watch which kept time but poorly, and that this again had proceeded from a structure which could hardly be called a watch at all – seeing that it had no figures on the dial and the hands were rudimentary; and that going back in time we came at last to a revolving barrel as the earliest traceable rudiment of the whole fabric. And imagine that it had been possible to show that all these changes had resulted, first, from a tendency of the structure to vary indefinitely; and secondly, from something in the surrounding world which helped all variations in the direction of an accurate time-keeper, and checked all those in other directions; then it is obvious that the force of Paley's argument would be gone. For it would be demonstrated that an apparatus thoroughly well adapted to a particular purpose might be the result of a method of trial and

[6] Quoted from R. Dawkins, *The Blind Watchmaker* (Penguin Books, 1988), 4–5.

error worked by unintelligent agents, as well as of the direct application of the means appropriate to that end, by an intelligent agent.[7]

Today calculations tell us that a lens eye could have evolved by natural selection in 364 000 generations and that 'eyelike organs have developed in the animal series independently at least 40 times'.

Natural theology was one of the rival explanations, which the evolutionists sought to disprove. They labelled it the theory of special creations. According to this account, all diversity of life is the fruit of special acts of creation: species were created, in their natural environments, in their present states. Species were fixed and did not change over their lifetimes. The *fixity* of species is a basic assumption of the natural theologian, and most of the 18th century. The celebrated anatomist, George Cuvier, who staunchly defended the fixity of species and teleology, had a much greater impact on the beginning of the 19th century than his rivals J. B. Lamarck and E. Geoffroy Saint Hilaire.

Design arguments depend on the assumption of the existence of a Supreme Being. His role may simply be that of an original creator, who offers no further interference. Or it may be that of a cosmic mechanic who keeps the cosmic engine running, by occasional intervention. Two creation scenarios are possible. Such a Supreme Being could have established the Scale of Beings in one sweep: a hierarchical and immutable ladder of organic creatures, a Great Chain of Being. The Great Chain of Being shares with Paley's natural theology the belief in the fixity of species, but there is also a strong sense of hierarchy, of a necessary ascending order from the lowliest creatures to the highest organisms. In this hierarchy, humans occupy the top rung. Geocentrism granted man a privileged habitat at the cosmic centre of the universe. The Great Chain of Being reserves for man an elevated place in the hierarchy of natural beings. The Great Chain of Being depicts the natural world as one of ascending complexity, with clear boundaries between species. Each species inhabits a particular rung on the ladder. No species moves along this ladder. Species do not evolve. No new forms of life arise.

Voltaire questioned the logic of the *static* Scale of Being. *Firstly*,

[7] T. H. Huxley: 'Criticisms of the Origin of Species' (1864), in *Collected Essays* Vol. II (London: Macmillan, 1907), 83–4. On the evolution of the eye, see Dan-E. Nilsson/S. Pelger, 'A pessimistic estimate of the time required for an eye to evolve', in M. Ridley, *Evolution* (op. cit. note 3), 299; E. Mayr *Evolution* (op. cit. note 4), 205.

species may face extinction (the wolf disappeared in England). *Secondly*, imaginary species may be inserted into the Chain of Being.

In response, the Great Chain of Being became temporalized. In its temporalized form it acquires motion. The unfolding of complexity out of simplicity takes time. Jean Baptiste Lamarck has been much ridiculed for his ideas on use-inheritance. Darwin held his achievements in low esteem. It is the idea of the giraffe, which stretches its neck to reach the leaves of tall trees; the neck grows longer and the giraffe passes its elongated neck on to the next generation of giraffes. Lamarck had much more to say. For Lamarck worked out a way of temporalizing the Great Chain of Being. In doing so, Lamarck abandoned the idea of the fixity of species and the theory of special creations. In place of the fixity of species Lamarck proposes the mechanism of *progressive modification* (anagenesis). Lamarck was also a stern materialist, in the best tradition of the French school. So Lamarck did not assume an act of divine creation at the beginning of organic life. Life starts by spontaneous generation. Through this process very simple creatures are born. If it were left undisturbed, the complexity of life's scale would slowly evolve through progressive modifications. Would the simpler creatures not disappear? No, because spontaneous generation works continuously, always replenishing the world. Necessary inner propulsion would turn the simpler creatures into more complex organisms. Complications arise. Changes in the environment disrupt the mechanism of progressive modification and challenge the organisms to adapt themselves. Changing environmental conditions lead to changes in organisms. Some organs experience a reinforced use and others fall into desuetude. Strengthened organs are passed on, through use-inheritance. Organisms change within a few generations. The complexity of the organic world slowly unfolds. This is *linear* evolution, because the idea of hierarchy is retained. For Lamarck man is a model of perfection and all other creatures are measured against man. Although Lamarck temporalizes the Great Chain of Being and abandons the idea of the fixity of species, he is still committed to teleology. That is, Lamarck thinks that the evolution of the Ladder of Existence follows some preset aim. The *telos* is to produce humans. Nature evolves from simpler to more complex organisms with the aim of bringing forth the most perfect being of them all: Homo sapiens. This has proved to be such a compelling image that even today evolutionary theory is often conflated with progressive modification, a confusion, to which many contemporary documents testify (Figure I).

Figure I: *The Seven Ages of an Academic.* A *Guardian* Ad to draw attention to Tuesday's academic job ads.

So a number of theoretical, highly speculative approaches existed before Darwin's revolutionary view of 1859. But neither Lamarck nor Paley could muster much empirical support. Yet important empirical discoveries were made in anatomy, embryology, geology and palaeontology. For instance, geology established a link between the position of rock strata and the age of the fossil finds. The rock strata contained an arrow of time.

Of particular importance were humanlike fossil finds, like Neanderthal Man (1856) and Java Man (1891/2). Human fossil records were found amongst fossils of extinct animals, like the mammoth, reindeer and the wild horse. Also found were tools and weapons, made of flint stone. This suggested that hominoid creatures inhabited regions of Europe, which were once home to now extinct animals.

The antiquity of man was a debate of central importance well before Darwin formulated his theory of natural selection. The empirical establishment of the antiquity of man showed two things: **a)** Humans were much older than the Biblical 6000 years. Hominids existed already during the Stone Age. There was also evidence of the migration of human groups into Europe. All this threw serious doubt on Cuvier's dictum that human fossil remains do not exist. It also suggested that species could become extinct, giving way to new species. Structural similarities between humans, hominids and apes became a serious scientific topic. All these findings challenged the view of the fixity of species. **b)** They also undermined the idea of progressive modification, which required that certain organism types must appear on earth before more complex ones can make their entry. If early humans cohabited the earth with now extinct animals, then progressive modification cannot be an adequate explanation. In the 1860s writers were unclear about the extent of the Stone Age in the history of the earth, but it pointed well beyond the Biblical limits. The determination of the ages of the earth through radioactive dating had not been developed. In 1868 Thomson (wrongly) estimated the age of the earth as no greater than 100 million years. Only Darwin was seriously troubled by this estimate. Global as it was, it said nothing about the ages of the earth and their extent. By the reasoning of that time, if hominids cohabited regions of Europe with the mammoth, the reindeer and the wild horse, they must have lived 57 000 years ago. Today, this period of the Stone Age is estimated at 100 000 years.

Then, in 1859 Darwin proposed a testable mechanism, which threw an explanatory grid over all these facts and many others like the bio-geographical distribution of species.

III. *Darwin's Revolution*

Darwin's title *The Origin of Species* is misleading. It is not the book's intention to explain the origin of life at the dawn of time. His theory attempts a naturalistic explanation of the persistence and modification of organic beings of the recent past and present. Darwin explains the appearance of variants of established species and the emergence of new species through his celebrated theory of natural selection. The theory of natural selection is an extrapolation of the practice of artificial selection to the natural environment. The gist of Darwin's insight is captured in his subtitle: *The Preservation of Favoured Races in the Struggle for Life.* The basic logic of Darwin's argument is inductive in nature. But it is induction of a sophisticated kind. Darwin does not inductively generalize from a few observed cases of artificial breeding to natural selection in nature. This would not have been an effective method because several theoretical attempts existed already, which had not yet been decisively disproved. And many geological and biological facts had been established, which called for accommodation. The geological discoveries revealed the recognition that geological strata indicated an arrow of time. The biological discoveries consisted in an accumulation of fossil records, which documented the existence of extinct animals (like the

of physicists and medical practitioners as much as in the pages of biologists. According to Ernst Haeckel,

the science of evolution made it clear that the same eternal iron laws that rule in the inorganic world are valid, too, in the organic and moral world.[10]

Implicit in Haeckel's statement is the rule of materialism, which many of Darwin's disciples shared. T. H. Huxley harbours as little doubt as Haeckel that science will discover the law of evolution of organic forms:

(the law) of the unvarying order of that great chain of causes and effects of which all organic forms, ancient and modern, are the links.[11]

Equally combining determinism with materialism, Huxley expresses the ultimate philosophical beliefs of his time: the reliance on mechanical and deterministic laws.

As a natural process evolution excludes supernatural intervention. As the expression of a fixed order, every stage of which is the effect of causes operating according to definite rules, the conception of evolution no less excludes that of chance.[12]

We should note in this connection that Darwin shared the commitment to materialism but not to strict determinism. Evolution is a stochastic process, in which contingency rather than necessity is the order of the day. The principle of natural selection acts on isotropic variation. It tends to select favourable variations and to weed out unfavourable variations. But it acts in a strictly local context, which is shaped by a changing environment. Darwin left his readers in little doubt about the contingency of evolution.

I believe in no fixed law of development (...). The variability of each species is quite independent of that of all others. Whether such variability be taken advantage of by natural selection, and whether the variations be accumulated to a greater or lesser amount (...) depends on many complex contingencies...[13]

[10] E. Haeckel, *The Riddle of the Universe* (London: Watts & Co., 1929), 285 (translation of *Die Welträtsel*, 1899).

[11] T. H. Huxley, 'Geological Contemporaneity' (1862), in *Collected Essays* VIII (London: Macmillan, 1910), 288.

[12] T. H. Huxley, 'Evolution and Ethics' (1894), in *Collected Essays* IX (London: Macmillan, 1911), 6.

[13] C. Darwin, *Origin* (op. cit. note 8), 318.

Friedel Weinert

The Darwinians were also committed to *materialism*, again a heritage of the Scientific Revolution. This commitment became particularly trenchant when Darwin's evolutionary model was applied to the appearance of man on earth. Darwin's contemporaries found it especially difficult to accept the earthly, common descent of man. Why did they feel such revulsion when materialism had been a venerable theme amongst the Enlightenment philosophers?

In his *Système de la Nature* (1770) Paul Thiry d'Holbach declared humans to be products of nature, both with respect to their emergence and their moral and intellectual faculties. Claude A. Helvetius defended a materialist system of morality and promptly saw his book *Sur l'Esprit* (1758) burnt in the same year in which Darwin's *Origin* was published. La Mettrie's *L'Homme Machine* was so provocative that shortly after its publication, in December 1747 in Leiden (Holland), it was forbidden there. A year later it was burned in The Hague. In this essay, La Mettrie declares that the human body is nothing but a clock. Everything is made of the same material, revoking the distinction between body and mind.[14] Lamarck, too, was a materialist. In his *Philosophie Zoologique* he declares that

> All the faculties without exception are purely physical, i.e. each of them is essentially due to activities of the organisation, from humblest instinct to intellectual faculties.[15]

The biggest challenge to the materialist is to explain the phenomena of mind and consciousness. As Lamarck admits, materialism faces the objection that the connection between brain and mind cannot be understood.

> What is the mind? It is a mere invention for the purpose of resolving the difficulties that follow from inadequate knowledge of the laws of nature. Physical and moral have a common origin; ideas, thought, imagination are only natural phenomena.[16]

Lamarck was ignored in his own time and later eclipsed by Darwinism. When Darwin published the *Origin of Species* his theory entered a crowded conceptual space. It harboured several

[14] J. O. de La Mettrie, *L'Homme Machine* (1747) (Paris : Editions Mille et Une Nuits, 2000), 68, 49.

[15] J. B. Lamarck, *Philosophie Zoologique* (1809), translated with an introduction by Hugh Elliot (New York/London: Hafner, 1963), Pt. II, Introduction.

[16] op. cit. note 15.

competing accounts of the transmutation of species. Next to it, an empirical space subsisted, which had yielded a vast amount of biological, embryological, geological and palaeontological records. The antiquity of man was one of the areas, in which the two spaces could mesh. It lent credence to the Darwinian view at the expense of rival attempts.[17]

V. *After Darwin*

With the publication of Darwin's *Origin* the issue of the origin and nature of humanity suddenly acquired a new theoretical framework. Darwin's famous promise:

Light will be thrown on the origin of man and his history,[18]

was immediately taken up by a number of researchers who attempted to provide an answer in terms of natural selection. When Darwin finally published *The Descent of Man* (1871) he was not entering an uncharted terrain. Any application of the theory of natural selection to the origin of mankind has to grapple at least with two issues: 1) the *empirical* challenge of placing the origin of humans within the realm of the organic order and 2) the *philosophical* challenge of accommodating man's superior mental and moral faculties. Until Darwin's *Descent* these attempts were undertaken without a major change in the fundamental philosophical presuppositions of determinism, materialism and mechanism.

---

[17] See C. Lyell, *The Geological Evidences of the Antiquity of Man* (London: Murray, 1863), Ch. XX, where Lyell discusses theories of progressive modification and transmutation with respect to man.

[18] Darwin, *Origin* (op. cit. note 8), 458. The evolutionist, materialist explanation was fiercely resisted in some quarters. But the literature of the period from 1859 to 1871 also testifies to numerous cases of instant conversion to the Darwinian cause. In order of national impact, Darwinism had its greatest effect in England and Germany, its least in France. And some of the most advanced men of science, like E. Haeckel and T. H. Huxley, lent their intellectual support to the evolutionary theory. This observation throws some welcomed doubt on Max Planck's often-quoted comment that a revolutionary idea gains acceptance in science not because of the conviction but the death of its critics. See Max Planck, 'Ursprung und Auswirkung wissenschaftlicher Ideen', in *Vorträge und Erinnerungen*, (Darmstadt: Wissenschaftliche Buchgesellschaft, 1965), 275. This is as little true of the early reception of Darwinism as it is of the early reception of the Special theory of relativity.

Friedel Weinert

1. The most important *empirical* argument in favour of the human origin in the animal world lay in structural similarities. Today we are told that humans and chimps share 98% of the genetic code. In the 1860s the argument from similarity had to rely on embryology, comparative anatomy and palaeontology. Researchers undertook painstaking anatomical comparisons, especially between the skeletons of old-world monkeys and humans. Blumenbach named monkeys *Quadrumana*: four-handed creatures and humans *Bimana*: two-handed creatures. This distinction was popular till Huxley showed to be inadequate. But the resemblance between their body plans, extremities and their skulls was plain to see.

The antiquity of man and his close structural similarity with the ape was established. Once the principle of natural selection became available, the hypothesis of man's descent from the ape was a natural conclusion. But which form did this descent take? Lamarck had already offered his theory of progressive modification, which defined man as the crowning moment of linear evolution. Man therefore appears as the most complex and highest form of life. Lamarck then proceeds to compare the perfection of humans with the graded imperfection of lower organic forms. However, the fossil records did not speak in favour of progressive modification. Although Huxley and Haeckel rejected the Lamarckian theory of progressive modification through use-inheritance, they both accepted some form of direct descent of man from lower organic forms. According to Huxley it is plausible that man may have originated by the gradual modification of a man-like ape:

> But if Man be separated by no greater structural barrier from the brutes than they are from one another – then it seems to follow that if any process of physical causation can be discovered by which the genera and families of ordinary animals have been produced, that process of causation is amply sufficient to account for the origin of Man.[19]

In an address to the French Association of Science (1878), Haeckel dismissed the popular belief of man's direct descent from any existing anthropoids. The more accurate picture was that 'man and the apes of the Old and New World are descended from a common

[19] T. H. Huxley, *Man's Place in Nature* (1863) (Chicago: The University of Chicago Press, 1959), 125; reprinted in *Collected Essays* VII (London: Macmillan, 1910), 77–156; see also *Collected Essays* II (op. cit. note 7), 151: 'There is nothing in man's physical structure to interfere with his having been evolved from an ape.'

ancestor.'[20] But in a popularisation of his new philosophy, Monism, Haeckel advanced a more radical claim. It is an 'incontestable historical fact'

> that man descends immediately from the ape, and secondarily from a long series of lower vertebrates.[21]

But Huxley was wise enough to remain in the slipstream of the Darwinian account:

> man might have originated (...) as a ramification of the same primitive stock as those apes.[22]

The menacing thought that man may have descended directly from the apes was grist to the mill of Darwin's friends and foes. The celebrated exchange between Wilberforce and Huxley at the Oxford meeting of the British Association feeds on the assumption of direct descent. Haeckel uses it to shock his audiences into humility. Even today a poster of a massive gorilla, bearing the rhetorical title: 'Is this your granddad?' exploits the linearity to ridicule the Darwinian view of descent. More mundanely, the linearity may be put to the service of wine sales (Figure II).

Figure II: A South African Chardonnay Wine called *Evolution*. The label on the back states: 'From the earth to the vine, from the vine to the fruit, from the fruit to the wine, from the wine to the soul—an evolution of nature.'

[20] E. Haeckel, *Nature* **18** (1878), 509.
[21] Haeckel, *Riddle* (op. cit. note 10), 69.
[22] T. H. Huxley, *Man's Place in Nature* (op. cit. note 10), 125.

Friedel Weinert

In his more radical mood, Haeckel attributes to Darwin and Huxley the view of man's direct descent from the apes. But Darwin was as circumspect as Huxley. In his *Descent of Man* (1871) he staggers towards the image of commonality of descent. Within the span of a few pages in this long book, he speaks of man as *descending* from some lower form (*Descent*, Pt. I, VI, 185), as the *co-descendant* with other mammals of some unknown or lower form (186), as having *diverged* from Old World monkeys (199, 201). Then, finally he suggests the image of **branching** (Figure III).

> The Simiadae then branched off into two great stems, the New World and Old World monkeys; and from the latter, at a remote period, Man, the wonder and glory of the universe, proceeded.[23]

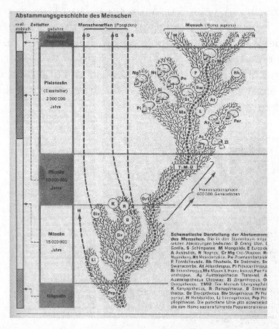

Figure III: An evolutionary tree of human descent, showing both the development of anthropoid apes (*left*) and the human branch (*right*). The tree shows that certain hominids became extinct on twigs. Only Homo sapiens, with several races, survived to the present (*dotted line*).

Source: *Knaurs Lexikon* A-Z, 1987, 571

[23] Darwin, *Descent* (op. cit. note 1), Pt. I, 213. But this terminology was so little fixed that the idea of branching also appears in J.B. Lamarck, *Zoological Philosophy* (op. cit. note 15), 37: "I do not mean that existing

250

But even if we accept the branching idea: not that humans descended directly from the ape but that both share a common ancestor—a formidable objection remained. Even the staunchest materialist cannot deny the intellectual gulf between men and brutes. Man's mental and moral faculties are far superior to the apes'. So man cannot have descended from the ape. It became a formidable challenge to Darwin's supporters to explain the appearance of mental and moral abilities within the limits of natural selection and materialism.

2. Many materialists faced up to this *philosophical* challenge. Not so Alfred Wallace. The co-discoverer of the principle of natural selection never accepted its implications for the emergence of human beings on this planet. Wallace adopted a compromise position, which is very reminiscent of that of Tycho Brahe with respect to Copernicanism. Brahe could not accept the loss of centrality of the earth, which follows from Copernicanism. He kept the earth in its central Aristotelian position and made the moon and the Sun orbit the central earth. The other planets, however, spin in orbits around the sun. Wallace reverts to the Cartesian mind-body dualism. In his apelike state, man was subject to the forces of natural selection. But then, in the distant past, a revolution occurred. It brought forth a creature with a mind and blessed with consciousness. Man's bodily development ceased. His ascent was henceforth focussed on the blossoming of his mental capacities. Natural selection shifted to cultural selection, in which superior races will replace inferior races. As the mental abilities of man far exceed what would have been useful for his survival, Wallace concludes that a superior being must have guided the 'development of man in a definite direction.'[24]

But a materialist explanation of mental functions cannot reach for supernatural causes. They would constitute a breach of determinism, which for almost all 19th century scientists presented a unique chain of physical events stretching from the past to the future. They would also constitute a breach of materialism, for they

[24] A. R. Wallace, 'The Limits of Natural Selection as Applied to Man' (1870), in *Natural Selection* (op. cit. note 2), 204.

animals form a very simple series, regularly graded throughout; but I do mean that they form a branching series (*série rameuse*), irregularly graded and free from discontinuity, or at least once free from it." For Lamarck this branching is the unavoidable result of environmental interferences with the ideal, necessary progressive evolution of the tree of life. For Darwin, branching is a contingent event.

shun the reduction of the mental to the physical. On the basis of these presuppositions the materialist must seek a plausible explanation of the emergence of mental functions, without falling outside the scope of the set limits. How can this be achieved? Firstly, the similarities between man and lower organisms, as established through the study of embryology, comparative anatomy and palaeontology, carry much of the evidential weight. The structural similarities suggest the emergence of humans from lower forms of life, from an ape-like progenitor. The intellectual gulf between man and the brutes, however, cannot be denied. The materialist must find a bridge: accepting the gap but explaining it from below. Huxley once more reaches for the watch analogy. All faculties depend on structures. The organ shapes the function. But a certain variation in structure does not correspond to a similar variation in function. The function is just an expression of molecular arrangements. A small change in structure can lead to a vast change in function. The smallest grain of sand will adversely affect the working of a clock mechanism. In a similar vein variations in the human body—upright position, the freeing of the hands and increasing brain capacity—have led to vast functional differences between humans and apes: the development of language and other symbolic forms. This explanation relies on Darwin's principle of the *correlation of growth*. In his *Descent* Darwin argues that there is no fundamental difference in kind between the mental functions of humans and higher organisms. Complex animals feel emotions and manifest signs of intelligence. Organisms are integrated systems and adaptive change in one part can lead to non-adaptive modifications of other features. An organ built under the influence of selection for a specific role may be able, as a consequence of its structure, to perform many other, unselected functions as well. Our large brain may have originated 'for' some set of necessary skills in gathering food, socializing etc., but these skills do not exhaust the limits of what such a complex machine can do.[25] The principle of natural selection is able to explain the evolution of large human brains.

The materialist hopes to explain how the brain can produce the mind. Mental states are supervenient on brain states, if not identical with them. Must the materialist also explain how the brain

---

[25] C. Darwin, *Descent* (op. cit. note 1), Part I, Ch. IV; *Origin* (op. cit. note 8), Ch. V; S. J. Gould, *The Panda's Thumb* (Penguin Books, 1987), 50; A. C. Crombie, *Styles of Scientific Thinking in the European Tradition* (London: Duckworth, 1994), Vol. III, 1759.

can produce public manifestations of mental processes, like moral rules and social norms? Is there a need to go one step further, from form to content? For non-materialist evolutionists like A. Wallace, the quality of the products of mental functions precludes an explanation in terms of natural selection. But materialist evolutionists, like Darwin and Huxley, want to account for the function as well as the content by appeal to natural selection. This explains why Huxley, in his *Essays*, feels compelled to reflect on evolution and ethics. Darwin has an altogether naturalistic view of moral values, presenting them as an outcome of the operation of social instincts in humans. Instincts form a bridge between humans and other primates. Humans inherited social instincts from the hominids. Social instincts bond humans together into groups. The survival of the tribe is a function of its social cohesion. Altruism and cooperation are favourable characteristics in the struggle of human groups with rival groups. Social values arise out of the struggle for existence between human tribes (and not from Mill's Greatest Happiness Principle.) A tribe, which functions internally, will thrive externally. Even religious values, like the belief in God, are cultural products.[26]

VI. *The Loss of Rational Design*

Clearly, this naturalistic explanation constitutes a complete loss of rational design. No supernatural intervention sets up the cradle of humanity. Materialist Darwinians reject Wallace's compromise position. Nor are humans, in a *literal* sense, the crown of creation. The Darwinians deny the Lamarckian solution of making humans the target of the process of progressive evolution. As a mechanism, progressive evolution does not exist. With the emergence of human beings the evolutionary process does not reach its pinnacle. Humans are not the peak of perfection, to which all other creatures are unfavourably compared.

Can humans figure as the crown of creation at least in a metaphorical sense? Even amongst materialists, reactions to the loss of rational design differed widely. Ernst Haeckel was the most

---

[26] On the question to which extent man's aesthetic, moral and religious sense can be explained in evolutionary terms, especially in the light of evolutionary psychology, see A. O'Hear, *Beyond Evolution* (Oxford: Oxford University Press, 1999). In *Invariances* (Cambridge, Mass./London: The Belknap Press at Harvard University Press, 2001), Ch. 5, Robert Nozick provides an evolutionary account of the genealogy of morality.

pessimistic. He equated the loss of rational design with the cosmic insignificance of man:

> It not only clearly indicates the true place of man in nature, but it dissipates the prevalent illusion of man's supreme importance, and the arrogance with which he sets himself apart from the illimitable universe, and exalts himself to the position of its most valuable element. This boundless presumption of conceited man has misled him into making himself "the image of God", claiming an "eternal life" for his ephemeral personality, and imagining that he possesses unlimited "freedom of will."
>
> Our own "human nature", which exalted itself into an image of God in its anthropistic illusion, sinks to the level of a placental mammal, which has no more value for the universe at large than the ant, the fly of a summer's day, the mircroscopic infusorium or the smallest bacillus.[27]

Charles Darwin and Thomas Huxley, by contrast, did not read cosmic inconsequence from man's lowly origin. Huxley rejects materialism if that means that all is matter and motion. Consciousness operates in the world as a third force. But consciousness is, in true materialist style, a cerebral function. Ideas change the world. Darwinism is a prime example. The development of civilization consists in the gradual deflection of the forces of natural selection. Social life in civilized societies is suspended from the cosmic process of nature, in which the brutish struggle for existence prevails. Civilized life resembles the horticultural process, in which the struggle for existence is largely eliminated. Like the good gardener, humans modify the conditions of existence to suit their needs. Social Darwinism is a false extension of evolution to the human sphere.

Darwin concurred with these views. The argument is open to the materialist that human values, whether their roots lie in social instincts or transcendent realms, take on a life and dynamic of their own. They channel social life in a direction opposite to the struggle for existence. Darwin saw the cosmic significance of humans in their ascent from humble beginnings to the summit of the organic scale, through cultural evolution.

In its temporalized form, the Great Chain of Being has a built-in dynamics, propelling evolution towards the highest perfection, which is invested in the human race. Humans therefore literally become the *crown of creation*. This is meant in a spatial sense.

---

[27] Haeckel, *Riddle* (op. cit. note 10), 12, 199–200.

Darwin and the Darwinians reject the teleology, which is central to progressive modification. The emergence of human beings does not constitute the pinnacle of progressive modification. Humans are an offshoot of evolutionary branching. The tree of life may have grown without sprouting a human branch. Rather than necessity it is contingency, which builds the cradle of humanity. The assessment of the place of humans in the cosmos must necessarily change. It need not be as sombre as Haeckel's.

Man's grandeur lies in the fruits of his superior mental capacities. Humans have descended from a lower form of organic life, but their ability to comprehend the world, to harness natural forces and to learn about the unknown from the known is unsurpassed in the animal kingdom. For Darwin and Huxley man remains the highest creature on the organic scale. But this is meant in a temporal, not a spatial sense.[28]

VII. *Some Philosophical Lessons*

There are some philosophical lessons to be learned from the study of the application of the principle of natural selection to the origin of the human race. They teach us something about the interaction between science and philosophy.

The *first* lesson tells us that purely scientific theories can have an immediate impact on worldviews. The evolutionary theory is not the first example in the history of science of such a direct influence. In terms of raw impact, Copernicus is Darwin's direct predecessor. Copernicus's heliocentric view led to the loss of centrality. The Copernican Revolution consisted in a shift of perspective from a stationary to a moving earth. Copernicus destroyed the ancient anthropomorphic belief that humans resided at the very hub of the universe. The Darwinian change of perspective leads to a loss of rational design. The conceptual network is rearranged. Old elements, like teleology and special creations, are erased. New elements, like materialism and history, enter. New questions arise: man's cosmic status in the face of the loss of centrality and rational design. To appreciate how scientific findings can infiltrate the capillaries of worldviews, note that humans use sophisticated

[28] R. Wendorff, *Zeit und Kultur* (Opladen: Westdeutscher Verlag, ³1985), 403; Darwin, *Descent* (op. cit. note 1), Chapter XXI; T. H. Huxley, 'Ethics and Evolution' (op. cit. note 12), 1–45; L. Büchner, *Sechs Vorlesungen* (op. cit. note 5), 210, 253–6.

conceptual networks to explain and understand the material world around them. The networks consist of a meshing of conceptual and empirical elements. And this points to the *second* philosophical lesson.

Like many 19th century scientists Darwin likes to portray himself as a pure inductivist—the fact-gathering ant of Bacon's apt analogy. But we have already seen that Darwin does not patiently collect the facts, from which, after a careful search for exceptions, he draws general inferences. Many of the facts were already in place. And Darwin, like his supporters, was imbued with scientific and philosophical presuppositions, which guided their construction of the theory of evolution. His was inspired by the work of Charles Lyell and the school of uniformitarianism. Reading Mathus impressed on him the gap between the arithmetic growth of food resources and the exponential rise of populations. The Darwinians embraced the *mechanical worldview*. This was not the austere mechanism of the physicists, for they had to cope with mental phenomena in a material world. Animals are not senseless automata, Huxley holds against the Cartesians, but conscious automata. Haeckel, too, finds little comfort in the physicists' view of matter ('a heap of dead atoms'). The universe consists of matter and spirit. Yet spirit is just energy. The Darwinians' commitment to *materialism* is an endorsement of a philosophical belief, which cannot be derived from the study of empirical facts. It leads to a denial of mind-body dualism. It encourages an explanation of mental processes as a material manifestation of brain activities. The symbolic mind becomes a function of an increased brain capacity. This leads to language and the power of reasoning.

The Darwinians carried philosophical baggage. If itemised, we see how they handled it differentially. Huxley wanted determinism, materialism and consciousness. Haeckel's Monism carries the slogan 'no matter without spirit, no spirit without matter.' Darwin's bugbear was determinism. After some terminological groping he eventually settles for the descent of humans from ape-like progenitors in terms of branching, not linear evolution. The branching descent is riddled with contingencies. So Darwin stands apart from other Darwinians by his rejection of ontological determinism.

Philosophical presuppositons do not constitute a closely-knit set. They constrain differentially. Darwin believed in materialism but not determinism. The combination of materialism and contingency turned Darwin, unwittingly, into one of the dismantlers of the mechanical worldview, which already had begun to lose sway in the physical sciences.[29]

Having observed the constraining and liberating play of philosophical presuppositons in the thoughts of great scientists, we can finally attempt to answer the question raised at the beginning of this paper. Why did the Victorians find the Darwinian perspective on human origins so unpalatable when determinism, materialism and mechanism had taken root in the intellectual life of European culture since the Scientific Revolution? The answer seems to be that the particular remix of facts and concepts, of science and philosophy played a major part. Accounts of the origin of species prior to Darwin erected a heavy structure of philosophical speculations on a slender base of empirical facts. These ideas, flapping like sails in the wind, could simply be banished as sacrilege (the fate of the French materialists) or ignored as guesswork (the fate of Lamarck) because they were not bolted to the material deck. And the alternatives were still reassuring: a respected authority like Cuvier affirmed the fixity of species, which was consonant with the prevalent belief in the Great Chain of Being, carefully built by a benevolent designer God. Teleology still had an anchor in biological thinking. All this changed with Darwinism. For the rich collection of facts, Darwin offered a testable mechanism, natural selection, and a coherent scientific theory. A scientific theory is a complex edifice, consisting of a mathematical frame, a raft of facts and philosophical presuppositions. Darwinism threatened conventional views about the place of humans in organic nature because a) it rejected special creations, b) it destroyed teleology, c) it embraced materialism and d) placed contingency at the heart of evolution. No wonder that biologists from Wallace to Gould rank Darwin as one of the greatest scientific revolutionaries.

[29] op. cit. note 9, Ch. 2.

Under Darwin's Cosh?
Neo-Aristotelian Thinking in
Environmental Ethics

MICHAEL WHEELER

1. Standing on Darwin's shoulders; or is that on his toes?

As a first shot, one might say that environmental ethics is concerned distinctively with the moral relations that exist between, on the one hand, human beings and, on the other, the non-human natural environment. But this really is only a first shot. For example, one might be inclined to think that at least some components of the non-human natural environment (non-human animals, plants, species, forests, rivers, ecosystems, or whatever) have independent moral status, that is, are morally considerable in their own right, rather than being of moral interest only to the extent that they contribute to human well-being. If so, then one might be moved to claim that ethical matters involving the environment are best cashed out in terms of the dutes and responsibilities that human beings have to such components. If, however, one is inclined to deny independent moral status to the non-human natural environment or to any of its components, then one might be moved to claim that the ethical matters in question are exhaustively delineated by those moral relations existing between individual human beings, or between groups of human beings, in which the non-human natural environment figures. One key task for the environmental ethicist is to sort out which, if either, of these perspectives is the right one to adopt—as a general position or within particular contexts. I guess I don't need to tell you that things get pretty complicated pretty quickly.

Some issues that energize environmental activists are essentially local in scale. Examples might include the pollution of a river by toxic waste or the building of a road through an area of natural beauty. It seems fair to say, however, that environmental ethics has become an important feature of the contemporary philosophical landscape mostly as a reaction to various high-profile environmental issues that confront humankind as a whole, issues that engage environmental activists world wide. The list includes

Michael Wheeler

disasters (or potential disasters) such as global warming, excessive deforestation, and the landslide extinction of large numbers of animal and plant species. But while it may be true that the latter class of issues has typically provided the real-world spur to environmentally oriented philosophizing, the core questions that more abstractly characterize the field of environmental ethics are not themselves essentially crisis-driven. What are the normative principles that regulate the ways in which human beings should intervene in the non-human natural world? Which, if any, non-human natural entities have independent moral status? Is it possible to generate stable ethical principles of an environmentally sensitive kind from a perspective on moral value which is purely anthropocentric? These sorts of philosophical questions would be worth asking even if the world were free from global environmental challenges.[1]

As the title of this paper suggests, one of my present goals is to say something of interest to thinkers engaged with environmental ethics. I am, however, no ethicist—environmental or otherwise. The arguments I shall develop are launched entirely from within the intellectual borders of philosophy of biology. This might look like a case of unprovoked philosophical imperialism—but it isn't. Indeed, at the risk of sounding petulant, they (some environmental ethicists that is) started it, by (implicitly at least) making claims about the fundamental character of biological systems.

Here, then, is where we are going. I begin (section 2) by describing how a prominent position in environmental ethics—Paul Taylor's biocentric individualism—is committed to a particular explanation of the way in which the ethical norms that ought to regulate environmental decision-making might be based on biological facts. This explanation rests in turn on what is (I argue) a recognizably Aristotelian style of thinking about the biological realm. And that's where, on the face of it, the trouble lies. For if the received view of Darwinian theory and its place in evolutionary

---

[1] My description of environmental ethics has, of necessity, been very brief. For recent book-length introductions to the field, see, for example: R. Attfield, *Environmental Ethics: an Overview for the 21st Century* (Cambridge: Polity, 2003); J. Benson, *Environmental Ethics: an Introduction with Readings* (London and New York: Routledge, 2000); D. Jamieson (ed.), *A Companion to Environmental Philosophy* (Oxford: Blackwell, 2001); D. Schmidtz and E. Willott (eds.), *Environmental Ethics: What Really Matters, What Really Works* (Oxford: Oxford University Press, 2002); M.E. Zimmerman (ed.), *Environmental Philosophy: from Animal Rights to Radical Ecology* (NJ: Prentice Hall, Third Edition, 2001).

biology is correct, then there is a case that the Aristotelian thinking in question, and thus the ethical framework at issue, are utterly indefensible. I scout this conditional conclusion (section 3) by drawing on some old work due principally to Elliott Sober. Things then take (what I hope is) an unexpected turn. I claim (section 4) that recent work on the phenomenon of self-organization in biological systems might provide an alternative source of *support* for the supposedly discredited Aristotelian view in biology, and thus, by extension, for any position in environmental ethics which depends on that view. Faced with what appears to be a disconcerting choice—between (i) the mighty theoretical edifice of Darwinism, and (ii) an impressively rejuvenated Aristotelianism in biology and environmental ethics—I spend some time looking at exactly how the land lies in the disputed region of biological theory (section 5). I close by drawing some general conclusions for environmental ethics (section 6).

As I see it, then, this paper is, at heart, an exercise in the philosophy of biology, but one with consequences for the kind of considerations to which environmental ethicists might legitimately appeal. In my more mischievous moments, however, I am tempted to put a different spin on things, and to portray the argument as a sort of Trojan horse parked in the middle of philosophy of biology. To see why, let's focus on exactly how the central claims unfold, when seen from a narrower philosophical perspective. For a while things progress without much incident. Under cover of a critical response to a leading position in environmental ethics, I requisition and adapt for my own purposes an analysis, due primarily to Sober, according to which there exists a deep incompatibility between (i) a certain aspect of Darwinian theory and (ii) a generically Aristotelian account of biological systems (sections 2 and 3). If (i) is true, then (ii) is false—or so it seems— and who would dare deny Darwinism? At this juncture, however, I unleash a controversial thesis about the primary source of biological form, a thesis that locates that source in the phenomenon of self-organization during organismic development (section 4). As I shall argue, this thesis is recognizably neo-Aristotelian in character. Thus the conflict between Darwinism and Aristotelianism, far from being an interesting historical curiosity, appears to be back squarely on the biological agenda. The remaining task for this paper (when viewed from the present, narrower perspective) is to say something about the principles by which this apparent conflict might ultimately be resolved (section 5).

261

Michael Wheeler

2. Wearing Aristotle's Boots

Earlier I identified the following as one of the core questions in environmental ethics: which, if any, non-human natural entities have independent moral status (are morally considerable in their own right)?[2] Let's say you believe the answer to this question to be that human beings alone have independent moral status, with the only moral status enjoyed by non-human natural entities being derived from human needs and interests. How might you justify this view? The most obvious strategy would be to claim that the possession of some particular property or combination of properties is necessary for independent moral status, and that humans alone posssess that property or combination of properties. One might then expect psychological achievements such as being rational, being reflectively self-aware, and/or having the capacity for complex generative language-use to be prime candidates for the properties in question. But now let's say you are of a more inclusive ethical disposition, in that you believe the answer to the target question to be that a large sub-set of (and maybe even all) animals—human and non-human—enjoy independent moral status. In this case the properties just mentioned would be too restrictive to figure as necessary conditions here, although they might still be sufficient conditions. The default strategy for you now would most likely be to appeal to sentience, marked standardly by the capacity to feel pain. Sentience is a property that most people (including most philosophers) would be happy to attribute to many (although perhaps not all) non-human animals, but not to plants. Moreover, on the face of it, causing pain is a reasonable candidate for a morally reprehensible act. So sentience might be promoted as both a necessary (plants are plausibly ruled out) and a sufficient (most animals at least are plausibly ruled in) condition for independent moral status.

Those without experience of environmental ethics might think that this sort of animal-centred position is about as inclusive as the

[2] Wading into the debate over which entities have independent moral status is a convenient way of seeing how the specific philosophical position in which we are principally interested here gains its plausibility. The debate in question is complex, however, and I cannot do anything like proper justice to it here. Indeed, I shall do no more than touch on a small sub-set of the myriad issues and, aside from our target view, I shall content myself with greatly simplified versions of the alternative positions discussed. Anyone whose interest is aroused may follow up the details in the introductions to environmental ethics listed in note 1.

independent moral status club ever gets; but that would be a misconception. In environmental ethics it is not uncommon for theorists to extend independent moral status to plants.[3] Once we take this bold step, it is no longer possible to adopt being sentient as necessary for independent moral status, although it may still be sufficient. (I am simply going to ignore the protestations of those brave and unembarrassed souls who maintain that plants are sentient, and who thus see no difficulty in maintaining the necessity of sentience.) So how are we to stake out this new boundary to independent moral status? The rather obvious move is to extend independent moral status to *each individual living thing*, a position known in the trade as *biocentric individualism*.[4]

For my money, the most worked out, systematic, and compelling version of biocentric individualism remains Paul Taylor's *attitude of respect for nature*.[5] At the heart of Taylor's framework is the idea of an entity having *a good of its own*. If an entity has a good of its own, then it makes sense for us to speak in terms of what is good or bad *for* that entity, without us having to make reference to any other

[3] Another way of extending independent moral status is to be a holist, and to hold that certain environmental wholes (e.g. species, ecosystems, the Earth) are morally considerable in their own right. Holism will not concern us in this paper. The introductions to environmental ethics listed in note 1 all discuss holism at some point.

[4] Of course, someone who holds that each individual living thing is morally considerable in its own right isn't thereby committed to the thought that we would never be justified in harming any living thing, but only to the thought that when one is deciding upon a course of action, the independent needs and interests of each living thing affected by that decision must be taken into account.

[5] See P. W. Taylor, *Respect for Nature: A Theory of Environmental Ethics* (Princeton, NJ: Princeton University Press, 1986); P. W. Taylor, 'The Ethics of Respect for Nature', *Environmental Ethics*, **3**, No. 3 (1981), 192–218, reprinted in *Environmental Philosophy: from Animal Rights to Radical Ecology*, M.E. Zimmerman (ed.) (NJ: Prentice Hall, Third Edition, 2001), 71–86. To be precise, Taylor restricts the application of his biocentric individualist framework to wild organisms, and so suggests that the moral status of domesticated organisms is a separate issue. However, this qualification is a questionable wrinkle that we can simply ignore. For a prior and less sophisticated example of biocentric individualism, see Albert Schweitzer's 'reverence for life,' as developed in his *Cultural Philosophy II: Civilization and Ethics* (London: A. and C. Black, 1929, Translated by John Naish from the 1923 German text). For a biocentric position that builds on Taylor's work, see J. Sterba, 'From Biocentric Individualism to Biocentric Pluralism', *Environmental Ethics*, **17**, No. 2 (1995), 191–207.

entity. Consider my watch. In ordinary conversation we might happily talk in terms of it being good for this watch to be regularly serviced. However, a moment's reflection shows that if we really want to understand the meaning of this sort of statement, we will be forced to make reference to the purposes and/or the needs of some other (in this case, human) entity. This additional entity might be the designer of the watch (whose purpose was to bestow an accurate timekeeper on the world) or its current user (whose needs and goals, such as arriving at the railway station on time, are furthered by having a precision timepiece). In the final analysis, it is the goods of these other entities that are furthered by the watch being regularly serviced. By contrast, suppose I say that it would be good for my father to have a hernia operation. That statement will be true or false, depending on whether it really would advance my father's good to have such an operation, but unpacking the meaning here requires no reference to the purposes and/or needs of any entity in addition to my father. In familiar ethical language, then, a watch is merely a means to an end, and never an end in itself, whereas a human being, who may at times be a means to an end, is always also an end in his or her self.

So, for some entities, it is true to say that they have goods of their own; for others, it isn't. But where do we draw the line? According to Taylor—and here's where the biocentric individualism kicks in—for each *individual living thing*, it is true to say that that entity has a good of its own. What grounds this claim? Here it is useful to consider Taylor's analysis of butterfly life:

> ...once we come to understand [the butterfly's] life cycle and know the environmental conditions it needs to survive in a healthy state, we have no difficulty in speaking about what is beneficial to it and what might be harmful to it. A butterfly that develops through the egg, the larva, and pupa stages of its life in a normal manner, and then emerges as a healthy adult that carries on its existence under favorable environmental conditions, might well be said to thrive and prosper. It fares well, successfully adapting to its physical surroundings and maintaining the normal biological functions of its species throughout its entire span of life. When all these things are true of it, we are warranted in concluding that the good of this particular insect has been fully realized. It has lived at a high level of well-being. From the perspective of the butterfly's world, it has had a good life.[6]

[6] Respect for Nature, op. cit. note 3, 66.

According to Taylor, then, the individual butterfly has a good life when (a) it undergoes the normal developmental process that butterflies standardly undergo, (b) it has a healthy adult life (in the context of the lives normally led by members of its species), (c) it successfully adapts to its physical surroundings, and (d) it maintains the normal biological functions of its species throughout its life. As far as I can see, satisfying conditions (a)-(c) constitutes part of what it means to satisfy condition (d). An organism couldn't be said to maintain the normal biological functions of its species throughout its life if it didn't undergo a normal species-specific developmental trajectory, have a healthy adult life, or successfully adapt to its physical surroundings. Here, then, is the key point: for each individual living thing, we can make sense of that organism as flourishing when, throughout its life, it succeeds in realizing the biological functions that are normal for organisms of that species, and as failing to flourish whenever it fails to realize those functions. It is because we always have this benchmark for what counts as the flourishing of a particular individual living thing that we can rightly speak of each individual living thing as having a good of its own.[7]

Four features of Taylor's concept of an entity's own good deserve emphasis:

1. What counts as the good of a particular animal or plant is fixed relative to the species of which that animal or plant is a member. As Taylor explains, in 'order to know what a particular organism's good consists in... it is necessary to know its species-specific characteristics. These characteristics include the cellular structure of the organism, the internal functioning of its various parts, and its external relations to

[7] For Taylor, being an individual living thing may not quite constitute a necessary condition for an entity to have a good of its own. Parenthetically he raises the issue of artificial intelligence, and resolves to remain open-minded about a possible future in which we feel compelled to say of a robot that it genuinely has a good of its own, independently of its designer's purposes. Taylor's position here is not quite clear. If he were prepared to say that such a robot were literally alive, then he might hold that being an individual thing is a necessary condition for an entity to have a good of its own. But, in the following passage, Taylor hesitates to extend the concept of life to robots, and suggests that a different system of ethics might be required in such a case: 'If mechanisms (*organisms?*) of artificial intelligence were ever to be produced, another system of ethics might have to be applied to the treatment of such entities by moral agents' (Respect for Nature, op. cit. note 3, 125, emphasis added).

other organisms and to the physical-chemical aspects of its environment. Unless we learn how the organism develops, grows and sustains its life according to the laws of its species-specific nature, we cannot fully understand what promotes the realization of its good or what is detrimental to its good.'[8]

2. Although Taylor is not entirely clear about the conceptual relation that obtains between a species-specific biological function and a species-specific characteristic, it seems, on the whole, that he conceives of species-specific characteristics as material factors that underlie or support some biological function. (The cellular structure of the organism, for example, fits this profile.). Re-reading the quotation immediately above through this lens, we can now see that, for Taylor, understanding organisms, and thus in what the goods of those organisms consist, requires two interlocking explanatory domains, that of biological function and that of material underpinning.

3. Whether or not an entity has a good of its own is independent of whether or not that entity is, even in principle, consciously aware of in what that good consists, and so may consciously organize its behaviour with the goal of furthering that good. In other words, for Taylor, sentience is not a necessary condition for an entity to have a good of its own. That's why individual non-sentient animals (if there are any) and individual plants have a good of their own in just as robust a sense as individual sentient animals. This is, of course, exactly what one would expect from a biocentric individualist position.

4. Whether or not an organism is flourishing is a fully objective fact about that organism, a fact that is susceptible to human investigation once we have the requisite knowledge about the organism's species-specific characteristics. This state of affairs means that human beings are, in principle, able to make judgments from the standpoint of an organism's own good, even if that organism is not itself capable of making such judgments.

As we shall see, Taylor's concept of an entity's own good is far from the whole of his biocentric individualism. Indeed, sharp-eyed readers will have noticed that, so far, I haven't even mentioned the notion of independent moral status. More on that soon. First though I want to take a brief stroll through some familiar historical territory, in order to substantiate the claim that Taylor's concept of

[8] Respect for Nature, op. cit. note 3, 68.

an entity's own good is recognizably and robustly Aristotelian in character.

Aristotle's term *psuche* is usually translated as 'soul.'[9] This can be misleading, however, since to the modern ear the word 'soul' suggests a spiritual mode of existence; and that clashes unhelpfully with most of what Aristotle says about the *psuche*, which is resolutely naturalistic. (I say 'most of' here in view of Aristotle's notorious cave-in over the intellect, the one component of the *psuche* that he claims is immortal and eternal.[10]) In view of the shortcomings of the term 'soul' in this context, it is better, I think, to start with Aristotle's claim that each species of organism may be identified by a set of biological capacities that, under normal circumstances, any individual member of that species will come to express. Correlatively, each organism will have associated with it one of these sets of (what I shall call) life-capacities; and that set constitutes its *psuche*. The master-list of such life-capacities, from which the lists that specify particular *psuches* will be drawn, looks something like this: self-nourishment (including growth and decay), reproduction, appetite, touch, non-tactile forms of perception, self-controlled motion, imagination, and intellectual reasoning. Here the various life-capacities have been arranged in order of, as Aristotle would see it, increasing sophistication. This is not an idle presentational move, since, according to Aristotle, the possession of

[9] Aristotle, '*De Anima* (On the Soul)', *The Complete Works of Aristotle*, J. Barnes (ed.) (Princeton, NJ: Princeton University Press, 1984, Revised Oxford Translation, Volume 1), 641–92. The brief analysis of the psuche which I include here draws, in part, on the following paper of mine: M. Wheeler, 'Cognition's Coming Home: the Reunion of Life and Mind', *Fourth European Conference on Artificial Life*, P. Husbands and I. Harvey (eds.) (Cambridge, Mass.: MIT Press, 1997), 10–19. That paper constitutes a very different philosophical project (the goal of which is to show that the discipline of artificial life has the credentials to be the intellectual core of a distinctively biological cognitive science, one which holds that life and mind share a common set of organizational principles). Nevertheless, in that work I pursue issues that surface again here. In particular, my later discussions in this paper of (i) the Aristotelian nature of certain recent self-organization-based accounts of biological form and (ii) the implications of Kauffman's N-K model draw, in part, on that previous investigation.

[10] '*De Anima*' op. cit. note 9, Book 3, chapter 5. For discussion, see, for example, K. V. Wilkes' 'Final Embarrassed Postscript' (her words not mine) in her 'Psuche versus the Mind', *Essays on Aristotle's De Anima*, M. C. Nussbaum and A. Oksenberg Rorty (eds.) (Oxford: Clarendon, 1992), 109–127.

Michael Wheeler

any particular life-capacity presupposes the possession of the less sophisticated life-capacities from this list. So, for example, the possession of touch presupposes the possession of appetite, reproduction, and self-nourishment. On this picture, then, self-nourishment, the most primitive of the life-capacities, is possessed by every living thing. Moreover, it emerges as being necessary and sufficient for life. This, I think, is the right way to understand Aristotle's claim that 'the nutritive soul is found along with all the others and is the most primitive and widely distributed power of soul, being indeed that one in virtue of which all are said to have life'[11]

Next we need to add in a well-known aspect of Aristotle's account of the *psuche*. Famously, Aristotle draws what he takes to be a widely applicable distinction between *form* and *matter*. To a first approximation, the form of an entity is its distinctive mode of organization. Thus Aristotle tells us that a statue's shape is its form, while its matter is the physical stuff (bronze, stone, or whatever) out of which it is made. The form of an axe is its capacity to chop, while its matter is the wood and metal out of which it is made. Moving into the biological world, the form of the eye is capacity to see, while the matter, according to Aristotle's ancient biology, consists largely of water. When Aristotle applies the form-matter distinction to whole living organisms, we are told that the form of a living creature is its *psuche*, its set of life-capacities; the matter is the organic body which underlies those capacities.[12] Against this back-

---

[11] '*De Anima*' op. cit. note 9, Book 2, chapter 4, 415; p. 661 in the cited edition.

[12] Here I am ignoring all sorts of nuances and difficulties. For example, it is clear that while the canonical example of a form (a statue's shape) allows form to be interpretable as structure, other examples (an axe's capacity to chop, an eye's capacity to see) somehow involve an additional notion of function. My use of the phrase 'distinctive mode of organization' is supposed to fudge this distinction (which is why I called my characterization a 'first approximation'). The issue of form and function (and so functionalism) in Aristotle is now an industry in Aristotelian scholarship. (See many of the papers in the aforementioned Nussbaum and Oksenberg Rorty collection on *De Anima*. For an evolutionarily oriented take on the issue, see my 'Cognition's Coming Home: the Reunion of Life and Mind', op. cit. note 9.) In addition, Aristotle himself characterizes the relationship between form and matter in a different way when he turns from a non-biological to a biological context. Roughly, he suggests that the matter of a statue is only contingently enformed by its shape, whereas the organic body is essentially enformed by the relevant psuche. See, famously, J. L. Ackrill,

ground, an Aristotelian organism may be glossed as what Charles calls an 'interactive unity' of matter and form.[13] One way of playing out this idea is as follows. On the one hand, the material (neurobiological/biochemical) aspects of an organism must be understood in terms of the biological forms (life-capacities) which those aspects generate and maintain. On the other, to do justice to this explanatory demand, one needs an account of organic matter as essentially a dynamic potentiality for generating biological form.[14]

The concept of the *psuche* also grounds Aristotle's own version of the idea that every organism may be said to have a good of its own. One can see Aristotle appealing to the idea of organisms having goods of their own when he says, for example, that 'mutilated or imperfect growths' occur when organisms fail to 'produce their species and rise to completeness of nature and decay to an end.'[15] Given that the terms 'mutilation' and 'imperfect' clearly signal failures to flourish, it seems that the notion of a 'completeness of nature' is equivalent to the concept of an organism's own good. Moreover, when an organism 'rises to completeness of nature,' before decaying naturally to an end, it may be understood as having flourished by fully expressing the set of life-capacities associated with its species. Thus the good of an organism consists in the full expression of the appropriate species-specific set of life-capacities.[16]

[13] D. Charles, *Aristotle on Meaning and Essence* (Oxford: Oxford University Press, 2000).

[14] See A. Code and J. Moravcsik, 'Explaining Various Forms of Living', *Essays on Aristotle's De Anima*, M. C. Nussbaum and A. Oksenberg Rorty (eds.) (Oxford: Clarendon, 1992), 138-41.

[15] *'De Anima'* op. cit. note 9, Book 3, chapter 9, 432; p. 688 in the cited edition.

[16] I should confess that Aristotle's account of the psuche is not quite as straightforward as I have made out in the main text. For one thing, he gives different master-lists of life-capacities in different places. For another, there are exegetical disputes among scholars about exactly how the various life-capacities ought to be divided-up. Finally, the relationship of presupposition may not always be as straightforward as I have suggested. These admissions need not concern us here, however, because these fine-grained details of the psuche, while important in other contexts, do not bear on the argument of this paper. For a systematic analysis of the structure of the

'Aristotle's Definitions of Psuche', *Proceedings of the Aristotelian Society* **73** (1972–3), 119–33. For one response to this problem, see C. Shields, 'Aristotle's Psychology', *The Stanford Encyclopedia of Philosophy (Fall 2004 Edition)*, Edward N. Zalta (ed.), URL = http://plato.stanford.edu/archives/fall2004/entries/aristotle-psychology

Michael Wheeler

There are obvious similarities between Taylor's notion of a set of biological functions and Aristotle's notion of a set of life-capacities. Both are to be unpacked as species-specific suites of biological traits, both determine in what the goods of particular organisms consist, and both need to be understood as specifying the formal (or functional) half of the form-matter (function-matter) unity that, on either account, constitutes an organism. But just how deep do the similarities go? My answer to this question will come in two parts. First I shall argue that while it is true that Taylor's ethical thinking endorses a fact-value distinction in a way that Aristotle's (arguably) doesn't, this divergence is not as important as it might initially appear. Crucially, both theories use the concept and the details of an organism's own good as the basis for specifying certain moral norms. This shared strategy is built on the principle that for an organism to have independent moral status, it is necessary that that organism can rightly be said to have a good of its own. Having identified this structural parallel, I shall argue (second part) that in order for ethical norms to be based on biological facts in this way, a certain understanding of biological systems—crucially, an Aristotelian one—must be in play. So it turns out that Taylor's position in environmental ethics implicitly buys into a fundamental feature of Aristotelian biology. And that's where the fun really starts.

Consider, then, the following question: how do we get from biology to ethics? For Aristotle, the distinction between biological (more generally, scientific) fact and ethical value did not loom large in the way that it does for many contemporary philosophers. Indeed, as far as the Aristotelian framework is concerned, it seems that the following position is licensed: once one has correctly identified the set of life-capacities associated with a particular species, one not only knows in what the good of an individual member of that species consists, and thus what would count as harming that individual (namely preventing that individual from coming to express fully its complete set of life-capacities), one also has a duty, in one's moral deliberations, to factor in the causing of such harm as a negative component.[17]

[17] This point is nicely made by Des Jardins. See J. R. Des Jardins, *Environmental Ethics* (Belmont, CA: Wadsworth, 2001), 24–5.

psuche, see G. B. Matthews, 'De Anima 2. 2-4 and the Meaning of Life', *Essays on Aristotle's De Anima*, M. C. Nussbaum and A. Oksenberg Rorty (eds.) (Oxford: Clarendon, 1992), 185-93. Reprinted as 'Aristotle on Life,' *The Philosophy of Artificial Life*, M. A. Boden (ed.) (Oxford: Oxford University Press, 1996), 304–13.

For Taylor, by contrast, one cannot simply read off ethical norms from biological nature in this way. He argues as follows:

1. In order for an entity to be granted independent moral status, it must be true to say, of that entity, that it has a good of its own.
2. Each organism has a good of its own.
3. However, to say that an organism has a good of its own is a statement of biological (i.e. scientific) fact.
4. Ethical norms are not logically deducible from such facts.
5. So it is consistent to assert that a particular organism has a good of its own while simultaneously denying that moral agents have a duty (all things being equal) to promote or preserve that good.

In other words, an entity having a good of its own is a necessary but not a sufficient condition for that entity to be granted independent moral status. It is not a sufficient condition because there exists a gap between scientific facts and moral values. Nevertheless, Taylor does hold that each organism enjoys independent moral status. So what carries us across the fact-value divide? Here Taylor identifies four nature-regarding beliefs that, he argues, one ought to hold. Together these beliefs make up (what he calls) the *biocentric outlook* on nature. In banner headline terms, the beliefs in question are (i) that human beings, along with all other organisms, are members of a community of life on Earth, (ii) that organisms form webs of ecological interdependence, (iii) that each organism is a unique individual pursuing its species-specific good in its own way, and (iv) that humans are not inherently superior to other living things. The plausibility of, and the relations between, these four beliefs need not concern us here. Our interest is in Taylor's claim that once one endorses the biocentric outlook, a commitment to the independent moral status of individual living things becomes the *only suitable* moral stance to adopt. So once one adopts the biocentric outlook, one is rationally (although not logically) compelled to grant individual organisms independent moral status. In Taylor's framework, this means that one must regulate one's actions by reference to an affected organism's own good, that is, by reference to the ways in which the action in question promotes or hinders that organism in coming to express the scientifically identifiable set of species-specific biological traits in which its own good consists. In effect, this move forges a *non-demonstrative connection* between biological facts and moral values. Moral values are, as Taylor puts it, 'based on' biological facts.

Michael Wheeler

The common core of our two theoretical frameworks may now be revealed. For the sake of simplicity, let's stipulate that an action is to be considered in isolation from other actions, and in relation only to a single affected organism. Then, for both our theories, the moral permissibility or otherwise of an action, when performed by some moral agent (see below), will be determined by the (positive, neutral, or negative) effects which that action will have on the likelihood of an affected organism coming or continuing to express the distinctive species-specific set of biological traits in which that organism's own good consists. This shared strategy for specifying ethical norms by reference to biological facts (what I shall from now on call, simply, 'the shared strategy') rests on the similarly shared claim that it is a *necessary* condition for an entity to be morally considerable in its own right that that entity have a good if its own. The Aristotelian theory differs from Taylor's here by making the possession of such a good a sufficient, as well as a necessary, condition for independent moral status. This move renders the route from biology to ethics direct, of course, but, as long as there exists some alternative machinery for making the fact-value transition (in Taylor's theory this is the biocentric outlook), the sufficiency claim is not required for the target strategy to get off the ground. The necessity claim, however, is. In both theories, certain biological facts are always available to play the key norm-specifying role precisely because, for each individual living thing, there always exists a set of scientifically identifiable species-specific biological traits (those in which the good of that organism consists) that can be used as a kind of moral manual.

Given the shared strategy, to what understanding of biological systems are our two theories committed? This is where we run headlong into what Elliott Sober calls Aristotle's *natural state model*.[18] As Sober explains, this model supplies us with a procedure for thinking about diversity and variation in nature. Aristotle

[18] E. Sober, 'Evolution, Population Thinking, and Essentialism', *Philosophy of Science* **47** (1980), 350–83; reprinted in *Conceptual Issues in Evolutionary Biology* E. Sober (ed.) (Cambridge, Mass.: MIT Press, 1994, second edition, from which page numbers are taken), 16–89. See also E. Sober, 'Philosophical Problems for Environmentalism', *The Preservation of Species: the Value of Biological Diversity*, B. Norton (ed.) (Princeton: Princeton University Press, 1986), 173-95; reprinted in *Environmental Ethics*, R. Elliott (ed.) (Oxford: Oxford University Press, 1995), 226–47. In the latter paper, Sober argues that some positions in environmental ethics are problematic because they implicitly endorse the natural state model. More on this in note 25 below.

argued that all natural objects, including organisms, have a natural state towards which they will inevitably gravitate, in the absence of interfering forces. In other words, interfering forces obstruct the natural tendencies of natural objects to reach or to stay in their natural states. Diversity and variation in natural objects are thus conceived as deviations from the natural states of those objects, caused by the operation of interfering forces. For example, in Aristotle's physics, the natural state of all sublunar heavy objects is to be located at the centre of the Earth, although the natural tendency that such entities have to achieve this state is often thwarted by interfering forces. Similarly, and crucially for us, although the natural state of all organisms is to express their full set of life-capacities, interfering forces may frustrate the natural tendency that such entities have to achieve this state.

Interlude: In Aristotle's own thinking, the natural state model of biological systems was, of course, embedded within a strongly teleological picture in which the natural world *in general* was conceived as literally purposeful and as literally goal-driven. This perspective has largely been discredited by the advance of modern science and its philosophical bedfellows. It is worth noting here that the widespread rejection of the strongly teleological view of nature does not herald the demise of the natural state model in science. Indeed, if we put an Aristotelian gloss on Newton's first law of motion, then that law says that a body will remain in its natural state of being either at rest or in uniform motion unless it is acted upon by a force. (Here, any force counts as an interfering force.) So the natural state model remains enshrined in Newtonian physics, and no one who is thinking in a non-metaphorical key believes that it is the goal or purpose of a body to remain either at rest or in uniform motion.[19] The message is that the strongly teleological dimension of Aristotle's own natural state model can, in principle, be discarded, leaving the rest of the model intact. Still, physics is physics and biology is biology. In biology, teleological language remains in force. The *purpose* of the heart is to pump blood, the male peacock's tail evolved to be large and decorated *in order to* attract mates, and so on. The standard trick, of course, is to reconceive one's teleology within a Darwinian framework. Ignoring all sorts of nuances and complications, the story goes like this. Where natural selection has been operative, individual organisms in the present generation will tend to express those phenotypic traits that have bestowed fitness

[19] This Aristotelian gloss on Newton's first law of motion is also to be found in Sober; see Sober, 'Evolution, Population Thinking, and Essentialism', op. cit. note 18, 168–9.

advantages on their ancestors. Such traits are adaptations; and the purpose, function or goal of an adaptation will be to carry out the fitness-enhancing task that it performed in ancestral populations. By way of this Darwinization, teleological concepts are underwritten historically, and are thereby made to behave themselves in relation to a physics that has discarded teleology altogether. I take it that Aristotle would most likely have approved of this naturalization of teleology. So that's not where the clash with Darwinism arises.[20]

Back to the main plot: it is easy enough to see how what I am calling the shared strategy may lean on the natural state model of biological systems, so let's spell it out. Buying Aristotelian physics for a moment, there is a clear sense in which, for heavy objects (and that includes organisms treated purely as heavy objects), all interfering forces are on a moral par: since heavy objects (qua heavy objects) are not the kinds of entities that have goods of their own, none of the interfering forces that prevent those objects from reaching their natural states are ethically significant. By contrast, in the case of organisms, all of which have goods of their own, and all of which are morally considerable in their own right, some interfering forces are ethically significant, namely those interfering forces that emanate from the actions of moral agents. When the action of a moral agent frustrates the natural tendency of an organism to reach its natural state (to express the species-specific set of biological traits in which its good consists), that action, considered in isolation from other actions, and only in relation to that organism, ought to be judged morally reprehensible.

---

[20] To keep everything above board, I should confess that there is a tension between Taylor's biocentric individualism and a Darwinized teleology. Taylor often writes of organisms as *teleological centres of life*. This locution signals the belief (a component of the biocentric outlook, see main text) that each organism is a unique individual pursuing its species-specific good in its own way. In unpacking this idea Taylor explicitly resists a move that might seem to be on the cards following the proposed Darwinization of teleology, namely to identify the concept of an organism realizing its own good with the concept of Darwinian fitness (See *Respect for Nature*, op. cit. note 3, 121, footnote 7.) Taylor points out that some individual organisms (e.g. some social insects) sacrifice their lives (and thus their own goods) to enhance the probability that their genes will survive into future generations (thus increasing their inclusive fitness), and he observes that some human beings freely choose to forego having children (thus reducing their fitness) in order, as they see things, to realize a good life.

The connection between the shared strategy and Aristotle's natural state model of biological systems may be even tighter than I have just suggested. Indeed, unless it is true to say that each individual organism has a natural tendency to develop and maintain the very set of biological traits which putatively constitutes that organism's own good, it is hard (I think) to see how the strategy of delineating ethical norms by reference to such sets of traits is supposed to work at all. Put very crudely, the underlying dependency looks like this: if the organism's life isn't going somewhere, then nothing we might do to that organism can count as hindering the flourishing of that life, in which case the suggestion that such allegedly obstructive interference on our part ought to count as morally reprehensible is a non-starter. The shared strategy requires, in addition, that the 'somewhere' in question is the full expression of a distinctive set of species-specific biological traits. But if all this is right, then that strategy, and thus Taylor's biocentric individualism, *requires* that some version of the Aristotelian natural state model of biological systems be correct, a version in which the relevant class of natural states is fleshed out in terms of certain species-specific sets of biological traits.

The conclusion of this section is that a prominent position in contemporary environmental ethics, namely Taylor's biocentric individualism, is, at heart, a neo-Aristotelian venture. In the next section I review some powerful reasons for thinking that if modern evolutionary theory is true, then the requirement that we have just located at the base of this framework—the requirement that the Aristotelian natural state model of biological systems be correct—will not be met. In other words, as far as this paper is concerned, the Aristotelian natural state model of biological systems is the principal target of Darwin's cosh.

3. Against the Natural State Model

According to Ernst Mayr, Darwin's legacy was threefold. He presented a mass of evidence that evolution occurs, he proposed natural selection as the mechanism of evolutionary change, and (crucially given our present interests) he replaced typological thinking by population thinking.[21] At root, the natural state model

---

[21] Ernst Mayr, 'Typological versus Population Thinking', in his *Evolution and the Diversity of Life* (Cambridge, MA: Harvard University Press, 1976), 26–9; reprinted in *Conceptual Issues in Evolutionary Biology*, E. Sober (ed.) (Cambridge MA: MIT Press, 1994, second edition, from which page numbers are taken), 157–60.

in biology is an example of typological thinking. There are species-*types*, identified as species-specific sets of biological characteristics. Individuals realize these species-types only imperfectly, due to the operation of interfering forces. Darwinian population thinking, by contrast, finds no place for types of this sort. The biological realm is not conceptualized as a place in which individual organisms have a natural tendency to realize some set of common characteristics that constitutes their generic species-type, or in which diversity is the product of interfering forces that deflect individuals from the path towards that state of species-wide uniformity. Rather, as Mayr puts it, '[all] organisms and organic phenomena are composed of unique features and can be described collectively only in statistical terms.'[22] In other words, individual variation is the fundamental way of things—the base-line of biological nature.

One way to illuminate the deep differences between these approaches is to see how they would handle some data from developmental biology. So let's call on the geneticist's best friend, the fruit-fly *Drosophila*. There are usually about 1000 light-receptor cells in the *Drosophila* compound eye. Genetic mutations can reduce the number of receptors dramatically, but genetic events are not the only causal factors in the developmental equation. As Lewontin reports,[23] the final number of receptors also depends on the environmental temperature at which the flies develop. For example, if flies with the wild (statistically most common in nature) genotype develop at a temperature of 15° centigrade, they will end up with 1100 receptors; but they will have only 750 receptors if the

[22] Op. cit. note 21, 158. Mayr's analysis gives us a template for how to explain biological nature. However, in the paper in question there is, intertwined with this explanatory template, a picture of the different metaphysical commitments that underlie typological and population thinking respectively. Mayr argues that for the typological thinker types are real while individual variation is an illusion, whereas for the population thinker varying individuals are real while 'types' (understood as statistical abstractions, as averages over populations of individuals) are not. Sober, rightly in my view, rejects both halves of this claim. (See Sober, 'Evolution, Population Thinking, and Essentialism', op. cit. note 18.) In the present context Mayr's questionable metaphysical picture need not be a cause for concern. His key insight concerning the explanatory priority of individual variation in population thinking does not depend on the dubious metaphysical window-dressing he supplies, and so may be formulated without it (which is what I have endeavoured to do in the main text). I take it that this is Sober's view also.

[23] R. Lewontin, 'The Organism as the Subject and Object of Evolution', *Scientia* **118** (1983), 63-82.

developmental temperature is as high as 30° centigrade. And things get more complicated once we allow, in addition, variations in the genotype, and consider the ensuing pattern of interactions with the relevant environmental factor. For example, *Drosophila* with a mutation known as *Ultrabar* always end up with less visual receptors than those with wild genotype. The same is true of *Drosophila* with a different mutation, *Infrabar*. However, the two mutant genotypes have opposite relations to temperature, such that the number of receptors possessed by *Ultrabar* flies decreases with developmental temperature, while the number possessed by *Infrabar* flies increases. In fact, if we make two plots of the number of light receptors against developmental temperature, one for *Ultrabar* and one for *Infrabar* (more on this idea in a moment), the two curves will cross over.

How is this developmental space to be conceptualized?[24] Let's begin with the natural state model. According to the strict interpretation of this model, there will be a unique number of light receptors that constitutes the natural phenotypic outcome for insects of this species, although interfering forces during morphogenesis may well mean that this number is often not realized. (In a more relaxed frame of mind, we might allow that the relevant natural state may be specified in a mildly disjunctive way, such that, for example, the natural state will be realized if the number of light-receptors takes any one from a limited, small range of values. This does not alter the fundamental character of the explanation, so, for ease of exposition, I shall continue to work with the strict interpretation.) Each of the mutation-driven, temperature-driven, or interactive variations in phenotypic form that we identified in the data above needs to be characterized as a deviation from some natural state—the natural phenotype. The most likely candidate for the natural phenotype is a compound eye with 1000 light-receptor cells (or some appropriately relaxed take on that phenotype). However, this is not the only option. There is no requirement in the natural state model that the privileged phenotype be statistically the most common.

Now let's turn to the approach recommended by population

---

[24] My brief analysis of *Drosophila* morphogenesis that follows is, in essence, the local application of a general theoretical analysis, advanced by Sober, of the different ways in which natural state thinking and population thinking approach development; see his 'Evolution, Population Thinking, and Essentialism', op. cit. note 18. In that paper Sober considers, only to reject, a number of different moves designed to reduce the tension between the natural state model and population thinking.

biology. The population geneticist will appeal to the concept of a *norm of reaction*. We've just seen this idea at work. A norm of reaction is a curve generated by taking a particular genotype, and plotting changes in a phenotypic trait of interest (in our example, the number of receptors) against an environmental variable (in our example, the developmental temperature). In effect, a norm of reaction shows how an organism of a particular genotype would develop in different environments. So one might conceptualize our fruit-fly developmental space in terms of a set of norms of reaction. This way of thinking enshrines individual variation at the root of biological nature. Each norm of reaction identifies a range of possible developmental outcomes for a particular genotype. Moreover, there is a deep sense in which, in terms of our understanding of the fundamental character of biological systems, each of these outcomes, and each of the outcomes for each of the different possible genotypes, is conceptualized as being on an equal footing. Of course, it may be true to say of the fruit-fly not only (a) that there is a wild genotype, but also (b) that in its ordinary developmental ecology, the temperature is regularly within a small range of values. This might explain why the number of light-receptor cells in the *Drosophila* compound eye is usually about 1000. Nevertheless this situation, riddled as it is with statistical and environment-relative contingency, seems to fall short of establishing the dual presence of a uniquely privileged developmental outcome and an associated tendency for the organism in question to realize that outcome—the kind of constrained developmental profile that the natural state model requires.

These apparent problems with the natural state model reverberate into environmental ethics. If the third Darwinian contribution identified by Mayr is on the mark, and the base-line of biological nature really is that actual organisms are, at root, no more than points on a vast landscape of phenotypic diversity, rather than enforced offshoots from a path that leads to a preferred species-specific destination, then it is hard to give any conceptual weight to the idea that in perturbing the developmental trajectory of an organism, we are preventing it from realizing its natural state. Any philosophical strategy for specifying ethical norms that rests on that idea is thereby undermined; and that includes Taylor's biocentric individualism.[25] But have we got the base-line right? Our first

[25] As mentioned above, in his paper 'Philosophical Problems for Environmentalism' (op. cit. note 18, 233–40), Sober traces certain difficulties facing some environmentalist positions to their implicit adoption of the natural state model. Sober's target is the very general claim, plausibly

flirtation with contemporary developmental biology certainly suggests that we have; but perhaps all is not as it seems.

4. Kick-Starting Aristotelianism

I now want to suggest that we have been moving too fast, and that there is, in truth, growing support in contemporary biological science for something which looks very much like an Aristotelian natural state model of organismic development.[26] Self-organization is a phenomenon that is now recognized as being widespread in nature—and that includes human nature. Indeed, it appears that wherever we look (e.g. at chemical reactions, lasers, slime moulds, foraging by ants, flocking behaviour in creatures such as birds,

[26] I am not the only person to have claimed recently that modern biological science is inadvertently rediscovering supposedly discarded Aristotelian concepts and principles. For example, Denis Walsh has been arguing that contemporary evolutionary developmental biology explains why organisms have the particular phenotypes they do (and in particular, the organismal capacities that underlie the evolvability of organismal lineages) by appealing to a reciprocal relation between the goal-directed plasticity of organisms and the causal powers of their underlying developmental systems. According to Walsh, this reciprocal arrangement maps onto, and, in the end, plays the same fundamental explanatory role as, the kind of interactive unity between a biological form and its realizing matter that constitutes an Aristotelian organismal nature. See D. Walsh, 'Evolutionary Essentialism', unpublished conference paper given at Teleology, Ancient and Modern, University of Edinburgh, 16–18 August 2004. Although the analysis that follows in this paper exploits different aspects of Aristotelian philosophy of biology and of contemporary developmental biology, it is clearly an overlapping and complementary approach.

at work in a number of environmentalist positions, that what is morally reprehensible about an action that frustrates an organism's endogenous developmental tendency to reach its natural state is that any such action places the organism concerned in an unnatural state. As Sober points out, once development is conceptualized on the population biology model, the idea that any one phenotype is the only natural one is deeply problematic. The worry about neo-Aristotelian environmentalism that I present here clearly reprises Sober's critique in certain respects, although I have endeavoured to add fuel to the fire by showing in detail exactly how that natural state model underlies the detailed neo-Aristotelian structure of one prominent environmental-ethical framework. More importantly, as we shall see, I think the natural state model lives to fight another day, whereas Sober doesn't.

Michael Wheeler

human infant walking, neural processing in the brain, traffic jams... the list is just about endless), there is compelling research to suggest that the concept of self-organization will contribute to our understanding of how things work. Biological systems, and more particularly organismic development, have, as we shall see, provided a particularly fertile breeding ground for self-organization-based thinking.[27] So what is self-organization? A system is said to self-organize when its components causally interact with each other so as to produce the autonomous emergence and maintenance of structured global order. The term 'autonomous' is here being used to indicate nothing more fancy than (i) that the global behaviour of the system in question is *not* being organized by some (inner or outer) controlling executive that dictates or orchestrates the activity of the individual components, and (ii) that those individual components do *not* make their contributions by accessing and following some comprehensive plan of the global behaviour, but rather by following purely local principles of causal interaction. Formal definitions aside, the best way to get a grip on self-organization is to consider an example. So let's take one from the arena that is of principal interest to us, namely organismic development.

To the untrained eye, the higher plants realize a bewildering and stunning variety of leaf arrangements. However, there are really only three generic forms present in nature. The most frequent of these is spiral phyllotaxis (phyllo-taxis = leaf-order). Spiral phyllotaxis is a pattern of organization in which successive leaves on the stem appear at a fixed angle of rotation relative to each other. Amazingly, natural instances of spiral phyllotaxis are such that only a very few angles of rotation are ever realized; and the most common angle of rotation to be found is 137·5°. How might one explain these facts? I shall focus on an account due to Brian Goodwin.[28]

[27] For seminal appeals to self-organization in biology, see, for example: B. Goodwin, *How the Leopard Changed its Spots: the Evolution of Complexity* (London: Phoenix, 1994); S. Kauffman, *The Origins or Order: Self-Organization and Selection in Evolution* (New York: Oxford University Press, 1993). For typically lively and incisive discussion, see J. Maynard Smith, *Shaping Life: Genes, Embryos and Evolution* (London: Weidenfeld and Nicolson, 1998).

[28] Op. cit. note 27, 105–19. I have used this example a number of times before to introduce the idea of self-organization in biological development, but then it is such a good example. See, for example, M. Wheeler, 'Do Genes Code for Traits?', *Philosophical Dimensions of Logic and Science: Selected Contributed Papers from the 11th International Congress of Logic, Methodology, and Philosophy of Science*, A. Rojszczak, J. Cachro and G. Kurczewski (eds.) (Dordrecht: Kluwer, 2003), 151–4.

According to Goodwin, as leaf-tissue grows, it places pressure on an elastic surface layer of epidermal cells. This pressure causes the epidermal cells to synthesize cellulose microfibrils to resist the force. Where the next leaf will grow is determined by the fact that, as a result of exactly where the stress has been placed, and exactly how the cellulose defences are laid down, the resistance to growth will be stronger in some areas of the epidermal layer than in others. Thus the global phenotypic leaf arrangement results from a sequence of local causal interactions between (i) the growing leaves under the epidermal surface, and (ii) the barricades of defending cellulose microfibrils. To provide support for such a view, Goodwin cites modelling studies which show that the phyllotactic arrangements observed in nature are stable patterns produced by such a system. This done, the challenge is to explain why these arrangements are the *only* stable arrangements generated by that system. Here Goodwin appeals to a second model which demonstrates that if (a) the rate of leaf formation is above a critical value, and (b) the system starts with the most-commonly-found initial pattern of leaf primordia in the growing tip, then the developing plant will tend overwhelmingly to settle on spiral phyllotaxis with an angle of rotation of 137·5°. In other words, given certain parameter-values and initial conditions, the most common phyllotactic arrangement found in nature is the generic form produced by the self-organizing dynamics in the model. Moreover, with different values for certain key parameters in the model (e.g., the growth rates and the number of leaves generated at any one time), the other phyllotactic arrangements observed in nature may be generated from the same basic self-organizing dynamics.

Examples of developmental self-organization could be multiplied—Goodwin himself describes a good number of compelling cases—but you get the idea. The question for us is this: why is this way of understanding organismic development fundamentally Aristotelian in character? The immediate answer (although one that stands in need of refinement) is that developmental self-organization puts back on the theoretical map the supposedly heretical thought that organisms have natural states towards which they will inevitably gravitate, in the absence of interfering forces. The idea here has two facets: (i) developmental gravitation may be conceived in terms of the underlying principles of change that explain the generic dynamics exhibited by particular developmental self-organizing systems; (ii) natural states may be conceived as the stable states of emergent global order produced in such systems.

Michael Wheeler

For an extra nudge in Aristotle's direction, one might also add in the following thought. As mentioned earlier, Aristotle has an account of organic matter as essentially a dynamic potentiality for generating biological form. And that is precisely what one gets, if one understands organic development in terms of a certain sub-class of self-organizing physical systems.

It may seem that my flagship example of self-organized form doesn't line up too well with Aristotelian life-capacities, since while the latter takes forms to be species-specific, the emergent order in the phyllotaxis case (spiral phyllotaxis, or even spiral phyllotaxis with a certain angle of rotation) is seemingly more general, in that many species may realize the same generic pattern. In fact, we just need to be rather more subtle in our understanding of Aristotle. As Lennox points out, for Aristotle, biological kinds are 'a set of general differentiae, features common to every bird or fish, *qua* bird or fish... Birds, *qua* birds, have beaks, for example. Different sorts [species] of birds may have beaks of differing length, width, hue, hardness, curvature. It is these sorts of differences, throughout all the differentiae of the general kind, which differentiate one form of bird from another.'[29] Pursuing our parallel, it seems likely, then, that specific forms—a distinctive sunflower leaf-structure, for example— may be understood as local variations on more fundamental patterns of self-organization, variations determined by the ways in which genes, in particular, act so as to parameterize the self-organizing dynamics realized by the species of organism in question.[30]

If Aristotelian natural state thinking in biology has indeed been successfully resurrected, then Taylor's biocentric framework for environmental ethics is also back on the map. Still, the observations that I have submitted so far, in favour of the view that self-organization-based developmental biology has Aristotelian credentials are manifestly the beginning, rather than the end, of a story. I can't hope to complete that story here. However, in the next section I shall attempt to take us part of the way, by clarifying the basic proposal, and by shoring it up against some prima facie objections.

[29] J. Lennox, 'Kinds, Forms of Kinds, and the More and the Less in Aristotle's Biology', in his *Aristotle's Philosophy of Biology* (Cambridge: Cambridge University Press, 2001), 162.

[30] Goodwin is one source for this conceptualization of how genes contribute to development. As he puts it: 'During reproduction, each species produces gametes with genes defining parameters that specify what morphogenetic trajectory the zygote will follow' (op. cit. note 27, 102). For further discussion, see M. Wheeler, 'Do Genes Code for Traits?' (op. cit. note 28).

5. Twists, Turns, and where the Road Runs Out

I have argued that the kind of developmental gravitation that must exist for Aristotelian biology to have any real purchase may be cashed out in terms of the underlying principles of change that specify the generic dynamics exhibited by particular developmental self-organizing systems. I have also suggested that Aristotelian natural states may be identified with the stable states of emergent global order produced by such self-organizing systems. But these claims need attention. As was clear from Goodwin's explanation of phyllotaxis, exactly which stable states of emergent global order are produced during development will typically depend on the values taken by the parameters of the system and by the initial conditions that obtain. This qualification might seem to be the population-biological fly in the natural state ointment. As we know, the natural state thinker needs it to be the case both that there is a privileged phenotype (the organismic natural state) and that each organism of the appropriate kind has a natural tendency to realize that phenotype. In response the population geneticist argues, with the apparent backing of mainstream contemporary evolutionary theory, that biological nature offers only norms of reaction (genotype-phenotype mappings in particular environments) and thus that the interlocking conditions required to support natural state thinking are simply not satisfied in the actual world. Now, given the way in which the population geneticist appeals here to the environmental embedding of development, one way of hearing the natural state thinker's predicament is that she wishes to specify what counts as the natural state of an organism (the privileged phenotype) independently of *any* developmental environment. Seemingly in this vein, Sober observes that the 'natural state model presupposes that there is some phenotype which is the natural one *that is independent of a choice of environment.*'[31] If this interpretation were correct, the attempt to understand self-organization-based thinking as a rediscovery of the natural state model would be doomed to failure. For the developmental environment will typically be the source of some of the parameter values and initial conditions that will partially control exactly which states of emergent order will be generated by any particular set of self-organizing dynamics. Under these circumstances, it might seem that 'all' that the self-organization-based thinker is doing is

[31] 'Evolution, Population Thinking, and Essentialism' op. cit. note 18, 179 (original emphasis).

detailing the processes underlying particular norms of reaction; that is, she is 'merely' identifying the mechanisms by which the transitions from a specific genotype to specific phenotypes are realized in specific environments. She is not rediscovering Aristotelianism. And a good thing too, one might think. For if the Aristotelian theorist really is committed to the claim that the natural state of an organism is a privileged phenotype in that it may be specified independently of any developmental environment (with only deviations from that natural state being traceable to environmental influence), then she is guilty of radically misconceiving the relationship between organism and environment. As population genetics makes clear, every phenotype is a product of interactions between genetic and environmental factors; so no sense at all can be given to the idea of an environment-independent phenotype.

If natural state thinking is to be revived, it needs to free itself from the troublesome thesis of phenotypic environmental independence. In this context it is interesting that, in the very next sentence after Sober states this thesis, he glosses it as follows: the 'natural state model presupposes that there is some environment which is the natural environment for the genotype to be in, which determines, in conjunction with the norm of reaction, what the natural phenotype for the genotype is.'[32] This is not equivalent to the environmental independence thesis. Indeed, Sober's putative gloss changes the picture in a highly significant way. On this new understanding, the natural state model incorporates environmental dependence, but makes the identification of a privileged environment (the natural one) part of the process by which the natural phenotype is picked out. In other words, all phenotypes are equal (with respect to environmental dependence), but one is more equal than others.

So how is this first-among-equals position to be secured? One option that suggests itself is to observe that some developmental environments will be statistically more common than others, and to claim that by virtue of their sheer numerical pervasiveness, the more common environments ought to count as the natural ones. But we have already rejected mere statistical prevalence as failing to secure the kind of constrained developmental profile that the natural state model requires. Another, seemingly more promising approach, is to hoist the fan of population genetics by her own

[32] 'Evolution, Population Thinking, and Essentialism' op. cit. note 18, 179.

petard, and to appeal directly to Darwinian theory. The idea here is to exploit the concept (often used in adaptationist evolutionary psychology) of the *environment of evolutionary adaptedness* (or EEA) of a phenotypic trait.[33] Roughly, the EEA of a phenotypic trait is the historical environment to which that trait is adapted, the environment within which its fitness enhancing effects resulted in it being selected for within the population. Statistically speaking, the EEA need not be the most common historical environment. Moreover, as long as the organism in question remains viable, adapted traits may hang around long after their historically present fitness-enhancing effects have been neutralized by environmental change. (The persistence of the human sweet tooth in an environment rich with refined sugar is a nice example.)

The present suggestion results in a more complicated strategy than Sober's passing reference to a privileged developmental environment suggests, although the core idea remains the same. The natural phenotypic form is now relativized not to a single environment, but rather to a set of historical environments, each of which is the EEA of one or more of the relevant phenotypic traits. Other extant environments may result in different phenotypic forms being generated (if, for example, different environmental factors result in different parameters for the developmental self-organizing system). Nevertheless, we certainly seem to have a handle on the idea of a privileged (natural) environment, and thus, despite the environmental dependence of development, on the idea of a privileged (natural) phenotype.

In spite of any off-the-shelf, tried-and tested attractiveness that this proposal might seem to have, I'm afraid that it is far from unproblematic as a way of salvaging Aristotelian natural state thinking. One worry that, in the end, has only limited bite turns on the fact that Aristotle characterized biological modes of organization as *internal* to the entities concerned. In other words, the modes of organization in which we are interested, for the purposes of biological explanation, are not externally imposed upon biological systems, but rather are essential aspects of the intrinsic natures of those systems.[34] This feature of Aristotle's account is

[33] See C. Crawford, 'Environments and Adaptations: Then and Now', *Handbook of Evolutionary Psychology: Ideas, Issues, and Applications*, C. Crawford and D. L. Krebs (eds.) (Mahwah, NJ: Lawrence Erlbaum, 1998), 275–302.

[34] See, for example, M. Frede, 'On Aristotle's Conception of the Soul', *Essays on Aristotle's De Anima*, M. C. Nussbaum and A. Oksenberg Rorty (eds.) (Oxford: Clarendon, 1992), 93–107.

Michael Wheeler

difficult to square with the tabled appeal to Darwinian selection—difficult, but not impossible. The problem, on the face of it, is that, given a certain neo-Darwinian outlook that characterizes evolution as a process of random genetic mutation plus environmentally driven gene-sifting, the appeal to selection seems to shift the source of biological form away from the organism and towards the environment (of evolutionary adaptedness), the external location of the relevant selection pressures. This looks to be incompatible with Aristotelian 'internalism'.

Fortunately the tension here can be relieved. First we need to remind ourselves of the rich, organism-centred processes of developmental self-organization that we are now taking to mediate the genotype-to-phenotype mapping. Second we need to adopt a certain interpretation of what Aristotle meant by 'internal'. Given that we are rejecting the problematic thesis of phenotypic environmental independence, it seems we are free to read 'internal' as 'autonomous', in the sense introduced earlier, that is as indicating (i) that the global behaviour of the system in question is not being organized by some (inner *or outer*) controlling executive that dictates or orchestrates the activity of the individual components, and (ii) that those individual components do not make their contributions by accessing and following some comprehensive plan of the global behaviour, but rather by following purely local principles of causal interaction. Finally we need to characterize the influence of the environment on the organismic dynamics here in the right way. Fans of developmental self-organization often speak of factors that affect the behaviour of some system without themselves being affected not merely as setting parameters of the system, but as setting control parameters. In this term of art, the word 'control' is being used not to signal a process in which the states of the other elements of the system are specified directly by the value of the control parameter, or in which the control parameter 'instructs' those other elements as to how they should change. The idea, rather, is that variations in the values of a control parameter may have the effect of transforming the way in which the target system is changing over time.[35] This notion of a substantial influence on the underlying dynamics of the target system is fully compatible with the claim that the processes that are fundamentally responsible for the generation of biological form are

---

[35] See, for example, E. Thelen and L. B. Smith, *A Dynamic Systems Approach to the Development of Cognition and Action* (Cambridge, Mass.: MIT Press, 1993), 62.

organism-internal, *if*, that is, 'internal' is read as 'autonomous' in the way that I have suggested. Thus we can have the cake of appealing to the concept of an environment of evolutionary adaptedness, while happily consuming a notion of biological form in which such forms are robustly traceable to organism-centred processes.

Here is a more serious worry about the compatibility of our emerging neo-Aristotelian framework with the suggested appeal to selection. The fact is that, under certain circumstances, selection and self-organization may pull phenotypes in different directions. The seminal exploration of this possibility is due to Stuart Kauffman.[36] An example from Burian and Richardson's discussion of Kauffman's work will help to focus the issue.[37] Assume that the generic order of a particular self-organizing system under evolutionary influence is to be blue, but that selection favours red. After many generations of evolution, will blue persist in the population, even though it is being selected against, and to what extent will it be visible? Kauffman's work suggests that, given certain conditions, the answer is that blue (the generic order) will be common, even in the face of strong selection in favour of red.

Let's be more specific. At the heart of Kauffman's work is a formal tool for biological investigation known as the NK model. If we adopt an interpretation of the NK model such that the parameter N is the number of genes in each genotype, and the parameter K is the degree of epistasis, then, as K increases, the fitness landscape becomes increasingly random, such that the fitness values of genotypic neighbours are uncorrelated. Since evolution by mutation and selection will be unlikely to find global optima in this random space, sub-optimal generic forms will persist. If K is low, then the fitness landscape will be smooth and gradual, but may have very shallow inclines (if N is high), in which case only small fitness differences will be available for selection to exploit, or very steep inclines (if N is low), in which case small mutations will tend to have relatively large disruptive effects. In either case, one cannot expect to find populations converged at the fitness peaks,

---

[36] S. Kauffman, *The Origins or Order: Self-Organization and Selection in Evolution*, op. cit. note 27.

[37] R. M. Burian and R. C. Richardson, 'Form and Order in Evolutionary Biology', *PSA 1990: Proceedings of the 1990 Biennial Meeting of the Philosophy of Science Association ii*, A. Fine, M. Forbes, and L.Wessels (eds.) (East Lancing, Mich., 1991), 267--87. Reprinted in *The Philosophy of Artificial Life*, M. A. Boden (ed.) (Oxford: Oxford University Press, 1996), 146–72.

and sub-optimal generic forms will survive. The upshot is that, for a wide range of parameter values, the results of self-organization rather than those of selection will be dominant.

Now notice that our strong inclination, in describing this result, is to say that because of the power of endogenously driven self-organization, a natural biological form has persisted in the face of a strong selection pressure against it. On the plus side (for the neo-Aristotelian), this means that the idea of the wellsprings of biological form being autonomous and organism-centred ('internal' in Aristotle's terms) rewards a more straightforward interpretation that it has hitherto enjoyed. But there is a significant cost. First note that in Kauffman's mathematical model the only environmental factor is the selection pressure against the pre-specified generic order. In real organismic development, however, there will, as we have seen, be a range of additional environmentally determined parameters that will have an influence on exactly which phenotypic outcome results. To preserve a vanilla version of Kauffman's scenario these influences will need to be selectively neutral. Nevertheless, for the reasons that we have explored previously, the natural state model needs to take them into account. And our preferred strategy for identifying the natural phenotype in the midst of such environment-relative variation has been to single out that phenotype by way of the privileged developmental environment that is the EEA. In the Kauffman scenario, however, there is no EEA, since adaptation has not taken place. So that strategy doesn't even get a foothold. In short, *if* the results of the NK model are robust, and *if* analogues of Kauffman's theoretical evolutionary scenario are widespread in nature, then we cannot adopt a general strategy of identifying the natural phenotype by way of an EEA.

Of course there are some big empirical ifs here. For example, Harvey and Bossomaier have focused on a key assumption of Kauffman's NK model, namely that update is synchronous. They show that if this assumption is relaxed, then very different systemic behaviour ensues, behaviour that would cast doubt on the idea that Kauffman's conclusions about selection and self-organization could be generalized to asynchronous systems.[38] This result is potentially telling since, as Harvey and Bossomaier themselves observe, one might expect many biological systems to be asynchronous in character. Perhaps then there is, after all, light at the end of the

[38] I. Harvey and T. Bossomaier, 'Time Out of Joint: Attractors in Asynchronous Random Boolean Networks', *Proceedings of the Fourth European Conference on Artificial Life*, P. Husbands and I. Harvey (eds.) (Cambridge, Mass: MIT Press, 1997), 67–75.

tunnel for the strategy of identifying natural phenotypes by way of EEAs, and thus for a reconstructed 21st century version of the Aristotelian natural state model in biology.

6. Conclusion: the Prospects for an Aristotelian Environmental Ethics

It's been a while since environmental ethics occupied the foreground in this paper, so it is time to draw together the threads of what we have learned into something approaching a take-home message for that particular area of philosophical inquiry, delivered courtesy of philosophy of biology. It seems that environmental ethics, by its very nature, is going to be more attracted to a biological grounding for ethics than some of its philosophical near-neighbours. Of course, basing one's ethics on biological science—any kind of biological science—is always going to be a hazardous business fraught with dangers relating to exactly how that science and the conceptual theorizing that surrounds it will turn out; but that's life, at least for the naturalistically inclined. If I'm right, the biocentric environmental-ethical framework developed by Taylor is positioned precariously at a crossroads in biological theory. For, as we have seen, that framework depends on the Aristotelian natural state model of biological systems, a model that stands in a complex relationship with (a) Darwinian population biology and (b) the interface between self-organization-driven accounts of organismic development and mainstream evolutionary thinking about the power and ubiquity of Darwinian selection. The prospects for bio-centric individualism of Taylor's stripe (and for any other environmental-ethical accounts that share its character) are contingent upon the outcomes of those debates. Faced with such uncertainty, the wiliest of environmental ethicists may ultimately decide (or may have decided already) to resist the charms of an evolutionary grounding in favour of some other philosophical underpinning. Given the acute and pressing nature of the world's environmental problems, that's what I would do.[39]

---

[39] For important discussions many thanks to Denis Walsh, Matthew Elton, Timothy Chappell, and audiences at the University of Dundee and the Royal Institute of Philosophy in London.

The Cultural Origins of Cognitive Adaptations

DAVID PAPINEAU

1 Introduction

According to an influential view in contemporary cognitive science, many human cognitive capacities are innate. The primary support for this view comes from 'poverty of stimulus' arguments. In general outline, such arguments contrast the meagre informational input to cognitive development with its rich informational output. Consider the ease with which humans acquire languages, become facile at attributing psychological states ('folk psychology'), gain knowledge of biological kinds ('folk biology'), or come to understand basic physical processes ('folk physics'). In all these cases, the evidence available to a growing child is far too thin and noisy for it to be plausible that the underlying principles involved are derived from general learning mechanisms. This only alternative hypothesis seems to be that the child's grasp of these principles is innate. (Cf. Laurence and Margolis, 2001.)

At the same time, it is often hard to understand how this kind of thing *could* be innate. How exactly did these putatively innate cognitive abilities evolve? The notion of innateness is much contested—we shall return to this issue at the end of the paper—but on any understanding the innateness of some complex trait will require a suite of genes which contributes significantly to its normal development. Yet, as I shall shortly explain, there are often good reasons for doubting that standard evolutionary processes could possibly have selected such suites of genes.

In this paper I want to outline a *non-standard* evolutionary process that could well have been responsible for the genetic evolution of many complex cognitive traits. This will in effect vindicate cognitive nativism against the charge of evolutionary implausibility. But at the same time it will cast cognitive nativism in a somewhat new light. The story I shall tell is one in which the ancestral *learning* of cognitive practices plays a crucial role, and in which this ancestry has left a mark on contemporary cognitive capacities, in a way that makes it doubtful that there is anything in them that is strictly 'innate', given a normal understanding of this term. For, if my account of the evolution is right, it seems likely that acquisition of information from the environment will always continue to be involved alongside genes in the ontogeny of such traits. On the picture I shall develop, then, we pay due respect to 'poverty of the stimulus' considerations—certainly the ease and reliability with which many cognitive powers are acquired shows that there are genes which have been selected specifically to facilitate these powers—but this does not mean that they are 'innate' in any stronger sense—for their acquisition will still depend crucially on information derived from environmental experience.

2 An Evolutionary Barrier

Why do I say that that standard evolutionary processes cannot account for the selection of the suites of genes behind complex cognitive traits? Cannot nativists simply offer the normal adaptationist explanation, and say that the relevant genes were selected because of the selective advantages they offered? However, there is a familiar difficulty facing such adaptationist accounts of *complex* traits, which we might call the 'hammer and nail' problem. If some phenotypic trait depends on a whole suite of genes, it is not enough for an adaptationist evolutionary explanation that the phenotype as a whole should be adaptive. After all, if the relevant genes originally arose by independent mutation, then the chance of their all occurring together in some individual would have been insignificant, and even if they did co-occur, they would quickly have been split up by sexual reproduction. So the fact that they *would* have yielded an advantage, *if* they had all co-occurred, is no explanation at all of how they all became common. Rather each gene on its own needs to bring some advantage, even in the absence of the other genes. It is by no means clear that this requirement will satisfied for the paradigm examples of putatively innate cognitive powers. Is there any advantage to the 'mind-reading' folk psychological ability to tell when someone else can see something, if you don't yet know how this will lead them to behave, or vice versa? Is there any advantage to being disposed to identify anaphoric linguistic constructions, if you don't yet know that languages have a systematic way of marking subject-object position, or vice versa?[1]

[1] The socially cooperative nature of language presents another kind of evolutionary hurdle: what if the use of one person having genes for language, if nobody else yet has them? In the interests of generalizing over non-cooperative cognitive capacities as well, I shall not stress this particular difficulty in what follows. However, the points made about social learning in section 6 indicate the obvious mechanism by which it could have been surmounted.

The Cultural Origins of Cognitive Adaptations

(Is there any advantage to a hammer, if there are no nails to hit with it, or any advantage to nails, if there is no hammer to hit them with?)

Notoriously, the major proponents of cognitive nativism have dealt with this challenge by largely ignoring it. Both Noam Chomsky and Jerry Fodor are famous for insisting that evolutionary considerations have no relevance to cognitive science. In their view, attempts to pin the down the evolutionary origin of cognitive traits are at best entertaining speculations, and at worst a distraction from serious empirical investigation (Chomsky, 1972, Fodor, 2000). However, this attitude simply fails to engage with the above challenge.[2] Questions about evolutionary origins may be difficult, but this doesn't alter the fact that a posited suite of genes can't actually exist if they can't possibly have evolved.

In the last decade or so, the self-styled 'Evolutionary Psychology' movement has married the nativism of Chomsky and Fodor with a positive concern for evolutionary questions, suggesting that a greatly expanded range of cognitive 'modules' (including modules for cheater-detection, mate-selection, and so on, as well as for language and the folk theories mentioned above) are evolutionary adaptations produced by selective pressures operating in the 'Environment of Evolutionary Adaptation' (Barkow, Cosmides and Tooby (eds), 1992). However, it cannot be said that the Evolutionary Psychology movement has properly engaged with the 'hammer and nail' issue. By and large, its adherents have been content to adopt a simple 'adaptationist' stance, assuming from the start that natural selection has the power bring about adaptive traits when they are needed. There is little in the writings of committed Evolutionary Psychologists to assuage the doubts of sceptics who feel that the selective barriers faced by innate cognitive modules are reason to doubt that such innate modules exist. (However, see Pinker and Bloom, 1990, esp. section 5.2.)

---

[2] Sometimes Chomsky and Fodor suggest that our innate linguistic powers may not be adaptations after all, but simply 'spandrel'-like by-products of other evolutionary developments (Chomsky, 1988, Fodor, 2000). This could be read as an implicit recognition of the 'hammer and nail' problem facing any simple adaptationist story. Still, the idea that all our innate linguistic powers are spandrels is difficult to take seriously. If a simple adaptationist account is ruled out, a far more plausible alternative is a complex adaptationist account, not a miracle. In effect, this is what I offer below.

David Papineau

3 Learning as a Basis for Genetic Advantage

In this paper, I want to consider a possible mechanism which might explain how the evolution of complex cognitive abilities might overcome 'hammer and nail' hurdles. Such hurdles arise when a specific gene is only selectively advantageous given a context of pre-existing cognitive traits. I shall show that such a gene can nevertheless be selected even in the absence of other *genes* which fix the pre-existing traits. The central thought of this paper is that it will be enough for such selection if those other traits are being *learned*. After all, what is required is that the other pre-existing traits should be *present*, not that they be genetically fixed, and there is no obvious reason why learning should not suffice for this.

The details of this suggestion will be examined at length in what follows. But I hope it will be immediately clear how it promises to overcome the 'hammer and nail' problem. Take some complex cognitive ability. As long as this ability is being *learned*, then this itself may create an environment in which genes that contribute elements of this ability will be selected. In effect, once the ability is being learned, then the relevant genes will start being selected precisely because they lighten the burden of learning.

This suggests the intriguing possibility that the innate modules so emphasized by recent nativist opinion are all 'fossilized' versions of abilities which originally arose from general learning mechanisms. If this right, then the genetic shaping of the modern human mind, far from demonstrating the impotence of general learning, is a testament to its fecundity.

I have introduced this suggestion by emphasizing the possibility of selective obstacles of the 'hammer and nail' variety. Some readers may remain unconvinced that this is a real problem. In particular, they may have felt I was too quick to dismiss the possibility that genes for the various components of complex cognitive traits might each be selectively advantageous on their own. Why shouldn't there be room for the strategy Richard Dawkins employs in *Climbing Mount Improbable* (1996), where he shows, against those who argue that a part of a wing is no advantage at all, say, how even a part of a wing may be better than nothing? Similarly, despite first appearances, maybe there is some advantage to being able to tell whether another organism can see something, even without knowing what this will make them do ... (Maybe hammers would be useful, even without nails, for banging other things ...)

I shall not take direct issue with this response. For what it is worth, I suspect that 'hammer and nail' obstacles are common enough in cognitive evolution, and that many of the cognitive traits that interest us simply could not have evolved with the help of prior stages when they were learned. But I do not need to defend this strong claim here. This is because the selective process I shall focus on does not require the absolute impossibility of evolving hammers without nails. Maybe many of the elements in the human understanding of mind, say, are of some biological advantage on their own, and maybe this alone could have led to the independent selection of genes which variously fix these elements. It is consistent with this that each of these elements are much *more* advantageous when found in conjunction with the rest of the understanding of mind, and thus that the initial selection of the relevant genes would have proceeded all the faster in contexts where other parts of understanding of mind was already being acquired from general learning processes. This argues that the kind of selection pressures I shall be exploring would have played a significant role whenever learning helped to foster complex cognitive structures, including cases when there was no absolute 'hammer and nail' obstacle to the selection of genes for those structures in the absence of learning. Given this, even readers who feel that I have overstated the 'hammer and nail' issue should still find what follows of interest.

4 Genetic Takeovers

Let me now give a more detailed analysis of the basic selective process I am interested in. It will be helpful in this connection to turn away from human cognition for a while and consider a simple example of bird behaviour. The woodpecker finches of the Galapagos Islands use twigs or cactus spines to probe for grubs in tree braches (Tebbich et al. 2001; see also Bateson 2004). This behaviour involves a number of component dispositions—finding possible tools, fashioning them if necessary, grasping them in the beak, using them to probe at appropriate sites. As it happens, the overall grub-seeking behaviour of the finches displays a high degree of innateness (though see section 14 below). Yet the evolution of this innateness would seem to face a severe version of the 'hammer and nail' obstacle. None of the component dispositions is of any use by itself. For example, there is no advantage in grasping tools if you aren't disposed to probe with them, and no advantage to being disposed to probe with tools if you never grasp them. This makes it very hard to see how genes for the overall behaviour could possibly have been selected for. In order for the behaviour to be advantageous, all the components have to be in place. But presumably the various different components are controlled by different genes. So any biological pay-off would seem to require that all these genes be present together. However, if these genes are initially rare, it would be astronomically unlikely that they would ever co-occur in one individual, and they would quickly be split up by sexual reproduction even if they did. So the relevant genes, taken singly, would seem to have no selective advantage that would enable them to be favoured by natural selection.

However, now suppose that, before the grub-seeking behaviour became innate in the finches, there was a period where the finches *learned* to catch grubs, by courtesy of their general learning mechanisms. This could well have itself created an environment where each of the genes that facilitate the overall behaviour would have been advantageous. For each of these genes, on its own, would then have the effect of fixing one component of the grub-seeking behaviour, while leaving the other components to be acquired from learning. And this could itself have been advantageous, in reducing the cost and increasing the reliability with which the overall behaviour was acquired. The result would then be that each of the genes would be selected for, with the overall behaviour thus coming increasingly under genetic control. (There is a general issue here, to do with the relative selective advantages of genes and learning, which I shall address in the next section. For the moment let us simply suppose that the advantages due to genes, such as increased speed and reliability of acquisition, are not outweighed by any compensating disadvantages, such as reduced ontogenetic plasticity.)

Here is a general model of this kind of process, which I shall call 'genetic takeover'.[3] Suppose n sub-traits, P_i, $i = 1, ..., n$, are individually necessary and jointly sufficient for some adaptive phenotype P, and that each subtrait is no good without the others. (Thus: finding tool materials, fashioning them, grasping them, ...) Suppose further that each sub-trait can either be genetically fixed or acquired through learning, with alternative alleles at some genetic

---

[3] A common alternative term for this process is 'genetic assimilation' (cf. Hinton and Nowlan, 1987, Turney *et al.*, 1996, Avital and Jablonka 2001, Godfrey-Smith 2003, Papineau, 2005). However, this term was originally coined by C. H. Waddington (1953, 1957, 1961), and there is some controversy as to whether he had the same process in mind (Bateson 2004, Griffiths 2006, Papineau, 2006). 'Genetic takeover' avoids this exegetical issue.

locus either genetically determining the sub-trait or leaving it plastic and so available for learning. So, for sub-trait P_i, we have allele G_i which genetically fixes P_i, and allele(s) L_i which allows it to be learned.

To start with, the G_is that genetically determine the various P_is are rare, so that it is highly unlikely that any individual will have all n P_is genetically fixed. Still, having *some* P_i genetically fixed will reduce the amount of learning required to learn the overall behaviour. (If you are already genetically disposed to grab suitable twigs if you see them, you will have less to do to learn the rest of the tool-using behaviour.) Organisms with some G_is will thus have a head start in the learning race, so to speak, and so will be more likely to acquire the overall phenotype. So the G_is that give them the head start will have a selective advantage over the L_is. Natural selection will thus favour the G_is over the L_is, and in due course will drive the G_is to fixity.[4]

This genetic takeover model is a simplification of one developed by Hinton and Nowlan (1987). They ran a computer simulation using a 'sexually reproducing' population of neural nets, with an 'advantageous phenotype' that required the 20 connections in their neural nets all to be set at '1' rather than '0'. Insofar as it was left to solely to 'genes' and sexual sorting, there was a miniscule chance of hitting the advantageous phenotype, and so genes for '1's were not selected. However, once the nets could 'learn' during their individual lifetimes to set their connections at '1', then this gave genes for '1's an advantage (since they increased the chance of so learning the advantageous overall phenotype), and in this context these genes then progressively replaced the alternative alleles which left the connections to learning.

It is worth spelling out exactly how the genetic takeover model offers a way of overcoming selective 'hammer and nail' obstacles. At

---

[4] This model should be handled with care. There is no need to think of the relevant loci as somehow 'dedicated' to the related phenotypes—the idea is only that each may be occupied by an allele G_i which (produces a protein) that causes the phenotype P_i in question; the alternative allele(s) L_i needn't be thought of as somehow specifically ensuring that P_i is learnable, as opposed to simply doing nothing to stop P_i being one of the many phenotypes that can be acquired from general learning mechanisms. Relatedly, it is only for purposes of expository simplification that I assume that the G_i alleles on their own determine recognizable phenotypic components P_i; what is crucial is solely that the G_is determine proteins that somehow make learning the overall P easier. I shall return to this point in my final section.

first it may seem that each G_i will have no selective advantage on its own, given that it only fixes one P_i, which isn't of any use without the other P_is. But in a context where the various P_is can also be learned, each G_i *does* have a selective advantage on its own, even in the absence of the other G_is, precisely because it makes it *easier to learn* the rest of P. Even in the absence of other G_is at other loci, any given G_i will still be favoured by natural selection, because it will reduce the learning load and so make it more likely that its possessor will end up with the advantageous phenotype P. This is what drives the progressive selection of the G_is in the model. Each G_i is advantageous whether or not there are G_is at other loci, simply because having a G_i rather than an L_i at any given locus will reduce the amount of further learning needed to get the overall P.

Much previous discussion of this kind of model has taken place under the heading of the 'Baldwin Effect'. This notion traces back to James Mark Baldwin (1896) and others evolutionary theorists at the end of the nineteenth century. While it is not always clear what these thinkers originally had in mind, the 'Baldwin Effect' is now standardly understood to refer to any selective process whereby some trait P is brought under genetic control *as a result* of previously being under environmental control. At first pass, of course, the Baldwin Effect sounds like Lamarckism, and indeed many commentators have argued that there can be no legitimate Darwinian mechanism fitting the specifications of the Baldwin Effect. (How can the prior environmental control of P possibly matter to selection, given that those who benefit from *environmentally acquiring* some trait won't pass on any genes for that trait to their offspring? Cf. Watkins, 1999.)

In this paper I shall generally steer clear of the intricate literature on the Baldwin Effect. But, for what it is worth, the genetic takeover model does at least provide one legitimate way in which a trait can come under genetic control *as a result* of previously being under environmental control. In this model the population of organisms moves from a stage in which the overall P is initially acquired by learning to a stage where it is genetically fixed. Moreover, the first stage is essential to the second, in that the alleles G_i which together genetically fix P would have had no initial selective advantage were P not previously learned.

5 Genes versus Learning

Let me now address the question of the relative benefits of learning and genetic control. In the last section I took it for granted that genetic takeover will generally be selectively advantageous. That is, I supposed that the L_i alleles which leave some element of an adaptive phenotype to learning will in general be outcompeted by the G_is which ensure that that those components become genetically fixed. However, it is by no means automatic that this should be so. There are costs as well as benefits to genetic control, and genetic takeover therefore requires that the latter outweigh the former.

Let me begin by detailing the possible advantages of genetic takeover. At first sight it may be unclear why there should be any such advantages. If the relevant phenotype will be acquired by learning in any case, as in our cases of possible genetic takeover, what extra advantage will derive from genetic determination? The immediate answer is that the relevant phenotype *won't* always be acquired in any case, if it is not genetically fixed. Learning is hostage to the quirks of individual history, and a given individual may fail to experience the environments required to instil some learned trait. Moreover, even if the relevant environments are reliably available, the business of learning some phenotype may itself involve biological costs, delaying the time at which it becomes available, and diverting resources from other activities. In particular, the fact that the phenotype needs to be learned, rather than coming for free with the genome, may mean that that organisms are limited in their opportunities to learn *further* adaptive traits, and are thus biologically disadvantaged for this reason.[5]

On the other side must be placed the loss of flexibility that genetic fixity may entail. Learning will normally be adaptive across a range of environments, in each case producing a phenotype that is advantageous in that specific environment. By contrast, genes which fix traits that are only adaptive in some given environment will be of no biological advantage if the environment changes so as to render that trait maladaptive. In circumstances of environmental variability, an organism with genes that fix some trait may thus be less fit than one which relies on learning to tailor its phenotype to its environment.[6]

[5] A side-effect of genetic control is thus the 'assimilate-stretch' process emphasized in Avital and Jablonka (2001): once some cognitive capacity is taken under genetic control and learning resources are thereby freed up, then organisms gain the opportunity to learn more sophisticated elaborations of that capacity, which may in turn be taken under genetic control, ... and so on.

[6] The loss of flexibility due to increased genetic control may well extend beyond the specific phenotype that is taken over genetically. When some trait that is originally shaped by some suite of relatively general learning mechanisms comes under genetic control, this may not be a simple matter

David Papineau

As a general rule, then, we can expect that genetic fixity will be favoured when there is long-term environmental stability, and that learning will be selected for when there are variable environments. Given environmental stability, genetic fixity will have the afore-mentioned advantages of reliable and cheap acquisition. But these advantages can easily be outweighed by loss of flexibility when there is significant environmental instability. Exactly how the plus-es and minuses of genetic control versus learning work out will depend on the parameters of particular cases.[7] For the moment, I shall continue to assume that we are dealing with cases where genet-ic control has the overall biological advantage. I shall have more to say about this issue in section 12 below.

6 The Significance of Social Learning

It may seem that my hypothesized mechanism for circumventing hammer-and-nail obstacles simply trades in one kind of improba-bility for another, substituting improbabilities of complex learning for improbabilities of genetic co-occurrence. I have focused on cases where some complex adaptive phenotype P consists of various sub-parts P_i, none of which are adaptive on their own. And I have answered the puzzle of how genes for these P_is could be selected, if none is advantageous on its own, by suggesting that these genes will become advantageous if the overall P can be *learned*. However, if the overall P is complex, and none of its parts advantageous on their own, won't there equally be a problem about *learning* all of P?

Consider our Galapagos finches once more. The P_is there were finding tools, fashioning them, grasping them, using them to probe

[7] For a detailed quantitative analysis of the relative costs of learning and genetic control, see Mayley (1996). Note that, in contexts where learning has the biological advantage over genetic fixity, then we might well find 'reverse Baldwin effects', where some trait originally under genetic control comes to depend on learning instead.

of that trait alone being switched, so to speak, from the control of those general learning mechanisms. For it is possible that the general learning repertoire will itself be affected by such switching. Perhaps bringing one trait under genetic control can make an organism less efficient at learning other traits. For example, if you are genetically predisposed towards folk psychology, then perhaps this will limit your ability to learn about non-psychological mechanisms. Commentators are somewhat divided on how far this danger is real (cf. Godfrey-Smith, 2003, Bateson, 2004).

The Cultural Origins of Cognitive Adaptations

... Now just as there was no *reproductive* advantage in finding tools, or fashioning them, if you don't know how to grab them, or probe, and vice versa, neither will there be any *psychological* reward in having any of these dispositions without the others. However, this is likely to block the individual learning of the various dispositions, since such learning hinges on psychological reward, and it is extremely unlikely that random behaviour generation will ever lead some animal to perform all the requisite actions in sequence. Maybe the improbabilities involved in learning won't be as bad as those operating at the genetic level. But they may still be bad enough to ensure that, even after you have one gene G_i for one of the P_is, there is no real chance of learning the rest of P, and so no real selective pressure in favour of that G_i. So we still seem to face a 'hammer and nail' problem even after we introduce the possibility of learning, and for the same reason—the component P_is don't bring any pay-off on their own.

However, suppose now that we are dealing with organisms that are capable of *social* as well as *individual* learning. Maybe there is a very low probability of any individual with some one G_i acquiring all the further elements of P via individual trial-and-error learning. But now suppose that the relevant population of animals has a *culture* of doing P—imagine, say, that the ancestors of the present Galapagos finches acquired their tool-using behaviour, not from individual trial-and-error learning, but via social learning from other finches who were already displaying it. This could then radically reduce the improbability of learning the various elements of P, and so could serve to render the G_is advantageous after all. If there is a real chance of learning all the requisite elements of P from others, then as before each G_i could be selected because it increased the speed and reliability with which P is learned.

It is interesting to note that, when social learning plays a role in this way, then the 'genetic takeover' of P will qualify as a 'Baldwin Effect' for a reason over and above that outlined in the last section. The requirements for a 'Baldwin Effect', recall, were that some trait P is brought under genetic control *as a result* of previously being under environmental control. When a genetic takeover of P is facilitated by *social* learning, then we have this requirement being satisfied for the reason that the relevant genes would not be selected without the prior *culture* of P. The relevant G_is have a selective advantage specifically because of the pre-existing socially learned culture—without the culture, it would be too hard for individuals to learn the further elements of P needed to render G_is advantageous. A gene which helped a finch to identify suitable twigs would have no biological virtue if the finch's only way of acquiring the rest of the tool-using behaviour was by individual trial-and-error learning. However, once these things can be learned by example from the other finches, then the gene becomes advantageous in a way it wasn't before. In short, the genes for P get selected as a result of P previously being socially learned.

This way of satisfying the Baldwin requirement is not the same as that described in the last section. There the idea was simply that each G_i would get selected because it made it easier to learn the rest of P. There was no assumption there that this learning depended on some prior *culture*. Any kind of learning, even non-social trial-and-error learning, would ensure that the G_is moved towards fixity via intermediate stages where the components of P were learned—and this in itself, as I pointed out, would give us one kind of 'Baldwin Effect'. I have now added in the *further* thought that in many cases learning the components of P may only be possible because other animals are already displaying P as an exemplar for social learning—this gives us another way of satisfying the Baldwin requirement that the selection of genes for P depends on P previously being learned. (To see clearly that these ways are different, note that, if there *were* any cases where individual trial-and-error learning created selection pressures for the G_is in the absence of social learning, counter to this section's line of argument, then we would *still* get genetic takeover even in radically unsocial species where no individual ever observes P in another organism at all. Here we would have a Baldwin Effect in the first sense—the G_is will get driven to fixity via helping each organism to learn P individually—but not in the second sense—the genetic takeover doesn't depend on other animals already learning P and providing a model for learning.)

In what follows, I shall focus on cases where social learning does play a crucial role in facilitating genetic takeover, and thus where the Baldwin requirement is satisfied twice over. In itself, this double satisfaction of the Baldwin requirement is merely a conceptual oddity. It is of no special theoretical significance that certain possible processes should fit the half-formed ideas of an unimportant nineteenth-century theorist in two different ways.[8] However, there is independent reason to think that these doubly

[8] Did Baldwin himself have my doubly Baldwinian process in mind? It is not clear. He did on occasion mention social learning as important for his topic, and later writers have also alluded specifically to social learning when discussing the Baldwin Effect (Baldwin, 1896, Watkins, 1999). But I have found no explicit analysis in the literature of why social learning matters in this context.

Baldwinian processes are biologically significant—they offer a plausible selective mechanism whereby complex cognitive adaptations can come under genetic control. To repeat the argument so far, it is often puzzling how complex cognitive abilities can be selected for, given that their various components seem of no biological components on their own. However, we have seen how such selection can indeed take place if the ability in question is initially *learnable*; moreover, we have seen how such learning can be rendered possible by *cultural* transmission, even in cases where it would be beyond the powers of individual trail-and-error learning. These points in themselves provide reason seriously to investigate the genetic takeover of culturally transmitted traits, quite apart from the fact that they satisfy Baldwin's requirements twice over.

7 Getting Cultures Started

In the last section I argued that social learning can facilitate behaviours that are beyond the reach of individual trial-and-error learning, and thus render those behaviours available for 'genetic takeover'. However, there are a number of complexities hidden under this simple appeal to 'social learning'.

For a start, there is an obvious worry that the appeal to social learning merely postpones the problem that many cognitive practices are too complex to be acquired by individual trial-and-error learning. After all, a culture has to get started somehow. There has to be some initial stage where the cognitive practice is introduced to the population, in order that individuals can start learning it from others who already display it. The only obvious way for this to happen is for some lucky or exceptional individual to strike on the practice by some individual means. However, this may seem to be in obvious tension with the idea that social learning helps precisely with practices that are too complex to be acquired by individual trial-and-error learning.

However, this tension is more apparent than real. Think of social learning as a process which takes us *from* one individual learning P *to* its becoming socially learnable by all. This can make it highly likely that P will become prevalent, even though it's very hard for any *given* individual to get P from trial-and-error. Suppose that the chance of any given individual learning P by trial-and-error is k, and that there are n individuals in the population. Then the probability of *at least one* individual arriving at P by trial-and-error will be $1-(1-k)^n$, and this can be high even if k is low. (For example, even if there is only a 10% chance that any given individual will get P from trial and error, it is 88% likely that at least one individual in a group of 20 will so get it.) In short, social learning switches the probability that any given individual X will somehow learn P, from the low (10%) probability that X will acquire P from individual trial-and-error, to the high (88%) probability that *someone* will acquire P from individual trial-and-error.

8 Varieties of Social Learning

Let us now look more closely at the idea of 'social learning' itself. My last section simply assumed that 'social learning' will ensure that any adaptive cognitive ability—any 'good trick', as Daniel Dennett terms it (1991)—will spread throughout a population as soon as any one member acquires it from trial-and-error learning. However, this cannot be taken for granted. There are different kinds of social learning, displayed by different species of animals, and by no means all of them will automatically transfer the kind of 'good tricks' at issue here from individual to population.

At its most general, 'social learning' refers to any processes by which the display of some behaviour by one member of a species increases the probability that other members will perform that behaviour. However, this covers a numbers of different mechanisms. We can usefully distinguish (cf. Shettleworth, 1998, Tomasello, 2000):

(i) Stimulus Enhancement. Here one animal's doing P merely increases the likelihood that other animals' behaviour will become conditioned to relevant stimuli via individual learning. For example, animals follow each other around— novices will thus be led by adepts to sites where certain behaviours are possible (pecking into milk bottles, say, or washing sand off potatoes) and so be more likely to acquire those behaviours by individual trial-and-error.

(ii) Goal Emulation. Here animals will learn from others that certain resources are available, and then use their own devices to achieve them. Thus they might learn from others that there are ants under stones, or berries in certain trees.

(iii) Blind Mimicry. Here animals copy the movements displayed by others, but without appreciating to what end these movements are a means.

(iv) Learning about Means to Ends. Here animals grasp that some conspecific's behaviour is a means to some end, and copy it because they want that end.

We can take it that the first two kinds of social learning will be present in a wide range of species. They require nothing more than a tendency for animals to move around together, plus powers of instrumental learning (i), or pre-existing abilities to exploit resources once they are detected (ii). Blind mimicry (iii) is less common: while it is possible that some non-human animals have this capacity, it is by no means universal, even in mammals and birds (Shettleworth, 1998). Full-blooded appreciation of the relevance of means to ends (iv) seems even more rare: there is little evidence that non-human animals can do this (Shettleworth, 1998; but see Akins and Zentall, 1998).

9 Social Learning and Genetic Takeover

Now, how far are these different modes of transmission suited for the role I have ascribed to 'social learning'—that is, spreading complex adaptive behaviours from individuals to populations, and thereby rendering those behaviours available for 'genetic takeover'? There are immediate problems with all but the last. Stimulus enhancement (i) and goal emulation (ii) seem ill-suited for transmitting *complex* behaviours, while there is nothing in blind mimicry (iii) itself to favour the transmission of *adaptive* over non-adaptive behaviour.

The trouble with stimulus enhancement (i) and goal emulation (ii), from our perspective, is that they don't transmit complex behaviours as such; rather, they transmit the environmental *opportunity*, so to speak, with the learner then using its own devices to exploit the opportunity. To see the problem, imagine that some unusual or lucky individual lights on some complex tool-using strategy with which to extract grubs from holes. Stimulus enhancement means that other individuals will be more likely to find themselves in the conditions where this behaviour would be rewarded; but this won't get these individuals performing the behaviour, if its complexity makes it unlikely that they will then randomly generate it. Again, goal emulation means that those observing the expert will learn that there are grubs in holes; but this won't get them performing any complex tool-using behaviour either, if nothing analogous is already present in their behavioural repertoire.

Blind mimicry (iii) suffers from a different problem. Here it is specifically the behaviour that is being transmitted, rather than the opportunity, and so a learner may well pick up some complex sequence of behaviours from a demonstrator. But there is nothing in blind mimicry to ensure that learners will preferentially copy *good* tricks rather than bad ones. To the extent that the behaviour is being picked up without any appreciation of what results it brings, it is as likely that useless patterns of behaviour will spread as useful ones. Blind mimicry on its own thus fails to provide a mechanism by which a good trick will spread throughout a population once acquired by one individual.

These difficulties with the first three modes of social learning are not insuperable. Perhaps the aimlessness of blind mimicry will be moderated if learners only persist with the copied behaviour if they subsequently find it psychologically rewarding. This will have the effect of keeping good tricks in the population—and making them available for further mimicry—and weeding out bad tricks. (Alternatively, learners may selectively mimic dominant or prestigious individuals—this too will discriminate in favour of advantageous cognitive strategies, to the extent that dominance and prestige depend on such strategies. Cf. Richerson and Boyd, 2004.)

Conversely, elements of blind mimicry might help overcome the limitations of the first two modes of social learning. Animals who are introduced to new opportunities by stimulus enhancement and goal emulation will be more likely to find some complex way of exploiting them if they are disposed blindly to mimic elements of the behaviour of others who have adopted some such means.

In any case, it is not as if there is some absolute level of reliable social transmission which needs to be reached. There will be cases and cases. We are interested in the possibility of genetic takeovers of complex adaptive learned behaviours. Such genetic takeovers will often require that the behaviour be reliably socially transmitted. There will be contexts where the requisite threshold of reliability is ensured by some mix of the three kinds of social transmission discussed so far, even if they are less effective at doing this than might initially have been supposed.

Even so, it should be clear that genetic takeover of complex behaviour is far more likely among individuals that are capable of the final mode of social learning, that is, learning about means to ends. Here there will no problem of bad tricks being as likely to be copied as good tricks—individuals will pick up specifically those behaviours that they can see give rise to attractive results, not just any behaviours they observe, as with blind mimicry. Nor is there any barrier to the copying of *complex* behaviours—individuals will here adopt the specific strategies they observe in their behavioural models, and will not be left to their own devices to develop ways of exploiting copied opportunities, as with stimulus enhancement and goal emulation.[9]

This suggests that, while there may be a relatively limited range of cases in other animals where complex behaviours come under a genetic control as a result of first being learned, there will have been ample opportunities for such 'Baldwinization' in our own recent hominid ancestry. Perhaps I am being unduly negative about other animals here: the points raised in this section by no means fully rule out the possibility that genetic takeover has often played a significant role in cognitive evolution outside the recent hominid lineage. But, be that as it may, our main topic in this paper is human cognition, and the availability of explicit learning about means to ends among our recent ancestors means that they would not have faced the same barriers to the cultural transmission of complex behaviours as other animals.

10 Maladaptive Cultures

This emphasis on the explicit learning of means to ends, however, raises a rather different query about the genetic takeover of cultural practices. A cultural practice will be a candidate for genetic takeover just in case it is *biologically* advantageous. Genes that help you to learn P will be subject to natural selection just in case P increases *reproductive* fitness. By and large, we can expect learned behaviour to be so biologically advantageous—after all, learning mechanisms have been designed by natural selection to select reproductively advantageous behaviours in the light of experience. Still, such learning devices are not sure-fire, and in some environments they will end up selecting biologically non-adaptive behaviour.

This will be a particular danger with social learning via the explicit appreciation of means to ends. This is a highly

[9] The reliable transmission of complex cognitive practices matters, not just for the possibility of genetic taleover, but also for the possibility of *cumulative* culture. This latter issue is the focus of Tomasello (2000). While Tomasello himself does not deny that the explicit appreciation of means-end relations matters for reliable transmission, he regards this as pretty much the same thing as the understanding of mind (and in particular, the identification of intentions). However, I think that non-human animals are blocked from an explicit appreciation of means to ends by far more fundamental cognitive barriers than their lack of understanding of mind. For discussion of this issue, see Papineau (2004) esp. sect. 7.

sophisticated form of learning, which depends on the vagaries of individual experience in complex ways, and which therefore leaves plenty of room for biologically deleterious results. We need only think of the way that contemporary individuals socially acquire such habits as drinking alcohol, smoking, and piercing body parts. While there is a certain sense in which such behaviours are indeed 'good tricks'—they are often genuinely effective means to feelings of well-being or to higher status—the social learning mechanisms of many individuals place far too much weight on these outcomes, and so instil behaviours which overall have a highly negative effect on reproductive fitness. And in such cases there will clearly be no question of genetic natural selection favouring genes which make you better at learning such behaviours, for the obvious reason that such genes will only decrease reproductive fitness even further.

Earlier in this section I argued that the explicit learning of means to ends is the mode of social learning most likely to facilitate genetic takeover. However, if this kind of social learning systematically gives rise to biologically maladaptive practices, in the way just described, then this suggests that genetic takeover may not be a significant evolutionary process after all.

11 The Adaptivity of Vertical Cultures

The danger of biologically maladaptive cultural practices depends crucially on who learns from whom. In this connection it will be helpful to distinguish between 'horizontal' and 'vertical' transmission of cognitive practices. While horizontal transmission is indeed prone to pass on biologically maladaptive practices, this is not true of vertical transmission.

Horizontal transmission is perhaps the most familiar way of thinking about the promulgation of culture. Here individuals learn cognitive traits from other unrelated individuals—traits are passed 'sideways' from one individual to another, so to speak. When cultural transmission proceeds in this manner, cognitive traits will become prevalent the more efficient they are at so 'infecting' new individuals. Given this, such horizontal transmission does indeed open the way for biologically disadvantageous traits to spread.

However, an alternative mode of transmission is 'vertical', from parents to children. And here things work rather differently. To the extent that transmission is vertical, cultural traits will spread just in case they increase the *reproductive success* of their possessors. This is because vertically transmitted traits will thus be subject to a process of natural selection entirely akin to the selection of genes which contribute to individual reproductive success. So when transmission is vertical, only biologically advantageous traits will spread through a population. Vertical transmission is thus likely to create conditions that will foster genetic takeover after all.

It is somewhat unusual to think of cultural traits as subject to the same selective pressures as genes. There is plenty of literature, of course, which treats cultural traits as 'replicators' in their own right, as 'memes', in Richard Dawkins' terminology (Dawkins, 1976, Blackmore, 2000). But most 'meme' theory focuses on horizontal transmission, and therefore views memes as being subject to quite different selective pressures from genes. With vertical transmission there is no such contrast, however. To the extent that cultural traits are passed from parents to children, they will be inherited in just the same manners as genes, and so are subject to entirely analogous selection processes.

Doesn't the idea that 'cultural traits are inherited in just the same manners as genes', as I just put it, run counter to a central plank in modern biological thinking, namely, that only genotypes and not phenotypes are passed down from parents to children? Surely this is the central message of Waismann's famous diagram: parental *genotypes* influence children's genotypes, but parental *phenotypes* per se have no effects on children. A proficient hunter may become expert at throwing spears, but this doesn't mean his children will automatically inherit this efficiency. However, it is easy to be misled by Waismann's diagram. It is of course true that parental phenotypes do not influence children's phenotypes *by altering children's genotypes*. There is no downwards causation from phenotype to germ line (cf. Crick's 'central dogma of molecular biology'). But it does not at all follow that parental phenotypes do not influence children's phenotypes *at all*. For there remains the possibility that they influence them directly, rather than by altering the germ line. And once this is in clear focus, then it is surely uncontentious that phenotypes can indeed so be passed down from parents to children. The expert hunter's proficiency will make no difference to his children's genotypes. But it may make plenty of difference to their phenotypes, if they learn their hunting techniques from him.

Biological evolution by natural selection requires heritable traits. But there is no obvious reason why it should require this inheritance to be genetic rather than non-genetic. It is arguable that the promulgation of non-genetically inherited traits via their differential influence on reproductive success is just as much biological evolution by biological natural selection as more familiar cases of genetic evolution.

It is common, even among those who regard themselves as opposed to a gene-centred view of evolution, to allow that a change in gene frequencies is a necessary and sufficient condition for biological evolution, if only at a 'book-keeping' level. I am suggesting that even this is too much of a concession to gene-centrism. To digress for a moment, consider Matteo Mameli's fable of 'the lucky butterfly' (2004). Suppose that there is a species of butterfly that imprints on the plant it hatches on. Butterfly larvae retain some trace of these plants, and when it is time for the mature butterflies to lay eggs, they return to the plants they hatched on. The tendency to lay eggs on a given type of plant is thus non-genetically inherited, passed from mothers to offspring via this imprinting mechanism. Now suppose that some population of these butterflies are all imprinted on plant type A. Then a freak accident—a storm, say—leads one butterfly to deposit her eggs on a plant of type B. Because of the imprinting mechanism, her descendants henceforth lay their eggs on plant B. Suppose plant B is more nutritious, with the consequence that the descendants of 'the lucky butterfly' start outcompeting the other butterflies in the general Malthusian struggle for survival. After a while the population consequently comes to consist entirely of these descendants. I say, following Mameli, that this is a standard case of biological evolution by natural selection, *even though there need have been no change whatsoever in the butterfly population's gene pool*. This might seem strange, but compare the scenario just outlined with one where the plant preference is indeed genetic, and the 'lucky' butterfly undergoes a genetic transformation that switches her from plant A to plant B, with the result, as before, that her descendants come to exhaust the population. There is of course no dispute that this would be biological evolution—one allele is favoured over another because of its advantageous effects. But if this would be biological evolution, why not regard the original lucky butterfly scenario in the same light? Why is it significant that the plant preference is determined by a gene rather than a memory trace, given that both are equally passed on from parents to off-spring?

The story of the lucky butterfly is an artificial example. But there is reason to suppose there is plenty of reliable non-genetic inheritance in nature and that in consequence there is natural selection of the non-genetic traits so inherited. Mameli (2004) lists many real-life examples. In addition to imprinting for locality, as in the lucky butterfly fable, he considers various other kinds of imprinting, including imprinting for kind of habitat and imprinting for food and sexual preferences. More generally, he points out that less channelled forms of learning than imprinting also lead to off-spring matching their parents in various respects. In the non-psychological realm, too, there are plenty of examples: various non-genetic zygotic materials are acquired by offspring from their parents, as are many symbionts. (See also Jablonka and Lamb, 1995, Avital and Jablonka, 2001.)

Mameli does not consider human cognitive traits. This is because the selective processes operating on these are complicated by the possibility of horizontal as well as vertical transmission. However, there is evidence that the vertical transmission of cogni-tive traits is an important mechanism among humans in tradition-al societies (Hewlett and Cavalli-Sforza, 1986, Gugliemino *et al.*, 1995). Perhaps this is itself the product of selection pressures operating within hominid history. Given that vertically transmitted traits will become common just in case they are reproductively advantageous, there will be extra genetic selection pressure in favour of learning from parents as soon as there is any tendency for selection to start operating on vertical transmission channels—for, once there is any such tendency, then genes which lead offspring reliably to copy their parents rather than other indi-viduals will be favoured precisely because they are more likely to engender reproductively advantageous practices. (Cf. Laland *et al.*, 2000, 142.)

I trust it is now clear how the selection pressures acting on vertically transmitted cognitive traits will favour reproductively advantageous traits, where this is not necessarily so for horizontally transmitted traits. Perhaps the point is most easily seen by considering the analogous pressures on parasites and symbionts. 'Infectious' parasites that are good at 'jumping sideways' may well be malignant to their hosts, for their long-term success is compatible with the reduced fitness or even death of those temporary hosts. But symbionts who spend extended periods of time in a single host, and whose descendants live in the offspring of that host, will outcompete their conspecifics just in case they help their hosts to survive and reproduce, for this is necessary condition for their reproductive success. Just the same applies to cognitive traits. Practices that spread sideways can be selected even if deleterious—like smoking, drinking and body-piercing. But practices that are transmitted from parents to children will spread only if they increase reproductive fitness, for their fates are bound up with the fate of the host lineages they inhabit.

Let us return from this digression into the biology of vertical transmission to our main topic, namely, the genetic takeover of complex cognitive practices. In section 9 I observed that the social learning of complex cognitive practices calls for explicit learning of means to ends, as opposed to less sophisticated forms of social learning. This then led in section 10 to the difficulty that there is no guarantee that this form of social learning will promulgate reproductively advantageous traits, as opposed to psychologically attractive ones. Explicit learning of means to ends is as capable of spreading unhealthy fashions as it is at instilling reproductive advantages. And if cognitive practices are reproductively unhealthy, then there will be no question of genetic takeover—genes get selected if they help foster traits that yield reproductive success, not traits that are psychologically attractive.

However, we are now in a position to see that this worry about the possibility of genetic takeover disappears if the primary mode of transmission of cognitive traits is vertical. True, explicit learning of means to ends will still be capable of leading offspring to copy psychologically attractive but reproductively disadvantageous practices from their parents. But if these traits are transmitted vertically, then any such reproductively disadvantageous traits will tend to disappear, through failure of their possessors to have descendants onto which to pass them. Vertical transmission ensures that only reproductively advantageous traits will become *prevalent* throughout the hominid population. And therewith vertical transmission will create the conditions for genetic takeover. Since vertical transmission ensures that prevalent practices will be reproductively advantageous, it also means that genes that foster those practices will have a selective advantage.

12 Environmental Stability

Back in Section 5 we noted a different kind of requirement for genetic takeover. If there is to be an advantage to genes that bring some cognitive practice under genetic control, then the environmental conditions that make those cognitive practices advantageous must remain stable over evolutionarily significant periods of time. Since genetic takeover reduces plasticity, there will be no selection for genetic control if the relevant environments are variable.[10]

It might seem that this argues against genetic takeovers of cultural practices in our recent hominid ancestry. Homo erectus and homo sapiens are among the most adaptable species that have ever existed, managing to establish themselves in a very wide range of environments offering many different kinds of exploitable resources. Techniques of hunting, foraging, and defence that work in one such environment will tend not to work in others. To the extent that hominid lineages experienced variable environments, we would thus not expect such techniques to come under genetic control. Our ancestors would surely have done much better to tailor these techniques to current environments in the light of experience, rather than committing themselves genetically to particular strategies. (Cf. Sterelny, 2003, ch. 9.)

However, these considerations do not necessarily apply to all adaptive hominid cognitive practices. If we focus on specific techniques for food-gathering and defence, involving specific weapons, tools and techniques, then the variability of the relevant natural environments may well have prevented any genetic takeovers. But the same point does not apply to such general cognitive powers as linguistic capacity, understanding of mind, folk physics, folk biology, and so on. The advantages of these cognitive powers will not be tied to some specific environmental condition, but will rather be available across all natural environments. These general cognitive powers enhance access to information, increase understanding, and facilitate social coordination, and this will be of benefit to the possessors of such powers in any human society, whatever the natural environment.

[10] Now that we have distinguished social from individual learning, we can add a wrinkle: social learning, rather than individual learning, will be advantageous when environments have an intermediate degree of stability, between the long-term stability that favours genetic control and the very low level of stability that demands individual learning. Social learning is less costly than individual learning, so will be better than individual learning when environments aren't so variable as to require re-calibration of traits to circumstances in each individual's lifetime; at the same time, it is more flexible than genetic control, and so will be favoured when environments don't display long-term stability over multiple generations. (Boyd and Richerson, 1985, Laland et al., 2000.) From the point of view of the argument of this paper, however, we can lump all learning together as suited to 'variable' environments, given that our focus is on scenarios with the very high degree of environmental stability required to favour genetic control over even social learning.

In effect, the prior existence of a *culture* of these general cognitive practices is the only environment required to give a selective advantage to genes that will accelerate the learning of that culture. If a cognitive practice is advantageous in all natural environments, as language capacity, understanding of mind, folk biology and folk physics arguably are, then a culture that renders that practice learnable will itself constitute the environment that favours genes that lighten the learning load involved. As long as that culture persists, then those genes will be advantageous, increasing the reliability of learning and reducing the costs involved. Here genetic takeover does not depend on any stability of external, natural environments—it is enough that there is a cultural environment to provide a stable backdrop for the selection of the relevant genes.

13 Reliable Transmission

How stable are human cultures? Dan Sperber (1996) has stressed the point that cultural transmission is markedly less reliable than genetic transmission. Where sexual reproduction standardly transmits perfect copies of parental alleles, mutations aside, cultural transmission is subject to all manner of bias and noise. This argues that human cultures are unlikely to remain stable over significant periods of biological time, thus undercutting the last section's suggestion that such cultures can themselves provide the stable environments which will allow the selection of genes

Here it is worth distinguishing between vertical and horizontal transmission once more. In the section before last I observed that vertical transmission seems to play an important role among humans. Of course, there will be cases and cases. Humans certainly learn many things from individuals other than their parents. We need only think of contemporary adolescent teenagers, who generally regard their parents as absolutely the last people to adopt as role models. But this is consistent with the possibility that maturing humans acquire large amounts of cultural information specifically from their parents at earlier stages of their development. In particular, this seems likely for their acquisition of such basic cognitive powers as language capacity, understanding of mind, and so on. To the extent that these powers depend on cultural training, the most likely context is surely interaction between parents and maturing offspring.

If this is right, then it gives reason to suppose that the relevant cultures practices will constitute stable traditions rather than transient fashions. I have already observed that the prevalence of vertical transmission can create selective pressures in favour of genes that lead offspring to copy their parents. Let us now add in the point that, in cases where transmission is vertical, there will also be pressures for genes that lead parents to *teach* their children. This is a kind of mirror image of 'Baldwinization'. Here the possibility of offspring acquiring some practice via learning leads to the selection of genes which makes this learning more reliable and less costly—but here the genes operate though the parental teachers rather than the maturing learners.

Note that this latter possibility is peculiar to vertically transmitted learning. There is nothing in principle to rule out the genetic takeover of horizontally transmitted cultures. True, as we have seen, there is a question of whether horizontally transmitted practices will be *biologically* advantageous to their practitioners. And there is the issue, which we are presently discussing, of whether horizontal culture will be *stable* enough to sustain genetic takeovers. Still, as I say, there is no principled barrier to some horizontal culture satisfying both these requirements, and so yielding selective pressures for genes which make tyros better at learning the relevant practice. Yet even in such a case there will be no pressure for genes for *teaching* the practice, given that the transmission is horizontal. Since the beneficiaries of teaching will be unrelated individuals, it will not increase the *teacher's* reproductive fitness that the learners should acquire the trait. It works differently with vertical transmission. In that case, the beneficiaries of teaching will be the offspring of the teacher, and so any parental genes which make the offspring better at acquiring the advantageous practice will automatically be favoured by natural selection.

A familiar example of this kind of selection is the way in which parents in many species will help offspring to practice their food-gathering skills (cf. Avital and Jablonka, 2001, 307–9); for example, some species of mammals and birds offer captive prey for their offspring to practice with. Clearly here there has been genetic selection on the parents for behaviour that facilitates learning in their offspring. It seems highly plausible that the natural tendency of human parents to engage in sustained verbal and intellectual interaction with their children, even at an age when the children cannot respond in kind, is similarly the product of selection of genes to make their children learn better.

Taken together, these points give us reason to suppose that the vertical transmission of basic cognitive practices like language, understanding of mind, and other folk theories would have been highly stable. Offspring would be naturally predisposed to copy their parents, and parents would be naturally disposed to teach their children various specific practices. These factors would seem quite adequate to sustain cultures in place for biologically significant periods of time, and thereby ensure the stable environments required for genetic takeover.

14 Innateness Revisited

Let us now finally return to the issue of the innateness of cognitive capacities. The argument of this paper may seem to support the thesis that many of our basic cognitive powers are innate. After all, it has aimed specifically to explain how the process of genetic takeover can lead to increased genetic control of practices that were previously learned. However, the issue of innateness is not straightforward. As I shall now show, in one good sense of 'innateness', there is no good reason to suppose that any cognitive capacities ever become innate.

How exactly is the notion of innateness best understood? One weak, comparative way of understanding the notion is in terms of 'norms of reaction'. In this sense, a given genome makes some phenotype P innate *to the extent* that it ensures its appearance across a given range of environments. Accordingly, one phenotype will be more innate than another phenotype, relative to some genome, if it appears across a greater range of environments; similarly, one genome can make a given phenotype more innate than another genome would if it ensures the phenotype's appearance over more environments. On this comparative understanding of innateness, there is no doubt that genetic takeover makes phenotypes 'more innate' than they were previously. By reducing the amount of learning required to produce some phenotype, genetic takeover means that the phenotype will appear in environments involving only limited amounts of learning, as well as environments involving more extensive learning.

However, this notion of innateness is limited to comparative judgments (and moreover will be rarely applicable, given that it requires the ranges of environments being compared to be related by strict inclusion rather than mere overlap). Because of this, many theorists aim for a stronger notion. One attractive notion is that a phenotype is innate just in case its appearance in normal development does not depend on any psychological mechanisms, and in particular does not depend on any *learning* process. (Cf. Samuels, 1998, 2002, 2004. See also Cowie, 1999.) This proposal is not unproblematic, facing obvious difficulties it its right-to-left direction: it is by no means clear that appearing in normal development without the help of any psychological mechanisms is *sufficient* for innateness. (Cf. Mameli and Papineau, forthcoming, sect. 4.) However, we can by-pass this issue here, since I shall only be concerned with the converse left-to-right claim: something is *not* innate if it *is* produced by a psychological mechanism like learning. This seems relatively uncontroversial, and will plausibly be part of any non-comparative notion of innateness. What I now want to argue is that there is no reason to suppose that genetic takeover will ever lead to innateness in any such non-comparative sense, on the grounds that it is unlikely ever to replace learning *entirely* by genetic control.

By way of an illustration of this point, consider the Galapagos woodpecker finches once more. Here there is no question but that their tool-using behaviour is in a comparative sense highly innate. Very little in the way of environmental support is needed for the behaviour to emerge. In particular, the finches seem not to need demonstrations by existing adepts from which to copy the behaviour socially. Even so, genetic control has not entirely eliminated the need for learning. The birds still need to be able to experiment with twigs at a crucial stage in development, in order to move from a crude predisposition to fiddle with twigs to successful insect-catching. It takes a month or two for the juvenile birds to refine this skill via individual trial-and-error learning (Tebbich et al. 2001). Their genes may strongly predispose them to the behaviour, but its full emergence also hinges on learning-based informational input from the enivironment.

A similar phenomenon is displayed in Hinton and Nowlan's (1987) simulation. As I explained earlier, their simulation showed that, once their neural nets could *learn* to set their connections at '1' rather than '0', then the overall advantageous phenotype of all 20 '1's became accessible, and genes for '1' started being selected for, replacing the alternative alleles that left the connections to learning. However, Hinton and Nowlan's simulation did not lead to the *total* replacement of learning genes by those that fixed '1's without learning. Once the neural nets had something like 70% of their connections fixed by genes (with the exact percentage depending on the parameters of the specific simulation), then the selective pressures tailed off, and there ceased to be any significant further replacement of learning alleles. This was because it was a relatively easy task to learn to set the last few connections at '1', once most of the others were genetically fixed at '1', so at that stage extra genetic control ceased to be significantly advantageous.

There is a principled reason why genetic takeovers should display this kind of incompleteness, always leaving some role for residual learning. In order for genetic takeover to be possible at all, it cannot be too hard to learn the overall advantageous phenotype at the early stages when very little is genetically fixed. If there were no real chance of finding the phenotype via learning in these early stages, then genes that marginally lightened the learning load would not be favoured, for they would still leave the organism with little chance of finding the pay-off phenotype. (This, recall, was why I attached so much significance to *social* learning. The point of social learning was that it can make complex behaviours learnable even when they are beyond the reach of individual trial-and-error learning.)

So candidate phenotypes for genetic takeover cannot be too hard to learn, even when they have little genetic help. An obvious corollary is that they will become very easy to learn, once there is a significant amount of genetic help. At that stage there will be no marked advantage to continued genetic takeover. Why bother to write the last details into the genes, when they can be picked up with no significant effort from the environment? Moreover, there may well be loss-of-flexibility costs associated with further genetic control, in the form of inability to fine-tune the phenotype to detailed environmental contingencies. All in all, then, it seems only to be expected that genetic takeovers will characteristically remain incomplete, always leaving some role to learning in fixing the overall phenotype. And to the extent that 'innateness' implies an absence of learning, this will mean that those phenotypes are never innate.

15 Learning all the Way Down

An obvious retort to this line of argument is that it may show that advantageous overall phenotypes are never rendered fully innate, but that this does not mean that *components* of those phenotypes will not be fully innate. Thus consider my baby model from section 4: I decomposed some overall phenotype P into components P_i each of which could be fixed by some allele G_i or alternatively left to learning by L_i. The argument of the last section gives us reason to doubt that the overall phenotype P will ever become fully innate, since the selective pressure to bring the last P_is under genetic control will tail off. But this does not mean that none of the component P_is will be fully innate—and indeed my model assumes that they will be, whenever the specific G_is that fix them are present.

More generally, this is the natural line of response for anybody concerned to defend a strong cognitive nativism. Nobody, I take it, wants to argue that learning is unnecessary for the acquisition of natural languages, like English or Swahili, or for knowledge of specific biological categories, or even for the culturally variable elements of folk psychology and folk physics. Rather, according to nativist orthodoxy, it is the *structures that facilitate* these mature accomplishments that are innate, not the mature accomplishments themselves. Of course the full flowering of these accomplishments depends on some degree of learning. But this learning is made possible by some underlying structure (by some specialized learning mechanism, so to speak) which is itself fixed by the genes, and which owes nothing to informational input from the ontogenetic environment.

Within the classical computationalist tradition, this view gets cashed out as the claim that there are various bodies of *innate knowledge*. Since individuals get these bodies of knowledge from their genes, they do not need to extract them from their environments. Given this headstart, they are then in a position to learn the further items of information needed to complete the relevant capacities. Thus, 'universal grammar' is the innate body of knowledge that allows the acquisition of natural languages; similar innate bodies of universal knowledge are posited to account for the acquisition of folk psychology, biology and physics. Nor need this model be restricted to the classical computationalists. Connectionists will talk about prewired connection strengths, rather than innate sentences in the language of thought. But in the present context of argument this is not a substantial difference. There is nothing to stop us viewing connectionist prewirings as themselves embodying items of information, indeed just the same items of universal knowledge as are posited by classical computationalists.

I am happy to agree that, at some level of description, the genes that have been selected to foster specific cognitive capacities can be viewed in this way as fixing various elements of 'innate knowledge'. After all, these genes will have been selected because they combine with inputs from learning to produce mature cognitive phenotypes; given this, the 'informational content' of the genes can be equated with the inference from the learning input to the informational contents of those mature phenotypes. What remains open, however, is whether this kind of description will amount to anything recognizable as a component of linguistic knowledge, folk psychology, or other familiar cognitive accomplishment. For it may be that the contribution of the genes takes place at a very basic developmental level, altering neonatal perceptual saliences and building certain kinds of fundamental neural structures, with the construction of mature cognitive capacities requiring informational learning input at every stage from then points onwards. If this is right, then learning as well are genes is likely to be implicated in the acquisition of even the components of mature cognitive capacities, like the folk psychological ability to judge who can see what, or the linguistic disposition to identify anaphoric constructions, or the folk biological assumption that organisms have species-typical essences, and so on.

My earlier model of genetic takeover involving P_is and G_is was too restrictive in this respect. There I assumed that the overall phenotype P could be divided into recognisable phenotypic components P_i, each of which could either be entirely fixed by genes G_i or could be left to learning. But there was no essential reason, apart from expository simplification, to think of genetic takeovers in this way. Genetic takeovers require only that there are G_is which lighten the learning load somehow, not that they do this by each fully determining some perspicuous component of the phenotype. The process would work just as well even if each such salient component were a product of both genes and learning, provided the genes involved did *something* to make it easier to learn the overall phenotype. (Cf. Papineau, 2006, section 6.)

The point generalizes to real-life examples. To see this, note that the considerations rehearsed in the previous section will apply as much to the salient *components* of any cognitive capacities as to the overall capacities themselves. Consider, as above, the folk psychological ability to judge who can see what, or the linguistic disposition to identify anaphoric constructions, or the folk biological assumption that organisms have species-typical essences, or so on. On the assumption that these abilities are upshots of genetic takeover, then they were once derived from ancestral learning mechanisms, and only subsequently has there been selection of genes to foster them. Given this scenario, there seems no reason to suppose that the genes so selected would have entirely eliminated any role for learning in the production of even these components. As before, given that ancestral learning was feasible, and the environment required available, why would selection have bothered, so to speak, to render these components fully innate? The selection of genes that make such learning fast and easy is one thing; the selection of genes that replace learning altogether is another.

The Cultural Origins of Cognitive Adaptations

To urge this is not to deny the uncontentious point that genes resulting from genetic takeover will have *some* effects independently of contributions from learning. Moreover, as explained above, I have no objection to characterising these innate effects in informational terms, as items of 'innate knowledge'. However, to repeat the earlier point, there is no reason to suppose that these items of information will amount to anything recognizable as components of folk thinking. The fully innate effects of genes need not extend beyond the very earliest stages of development, fixing initial neural structures that bias learning in certain ways, but which from then on need to be combined with inputs from learning if further intellectual development is to occur.[11]

It is a familiar general point that genes determine scarcely anything on their own, without some help from environmental factors: genes are selected to produce advantageous phenotypes *in conjunction* with stably recurring features of the environment. With those specific genes that result from genetic takeovers of previously socially learned practices, the relevant stable features of the environment will be the continued existence of that practice, which will then contribute via learning to the acquisition of that practice by maturing individuals.

The process of genetic takeover thus yields cognitive capacities which derive from a deep interaction between genes and learning. The striking ease and rapidity with which children master their native language and acquire various elements of folk thinking, even in the absence of any explicit instruction, provides undeniable evidence that many genes have been selected specifically to foster these cognitive capacities. However, to the extent that this selection has derived from genetic takeovers of ancestral cultural practices, then no recognizable component of these capacities is likely to be innate, in the sense that it would appear even in the absence of any learning. Genetic natural selection will have ensured that such capacities emerge quickly and reliably across a wide range of human environments. But since all human environments, freak cases aside, contain ample opportunities for social learning, continued

---

[11] Animal studies suggest that mature phenotypes often depend on earlier learning in unexpectedly deep ways. Young chicks who are prevented from seeing their own feet for two days after hatching are later unable to pick up mealworms, a typical behaviour in normal chickens (Wallman, 1979); mallard ducklings need to hear their own embryonic calls while still in the egg in order to recognize maternal mallard calls later (Gottlieb, 1997); rhesus monkeys reared in isolation are incapable of sexual behaviour when adult (Mason, 1960, 1961).

dependence on some modicum of such learning will not detract from the speed and reliability of acquisition. In short, while genetic takeover selects genes for cognitive capacities, it does not make those capacities innate.[12]

References

Akins, C. and Zentall, T. 1998. 'Imitation in Japanese Quail: the Role of Reinforcement of Demonstrator Responding', *Psychonomic Bulletin and Review* 5, 694-7.

Avital, E. and Jablonka, E. 2001. *Animal Traditions: Behavioural Inheritance in Evolution*. Cambridge: Cambridge University Press

Baldwin, J. 1896. 'A New Factor in Evolution', *The American Naturalist* 30, 441-51, 536-53.

Barkow, J., Cosmides, L., and Tooby, J. 1992. *The Adapted Mind*. New York: Oxford University Press.

Bateson, P. 2004. 'The Active Role of Behaviour in Evolution', *Biology and Philosophy* 19, 283-298.

Blackmore, S. 2000. *The Meme Machine*. Oxford: Oxford University Press.

Boyd, R. and Richerson, P. 1985. *Culture and the Evolutionary Process*. Chicago: Chicago University Press.

Chomsky, N. 1972. Language and Mind. New York Harcourt, Brace, and World.

Chomsky, N. 1988. Language and Problems of Knowledge. Cambridge, Mass: MIT Press.

Cowie, F. 1999. *What's Within? Nativism Reconsidered*. New York: Oxford University Press.

Dawkins, R. 1976. *The Selfish Gene*. Oxford: Oxford University Press.

Dawkins, R. 1996. *Climbing Mount Improbable*. London: Penguin Books.

Dennett, D. 1991. *Consciousness Explained*. London: Allen Lane.

Fodor, J. 2000. *The Mind Doesn't Work that Way*. Cambridge, Mass: MIT Press.

Godfrey-Smith, P. 2003. 'Between Baldwin Scepticism and Baldwin Boosterism', in Weber, B. and Depew, D. (eds), *Evolution and Learning*. Cambridge, Mass: MIT Press.

Gottlieb, G. 1997. *Synthesizing Nature-Nurture: Pre-Natal Roots of Instinctive Behaviour*. Mahwah NJ: Lawrence Erlbaum.

Griffiths, P. 2006. 'The Baldwin Effect and Genetic Assimilation', in P. Carruthers, S. Laurence and S. Stich (eds) *The Innate Mind: Culture and Cognition*. Oxford: Oxford University Press.

Gugliemino, C., Viganotti, C., Hewlett, B. and L. Cavalli-Sforza. 1995.

[12] For helpful responses to earlier versions of this paper, I would like to thank Ruth Kempson, Richard Samuels, Gabriel Segal, and especially Matteo Mameli.

'Cultural Variation in Africa: Role of Mechanisms of Transmission and Adaptation', *Proceedings of the National Academy of Sciences* 92, 7585-7589.

Hewlett, B. and L. Cavalli-Sforza. 1986. 'Cultural Transmission among Aka Pygmies', *American Anthropologist* 88, 922-934.

Hinton, G. and Nowlan, S. 1987. 'How Learning can Guide Evolution.' *Complex Systems* 1, 495-502.

Jablonka, E. and Lamb, M. 1995. *Epigenetic Inheritance and Evolution*. Oxford: Oxford University Press.

Laland, K., Olding-Smee, J., and Feldman, M. 2000. 'Niche Construction, Biological Evolution, and Cultural Change', *Behavioural and Brain Sciences* 23, 131-75.

Laurence, S. and Margolis, E. 2001. 'The Poverty of the Stimulus Argument', *British Journal for the Philosophy of Science* 52, 217-76.

Mameli. M. 2004. 'Nongenetic Selection and Nongenetic Inheritance', *British Journal for the Philosophy of Science* 55, 35-71.

Mameli, M. and Papineau, D. Forthcoming. 'The New Nativism: A Commentary on Gary Marcus's *Birth of the Mind*', *Biology and Philosophy*.

Mason, W.A. 1960. 'The Effects of Social Restriction on the Behavior of Rhesus Monkeys: I', *Journal of Comparative and Physiological Psychology* 53, 82-9.

Mason, W.A. 1961. 'The Effects of Social Restriction on the Behavior of Rhesus Monkeys: II', *Journal of Comparative and Physiological Psychology* 54, 287-290.

Papineau, D. 2004. 'Human Minds', in A. O'Hear (ed.) *Minds and Persons*. Cambridge: Cambridge University Press.

Papineau, D. 2005. 'Social Leaning and the Baldwin Effect', in A Zilhao (ed) *Rationality and Evolution*. London: Routledge.

Papineau, D. 2006. 'The Baldwin Effect and Genetic Assimilation: Reply to Griffiths', in P. Carruthers, S. Laurence and S. Stich (eds) *The Innate Mind: Culture and Cognition*. Oxford: Oxford University Press.

Pinker, S. and Bloom, P. 1990. 'Natural Language and Natural Selection', *Behavioural and Brain Science* 13, 707-84.

Richerson, P. and Boyd, R. 2004. *Not in Our Genes Alone*. Chicago: University of Chicago Press.

Samuels, R. 1998. 'What Brains Won't Tell Us about the Mind', *Mind and Language* 13, 548-70.

Samuels, R. 2002. 'Nativism in Cognitive Science', *Mind and Language* 17, 233-65.

Samuels, R. 2004. 'Innateness in Cognitive Science', *Trends in Cognitive Science* 8, 136-41

Shettleworth, S. 1998. *Cognition, Evolution and Behavior*. Oxford: Oxford University Press.

Sperber, D. 1996. *Explaining Culture*. Oxford: Blackwell.

Sterelny, K. 2003. *Thought in a Hostile World*. Oxford: Blackwell.

Tebbich, S., Taborsky, M., Fessl, B., and Blomqvist D. 2001. 'Do

Woodpecker Finches Acquire Tool Use by Social Learning?' *Proceedings of the Royal Society* 268: 2189-2193.

Tomasello, M. 2000. *The Cultural Origins of Human Cognition.* Cambridge, Mass: Harvard University Press.

Turney, P., Whitely, D., and Anderson, R. (eds). 1996. *Evolutionary Computation, Evolution, Learning and Instinct: 100 Years of the Baldwin Effect.* Cambridge, Mass: MIT Press.

Waddington, C. 1953. 'Genetic Assimilation of an Acquired Character', *Evolution* 4, 118-26.

Waddington, C. 1957. *The Strategy of the Genes.* London: Allen and Unwin.

Waddington, C. 1961. 'Genetic Assimilation', *Advances in Genetics* 10, 257-90.

Wallman, J. 1979. 'Animal Visual Restriction Experiment: Preventing Chicks from Seeing Their Feet Affect Later Responses to Mealworms', *Developmental Psychobiology* 12, 391-7.

Watkins, J. 1999. 'A Note on Baldwin Effect', *British Journal for the Philosophy of Science* 50, 417-23.

Name Index

Name Index